Displacing Whiteness

Displacing Whiteness

Essays in Social and Cultural Criticism

Edited by Ruth Frankenberg

Duke University Press   Durham and London 1997

© 1997 Duke University Press
All rights reserved
Printed in the United States of America on acid-free paper ∞
Typeset in Berkeley Medium by Tseng Information Systems, Inc.
Library of Congress Cataloging-in-Publication Data appear
on the last printed page of this book.

Contents

Introduction: Local Whitenesses,

Localizing Whiteness

Ruth Frankenberg

THE essays in this volume critically examine contemporary meanings of whiteness and the circumstances of their construction from a range of national, racial, and ethnic locations. The result is whiteness unfrozen, whiteness viewed as ensembles of local phenomena complexly embedded in socioeconomic, sociocultural, and psychic interrelations. Whiteness emerges as a process, not a "thing," as plural rather than singular in nature.

Why talk about whiteness, given the risk that by undertaking intellectual work on whiteness one might contribute to processes of recentering rather than decentering it, as well as reifying the term and its "inhabitants"? But there are also tremendous risks in *not* critically engaging whiteness. Among these are, first, a continued failure to displace the "unmarked marker" status of whiteness, a continued inability to "color" the seeming transparency of white positionings. Second, to leave whiteness unexamined is to perpetuate a kind of asymmetry that has marred even many critical analyses of racial formation and cultural practice. Here the modes of alterity of everyone-but-white-people are subjected to ever more meticulous scrutiny, celebratory or not, while whiteness remains unexamined — unqualified, essential, homogeneous, seemingly self-fashioned, and apparently unmarked by history or practice (e.g., the notion of "racial-ethnic communities" as synonym for "communities of color"). Third (and Angie Chabram-Dernersesian's essay in this volume demonstrates this particularly well), critical attention to whiteness offers a ground not only for the examination of white selves (who may indeed be white *others,*

depending on the position of the speaker) but also for the excavation
of the foundations of *all* racial and cultural positionings.

For the most part, critical work on whiteness has emerged in the
context of, and very frequently in direct response to, critique of racism
and the racial order focused on positions of subordination, whether
the latter is undertaken by people of color (as has most often been
the case) or by white people. Indeed, I would argue that the essays in
this collection would lack much of their meaning and efficacy outside
the broad context of such work. Conversely, as suggested above, critical analyses of whiteness are vital concomitants of engagements with
racial subordination.

Recent work on whiteness has engaged a range of questions. Arguably, the fullest and best developed area of work is in historical studies.
This work, in social and economic history, at times building on but
also radically revising and extending Marxist and feminist historiography, has begun to map out the salience of whiteness to the formation
of nationhood, class, and empire in the United States and in the European colonial enterprise.[1] This scholarship helps make it evident that
the formation of specifically white subject positions has in fact been
key, at times as cause and at times as effect, to the sociopolitical processes inherent in taking land and making nations. Historical work on
whiteness thus builds from and adds to the much larger body of historical work on racism and on other racialized and/or colonized subjects (e.g., African American history, Native American history, Indian
colonial history). It is also enabled by, and advances, work arguing for
the fundamentally racialized character of U.S. and European histories.

In a second and related area, sociologists and practitioners of cultural studies have begun to examine the place of whiteness in the
contemporary body politic in Europe and the United States. Like the
historians, such scholars are interested both in the making of subjects and in the formation of structures and institutions. Here again,
their substantive work joins with that of theorists of race and critics
of racism about and/or from a range of subordinated racial locations.
They too assert the central rather than epiphenomenal location of race
in social formation.[2] Naming the temporality of this body of work is
challenging. While some historians, sociologists, and feminist or cultural critics (e.g., Baldwin, Smith, Horsman, Wellman, and Rich) have
published critical work on white identity over several decades, the
bulk of such work is more recent, dating from the second half of the
1980s and 1990s.

A third area of work asks how whiteness is performed by subjects, whether in daily life, in film, in literature, or in the academic corpus.[3] At times what is at stake in such research is the "revealing" of the un-named—the exposure of whiteness masquerading as universal. But at other times the stake is rather in examining how white dominance is rationalized, legitimized, and made ostensibly normal and natural.

A fourth area examines racism in movements for social change. The burden of this work is rather similar to that just named: the cri-tique of whiteness asserted as universal, and the critique of white dominance in social change movements (or a presumptive arrogation, by white subjects, of leadership of social movements). Feminist move-ments, are, I would suggest, one site of highly developed work in this last area.[4] And, relatedly, work on the "other side of the coin" moni-tors and analyzes the making of white supremacist identity and politi-cal movement ideology and practice. Here again we see a stream of criticism rather older than the work that has burgeoned from the mid-1980s into the present.[5]

Of course, these four areas cannot be segregated from one another; one cannot adequately examine questions of culture or performance or movement theory and activism outside their social context; nor does one usually undertake historical research in the absence of a set of ani-mating concerns in the present. This collection of essays engages all four areas just named but is centered between the second and third: attention to the contemporary body politic, at the levels of both struc-ture and subject formation, and engagement with cultural practice and performance in a range of genres. However, it must be noted that both history and the implications of authors' conclusions for activist prac-tice are frequently a part of their discussions.

This collection is interdisciplinary, both in that its authors are institutionally situated across a range of locations—departments of an-thropology, literature, sociology, humanities, African American studies, American studies (racially unmarked?!), Chicana/o studies, cultural studies, and women's studies—and in that each author works syncreti-cally with a repertoire of theoretical apparatuses and methodologies drawn from traditionally "humanities" *and* "social scientific" sources.

By naming this book *Displacing Whiteness* I indicate the authors' efforts to resituate whiteness from its unspoken (perhaps unspeak-able?) status; to displace and then reemplace it. The authors show how whiteness operates in particular locales and webs of social relations. And with the subtitle *Essays in Social and Cultural Criticism* I signal the methodologies by means of which these authors situate whiteness(es) in time and space, tracing rather than merely asserting its embeddedness in particular histories and class formations, in masculinity and femininity.

This collection breaks new ground in both theoretical and substantive terms. The overall effect, both of these essays and of whiteness as it is reconceived here, is well illustrated by the image of fractals that John Hartigan Jr. deploys in his essay. Hartigan draws on the work of Marilyn Strathern, who has said that thinking of fractals when modeling social processes calls attention to the partial connections that link such processes, generating patterns that are replicated at levels of increasing specificity.

Whiteness emerges in this book as historically constructed and internally differentiated. Whiteness as process is seen to be contested and contestable; yet these essays are also animated by their authors' cognizance of the fundamental coconstitution of whiteness and racial domination—a reality that is, if not intractable, clearly not amenable to elimination or evasion by textual fiat. This collection is thus both an effort to deconstruct and fragment the notion of whiteness and a contribution to ongoing critique of racism and (neo/post)colonialism at the turn of the twentieth century. And as will be manifest in the pages that follow, this volume does not conceive racial formation—whether in the United States or elsewhere—as biracial but rather as multiracial. By the same token, the volume as an ensemble clarifies that whiteness must be viewed both as emergent from multivalent historical processes and through multiple dynamics of alterity.

Haole, pakeha, ghost, gringo, wasiku, and honky—some names for white people given to them by people who are not white.[6] American, English, British, man, woman, white woman, white United Statesian— some names for white people given to them by people who are white.[7] When has whiteness been visible and when has it been "unmarked"? When has whiteness "disappeared" into national, ethnic, or cultural namings? First, it is crucial to take into account the position in the racial order of the person viewing whiteness. For as bell hooks points out in this volume, communities of color frequently see and name whiteness clearly and critically, in periods when white folks have asserted their own "color blindness" as well as in times of self-conscious white claims of superiority. And in examining white self-namings, one must further distinguish—although the separation is not always hard and fast—between assertions of white supremacism or superiority and critical self-examinations of whiteness (Rebecca Aanerud, this volume).

The more one scrutinizes it, the more the notion of whiteness as unmarked norm is revealed to be a mirage, or at least a phenomenon delimited in time and space. For I suggest that it is only in those times and places where white supremacism has achieved hegemony that whiteness attains (usually unstable) unmarkedness. In this volume, David Wellman and Phil Cohen analyze, from opposite sides of the Atlantic, the crisis in white masculinity that has resulted from the fall of that subject position from its prior state of unmarkedness (unmarked at least from its own purview). In times and places when whiteness and white dominance are being built or reconfigured, they are highly visible, named, and asserted, rather than invisible or simply "normative."

The notion of whiteness as unmarked in particular times and spaces should not be taken to invoke sequential or fully separable locales, for hegemony is never complete, never uniform. To take the United States as an example, white dominance, white normativity, or the presumption that "white" and "American" mean the same may be taken for granted in a small town but contested in a large city, presumed in a suburb but challenged downtown. Americanness as whiteness may be hotly defended at the United States–Mexico border, as when Californians challenge the efforts of border crossers by parking their vehicles with headlights blazing in the direction of potential incomers.

Less dramatic perceptions of the racial order vary by neighborhood, in part because not only racial identities but also income and class status vary by neighborhood. The vast majority of white, California-raised students whom I teach make it clear that they grew up with few or no peers of color. For them, whiteness is indeed unmarked, and race an apparently distant and abstract concept. For them, marking of whiteness frequently begins as an awakening—rude or otherwise—in women's studies, ethnic studies, or American studies classrooms. Elsewhere, whiteness may seem to be performed invisibly in one household while it is named and contested in the one next door. Meanings of whiteness can also be contested within households. For example, within the multiracial families France Winddance Twine studied, whiteness was often ostensibly invisible to a "genetically white" mother but visible to her young adult biracial daughter. Finally, as my own research with white U.S. women shows, "color blindness" is in fact difficult to maintain as a fiction, even for those most securely raised within it and those who try hardest to hold fast to it.[8] However, white people's conscious racialization of others does not necessarily lead to a conscious racialization of the white self. Indeed, here we return to the proposition with which we began: that whiteness makes itself invisible precisely by asserting its normalcy, its transparency, in contrast with the marking of others on which its transparency depends. And we return also to the necessity for this text, which is committed to marking whiteness. For it must be noted that the variability in how whiteness is seen is anything but random: rather, it can be accounted for, analyzed, and challenged.

In examining whiteness, in seeking to account for its variable visibility, one must recognize how continual processes of slippage, condensation, and displacement among the constructs "race," "nation," and "culture" continue to "unmark" white people while consistently marking and racializing others. We may take an example of this slippage from the current widespread efforts to increase immigration control in the United States. Popular sentiment in favor of immigration controls draws sometimes on explicit racism and sometimes on racism recoded in national and cultural terms. Thus there is expression of anxiety about the supposed "color" of the United States and the "darkening effect" immigrants will have on it; there is tension about the national origin of potential immigrants, with attention focused more on some nations of origin than on others; and finally, there is at times expression of whites' fears of being culturally and linguistically overwhelmed—and again, some cultures and languages are perceived to be more threatening than others.

Further, notions of race are closely linked to ideas about legitimate "ownership" of the nation, with "whiteness" and "Americanness" linked tightly together. Meanwhile, the repressed memory of the brownness of the original residents of this land ("owners" of the land was not a term many of them would have thought to use) and of the immigrant origins of white United Statesians forms another crucial dimension of the story. This dance of assertion and repression has been present throughout the history of the United States. It continues in the context of debates over whether immigrants, especially those who are not white, have the right to work, to own property, and to utilize resources ranging from water and fire departments to schools and social security. There are, indeed, perpetual question marks hanging over the heads of some categories of legitimate U.S. residents, especially Asian, Latino, and Chicano citizens and residents. By contrast, I, a British-accented resident of the United States, have rarely been questioned as to the legitimacy of my status as a teacher of American studies.

Formal politics are, of course, also racialized. Campaigns for the 1996 U.S. elections were unfolding at the time this manuscript was being completed. In those contests, support for immigration controls and for limiting immigrants' access to education and health and welfare services increasingly appeared as litmus tests of "electability." The other decisive issues were candidates' positions on abortion; on "crime," policing, and punishment; and on universal access to a health and welfare safety net. All of these domains are racialized in the popular imagination—crime is "black," with the need for protection against crime coded "white"; immigrants are "brown" and "yellow"; "black" *and* "brown" people are draining the welfare system; and "white" women want abortions. And finally, "Americans," but not foreigners, deserve jobs. As usual, "red" people—Native Americans of the mainland and Hawaii—were entirely absent from the campaign discourse.

It should perhaps be noted that popular imagination is not coterminous with objective fact—thus, for example, the majority of welfare recipients are white. Be that as it may, the political "middle ground" increasingly sees candidates taking up positions *against* immigrants but *for* reproductive rights, *against* socially guaranteed access to health services and welfare but *for* increasingly forceful policing, punishment, and incarceration. We see class and gender being forcefully racialized, and we also see polarizations of insiderness and outsiderness, organized at times around the axis of race, at other times around national status, and yet elsewhere around a race-national combination. I think it is also safe to assert that some women more than others—of the right class, the right "race"—are being seduced into a new kind of insiderness along with their male counterparts.

As the foregoing suggests, class interweaves with race in a complex way. In this volume, Twine points out how middle-class status helped to secure the whiteness of brown-skinned suburban children, at least prior to puberty. Elsewhere, Karen Brodkin Sacks's essay "How Did Jews Become White Folks?" examines the post–World War II transformation in the status of Jews and other Euroamericans of southern and eastern, rather than northern and western, origin within Europe, whereby, for the first time, the former were able to join with the latter in an expanded sense of white American identity.[9] Large numbers of European Americans achieved middle-class status, signaled by college education, homeownership, and suburban residence. In what amounted to a massive movement of upward mobility, differences between city dwellers and suburbanites were sharpened; simultaneously, racial segregation and inequality were further enforced. Sacks notes that "like most chicken and egg problems, it's hard to know which came first. Did Jews and other Euroethnics become white because they became middle class? That is, did money whiten? Or did being incorporated into an expanded version of whiteness open up the economic doors to a middle class status? Clearly, both tendencies were at work" (86).

Sacks's examination of economic mobility in post–World War II United States shows clearly the crucial roles played by the GI Bill, the Federal Housing Authority, and the Veterans Administration, both in underwriting the upward mobility of Euroamerican men and in systematically excluding African American men, and women of all ethnicities, from the benefits offered by these institutions. The middle class expanded by means of a process Sacks describes as "affirmative action" for Euroamerican men (79ff.), simultaneously building a more inclusive Euroamerican whiteness and reentrenching preexisting categories of racial alterity.

One may trace, in the United States, Canada, western Europe, Australia, New Zealand—in short, in all those places one might name as either colonizing nations or settler colonies—a history of the self-naming of white people as white that is linked to imperial and colonial expansion, simultaneous with the making of (white dominant) nation states. One powerful scholarly telling of this story, Reginald Horsman's *Race and Manifest Destiny: The Making of American Racial Anglo-Saxonism,* painstakingly maps the origin story of early white Americans.[10] (Here I use "origin story" in the anthropological sense, gesturing to how a community understands itself rather than to the "truth" or "objectivity" of its version of events.) Horsman documents the self-naming of early settler colonialists as the self-perceived true inheritors of an Anglo-Saxon lineage, purportedly traceable to a glorious golden age of rural collectivity that was tragically destroyed by the coming of feudal hierarchy to English soil.

It was in part on the basis of this self-description that white settlers justified to themselves their westward colonial expansion; their destruction of indigenous community, land, and life; the annexation of Mexican land "won" in the Spanish-American War; and their hopes of a domain that would one day span the globe. But the second part of self-justification called for the naming of a range of others as inferior, including indigenous Americans, Africans, and the "mongrel races" of Spanish and indigenous Americans further south. While beginning with a terminology of "peoples" and nations, a transatlantic literature on "race," purportedly systematic and scientific, supplanted nationalist and culturalist forms of supremacism through the nineteenth century.

Examining this history makes clear, indeed, why it is that race, culture, and nation slide so smoothly one into another in the present, providing alibis for each other in contemporary social, cultural, and political discourses about race, nation, identity, ownership, and belonging. "Race" is, in fact, a rather recent phenomenon; the hierarchical ranking of "peoples" is a much older measuring instrument in the Western lexicon of supremacism. And I should note, in case it is necessary to underscore this point, that the concept of race was born out of "racism avant la lettre," that is to say, out of earlier namings of supremacy. In other words, it is not the case that an innocent racialness was corrupted by a later ranking of races, but rather that race and racism are fundamentally interwoven.

From this recognition it follows that whiteness is a construct or identity almost impossible to separate from racial dominance. For the term *whiteness,* expressing the idea that there is a category of people identified and self-identifying as "white," is situated within this simultaneous operation of race and racism. White, then, corresponds to one place in racism as a system of categorization and subject formation, just as the terms *race privileged* and *race dominant* name particular places within racism as a system of domination.

In the historical moment with which Horsman is concerned, whiteness was *not* normative and thus unseen and unmarked, but rather named, marked, and still in the making. At the time of the founding of the first colonies in North America, to be white (and "white" is indeed the wrong word for that historical moment) was to be Anglo-Saxon (Germanic or English), self-identified as the best of the best, as the true inheritors of a long, Aryan legacy. Further, naming the dominant identity meant substantively naming a self (fictitiously or not) as well as naming in order to exclude a range of others. To be Anglo-Saxon was also to be culturally and intellectually superior, arguments developed in relation to the construction of Native American and African others.

Similar processes (although of course with substantive variation) are apparent everywhere in the making and marking of whiteness: the cycling of race, culture, and nation as naming systems for difference read hierarchically. Also visible is the marking of putative others— constituted by means, again, of race, culture, or nation—as sites for the resolution of contradictions faced by white selves, sites onto which that which is feared or desired may be displaced.

David R. Roediger's *Wages of Whiteness* broke new ground in analyzing the making of a U.S. white working class through the first two-thirds of the nineteenth century.[11] Then, as in other times, whiteness meant something specifiable: foremost, to be white was to be "not-black." But one would not fully tell this story without noting that to be "not-black" meant, crucially, to be nonenslaved. And in turn, to be nonenslaved meant *both* not being a plantation slave *and* not living in a monarchic society, but rather in a republic. One must also emphasize the ways difference was dramatized by being racialized. Roediger notes how all points of connection or similarity between the conditions of chattel slaves and wage slaves were vigorously suppressed, linguistically as well as through antiblack racism. Thus, for example, in the first decades of the nineteenth century, white American workers, both male and female, rejected the term *servant,* substituting *help, hired hand,* or later simply *hand* to describe their status as persons who worked for wages. In those decades this transformation was widely noted by Americans and overseas visitors alike; and whites' insistence on these terms as markers of their distinction from "negurs" and slaves was also common knowledge, remarked on both in the press and in visitors' and immigrants' letters home.[12] In a similar way, use of the terms *wage slave* and *white slavery* to describe the condition of white waged workers, common in proworker literature of the 1830s and 1840s, fell out of favor in later decades, for a number of reasons, but in part because "to ask workers to *sustain* comparisons of themselves and Black slaves violated at once their republican pride and their sense of whiteness."[13] Moreover, as Roediger notes, "for all but a handful of committed abolitionists/labor reformers, use of a term like white slavery was not an act of solidarity with the slave but rather a call to arms to end the inappropriate oppression of whites."[14]

Roediger also shows how, on the minstrel stage, as whites put on blackface makeup and performed (mis)representations of black culture, blackness became a site for the exploration of white male workers' own anxieties, both as new immigrants from Europe and as new urbanites fresh from the countryside.[15] Finally, Roediger documents Irish immigrants' struggle to become white.[16] Onto the site of "race," then, were condensed a range of contradictions. In this process potential cross-racial solidarities were skirted as difference was emphasized. Again, we see whiteness as being made rather than as self-evident. We see, too, its instability, its insufficiency as an autonomous location of identity. For these workers, whiteness meant a particular relationship to nationhood and the labor process. Simultaneously, particular forms of masculinity were being marked out, classed, and racialized. *Wages of Whiteness* shows, then, how in the process of nineteenth-century, northern U.S. class formation, constructions of whiteness were densely interwoven with constructions of femininity and masculinity as well as with class and nationhood.

One may trace, beginning within early colonial and racist discourses within and beyond the United States, and unfolding into the present, a repertoire of "images" or tropes that construct versions of femaleness and maleness divided by race, nationality, or peoplehood, depending on which mode of naming difference predominates in a given moment or place. The repertoire is small. Its themes are repetitive to a degree that would be banal were these tropes not so devastating in their effects. In them, both maleness/femaleness and whiteness/nonwhiteness are articulated, at times in simple pairings, at other times in more dizzying, more complex formations. These are at times complementary, and at other times more immediately contrastive; but in all cases these tropes are coconstructed, and always hierarchically so.

I shall demonstrate this interplay of complement and contrast by means of an unholy and unorthodox extended, or even distended, "family," a cast of characters to whom I give capitalized, and thus "proper," names for the purpose of underscoring their status as tropes rather than people. Let us begin with a simple quartet: White Woman, White Man, Man of Color, and Woman of Color. They have reappeared so frequently across time and space as to justify describing their primary characteristics, if only to complicate these immediately afterward. My namings here focus in particular on the North American and especially United Statesian versions of this cast of characters, although they share much with versions found elsewhere. White Woman is frail, vulnerable, delicate, sexually pure but at times easily led "astray." White Man is strong, dominant, arbiter of truth, and self-designated protector of white womankind, defender of the nation/territory (and here defense of the nation and its honor often also entails defending White Woman's racial chastity). Man of Color (most frequently this has meant African/Black Man, but it has also, through the course of U.S. history, meant indigenous American, Mexican American, Filipino, Chinese, or Japanese Man)[17] is sexually rapacious, sometimes seductive, usually predatory, especially toward White Woman; it is he, in fact, from whom White Woman must be protected by White Man. And, finally, Woman of Color (and again this might mean African/Black Woman, Asian Woman, Indigenous North or South American Woman, Latina) is also sexually eager, seductress, willing and able consort, especially for the White Man of this tropological family, personally unhygienic, overly fertile, but also usable for breeding, when this is beneficial for White Man, and for tending white children *and* adults, again when beneficial for White Man or White Woman. Woman of Color as trope is construed ambivalently, always on a slippery slope from exotic beauty to unfemininity and ugliness.

We may note, to begin with, the complementarities required for this trope-ical family to thrive: White Man as savior would founder without White-Woman-who-must-be-saved. Similarly, without Man of Color as predator, White Man loses much of his sense of worth and purpose. Within the terms of the discourse, White Man has most to gain by its perpetuation, and most to lose by its dismantling. By contrast, it should not be hard to recognize that Woman of Color and Man of Color have very little to gain in this setup. White Woman's ambiguous and ambivalent status in this family of tropes is striking: she is, on the one hand, accorded privileges and status by this race/gender positioning, and, on the other hand, confined by it. In any case she is advantaged only conditionally on her acceptance of the terms of the contract. This includes especially her sexual practices, for the trope-ical family is strictly heterosexual and monoracial in its coupling (with the exception that White Man may have unofficial liaisons with Woman of Color, with or without her consent). We may note, too, the binaries in the schema: White Woman's chastity and delicacy, her sexual modesty, contrast sharply with Woman of Color's apparently excessive appetites; the representation of White Man's sexual hungers as appropriate or acceptable contrasts with depictions of the sexual "uncivility" and inappropriateness of Man of Color. A parade of monstrous apparitions indeed.

I have, of course, dramatized the trope-ical family here; but, unfortunately, it seems to me that I have captured it accurately rather than caricaturing it. For elements of this discursive repertoire have been replayed endlessly through British imperial history, through the history of the United States, and elsewhere. And their potency continues into the present. The temptation to "laundry-list" examples to illustrate my point is strong, but I will avoid it. Suffice it to say, instead, that these tropes have served, first, to explain or justify (to the oppressor if to no one else) myriad forms of disciplining violence—physical, cultural, and psychic—in locations "structured in dominance."[18] Second, in multiple contexts, *actual* white women, white men, and men and women of color (as opposed to figures in a trope-ical diorama) continue to be enlisted into the service of elements and aspects of these tropic constructs, projecting and performing them with varying degrees of consciousness and unconsciousness, coercion, seriousness, and parody.

One might argue that the white members of the trope-ical family as I have characterized them here are of the elite, and there is some truth to this claim. Poor white women, for example, have at times not been seen as either delicate or deserving protectees of their (and the nation's) men. Here, the notion of "white trash" comes to mind,[19] as well as the fate of European women immigrants to the United States at the turn of the twentieth century.[20] For the women of both groups were characterized in terms similar to those I used to describe the trope-ical Woman of Color: excessive fertility and sexual appetite, lack of hygiene. But in fact these counterexamples serve to reinforce my argument, for "white trash" as a concept actually marks the borders of whiteness; and European immigrants, especially those from the south and east, also fought long and hard to be considered "white." The slipperiness of whiteness as a construct is revealed here: although ostensibly marked by the clearly distinguishable behaviors or characteristics of self-designated selves, and of others named as such by those self-designators just mentioned, whiteness turns out on closer inspection to be more about the power to include and exclude groups and individuals than about the actual practices of those who are to be let in or kept out. (This slipperiness is demonstrated in different ways in the essays by France Winddance Twine, Phil Cohen, David Wellman, and Vron Ware in this volume.)

Like white women, white men are also diversely located in relation to power and privilege. For the most part they are not possessors of territory to defend, and frequently they lack the wherewithal to protect anyone, female or male. Yet often whiteness as a mode of self-naming is precisely the leverage white men have sought to use in their efforts to manufacture a sense of inclusion (to varying degrees illusory) in the dominant, to claim and seek to enforce ownership of nation or neighborhood, however symbolically. David Roediger's work, for example, powerfully demonstrates the ways whiteness and a particular kind of imagined community of labor enabled the simultaneous manufacture of interwoven versions of whiteness, masculinity, and free labor, quickly displaced and condensed around a sense of national belonging and entitlement as "Americanness." We will see in David Wellman's essay how both nineteenth- and late-twentieth-century minstrel shows project stereotypic images of blackness in order to displace and externalize anxieties about transformations in white masculinity. Phil Cohen and Vron Ware address in different ways the interweaving of masculinity, labor, and the sense of national belonging in the making of British whitenesses.

Additional kinds of instability and place switching are possible within the trope-ical family. To offer only one example in this regard, in the United States, as noted above, Asian men have at times been positioned in the trope-ical family in the classic Man of Color category, as sexual threat to white women. At other times, however, Asian men have been feminized in the racist imagination of the United States. And at still other times, they have been promised partial and conditional access to some of the benefits enjoyed by white men. One can, however, contextualize and thus "explain" these positionings: Chinese, Japanese, and Filipino men were castigated as potential or actual sexual assailants of white women as part of strenuous efforts at anti-Asian immigration control organized by coalitions of white labor unions, media, and elected officials in the last decades of the nineteenth century and the first decades of the twentieth.[21] In turn, the successful imposition of immigration control, restricting the entry of Asian women, helped bring into being bachelor communities of Asian men who were then derided as effeminate.[22] In either case the categorization is premised on the otherness, the alienness, of Asian men and women. This example, albeit described in brief here, demonstrates how racist discourse moves in concert with other political and economic processes, as well as at other times simply rolling along by virtue of its own momentum.

In speaking of place switching, one may also raise the question of agency. Just as white men do not, in fact, consciously control the terms of racial discourse as the discourse itself proposes that they do, white women are in actuality not mere pawns in the mapping and making of racial categories, hapless victims of both Man of Color as predator and White Man as rescuer and stifling protector. Rather, like white men, white women are frequently agents of racism in their own right; less often, white men and white women are also agents of its subversion. Several essays in this collection examine the nature of white agency in the relations of racism and strategize about shifting the valence of "racial agency" from reproduction to challenge and transformation. Further, the deployment of whiteness as a term of power, as socio-cultural currency, is not solely the prerogative of "biologically white" persons (and I hope that this introduction has, if nothing else, served to render that category an uncertain one). For as Angie Chabram-Dernersesian shows in her discussion of Chicana/o and Mexicana/o constructions of whiteness, whiteness as a system of meanings may be deployed within a range of contexts, by a range of groups of people, and for diverse reasons which are, to paraphrase Hartigan, patterned, irregular, and yet still connected.

Finally, we must pause to note which figures and processes are excluded from this trope-ical nightmare. First, the trope-ical family is relentlessly heterosexual: no image, male or female, however racially marked, is projected as homosexual, for better *or* for worse. A "real" man or woman, white or of color, is presumably heterosexual. There is, for example, no threat of homosexual assault by Man of Color, and likewise no glorification of the homosexual charms of White Woman. Indeed, if the trope-ical family were to exist and confer, their one point of agreement would most likely be that homosexuality is either un-natural, wrong, or both.

Second, there is little place in the trope-ical family to name physical violence, from the standpoint of either the perpetrators or its targets. There is silence rather than praise or blame, for example, in trope-ical articulations of mass killings of Native Americans in the period of colonization and westward expansion, and of African Americans while being transported to the United States as slaves. (White Man is not, for example, glorified as killer; nor is Man or Woman of Color noted as actual or potential target.) In the end, I suggest, we begin to see the trope-ical family deliquesce into a morass of erasures, inversions, distortions, and partial namings of actual historical and sociocultural processes.

I began this discussion by proposing that to view whiteness as "unmarked marker," as empty signifier, is to universalize a particular, and rather recent, historical moment. I have sought to argue that a range of processes of inclusion and exclusion have gone into the making of the version of whiteness that has been handed down to many of us—whiteness as norm, as transparency, as national/natural state of being. It is only when the processes of constructing dominance are complete that whiteness enters the realm of the apparently natural, of doxa. Moreover, as the essays in this volume point out, the status of whiteness in doxa is unstable, to say the least. Rather, I would argue that whiteness is always constructed, always in the process of being made and unmade. Indeed, its characterization as unmarked marker is itself an "ideological" effect that seeks to cover the tracks of its constructedness, specificity, and localness, even as they appear.

In a process that has been gradually gathering force over the last several years in the United States and elsewhere, whiteness is once again leaving its location in doxa, becoming a focus of discussion and critique for some, and a treasured yet endangered object for others. In this latter regard, we may note that in the United States white supremacist, white patriot, and white militia terrorism is on the rise, with black churches, Southeast Asian schoolchildren, *and* government buildings among the targets. As analysts of white patriot and militia movements explain, in assaults on government buildings and agents we see white activists self-styled as an endangered race, ostensibly fighting back or striking preemptively against a government—probably run by Jews, possibly with multinational influences, and aided by African American "underlings"—whose intention is to withdraw all basic rights from white people (the self-described true and just inheritors of the land).[23] As extreme as this sounds, it is also important to recognize its eery resonance with more "mainstream" white fears and fantasies: of curricula overrun by African Americans and other people of color (perhaps aided or encouraged by Jews, homosexuals, and other liberals), of jobs withheld from white men and given to others, of the nation bankrupted by welfare and medical bills, and of NAFTA and illegal immigration ruining the economy. Electoral and legislative assaults are another mode of response to fears of this kind—"mainstream," perhaps, but arguably equally if not more violent in their long-term effects.

Meanwhile, other whites are also asking the question with which David Wellman ends his essay: What, or who, do white people want to be? Are there alternatives available to whitenesses coded as national and racial dominance? The answer remains unclear. In the efforts to form European American social clubs in junior high and high schools that parallel the African American and Filipino clubs (for example) that already exist, we see attempts to recode whiteness as ethnicity or culture rather than race. However, this shift is not one that comes easily. First, the founding of a European American club inevitably brings with it the image of white supremacism, however unintended. And given the recruiting work of white supremacists in junior high and high schools, cases of mistaken identity are perhaps understandable. Indeed, it is sometimes hard to tell whether such efforts are undertaken in the spirit of parallelism or as backlash. Next, it is unclear whether there is, truly, a culture group namable as "European American" in terms of language, practice, and activity. And this returns us to the question, can whiteness be deracialized any more than any other ethnicity in a racially hierarchical social order?

In the world of social life and activism beyond the far right, white adults as well as children are seeking to pose the question of whiteness in new terms. White participation in politics of solidarity, in civil rights and national(ist) liberation movements, is, of course, long-standing and ongoing. But until recently such activities had not for the most part interrogated whiteness close up. Certainly its effects— the reproduction of dominance and privilege—were critically examined and named in racial and class terms, and certainly whites were enjoined to eschew race privilege. But there was not much in the way of examination of what whiteness *is*, as daily practice, as cultural assemblage, as site of identity or identification.

More recently (that is to say, beginning in the first half of the 1980s), left-of-center activist engagement with whiteness has approached the terrains of subjecthood and culture. The earliest work dovetailed intentionally with (and actually often sprang from) solidarity-based activism and multiracial coalition efforts. It sought primarily to comprehend how white people learn their places in the racial order and what keeps them invested in those locations.[24] As noted above, significant studies in this area have been undertaken by feminists and other community activists, and their work is consciously antiracist in its intent. However, as I have argued elsewhere, if focusing on white identity and culture displaces attention to whiteness as a site of racialized privilege, its effectiveness as antiracism becomes limited.[25]

In an even newer twist, versions of these ideas have been "corporatized," widely taken into the worlds of business, education, and the nonprofit sector. "Sensitivity" and "diversity awareness" programs bring new difficulties along with them, since they ask trainers to, in effect, guide people, willing or not, toward greater racial and cultural awareness of themselves and others. Here, the intent is to act in increasingly diverse classrooms, workplaces, health maintenance organizations, and so on, to train whites (and others too, but mainly whites) in "cultural competence," the capacity to work effectively with cultural others. Such training sometimes, but by no means always, also seeks to help create racial and ethnic equity in the workplace. Depending on the trainers and their approaches, this activity may focus attention more on racial "others" than on dominant selves. This means that, in these processes, once again whiteness may reemerge as the generic place marker, with whites asked to become "competent" in relating to members of "marked" cultural groups, or with nonwhite and/or non-male and/or non-U.S. persons taught to communicate in apparently generic corporate languages.

Other issues are being worked through under the surface of this new discourse. One is whether white people and white culture are "good" or "bad" (a question that, according to some interpretations, is begged by critique of white privilege and complicity with advantaged locations in the racial order). Here, we see a displacement of practical and material questions about white people's location in racial hierarchy onto very static notions of essence and original sin. It follows naturally from this displacement that whites would embark urgently on the quest either to be proven innocent or to find redemption. From here, the effort to find reasons to be "proud" of white culture, or ways to nuance whiteness by reference to class or ethnic subordination, becomes comprehensible within the terms of the discourse. A second problem in these approaches is the reification of cultures and the erasure of the processes through which cultures as practices come into being. Rather than conceptualizing cultures as fluid, intersecting realms, one gleans the image of a toy merry-go-round, with each bobbing figure representative of a group hermetically sealed from all the others.

An example taken from a training handout designed for work with white employees in corporate and nonprofit institutions illustrates these efforts. I draw on it not because it is better or worse than others, but because in its clarity it expresses well the difficulties inherent in these approaches. The handout says: "Some of our issues [as white Americans] are unique. While minority cultures have struggled to obtain power, white Americans must struggle to share the power we have. While minority cultures have struggled to retain their autonomy, white Americans must struggle to make our culture exist without dominating other cultures. We need to develop a public discussion of issues that apply uniquely to us as white Americans in a multicultural

America."[26] Here, the goal is manifestly to generate an antiracist practice of whiteness and to name whiteness as simultaneously racial and cultural. But we also see the enactment of a complex linguistic dance, one painfully familiar to many antiracist educators in the United States and probably elsewhere, too. Its burden, in my view, is to speak to white people about race privilege and white dominance in ways that mimic the discourses of activists of color (although discordantly here using the term "minority"), while at the same time naming the oppositeness, the differentness, of the positioning of whites in the racial order. There is, I'd suggest, an effort to sneak in the critique of racism and white privilege or dominance rather than, as older organizations might have done, to express it more directly. The intent here is perhaps to speak to and reorient, without naming them, the white backlash, resentment, and "me-too-ism" that have manifested as all too common responses to civil rights discourse. Thus, the implications in this quote are that whites, too, are unique; whites, too, must struggle to name their culture and retain their autonomy; whites, too, have a place in a multicultural United States.

What becomes of whiteness in this process? Or, to put it a different way, what kinds of whitenesses are being constructed in the turn to identity and culture? Two things are evident, I suggest. First, there is a drift away from viewing whiteness as racial category to viewing it as cultural category. This simultaneously evades and mystifies the positioning of whiteness in the racial hierarchy. Second, such constructions frequently reify and homogenize whiteness. I suggest that the effort to name an entity called "white culture" mirrors the reification of "nonwhite" cultures that has been in place for much longer. For there is, of course, no singular delimitable space called "black culture," "Chicana/o culture," or "Indian culture," any more than there is one called "white culture."

At the heart of the problem is the history of the concept of culture itself. Assertions of cultural superiority and inferiority have been among the alibis of racism for at least three hundred years. Equally, the assertion of some white cultural practices as culturally normative has been one of the effects of the achievement of race dominance. And this imposition of white cultural normativity explains precisely why whiteness looks more amorphous than those other cultural assemblages intentionally bounded and delimited in the context of racial oppression. Whites have never been culturally identical, nor have all the cultural practices preferred by whites been culturally dominant. And an effort to erase these long "culture wars" and manifest a bounded white culture is not only doomed to failure but also irrelevant to an effort to challenge racial hierarchy.

The essays in this text certainly examine whiteness as culture—but as practice rather than object, in relation to racial formation and historical process rather than as isolable or static. The authors ask how whiteness is complexly and differentially deployed in mediating social relations, whether between whites and racial "others," among whites, or within communities of color. Each essay steps beyond the taken-for-grantedness of whiteness to examine particular aspects of whiteness, or particular whitenesses, through analytic matrices that engage whiteness in terms that are both local and translocal, contemporary and embedded in specifiable histories. The contributors' foci include the following:

Examination of the "performance" and production of whiteness and white identities in daily, local practices (Cohen, Hartigan, hooks)

Tracking of daily performances of whiteness as they move into formal and institutional political processes (Ware, Wellman)

Deconstruction of the ways whiteness marks literary, cinematic, and scholarly practice (Aanerud, Chabram-Dernersesian, Muraleedharan, Sandoval)

Excavation of the limit points of whiteness, enabling reflection on the disciplinary practices that reinforce race as a historically constructed system of differentiation, exclusion, and belonging (Aanerud, Hartigan, Twine)

Critique of white complicity with the reproduction of racial domination along a continuum from conscious to unself-conscious enlistment (all authors)

Articulation of strategies for the development of antiracist, activist practice (Chabram-Dernersesian, Cohen, hooks, Ware, Wellman)

These essays are *not* the proceedings of a conference, and there has been no direct contact among contributors except contingently. Nor have the authors read one another's essays. Yet they share much. Some authors have been directly influenced by the other contributors' work.

Many share a common pool of textual influences, in the area of white-ness in particular, in the history and theory of race, and in sociocul-tural and textual theory at large. Moreover, as will be clear, these au-thors have in common a set of guiding questions and expectations as they enter their discussions of whiteness. First and most obvious is a recognition that whiteness cannot be assumed, but rather must be ex-amined. Second, all undertake social constructionist analyses of race and whiteness. A third common theme, and here I start to name the ways these essays powerfully break new ground, is that these authors emphasize and document how whiteness is always emplaced, tempo-rally and spatially. They trace (rather than simply asserting) the inter-meshing of whiteness with other webs of relations, including those of gender and sexuality, class, nation, and region. Fourth, and relatedly, the authors' recognition of whiteness as a site where much power ac-crues is followed up by their innovative approaches to analyzing the workings of whiteness as a set of relations where power is most use-fully viewed as multifaceted rather than monolithic, and as less stable in some locations than in others. Last, and interwoven with all of the above points, is an insistence that analyzing whiteness is inseparable from the critique of racism. This lends a determination, a doggedness, and an urgency to the essays in this volume.

The essays are presented along a continuum, beginning with those primarily focused on written and filmic texts and moving on to those engaging social and/or ethnographic settings. It need hardly be said, though, that a clear separation of the essays into cultural versus social texts, much less into humanistic versus social scientific approaches, is impossible. For of course, none of these authors deals with writing or film outside social context, and conversely, none of those who engage social texts does so without situating them in relation to the cultural practices and performances that help to make them explicable.

Rebecca Aanerud's essay, "Fictions of Whiteness: Speaking the Names of Whiteness in U.S. Literature," examines constructions of whiteness in literature. Aanerud notes the questions framed by Toni Morrison in *Playing in the Dark: Whiteness and the Literary Imagina-tion:* What might be "the nature—even the cause—of literary white-ness? What is it *for?* What parts do the invention and development of whiteness play in the construction of what is loosely described as 'American'?"[27] Aanerud examines two distinct moments in literary whiteness: one is modernist and gender conscious, exemplified in Kate Chopin's 1899 novel, *The Awakening;* the second moment, postmodern and post–civil rights, is examined with two texts as foci of inquiry: Allan Gurganus's novella "Blessed Assurance" and Joanne Brasil's *Escape from Billy's Bar-B-Q*. Aanerud's intent is to develop a critical reading practice that foregrounds the construction and representation of whiteness in U.S. fiction and allows readers to recognize white authors' complicity with the discourses of white supremacy.

Aanerud argues that reading whiteness into texts that are not overtly about race is essential if we are to disrupt whiteness as the unchallenged racial norm. We also learn about the genderedness of whiteness and the racialness of gender from Aanerud's reading. She points out how in *The Awakening* whiteness signifies particular relationships to maternity and sexual propriety. Analyzing *The Awakening* also reveals how whiteness itself is socially constructed. The white female character works to preserve her whiteness, which, Aanerud argues, "is a highly orchestrated product of culture and nature."

The post–civil rights texts on which Aanerud focuses tell a different story, for in these works the authors self-consciously name and interrogate their own whiteness. These texts pose other questions for the critic, whose goals are now to analyze the meanings assigned to whiteness by examining how it is represented and constructed. Rather than challenging the terms of whiteness, however, these white authors seem most interested in establishing the innocence or distance of their white protagonists in relation to white dominance. Here we learn how, in fact, white solipsism can be reestablished in contemporary performances of literary whiteness.

Aanerud's essay sets the stage for themes that recur throughout this collection. First, her discussion indicates the constructedness of whiteness, which is established as performance rather than essence. Aanerud also indicates the possibility and necessity of situating performances of whiteness, literary or otherwise, in time and space. For we see in her readings of *The Awakening*, "Blessed Assurance," and *Escape from Billy's Bar-B-Q* how location, political moment, and standpoint place limits and priorities on the possible or likely range of enunciations of whiteness by subjects. Moreover, she articulates clearly the embeddedness of whiteness in racial formation and also in other sets of relations (in her essay, class and gender are especially to the fore). And finally, as do all the authors here, Aanerud emphasizes that as a racial category, whiteness cannot be other than embedded in racism.

T. Muraleedharan, like Aanerud, examines a textual enunciation of whiteness, but in film rather than literature. Muraleedharan's essay,

"Rereading *Gandhi*," asks the startling question, Is Gandhi white? Muraleedharan refers here to the Gandhi of Richard Attenborough's 1982 film of the same name. Muraleedharan shares Aanerud's recognition that part of the overall project of antiracism is the analytical emplacement of cultural artifacts—here, visual and literary texts—in their social contexts. In particular, Muraleedharan demonstrates the need to investigate the cultural products that sustain the racist foundations of the dominant order, and sets out to make explicit the "scarcely visible" racism evident in the narrative of *Gandhi*.

The social context is postwar, postempire Britain, and Muraleedharan situates *Gandhi* within a series of films, television shows, and novels offered in the late 1970s and early 1980s in a burst of Raj-nostalgic fascination with "British" India. He demonstrates that reading Gandhi in *Gandhi,* both formally by means of film theory and contextually by means of sociocultural analyses of postwar Britain, elucidates the participation of *Gandhi* and other Raj-nostalgia texts in the Thatcherite policies that dominated Britain in the 1980s.

And there is more, much more, at stake than the simple whitening of Gandhi (itself an extraordinary accomplishment on the part of the filmmaker!). For one thing, whiteness in this context stands for universality and civility. And we may also link Muraleedharan's reading of this postempire British filmic text with Aanerud's analysis of post–civil rights literary artifacts, for each author makes clear that the white liberal "stake" in the text is to prove the innocence of whiteness and of white people, specifically and in general. Muraleedharan's essay again serves to remind us of the localness of whiteness, of its pluralness. We may note, for example, that the nonwhite Other of Gandhi/*Gandhi* is not black but brown. And this recalls once again the nonbinariness of racial categories: the story of race is not a simple story of black and white, but rather one of more complex, intermeshing dyads crafted through nationally structured processes of history (in this collection instantiated as black-white, brown-white, African-European, Mexican-Chicano, Chicano-Anglo, Indian-British).

The burden of *Gandhi*'s whiteness is a particularly British one, and a particularly postcolonial and Thatcherite one. It is also a class-marked one. This means that even Phil Cohen's and Vron Ware's essays, while engaging whiteness in Britain a mere decade or so after *Gandhi*, by centrally focusing on working-class stakes in whiteness offer versions of whiteness different from the one "ambushed" in Muraleedharan's discussion although thoroughly interwoven with it.

Chéla Sandoval's essay is startling in a different way. She represents Roland Barthes to us not only as master semiotician but also as "one of the first white Western critical theorists to develop an analytical apparatus for theorizing white consciousness in a postempire world." Sandoval's "Critical Theory and White Mythologies: The Rhetoric of Supremacy" reads the works of Roland Barthes and Frantz Fanon with and against one another in a way that, like the essays of Chabram-Dernersesian, hooks, and Muraleedharan, brings our attention to the gaze and its socioracial location.

Fanon's *Black Skin, White Masks* (1951) recounts the "wounded forms of consciousness" developed by people of color forced to live under white supremacist rule. Barthes, in *Mythologies* and its analytical framing essay, "Myth Today," asks how "innocent" or well-intentioned citizens can enact the forms of being that are tied to racist colonialism. Sandoval argues that both texts engage empire and the making of consciousness. While on the surface one might argue that Fanon's text examines the subject formation of the oppressed, and Barthes's that of the oppressor, the two texts are by no means simple mirrors of one another. For one thing, Fanon's examination of the "masking" of subordinated subjects under colonialism cannot proceed without analysis of the making and the pathways of the dominant's consciousness. But in addition, Sandoval demonstrates how Barthes's analysis of dominant consciousness draws on, and then submerges, all traces of what she calls a "methodology of the oppressed."

Sandoval's exploration resituates Roland Barthes as a powerful critic of whiteness. But at the same time she offers insight into the limits of white self-scrutiny in this instance and the challenges faced by a critic, such as Barthes, seeking to analyze circumstances of his own making. What we have, then, is not only a discussion of two texts—not only a recognition of the ways in which we cannot, in fact, examine the subject position of the oppressed without engaging that of the oppressor, and vice versa—but also a powerful allegory of appropriation, of erasure, and of the loneliness and limitation that Fanon and Barthes engender. Further, Sandoval offers powerful lessons about canon formation and its "discontents."

Angie Chabram-Dernersesian's essay, "On the Social Construction of Whiteness within Selected Chicana/o Cultural Discourses," asks what the stakes are in Chicana/o constructions of whiteness. Just as Aanerud asks what literary whiteness is "for" in white literary contexts, and as Muraleedharan asks to what end Gandhi is whitened for the

English popular imagination, Chabram-Dernersesian asks what whiteness is "for" in Mexicana/o and Chicana/o discourse. She begins by noting that in a period of decreased satisfaction with "the essentialist brand of identity politics," Chicana/o critics have been active in "negotiating the hyphen between Chicana/o and Latina/o and attending to the gender linkages that are inscribed in this transnational movement through the Americas." But, she continues, critics have put much less effort into examining how Chicanas/os construct whiteness in order to position alternative and even oppositional identities within a conflicted social arena.

Chabram-Dernersesian goes on to examine Chicana/o and Mexicana/o constructions of whiteness sociohistorically, by means of closely reading performance and folk art—theater, literature, poetry, and music. Readers are taken to a range of discursive sites, including the Chicano movement and the theater and filmic performances that emerged from it; the U.S.-Mexican border and the violent remakings of identity that began with the making of that border in the 1848 Treaty of Guadalupe-Hidalgo; and, finally, feminist rereadings both of Chicana/o and Mexicana/o identities and of their interrelation in the present.

For Chicana/o and Mexicana/o cultural practitioners, to name whiteness has in general meant naming an Other. This characteristic, of course, immediately separates their concept from whites' own namings of whiteness. Further, Chabram-Dernersesian thinks it crucial to examine how, when, and why whites and Others are articulated as *aca* and *alla,* as "*within*" and "*without*" Chicano/Mexicano realms of belonging. Chabram-Dernersesian thus demonstrates how other positionings, other namings, are condensed into whiteness in Chicana/o and Mexicana/o discourses on whiteness. A key focus in this essay is la Malinche, the brown woman seen to have sold out her people to Cortés and to continue to sell out to white society. For Chabram-Dernersesian, la Malinche condenses with whiteness in a way that empties class and race of gender, wresting Chicanas out of the political imaginary of resistance and contestation. In a related way, the pocha or pocho, the brown woman or man north of the border, is "whitened" in Mexicano cultural discourse. This again flattens and erases aspects of historical and social process.

This essay translocalizes and pluralizes whiteness, indicating its shifting saliency across national borders, and indeed in the aftermath of the restaking of national borders. Chabram-Dernersesian makes evident the fruitfulness of examining the sociopolitical contexts within which and in response to which narratives of whiteness emerge. She also alerts us to the range of agendas and contexts within which whiteness has value, is currency—whiteness is not, from this purview, the exclusive "property" of a dominant ethnic group, internally undifferentiated and with no other claims to power than its whiteness. Rather, whiteness as a name may be deployed variously. It also follows that perhaps "power" must have other names besides whiteness in order to be fully effective.

Like Chabram-Dernersesian, bell hooks, in "Representing Whiteness in the Black Imagination," a 1992 essay reprinted here, examines whiteness from a vantage point ostensibly outside whiteness—and in doing so shows that the borders of whiteness are not, in fact, as fixed as they might seem at first glance. Hooks's essay examines, historicizes, and situates black gazes (not "*the* black gaze," for these are plural too) on whiteness. Her focus on whiteness as terror reminds us as forcefully as did Chabram-Dernersesian of the violently irreducible connection between whiteness and race dominance.

In a mirroring that is careful and complex, hooks also locates whites gazing at blacks gazing at whites. And she points out that whites' disbelief that there *is* a black gaze on whiteness is itself racism, a symptom of the twin presumptions of white invincibility and black inferiority. Hooks's discussion of whiteness as terror is at times autoethnographical in its method: a documentation of journeyings old and new through kinds of "white territory," including neighborhoods, classrooms, conference halls, and that infamous site of international white terror-induction, the airport arrival or departure gate. And hooks returns us again and again to that figure who is the counterpoint to the white terrorist—the disbelieving white liberal. Ultimately, however, for hooks as for all the authors in this volume, whiteness and blackness are historical, not essential, constructs, plural rather than singular, and potentially alterable by means of careful political practice. So that, like some others in this volume, hooks ends her paper by suggesting how we might begin remaking whiteness, how we might start to resituate whiteness and blackness in relation to each other.

John Hartigan Jr.'s essay, "Locating White Detroit," is drawn from an ethnographic study conducted in white underclass Detroit, part of a larger study of whites in Detroit whose purposes included determining how whites varied by class background in articulating their whiteness.[28] Like the other contributors, Hartigan proposes that the analysis of whiteness requires specification. Also like the others, Hartigan found it necessary to (re)create analytical and theoretical tools in order to accomplish this task. Adapting cultural anthropologist Marilyn Strathern's fractal theory of cross-cultural communication and using it to rework the racial formation theory of sociologists Michael Omi and Howard Winant, Hartigan asks, Where does whiteness end? Where do whites begin? The value of fractal theory as an analytic tool is borne out in Hartigan's examination of underclass Detroit, where, as Hartigan notes, whiteness diverges from national assumptions and understandings and is rarely the normative condition. In fact, whiteness is often considered out of place in this "black metropolis."

Through interviews, observation, examination of Detroit media, and participation as a resident of a poor, white and black neighborhood close to Tiger Stadium, Hartigan is able to examine whiteness across a range of sites: race and space, who "belongs" where, when, and why; neighborhood, class, and race, white "flight" to the suburbs and the complex relations between white family members who have left and those still in the " 'hood"; family, nuclear or extended, at times monoracial and at times not; sexual partnership; school; and public events such as the Saint Patrick's Day parade.

The fractal dance of transmission was, one might say, chaotically orderly. It became clear that the white, underclass Detroitans interviewed by Hartigan never "forgot" they were white. Yet their racialness might be passive or active from one site to the next, and from moment to moment. Hartigan's fieldwork convinced him that whiteness is not transmitted unchanged down through increasingly specific levels of society. Further, whites at different economic levels viewed whiteness in different ways.

Perhaps more than any other essay in this collection, France Winddance Twine's "Brown-Skinned White Girls: Class, Culture, and the Construction of White Identity" makes simultaneously visible the unnaturalness of whiteness as a racial category and the pathways of its enforcement. The essay draws on Twine's interviews with young women of known African ancestry raised by at least one parent of known European ancestry in the suburban United States who were first made "white" as children and later unmade, excluded from whiteness.

Twine states at the outset of her essay that feminists who theorize about whiteness have not addressed "white" women who are not exclusively of European ancestry. Further, she says, "cultural anthropologists have assumed that a white identity that does not involve 'passing' is not available to African-descent women who possess bio-

logical markers that place them in a nonwhite category." Even the challenge of finding accurate language with which to describe her interviewees underscores Twine's point—that whiteness is above all a *social*
construction, but one whose disciplinary practices work forcefully to
maintain the fictive biological "alibi" of race.

We learn from Twine's essay, and from the words of her interviewees, that whiteness is made out of materials that include socioeconomic
status, cultural practice, peer group acceptance, parental teaching, and
community participation in ideological constructions of what constitutes "racial neutrality." But before we are tempted to imagine that
race is after all subsumable as something else—perhaps class, perhaps
culture—we are shown when, how, and why these young women's
whiteness was challenged, made more complex, made less tenable, beginning in puberty and adolescence. Later, in the atmosphere of the
university campus, these women made diverse choices between whiteness, blackness, mixed-ness. We see their reflections on past, present,
and future. And as well, we see the delicate balancing of choice and
constraint within which these women move, naming themselves and
being named as racialized persons.

Like the other ethnography-based essays in this collection (Cohen,
Hartigan), this one powerfully localizes whiteness, examining it in
spaces as small as a college campus or neighborhood, yet explicating
also how the small space is linked temporally and territorially to far
larger expanses. And, again like other essays, this one takes us beyond
a mere "listing" of the systems within which race "lives" and moves, to
a careful tracing of how, in a given setting, race makes and is made by
relations of sex and sexuality, class, and culture.

Phil Cohen writes histories of the present, excavating and tracking makings and remakings of whiteness. His "Laboring under Whiteness" analyzes one version of working-class whiteness, a British, essentially male one. In his earlier extensive ethnographic studies in the
East End of London, especially with working-class white youth at
work and play—as secondary school students,[29] as soccer supporters—Cohen focused on the young men's collective sense of self and
other, and the explicit hostility to black people of Asian and African
descent that is central to its formation. He analyzed this racist whiteness within sociocultural and sociopsychic narratives, explicating the
simultaneous class and ethnic restructurings of the last two decades
in this part of London and the effects of these on the kinds of mascu-

linity achievable in this context. As one section heading of his essay in this volume has it (playing on a John Lennon cut later recorded by Marianne Faithful), "A working-class racist is something to be."

In "Laboring under Whiteness," Cohen includes excerpts from an interview and discussion of identity and ethnicity with a group of white high school students, analyzing it within a frame of Lacanian and post-Kleinian psychoanalysis, and against the backdrop of British labor history. Cohen's goals, like his analysis, are many stranded. Cohen asks how this young, male, working-class, East End–based whiteness came to be, and what implications the conditions of its making might have for antiracist strategy in Britain. Cohen's concern to localize whiteness stems in part from his sense of the analytic and strategic inadequacies of a "transatlantic wall against racism" that originated, he argues, in the United States in the aftermath of the Civil Rights movement and was elaborated on by left and feminist movements on both sides of the Atlantic. In Cohen's view, whether the outcomes of this overall framing entail a biologistic or a social constructionist naming of whiteness (and for that matter, of blackness and other racial positionings), "neither offers much purchase on the complexities of the encounters that are currently taking place in and across racial and ethnic divides." Cohen's alternative is an insistence on specification, for "the building of a new transatlantic wall against racism will have to wait on a proper recognition of what separates as well as what unites us."

Vron Ware's "Island Racism: Gender, Place, and White Power" also takes us to Britain, seeking to explore in the context of England's "prolonged identity crisis . . . how masculinity and femininity are involved in the representation of Englishness as an exclusively white identity." Ware frames her discussion around two events: the 1993 local election success of British National party member Derek Beackon with a winning slogan of "Rights for Whites" and a campaign focused on allegations of antiwhite and pro-Bengali discrimination by the local housing authority, and a 1995 soccer match between England and Ireland that ended abruptly when English-initiated riots broke out in the crowd.

Ware takes us on a complex analytical journey, engaging the local and national material and discursive histories in which each event is embedded. She is concerned to view each event as object lesson for theorists and activists against racism, asking where, how, and why we seem to lack tools adequate to the task of analyzing, much less challenging, racism in daily life. She is also concerned to link, analytically, "extremist" and "mainstream" racism, noting the evasive or distancing responses of the British press that tended to mark as extreme and unusual these events and their participants.

As important as her reading of what *is* said, Ware argues that other crucial questions are evaded in both media and analytical engagement with everyday racism. How are *women* positioned in the racist relations of these two events? What are the political and economic processes covered over and racialized by the electoral strategies of both the British National party *and* other, more mainstream, political parties, and how are these gendered? And, finally, how might gendered analyses of racism contribute to our ability to respond effectively to racist practices both in the daily life of communities and in the arena of formal politics?

David Wellman is also concerned to tell a familiar story in a new way, and thus to intervene in what in the first half of the 1990s most often appeared as a political gridlock: the struggle over the legitimacy or illegitimacy of affirmative action. And indeed, as we go to press the gridlock seems to be rapidly unjamming, with right-of-way ceded to the anti–affirmative action forces. "Minstrel Shows, Affirmative Action Talk, and Angry White Men: Marking Racial Otherness in the 1990s" begins by examining the myths and facts of affirmative action in a way that forcefully reminds us of the simple untruth of many of the anti–affirmative actionists' claims. But more significantly, Wellman explains what is at stake, on a deeper psychocultural level, in white males' responses to affirmative action. Drawing a powerful analogy between the 1990s discourse on affirmative action and the minstrel shows that were extraordinarily popular with white working-class men in the mid–nineteenth century United States, Wellman proposes directions our interventions might take if we are to meaningfully challenge the now commonplace images of the quota queen, reverse discrimination, and the unqualified beneficiary of affirmative action.

I will not steal Wellman's thunder by reiterating his argument here. Suffice it to say that while Wellman recognizes the necessity of attacking affirmative action myths on evidentiary grounds, he also thinks that other, unacknowledged issues are at stake. In seeking out and analyzing these issues, Wellman ends by offering analytic strategies that might both hone antiracist education *and* enhance popular consciousness about some of the key economic, social, and cultural processes currently unfolding in Western societies.

Notes

Thanks to the contributors to this volume for their inspiration, optimism, and energy, as authors and as thinkers. Thanks to Ken Wissoker for his proposal that I put this collection together, and for his enthusiasm and insight throughout the production process. Thanks to two anonymous readers for their care and comments in response to my first draft of this introduction. Finally, thank-you to my partner, Lata Mani, for her thoughtful interest and involvement in the completion of this project, and for providing this book with its title.

1   Among others, see Reginald Horsman, "Scientific Racism and the American Indian in the Mid–Nineteenth Century," *American Quarterly* 27 (May 1975): 52–168; Horsman, *Race and Manifest Destiny: The Origins of American Racial Anglo-Saxonism* (Cambridge: Harvard University Press, 1981); Theodore W. Allen, *The Invention of the White Race,* vol. 1: *Racial Oppression and Social Control* (London: Verso, 1994); David R. Roediger, *Towards the Abolition of Whiteness: Essays on Race, Politics and Working Class History* (London: Verso, 1994); Roediger, *The Wages of Whiteness: Race and the Making of the American Working Class* (London: Verso, 1991); Alexander Saxton, *The Rise and Fall of the White Republic: Class Politics and Mass Culture in Nineteenth Century America* (London: Verso, 1990); Vron Ware, *Beyond the Pale: White Women, Racism and History* (London: Verso, 1992); Tomas Almaguer, *Racial Faultlines: The Historical Origins of White Supremacy in California* (Berkeley: University of California Press, 1994); Kathleen Blee, *Women of the Klan: Racism and Gender in the 1920s* (Berkeley: University of California Press, 1991).

2   Significant texts here include David T. Wellman, *Portraits of White Racism,* 2d ed. (1977; Cambridge: Cambridge University Press, 1993); Phil Cohen, "It's Racism What Dunnit," in *Race, Culture and Difference,* ed. J. Donald and A. Rattansi (London: Sage, 1992); Cohen, "All White on the Night," in *The Good Society,* ed. M. Rustin (London: Verso, 1996); Cohen, "Backbone of the Nation, Race Apart," in Dockland Forum, *Twenty Years* (London: n.p., 1996); Cohen, *Rethinking the Youth Question* (London: Macmillan, 1997); Les Back, *New Ethnicities and Urban Youth Cultures* (London: University College London Press, 1995).

3   Examples here are, in film, Fred Pfeil, *White Guys: Studies in Postmodern Domination and Difference* (London: Verso, 1995); and Richard Dyer, "White," *Screen* 29, no. 4 (1988): 44–64; in daily life, Ruth Frankenberg, *White Women, Race Matters: The Social Construction of Whiteness* (Minneapolis: University of Minnesota Press, 1993; and London: Routledge, 1993); Wellman, *Portraits of White Racism;* a germinal text from a much earlier time is Lillian Smith, *Killers of the Dream* (1949; reprint, New York: Norton, 1978). James Baldwin, "On Being White and Other Lies," *Essence* (April 1984): 80–84 is a late piece by Baldwin but one that signals many years of critical work on whiteness. In literature, see Toni Morrison, *Playing in the Dark: Whiteness and the Literary Imagination* (New York: Vintage Books, 1993); in the academic corpus, Elizabeth V. Spelman, *Inessential Woman: Problems of Exclusion in Feminist Thought* (Boston: Beacon Press, 1988); Avery Gordon and Christopher Newfield, "White Philosophy," *Critical Inquiry* 20 (Summer 1994): 737–57. See also two just-published books: Michelle Fine, Lois Weis, Linda C. Powell, and L. Muu Wong, eds., *Off Whites Readings as Race, Power, and Society* (New York:

Routledge, 1977); and Matt Wray and Annalee Newitz, eds., *White Trash: Race and Class in America* (London: Routledge, 1997).

4   Feminist works on white identity and feminist practice include Adrienne Rich, "Disloyal to Civilization: Feminism, Racism, Gynephobia," in *On Lies, Secrets and Silence: Selected Prose, 1966–78* (New York: Norton, 1979); Minne Bruce Pratt, "Identity: Skin, Blood, Heart," in *Yours in Struggle: Three Feminist Perspectives on Anti-Semitism and Racism,* ed. Elly Bulkin, Minnie Bruce Pratt, and Barbara Smith (Brooklyn: Long Haul Press, 1984); Mab Segrest, *My Mama's Dead Squirrel: Lesbian Essays on Southern Culture* (Ithaca, N.Y.: Firebrand Books, 1986).

5   See, in particular, articles published by the Center for Democratic Renewal, P.O. Box 50469, Atlanta, GA 30302, including *The Christian Identity Movement* (1991); *Quarantines and Death: The Far Right's Homophobic Agenda,* (1992); *They Don't All Wear Sheets: A Chronology of Racist and Far Right Violence 1980–1986* (1987); and *Paramilitary Right Moves Center Stage: Overview of Militias, Hate Groups and Intolerance in 1995* (1995). Also the journals and articles from the Southern Poverty Law Center, 400 Washington Avenue, Montgomery, AL 36104, including *False Patriots: The Threat of Anti-Government Extremists* (1996); also see James Ridgeway, *Blood in the Face: The KKK, Aryan Nations, Nazi Skinheads and the Rise of a New White Culture* (New York: Thunder's Mouth Press, 1990).

6   Haole is an indigenous Hawaiian name for white people; pakeha is an indigenous New Zealander name for whites; wasiku is one of many indigenous mainland U.S. Native American names for whites; ghost is the name given to whites in the family Maxine Hong Kingston describes in her autobiographical novels about growing up in San Francisco's Chinatown: *The Woman Warrior* (New York: Vintage, 1976), and *China Men* (New York: Ballantine, 1981); gringo is a Mexican name for North Americans, especially white ones; honky is an African American name for white folk.

7   American, English, British—conflations of racial with national identity in white dominant nation-states; man—universalization of the white male subject, at times even by liberals (forty-somethings and those older will perhaps remember a line from a song from the early 1970s, "The family of man keeps growing"); woman—universalization of white female subject as the subject of feminism, frequently commented on in the last two-plus decades of critique of the feminist movements of North America and Western Europe; white woman—white female (feminist?) response to calls to locate herself more carefully in feminist discourse; white United Statesian—white male or female U.S. resident's response to the call to locate her/himself more carefully in the world order, localizing both race and nation within the continental Americas.

8   Frankenberg, *White Women, Race Matters,* esp. 142–57.

9   Karen Brodkin Sacks, "How Did Jews Become White Folks?" in *Race,* ed. Steven Gregory and Roger Sanjek (New Brunswick: Rutgers University Press, 1994).

10 Horsman, *Race and Manifest Destiny.* For another acute analysis of the significance of constructions of whiteness to the making of another part of the United States, California, see Almaguer, *Racial Faultlines.*

11 Roediger, *The Wages of Whiteness.*

12 Ibid., 47–50. See also, in the following pages, his discussion of the similarly moti-

vated transition, in workers' language use, from *master* to the Dutch *bos* (also meaning "master"), which became the now normative *boss*.

13   Ibid., 86.

14   Ibid., 68.

15   Ibid., 95–131.

16   Ibid., 133–63.

17   Some valuable discussions of comparative racialization in the United States are Almaguer, *Racial Faultlines;* Horsman, *Race and Manifest Destiny;* Megumi Dick Osumi, "Asians and California's Anti-miscegenation Laws," in *Asian/Pacific American Experiences: Women's Perspectives,* ed. Tsuchida Nobuye (Asian/Pacific American Learning Resource Center and General College, University of Minnesota, 1982).

18   I take this term from Stuart Hall, "Race, Articulation and Societies Structured in Dominance," in UNESCO, *Sociological Theories, Race and Colonialism* (Paris: UNESCO Press, 1980), 305–45.

19   Here, see the essays in Matt Wray and Annalee Newits, eds., *White Trash: Race and Class in America* (New York: Routledge 1997).

20   Kathie Friedman Kasaba, *"To Become a Person": The Experience of Gender, Ethnicity and Work in the Lives of Immigrant Women, New York City, 1870–1940* (Binghamton, N.Y.: SUNY Press, 1996).

21   On this history, see Osumi, "Asians and California's Anti-miscegenation Laws."

22   For a discussion of this process, see Elaine Kim, *Asian American Literature* (Philadelphia: Temple University Press, 1982), 173–213.

23   Southern Poverty Law Center, *False Patriots.*

24   Of considerable importance here is the legacy of the late Ricky Sherover-Marcuse, whose program "Unlearning Racism" was taught in workshops around the United States. Combining the tools of the Frankfurt school with those of the Reevaluation Cocounseling movement, Sherover-Marcuse's approach was to "heal" whites from their enlistment in racism through a combination of consciousness raising and sociopsychological counseling, rather than to enforce or coerce their rejection of what she viewed as their socially constructed complicity with the racial order.

25   Frankenberg, *White Women, Race Matters.*

26   Center for the Study of White American Culture, Inc., 245 West 4th Avenue, Roselle, NJ 07203.

27   Morrison, *Playing in the Dark,* 9.

28   Hartigan, *Cultural Constructions of Whiteness.*

29   "High school," in U.S. parlance.

Fictions of Whiteness: Speaking the Names of Whiteness in U.S. Literature

Rebecca Aanerud

One of the signs of our times is that we really don't know what "white" is.
—Kobena Mercer, in *How Do I Look? Queer Film and Video*

In our society dominant discourse tries never to speak its own name.
—Russell Ferguson, *Out There: Marginality and Contemporary Art*

Racializing Whiteness

THE final lines of Kate Chopin's novel *The Awakening* unmistakably mark Edna as white: "The foamy wavelets curled up to her white feet, and coiled like serpents about her ankles. She walked out. The water was chill, but she walked on. The water was deep, but she lifted her white body and reached out with a long sweeping stroke."[1] Yet despite this specificity of Edna's white subjectivity, little critical attention has been paid to her position as a white woman. Whiteness in the above passage is often understood to signal Edna's vulnerability, her innocence, even her purity associated with the rebirth to her true self. Certainly reading whiteness as such, although troublesome, is valid. I suggest, however, that *whiteness* has multiple meanings and significations, not the least of which is "race." In 1985 Henry Louis Gates Jr. wrote that "until the past decade or so . . . race has not been brought to bear upon the study of literature in any apparent way,"[2] to which I would add that whiteness as race has yet to receive adequate critical consideration in the field of literary studies. It is not my intent to appropriate discussions of race in an effort to recenter white subjectivity. Rather, I want to call into question what white subjectivity is by contributing to the recent work of making visible the "constructed, and contested character of 'whiteness.'"[3] Far too often, when race as a category of analysis is invoked, its meaning and significance are construed in terms of nonwhiteness. A classic example of this is illustrated in the following passage in which Teresa de Lauretis responds to a question concerning the absence of a racial component— despite the interracial relationship between the two main characters (Agatha, a black Latina Brazilian, and Jo, a white U.S. American)— in her analysis of the film *She Must Be Seeing Things*. "I thought a lot about the inscription of race in the relationship between Agatha and Jo, but I concluded that the film intentionally focuses on the other aspects of their relationship. And though it makes it clear that the role of Agatha is marked by her *cultural* difference as a Brazilian, a black Latina, it doesn't address the *racial* difference between the women. So it's not that race is not a crucial issue in lesbian and feminist relationships, politics, and theory. It certainly is. But it is not represented as an issue in this film."[4] Race, in this quotation, is understood as racial difference located in the characters of color or in the dynamics between characters of differing racial backgrounds. It would seem that discussions of race are applicable only to those individuals, real or fictitious, who occupy a subject position other than white. Within such a scheme, being white is equated with being unraced—or, to stress the political, being normal.

In fact, all people live racialized lives. Jo's subjectivity is as racialized as Agatha's. As social beings we are each implicated in an interconnected series of hierarchical systems, of race, class, and gender among others. These systems are read onto our bodies, and we in turn interpret and are interpreted through our understandings and misunderstandings of them. Our awareness of these systems is partially informed by the degree of privilege or oppression we experience as a result of our positioning. While it might seem that race is something that affects only people of color, in fact race is a meaningful and fundamental factor in all lives.[5] In film as well as literature race need not be an issue in order for it to be a relevant component. I am interested in expanding the theoretical discussions of race to include an examination of the constructions and representations of white subjectivity in literature. Relatedly, I wish to see how current power relations of gender, sexuality, race, and class are reproduced through the unspoken privilege of assuming racial neutrality.

This essay will take "whiteness" to be a socially and historically constructed category of racial identity. As such, whiteness cannot be understood as a singular entity, existing prior to or apart from other categories of identities. Its formation depends on the changing relations of gender, class, sexuality, and nationality. Thus, the meaning of whiteness, like all racialized identities in the United States, is not monolithic. Instead, its construction and interpretation are informed by historical moment, region, political climate, and racial identity.

As the epigraphs suggest, whiteness can be difficult to see. As Richard Dyer puts it, in a white supremacist nation, whiteness "secures its dominance by seeming not to be anything in particular."[6] This is not to suggest that representations of whiteness are similarly obscure to all "seers." In her article "Representing Whiteness in the Black Imagination," bell hooks argues that not only do many black authors (and her students of color) see whiteness clearly, they represent it in a way not seen in the works of white authors, namely, whiteness as terrorizing. I would add that one's ability to see whiteness is equally influenced by his or her relationship to white dominant society as a whole. In other words, the varying abilities to "see" whiteness are as much a result of consciousness as they are of race.

However, despite the "real" relations of readers of American fiction to that body of literature, all readers, to draw from Toni Morrison, "until very recently, and regardless of the race of the author, have been positioned as white."[7] From this position, whiteness as race operates as an unmarked racial category. Unless told otherwise, the reader, positioned as white, assumes the characters are white. (Un)marked whiteness is, of course, a type of marking. In an analysis of Hemingway's *To Have and Have Not*, Morrison writes that she easily identifies Eddy as white: "We know he is because nobody says so."[8] Such (un)marked whiteness is often reinforced by the overt racial marking of the nonwhite characters.

Although the construction of whiteness depends on dynamic social, political, and historical factors, a predominant construction in American literature is undoubtedly whiteness as "unraced," or racially neutral. This construction has significant political underpinnings. In this normative space, as Dyer argues, whiteness comes to stand for "the natural, inevitable, ordinary way of being human."[9] Occupation of this privileged position "is the source of its representational power . . . white domination is reproduced by the way white people 'colonise the definition of normal.'"[10] This essay seeks to unpack the construction of whiteness as the neutral way of being human through an examination of its representations in the literature of American authors. What are the various forms of whiteness in American literature? Or, as Toni Morrison asks, what is "the nature—even the cause—of literary 'whiteness.' What is it *for*? What parts do the invention and development of whiteness play in the construction of what is loosely described as 'American'?"[11] Here I will attempt to answer some of these questions by analyzing three works of American fiction by white authors: *The Awakening,* by Kate Chopin; "Blessed Assurance," by Allan Gurganus; and *Escape from Billy's Bar-B-Que,* by Joanne Brasil.

I have chosen these three texts in part because in each case the author is a white person writing about whiteness. The importance of looking at the way white authors write whiteness is twofold. First, white writers are more likely to assume whiteness as a (non)racial norm. Understanding how whiteness functions as the unspoken norm is, I believe, a crucial part of challenging its domination. Second, white writers occasionally recognize whiteness as a racial category, and some even take it as their central theme; this is especially true of some post–civil rights texts. Here, I will consider what, if anything, is revealed about whiteness when white writers self-consciously locate whiteness.

To address the first concern, I will discuss *The Awakening.* Although Kate Chopin's novel initially met with criticism as a result of its apparent advocacy of female adultery, today it is securely positioned within the ranks of the canon of American literature. As such, it functions as a representative of much of American literature written by white authors: its characters are assumed to be white. My reading, then, calls for locating whiteness in the main characters and analyzing the role whiteness plays. To address the latter concern, I will examine two noncanonized works written with the intent of thinking about whiteness. Both racially locate the white characters as white, thus interrupting the predominant representation of whiteness as racially neutral. My discussion of these three texts will work toward the development of a critical reading practice that foregrounds the constructions and representations of whiteness and will challenge the way in which many texts by white U.S. authors are complicit with the discourses of white supremacy.

(Un)marked Whiteness

In 1899 Kate Chopin published a novel about an unhappily married woman, Edna Pontellier. An upper-middle-class white woman and mother of two children, Edna lives a predictable and settled life with her husband, Léonce, in New Orleans. The opening scenes of the novel are set on an island off the Louisiana coast where the Pontellier family is vacationing. While on vacation Edna's dissatisfaction with her position in life crystallizes. Her marriage is empty. She feels distant from other women such as her friend Adèle Ratignolle, a woman perfectly happy as a wife and mother. And although feeling a kind of kinship with the pianist Mlle Reisz, Edna is hesitant to commit herself to the world of artistic expression and settles instead for dabbling in sketching. Her flirtatious friendship with Robert Lebrun advances to a love affair, which is, however, unconsummated. Robert leaves for business ventures in Mexico, and Edna returns to her life in New Orleans. In the space of nine months, Edna moves from an awareness of her dissatisfaction, to the awakening of her potential self, to the ultimate recognition that this world holds no place for that self. In the end she commits suicide by drowning.

Critical readings of *The Awakening* have examined, among other things, the paradoxes of Edna's womanhood.[12] Gender, often coupled with class, has been taken as the primary category from which to analyze Edna's status as wife and mother. Yet, can we so easily separate gender and race? Historian Vron Ware writes that "to be white and female is to occupy a social category that is inescapably racialized as well as gendered."[13] Instead of reading Edna's whiteness as incidental to her womanhood, I see it as inextricably tied to the construction of the feminine gender (understood especially as motherhood) and female sexuality (understood as Edna's desire), and I am interested in her struggle to find a space outside those constructions.[14]

The white characters in *The Awakening* are not overtly identified as white. Racially they are represented as normal or neutral. Nonetheless, and confirmed by Toni Morrison's method of white racial identification, they are white. Moreover, and true to the genre, characters of color are racially named: the quadroons, the little black girl, the dark women of Mexico, the mulattress. Although the white characters are not identified as occupants of a racially constructed social category, they are often described as having white skin. References to white skin and the imagery of white skin in Chopin's text not only reveal the main characters as white but are closely linked to the construction of motherhood and sexuality. During the early nineteenth century, motherhood and female sexuality were defined by piety, purity, submissiveness, and domesticity, or what is identified as the Cult of True Womanhood.[15] Hazel

Carby writes, "Within the discourse of the cult of true womanhood, wifehood and motherhood were glorified."[16] In truth, however, many women stood outside these glorified roles. Slave women in the ante-bellum South could expect neither the bonds of motherhood nor those of marriage to be respected by the white society.[17] Hortense Spillers, for example, argues that within the traditional symbolics of feminine gender, where motherhood is understood as the right to claim a child, the primary social subject is the middle-class white woman.

Against the backdrop of motherhood, the imagery of white skin can be read as a gauge of the acceptance of that gender role. Although both Edna and Adèle are white, it is Adèle who is exceedingly white. She is initially described as "the fair lady of our dreams" (KC, 888), with her spun-gold hair, her sapphire blue eyes, and her white neck. And later, when Edna visits Adèle at her home, it is "the rich, melting curves of her white throat" (KC, 937) that establish her extreme beauty and move Edna to muse about painting her friend. When the two women walked to the beach, it was Adèle who, "more careful of her complexion, had a twine of gauge veil about her head. She wore dogskin gloves with gauntlets to protect her wrists. She was dressed in pure white, with a fluffiness of ruffles that became her" (KC, 895). Likewise it is Adèle who excels at motherhood. Whereas Edna is "not a mother-woman," Adèle is the type of woman who flutters about "with extended, protecting wings when harm, real or imagined, threatened [her] precious brood" (KC, 888). Adèle's protection of her precious brood is not unlike her protection of her perfectly white complexion. Both represent the comfort and security she finds in her social role. In contrast, the text establishes Edna as far less attentive to her white complexion. Her husband, in the opening scene, chastises her because she has not fully covered her arms while swimming and sunbathing: "You are burnt beyond recognition" (KC, 882). Similarly, Edna is less attentive to her children, who, we are told, would be more apt to wipe the water out of their eyes and go on playing than to run to their "mother's arms for comfort" (KC, 887). The imagery of Edna's darkened white skin represents ambivalence, even rejection, of the social category in which she is positioned.

If, as Spillers argues, some women stand outside the traditional symbolics of the feminine gender, other women stand inside them with varying degrees of complicity. Yet these degrees, especially in reference to motherhood, are slight. There is little room for variation. To be an ambivalent mother is to be a "bad" mother. A woman can occupy an oppositional position within the gender scheme,—as Mademoiselle Reisz does—but she must possess a "brave soul", a "soul that dares and defies" (*KC*, 946). Edna Pontellier, unlike Mlle Reisz, is not a willing rebel in the gender scheme. Although she feels herself an outsider and is constructed as a kind of Other throughout the text—"She is not one of us; she is not like us" (*KC*, 900)—she initially struggles to be an insider. Her desire to paint, "to try herself on" her "fair companion" Adèle, who "was a tempting subject" (*KC*, 891), can be read as her desire to try to fit herself into the subject position of a contented wife and mother figure. It is not without frustration and discomfort that Edna finds herself unable to embrace the social category in which she is prefigured.

While whiteness functions overtly and is a central defining metaphor in the images of motherhood, it functions far more obliquely in the constructions and representations of sexuality. It is not defined by imagery of white skin or clothing; rather, its meaning is informed by the boundaries of nonwhiteness. The whiteness of Edna's sexuality is constructed in contrast to the dark women of Mexico and a "young barefooted Spanish girl," Mariequita. Edna's flirtation with Robert Lebrun is fueled to sexual longing when he suddenly moves to Mexico. Her inability to express her feelings to Robert before he leaves is informed by the boundaries of her social role: "Edna bit her handkerchief, striving to hold back and to hide, even from herself as she would hide from another, the emotion which was troubling—tearing—her" (*KC*, 926). Her exaggerated longing for him after he leaves is supported by the racially constructed fear of those same boundaries: the Mexican women "with their dark black eyes and their lace scarfs" (*KC*, 985).

The stereotype of the exotic, the promiscuous, the earthy and accessible female Other in part constructs white female sexuality.[18] Mariequita, with "her round, sly piquant face and pretty black eyes" and her "broad and coarse" feet, which she makes no attempt to hide (*KC*, 914), inspires both fear and longing in Edna. The gaze Edna focused earlier on Adèle is now turned to Mariequita: "She looked Mariequita up and down, from her ugly brown toes to her pretty black eyes, and back down again" (*KC*, 914). As Adèle represents unattainable motherhood, Mariequita represents unattainable sexuality.

The link between motherhood and sexuality is the site and substance of Edna's crisis as a white woman. Historically, white women's sexuality has been bridled by their role as mothers. In order for women to have esteem, value, and indeed power within white society, the role of mother must be maintained and honored. Moreover, the status and well-being of children reflect the success or failure of the mother. Mariequita's insouciant attitude in the story she tells of Sylvano's wife running off with Francisco and leaving all but one child behind represents a distant option for Edna. Barbara H. Solomon writes that "Edna could never adopt Mariequita's casual attitude toward marriage and infidelity, much as she struggles to escape the consequences of her unfortunate marriage to Léonce. Edna may not care whether her behavior hurts her husband, but she is haunted by her fear of harm she might cause her small sons, Etienne and Raoul." [19] Yet while Edna's position in the gender hierarchy is constraining, this constraint is offset by her position in the race and class hierarchies. Her abundant leisure time is made possible by women of color. As Anna Shannon Elfenbein comments, "the ubiquitous presence of dark women cushions everyday life for women of Edna's class." [20] These women cook the meals, clean the rooms, and, most important, tend the children. The work of the "quadroons" makes Edna's mothering role tolerable, but also renders it, in effect, unnecessary. Unless Edna is able to embrace motherhood, as Adèle does, the sexual restrictions placed on her are meaningless because her function is and can be replaced by the work of hired hands. Edna's suicide is the inevitable outcome of her awakening. Her unsuccessful attempts to occupy a subject position other than her own—whether that of Adèle, the one satisfied through the fulfillment of her social category (white and female); or that of Mlle Reisz, the woman who dares to occupy the oppositional stance within the social category; or that of Mariequita, who lives outside the boundaries of that social category—reveal Edna's struggle to find a space within the limitations of her white and female subjectivity. Unable to find that space, Edna enters the water and swims to her death. Ironically, her death by drowning finds her that space of gendered whiteness by placing her securely within the symbolics of the nineteenth-century white female literary tradition.

This reading of *The Awakening* that foregrounds Edna's white subjectivity has three intended goals. The first is to call into question literary conventions, such as "marking," which serve to maintain whiteness as *the* racially neutral category of identity. The second is to demonstrate how whiteness is represented through formal elements such as metaphor, imagery, and plot. The third goal, the farthest reaching of the three, is to interrupt conceptualizations of whiteness and race in general as essentialized. For example, the passages that contrast Edna and Adèle's attentiveness to protecting their white skin signify, as I argued above, their relative embrace of the mothering role. At the same time, and perhaps even more important, these passages reveal the social construction of whiteness itself. Adèle must work to preserve and reproduce her whiteness. The status of whiteness must be crafted and maintained through clothing, conduct, and attitude. Whiteness, like race in general, cannot be understood simply as a natural phenomenon. Rather, it is a highly orchestrated product of culture and nature. The recognition of whiteness as not a set condition of fact—that is, having white skin—but instead a product whose meaning and status must be sustained by a process of reproduction along preestablished lines is crucial to an interruption of whiteness as the status quo.

Reading whiteness into texts like *The Awakening* that are not overtly about race is an essential step toward disrupting whiteness as the unchallenged racial norm. Moreover, this critical reading practice will inevitably lead to a more complex and thoughtful understanding of whiteness and race in general. As readers of U.S. fiction and culture, we cannot avoid the politics of race that informs both the production and the reception of all texts. We must recognize that race is a vital and constant component of our literature even when all the characters are white. Of course, the recognition of race as a constant component does not mean that race must always be taken as the privileged component. I advocate situating Edna Pontellier as a white character not because I necessarily feel that race is the most important lens through which to view this text, but because she *is* a white character. Reading Edna as simply a woman, unraced and universal, erases the degree to which not only her whiteness but also her class position and her heterosexuality have everything to do with her frustration, her awakening, and her death. It also provides an opportunity to reexamine the initial controversy this novel inspired. As mentioned earlier, Chopin's apparently sympathetic rendering of female adultery contributed to the book's negative reception. However, if we consider *The Awakening* in the light of the period in which it was written, a period marked by the unprecedented lynching of black men, and if we further consider the "justifications" for these lynchings, we begin to see how the novel posed a threat beyond the potential loss of white male control of the female body. In her discussion of Ida B. Wells's campaign against lynching, Vron Ware writes: "As long as white women were seen to be the property of white men, without power or a voice of their own, their 'protectors' could claim to be justified in taking revenge for any alleged insult or attack on them. Whenever the reputation of white women was 'tainted' by the suggestion of immoral behaviour, it could always be saved by the charge that they had been victims of black lust."[21] Edna Pontellier is a white woman whose "immoral behavior" cannot be attributed to black male lust. As such her transgression threatens to destabilize not only the authority of white men over white women, but the authority of white men over black men. A reading that highlights Edna's whiteness places the novel solidly within national conversations and debates of race as well as gender, and demonstrates the degree to which these debates are intrinsically linked.

My reading draws heavily on the work of Russell Ferguson, who calls for "speaking the name" of dominant discourses as a necessary, albeit partial, means to challenging their authority. Unfortunately, this authority is not easily dismantled. The act of situating whiteness on the part of either the critic or the author himself or herself does not lead to a quick and easy reshuffling of power relations. It can, in fact, result in a reinscription of those power relations, as we shall see in the following section.

Naming Whiteness

Chopin's text, with its "unraced" white characters, is, as I suggested earlier, characteristic of much fiction written by U.S. white authors. Less typical are the texts by Allan Gurganus and Joanne Brasil. Each identifies the white characters as white, thus interrupting the predominant representation of whiteness. Instead of whiteness passing as an assumed norm, it is recognized as a particular racial category. Because both authors name their white characters as white, the reader's critical practice of situating whiteness is unnecessary. The goals of the reader are instead to analyze the meanings assigned to or associated with whiteness by examining its representations and constructions and, if possible, to assess what significance a self-conscious narrative can have in challenging white supremacy.

I have chosen the Gurganus and Brasil texts because each takes white guilt as a primary theme. In each text the central character undergoes a crisis associated with being white, and each illustrates a distinct strategy for attempting to resolve the crisis of white guilt. In the Gurganus text the crisis is negotiated through a series of rationalizations couched in a confessional narrative. In the Brasil text resolution is attempted by a gradual dismissal of race itself through a narrative marked by unrelenting simplicity.[22]

The novella "Blessed Assurance" is from *White People,* a collection of stories by Allan Gurganus.[23] Recognizing the perplexing nature of whiteness, Gurganus takes it as his central theme: "This book is very much about the joys and limitations of being a white Protestant American. In color theory, white is the absence of all color. Isn't it weird; we named ourselves for what is *not* in the world? We're like a vacuum people, distanced from pleasure. So the drama of the book is people in quest of meaning and pleasure in their lives."[24] This curious quotation is instructive to an analysis of Gurganus's work in two important ways. First, it sets up suffering as an outcome of being white. In interesting and certainly problematic ways, whiteness characterized as absent, empty, or that which is "not in the world" is prone to evade important considerations of power because far too often the privileges associated with being white are lessened, allowing the representation of white as victim to surface. Second, it sets meaning and pleasure as the goal of the characters' quests, when in fact the quests are less for meaning or pleasure than for innocence. In Gurganus's stories, meaning and pleasure for the white characters are deferred until innocence is secured. In his review of *White People,* Henry Louis Gates Jr. comments that "most of these stories are narrated by people who want some sort of forgiveness—it's what fuels their loquacity, speeds their confessions."[25]

Gates's critique is particularly apt for "Blessed Assurance," a story about a white man of southern working-class origins who has achieved the American Dream. Through hard work, exploitation, white-skin privilege, and a healthy dose of denial, this man, Jerry, rose from the ranks of laborers to become a successful business owner and lawyer. Jerry, now reaching the age of retirement, tells the story of one of his first jobs. He collected funeral insurance payments from poor black people. As a working-class young man, his need for steady income overcame his reservations concerning the ethics of this work. He was willing to be convinced by his employer, who assured him that selling funeral insurance to people who barely had money for shelter was honest: "Soon as some next-of-kin comes in here with a legal death certificate, I pay off like clock work. So, yeah, it's honest . . . I see that look on your face. Only thing, buddy, if they miss two weeks running, they forfeit. They lose the present policy and any other Windlass ones they've paid up. I don't care if they've put in thousands, and several of your older clients will have: if they let one, then two (count them) two big Saturdays roll by, their pile becomes the company's" (*BA,* 235).

During the months that Jerry held this job he slowly came to know and care about the people along his route. Despite the warnings of his employer not to "carry" a customer for even one week, Jerry began to make payments for customers, eventually reaching a total of nine. After a number of weeks Jerry reluctantly admitted to his employer that the policies for numerous clients were being maintained not by their weekly payments but by his. By his admittance the clients lost their policies and their money was turned over to the company. Although Jerry held this job for only a brief time, now, as an aging man, he is plagued by guilt for having agreed to such employment. The story he tells is his attempt to explain, rationalize, and obtain forgiveness for his actions. My analysis of "Blessed Assurance" examines the various representations of whiteness and white guilt, analyzes the way in which whiteness is situated, and, most important, looks at the way Jerry's quest for innocence is misguided.

The novella opens with Jerry reflecting on his early years, which have come back to haunt him: "I sold funeral insurance to North Carolina black people. I myself am not black. Like everyone else who was alive fifty-nine years ago, I was young then, you know? I still feel bad about what went on. My wife says: telling somebody might help. Here lately, worry over this takes a percentage of my sleep right off the top.—So I'm telling you okay?" (*BA*, 232). With these opening lines two narrative elements are evident. First, the confessional mode is established whereby readers are situated not only as the hearers of Jerry's confession, but also as the healers of his guilt; and second, Jerry is situated as white. Although potentially disruptive to dominant discourses in which whiteness functions as the unnamed and unnameable norm, Jerry's situated whiteness remains problematic because he does not actually name himself as white; instead he marks his whiteness by saying he is "not black." Gurganus's choice to have his character name his whiteness by not naming it could be read as an attempt to interrupt Morrison's "assumed whiteness" (we know characters are white because nobody says so); on the other hand, there is a reinscription of the assumption of whiteness. Readers are to assume that only a black person or a white person would sell funeral insurance to black people in the South, but certainly not a Latino/a, Korean American, American Indian—in short, any person of a racial identity other than black or white. Or perhaps, even further, we are to assume that in the United States there are really only two racial categories. If one is not black, one must be white. Further, not naming Jerry's whiteness underscores his shame *of* being a white person. It is as if he cannot bring himself to actually say the words that would unmistakably place him at the top of a racial hierarchy.

Following this initial representation of whiteness as shame come a number of other representations such as whiteness as authority and whiteness as guilt. Curiously, these two representations of whiteness occur along with opposite representations. For example, whiteness as the omniscient authority is paired with a representation of whiteness as empty or absent. Seen early in the text, whiteness as authority is marked as the ability to define the Other. The classic colonialist "those people" invoked unconsciously throughout Chopin's text is exposed and developed in Gurganus's. Jerry's clients are elderly black women whom he initially sees as the same, as "all one old black woman" (*BA*, 241). As Jerry develops a friendship with one of these women, Vesta Lotte Battle, a woman more than ninety years old who has invested heavily in insurance, the security he feels in his whiteness is shaken. His eventual friendships with numerous clients bring about an identity crisis constructed in racial terms: "The more vivid each dark person became, the blanker, blander and whiter I felt. A plug of stray cotton" (*BA*, 254). Jerry's transgressive act is his willingness to know the clients along his route as individuals. He pulls taffy with their grandchildren, helps out with odd jobs, and ultimately covers their insurance payments. Jerry goes against the "logic" of white supremacy, in which objectification of the Other is essential to a self-satisfied whiteness. Instead of Jerry's whiteness maintaining a claim to normalcy and possibly even full authorship of self and Other, he finds only emptiness and confusion, because whiteness, as he knows it, has meaning only when nonwhiteness is simplistic and undifferentiated.

The primary representation of whiteness, marked throughout the text, is guilt. Jerry's guilt seemingly stems from the funeral insurance job and his transition from working class to upper class, which stands in stark contrast to the lifelong poverty of the black women to whom he sold the insurance. But the true source of Jerry's guilt is located not in his actions but in his essentialized identity as a white person. We will examine the distinction between guilt located in identity versus guilt located in actions as we look closely at the confessional narrative employed by Gurganus.

As a literary technique the confessional narrative sets the stage for storytelling by way of flashbacks. And, as mentioned above, it functions to situate the reader as a potential exonerator of Jerry's guilt. Beyond the literary considerations of the use of a confessional narrative lies the cultural implication of a confession. Michel Foucault notes that the confession has become "one of the West's most highly valued techniques for producing truth."[26] However, the confessional narrative in "Blessed Assurance" functions not to bring about truth but to evade it, primarily because it is not, in fact, a confession at all, but rather a series of rationalizations. And like rationalizations in general, Jerry's function to explain the circumstances that informed his actions. Thus, Jerry's confession of collecting and selling funeral insurance is immediately followed by the details of his own humble beginnings. Like many people in his hometown, his parents worked in the local cotton mill. The long hours and poor working conditions at the mill eventually led to brown lung disease. Jerry assures us that he took the job selling funeral insurance only to finance his education in night school and to help pay for his parents' mounting medical bills: "See, I only did it to put myself through college. I knew it wasn't right" (BA, 232).

We learn that Jerry started making payments for some of his clients because he had come to genuinely care about them. He did not want to see them lose all their money to the insurance company because they were poor. His guilt is not associated with making the payments; rather, it arises from his decision to tell his boss that nine of his clients had been delinquent in their payments. Like the decision to take the job initially, this decision is explained and rationalized. It was a decision reached only after much pleading and many sleepless nights. First he tried to reason with his clients, arguing that he himself was poor: "Look, I'm poor too or else I wouldn't keep this job, believe me" (BA, 253). Finally, his own physical and emotional deterioration led his boss, Sam, to the conclusion that Jerry had been carrying customers: "Buddy? Something's off, right? College material like you, and with bags down to here. I'm seeing a wear-and-tear beyond normal wear of raking in their coins come Saturday. Know what Sam here's starting to think? Somebody's holding out on you, kid. You definitely got moochers. More'n one, too. Your face gives it away" (BA, 274). With his situation exposed, Jerry confessed to Sam and revealed the names of the nine clients in default.

Jerry's guilt does not rest simply on that one job, however. It encompasses the entire span of his career. He is especially guilt ridden about his remarkable financial success. His achievement, marked by material possessions such as businesses, homes, and trust funds for each of his children, brings him little comfort. It is again necessary to his confession to explain how someone like him became a wealthy man. In his characteristically humble and understated manner, Jerry explains his upward mobility as a combination of good luck, hard work, and "American ingenuity." At the age of twenty-five Jerry inherited two laundromats from "a rich ill-tempered bachelor" for whom he worked. By age thirty-one he had made the Law Review at Duke University. A few years later he patented an invention that clinched his financial security: an adjustable coin plunger for commercial washers and dryers. In short, Jerry achieved the American Dream.

If we look closely at what Jerry's pseudoconfession has accomplished, we can see that, first, it has moved Jerry from an active participant in his own life to a victim of circumstances. The narrative functions to establish his voice as apologetic but powerless. In his search for innocence and redemption Jerry struggles to reduce his own subjectivity to just "a plug of stray cotton." For a wealthy white man in North Carolina hoping to appease his guilt for selling useless insurance to poor black women, cotton is a loaded metaphor. The invocation of cotton links Jerry to a history of oppression in which he too is one of the oppressed. He empties himself of agency and attempts to believe that he is no more powerful than the black women to whom he sold funeral insurance so many years ago.

Second, the confession has moved the construction of whiteness from guilt to innocence. We are left wondering what exactly Jerry did that was so wrong. Certainly the insurance collection job was not wholly ethical; by his own admission he knew it was wrong. Yet his circumstances were difficult. The narrative maneuvers the reader into Jerry's dilemma by suggesting that most people, regardless of racial identity, would have done the same had they been in Jerry's shoes. This shift from guilt to innocence is predicated on the false assumption that a white person who does not participate in "extreme" racist acts (e.g., by belonging to a white supremacist group or subscribing to white supremacist ideology) is not racist. Despite this move from guilt to innocence, at the completion of his "confession" Jerry still seems unconvinced and again looks to the reader for reassurance: "Hey, I appreciate your listening. Really. I don't know—I've kept fretting over this, feeling it for all these years. I mean, basically I'm not all that bad of a man, am I? Am I?" (BA, 305).

This final appeal reveals that Jerry's sense of guilt stems not from what he has done but from what he is: a white person. The narrative which starts with a focus on acts, ends with a focus on identity. This critical shift from acts to identity is the inevitable result of a narrative that labors to establish the fact that Jerry has not really done anything wrong, leaving only his whiteness as the source of his guilt. Ultimately, the meaning of whiteness in "Blessed Assurance" depends on an essentialization. Whiteness is equated with and reduced to having white skin. This essentialization allows for a separation of identity from actions, leading the healer/reader to conclude that Jerry cannot be guilty for something that is beyond his control; that is, the "biological fact" of his white skin. The representation of whiteness and white guilt in "Blessed Assurance" is based on the false supposition that a clear distinction between identity and actions can, in fact, exist. This representation functions powerfully in current debates on race and racism in U.S. culture today. It is often used as a justification for white people to avoid examining racism because associating the concept of "guilt" with something beyond one's control makes no sense. I am not arguing that guilt ought to be associated with something beyond one's control. I am arguing that the rationale behind this representation of white guilt is flawed because it is based on an essentialized whiteness as opposed to a socially constructed whiteness.

For Jerry, the misconceptualization of guilt is characterized by his obsession to negotiate himself out of the position of "self as bad." There are various strategies for shedding guilt as a white person. They range from a denial of the historical and present-day reality of racial discrimination to a full acknowledgment of both the historical and current realities of racism and a willingness to accept accountability for those realities by challenging the power structures that ensure their continuance. The strategy Jerry employs falls between these two extremes. Although willing to concede the profound existence of racism, Jerry is not able to move beyond his own self-centering guilt. Instead of confronting his guilt as a means of dismantling its paralyzing effects, he seeks to evade it by confessing that he feels truly bad and rationalizing his actions as consequences of youth and economic need. Through the construction of an innocent whiteness, perhaps even a maligned whiteness, Jerry comes to stand for a kind of innocent white man who, through no fault of his own, is positioned as a beneficiary of a system that hands out privilege to some and oppression to others.

Joanne Brasil's text constructs whiteness and white guilt much as Gurganus's text does, but Brasil employs a different strategy for negotiating the crisis generated by whiteness.

As with "Blessed Assurance," whiteness in *Escape from Billy's Bar-B-Que* is characterized by guilt and an underlying sense of anxiety.[27] Whiteness is acknowledged rather than assumed, but the privileges that go hand in hand with whiteness are evaded. Being white for the novel's female protagonist, Cecyl, is a source of confusion and conflict.

Cecyl's confusion makes her an apt counterpart to Jerry. However, her narrative voice is less savvy; it is a voice marked by unrelenting naïveté. Moreover, throughout the novel Cecyl's prevailing construction is as an outsider to the social orderings of race, class, sexuality, and gender. Taken together, the outsider position and the naive voice function to ensure a place of innocence in the U.S. racial scheme. Unlike Jerry, who seeks the space of innocence through his narrative, Cecyl's narrative presumes innocence and thus attempts to speak from that most privileged of positions—objectivity.

The novel chronicles Cecyl's experiences as a young white girl living in the South. Southern racism, which seems to go unnoticed by other whites, horrifies her. Under the impression that racism is a southern phenomenon, Cecyl moves to the North. Although the North does not turn out to be the liberal, prejudice-free land she had envisioned, she remains there and takes advantage of the many experiences—personal, political, and academic—available to young white women during the late 1960s. Eventually she returns to the South and finds an environment of racial harmony. As with Gurganus's text, my analysis of *Escape from Billy's Bar-B-Que* examines the way whiteness is situated in the text and looks at the various representations of whiteness and white guilt.

The narrative begins by explicitly situating the black/white dichotomy in Cecyl's hometown, Phoebus, Virginia: "Since they still had racial segregation then (which they still do now, of course), they needed to have two barber shops and two bar-b-que places so they could keep all the Black people and White people separate. They had two grocery stores too, but everyone was allowed to shop at both of them. I don't know why. The White people just said that that's the way you were supposed to do it" (*EBB*, 1). Cecyl's racialized subject position stands somehow outside the constructions of "all the Black people and White people." As in the Gurganus text, there seem to be only two racial categories. Cecyl goes on to describe Big Mamma's Barbershop, which is located across the street from Billy's Bar-B-Que (owned by Cecyl's father). Because Big Mamma's is the town's black barbershop, it is off-limits to Cecyl, although she spends much of her time watching the dancing and fun that spontaneously occur on the (O)ther side of the street. Her spectatorship of this Otherness reveals a marked contrast to her own environment at Billy's, which is described as thoroughly normal: "Everything was normal. Normal formica tables, normal chrome chairs, and a row of normal stools" (*EBB*, 2). The construction of whiteness as boring and knowable is difficult to miss, especially in contrast to the highly stereotypic characterization of blackness.

Through Cecyl's frank and direct narration the novel explores her ambivalence about being white. She contrasts herself with her friend Betty: "One thing about Betty Baines, she was never confused, especially when it came to being White. She knew just what to do. The thing was, Betty took it for granted that she was White. . . . I didn't have that same feeling of Whiteness that other White people seemed to have" (*EBB*, 7). Cecyl's ambivalence toward whiteness reinforces her supposed position as an outsider to the racial order of the South. This positioning in part stems from her family's Irish immigrant status and suggests a construction of whiteness that depends on a long history of racial inclusions and exclusions in defining American citizenship.[28] Feeling white, for Cecyl, is linked to an awareness of the history of white supremacy. Her discomfort and confusion are clear as the narrative recounts a lesson about slavery: "The worst trouble started in sixth grade. Our teacher, Mrs. Matt, gave us a lesson on slavery in the Old South. In order to be as 'unbiased' as possible, Mrs. Matt carefully divided the blackboard into two equal parts. On the one side we were supposed to list the 'bad' things about slavery in the Old South, and on the other side, we were supposed to list the 'good' things about it" (*EBB*, 6). Cecyl's best friend, Betty, offers the first good thing ("It Christianized the African heathens") and is praised by the teacher. For Cecyl, "the worst trouble" refers less to slavery being taught as possibly having good qualities than to her own estrangement from white people and "being white." She sees herself and other whites as benefiting from white-skin privilege, but unlike the others she is not comfortable with feeling that this privilege is deserved. For every white person in the South but Cecyl, feeling white carries with it the feeling of superiority to anyone who is not white. This feeling of whiteness as superiority is for her the source of ambivalence and discomfort. In an attempt to alleviate (and escape) her racially constructed identity conflict, Cecyl migrates to Boston.

The novel unfolds chronicling Cecyl's various northern adventures: living with her black boyfriend, Crawdaddy; moving in with hippies; doing antiwar work and other 1960s-related activities; and finally marrying Mario, a Latino jazz musician from Brazil. The text continues to mark whiteness overtly as a racialized social category complicated by markings of sexuality, gender, class, and regional awareness. Despite these complications, the narrating voice of Cecyl remains remarkably simplistic and naive. This relentless simplicity becomes particularly apparent as Cecyl describes her first sexual relationship, in which her occupation of a racially gendered body reveals minimal agency: "Somehow or other I got to be Crawdaddy's girlfriend. I don't know how that happened. . . . I was just going with him just to be polite in case he thought I was prejudiced. Then I just started getting used to him, and then I got to like him and got a crush on him. It was embarrassing, but I didn't know how someone was supposed to act when they were someone's girlfriend, especially if it was a person of the opposite race's girlfriend I was supposed to be being" (EBB, 20).

The representation of Cecyl's naive white femininity, while striking, is not without precedent. In her analysis of films about Britain's colonial past, social historian Vron Ware identifies three white female types: the good, the bad, and the foolhardy. The good represents a character who is spiritually opposed to all injustice but is powerless. She is "destined to suffer because she feels so deeply."[29] The bad represents "the uncomplicated attitude of the wife" who enjoys imperialist trappings and disdains "natives" and colonial settings. The foolhardy has feminist inclinations signified by her unwillingness to conform; however, she is thoroughly naive about the privileged position she occupies. She is often involved in an interracial sexual relationship that has the potential to bring about her death. The tragic ending can be read not only as an obvious warning against such transgressions but also as reinstating the purity and victim status of her white womanhood. Ware's foolhardy type finds apt representation in Cecyl. As a heterosexual white female character who has not examined her own racism, Cecyl's most powerful means of expressing her unwillingness to conform to American racism is through an interracial relationship. True to her character, this expression seems to be accidental rather than the result of misguided agency or desire.

Brasil's representation of Cecyl's white sexuality via Crawdaddy is consistent with a Western and white aesthetic tradition in which characters of color often function as catalysts of the white characters' sexuality. Although Cecyl's second sexual relationship, with Mario, is also interracial, its construction varies significantly from the construction of the preceding relationship in that race as a marker of difference is invoked only briefly through tropes such as his national identity, his Spanish accent, and his interest in jazz. Ultimately, race and the racial difference between Cecyl and Mario fall out of the narrative completely. The absence of any attention to race or racial differences is striking in a narrative that previously marked race so clearly.

The fact that race remains central to Cecyl's relationship with Crawdaddy yet becomes all but nonexistent with Mario has some intriguing implications. One implication, in accordance with a white liberal ideology, is that race and racism are not issues for Cecyl in her relationship with Mario because they are truly in love. They interact with each other as "individuals," not as members of different races. This shift from "race matters" to "race doesn't matter" foreshadows the idealism of the novel's ending: despite the lack of any structural or institutional changes, racism disappears.[30]

A second, and perhaps more powerful, implication is the reinscription of the black/white racial paradigm articulated early in the novel. Race matters and is central to Cecyl's relationship with Crawdaddy but not with Mario because, as is also true in Gurganus's text, there are only two racial categories of any significance. As a result, race and racial difference are constant factors in the relationship between Cecyl and Crawdaddy but not between Cecyl and Mario. As a Latino, Mario does not fit into either of the two racial categories that frame Cecyl's narrative. He stands outside Cecyl's simplistic black/white dichotomy and like herself is constructed as "raceless" by the narrative.

Like Gurganus's Jerry, Cecyl attempts to negotiate a space where she can maintain a clear conscience despite her white-skin privilege. For both characters the "problems of whiteness" are located in narratives about race. However, constructions of race are always entangled with other constructions of identity. For example, the solutions to the crisis generated by "whiteness as bad" are informed by gender and articulated through the racialized gendered body. The history of the white female body as a commodity of exchange sets the stage for a reading of Cecyl's relationship with Crawdaddy as an attempt to "buy" a kind of "antiracism," or at the very least a nonconformist position in U.S. racism. Moreover, her gender constructs a plausible "innocence" for Cecyl, who, unlike Jerry, does not occupy a position of privilege via both gender and race. Although Jerry's climb up the economic and class ladders was far from easy, he had both his gender and his race working for him rather than against him. It is, of course, his remarkable upward mobility that contributes to his sense of guilt at having participated in the exploitation of others. Cecyl, on the other hand, cannot rely on her gender to work for her in the pursuit of economic success; this, compounded with her "outsider" position to a racial ordering and her ready naïveté, allows her to believe that she does not participate in the systematic exploitation of others. Thus, she has little need of the confessional narrative. Instead, her search for a clear racial conscience is expressed through a narrative marked by the absence of history and a lack of awareness of power relations.

In the end, Cecyl returns to the South and finds the racial relations of her town magically transformed. While Cecyl is helping her father at Billy's Bar-B-Que, Big Mamma enters: "She just walked in so matter of factly and ordered a bar-b-que sandwich and a coke. Billy stopped and told her a stupid joke" (*EBB*, 135). After Big Mamma leaves, Cecyl asks Billy why Big Mamma came in to get a sandwich when she never did before. Her father simply tells her, "It's the new days now, honey. It's the new days" (*EBB*, 135). With this line the novel ends. Through this assimilation narrative racism is resolved by the Other becoming "just like us." (Big Mamma comes over to Billy's place, not the other way around.) It is no longer necessary for Cecyl to "feel bad" or to position herself as an outsider. In the text racism ceases to be a problem because race itself seems to have disappeared.

As with the Gurganus text, Brasil's text generates a number of questions. With my epigraphs from Kobena Mercer and Russell Ferguson in mind, I see two questions in particular emerge. First, does Brasil's attempt to situate whiteness reveal characteristics of whiteness? Second, does the situated whiteness of the text interrupt the normative position white characters have occupied in much of American fiction? Certainly Brasil's text does reveal something of the characteristics associated with whiteness, albeit a fairly essentialized whiteness. Whiteness is cast as boring, bad, knowable, and somehow unchanging. Also important, and related to the second question, whiteness represents "the normal." So, while the situated whiteness does interrupt the normative position of white characters in these examples of American fiction, it does not interrupt a construction of whiteness as normal. Paradoxically, it reinscribes this position. We can see this reinscription most clearly in the regular use of stereotypic names such as Big Mamma and Crawdaddy for the characters of color, and markers such as jazz associated with Cecyl's transition to sexual adulthood. In her introduction to *Playing in the Dark: Whiteness and the Literary Imagination*, Toni Morrison discusses the association of certain "racialized" metaphors to the white imagination: "I was interested, as I had been for a long time, in the way black people ignite critical moments of

discovery or change or emphasis in literature not written by them."[31]
She goes on to say that "neither blackness nor 'people of color' stimu-
lates in me notions of excessive, limitless love, or anarchy, or routine
dread."[32] And while Morrison could rely on these established tropes,
she chooses not to. Moreover, she offers the challenge to other writers
to likewise decide against the use of such metaphors. Brasil's use of
these tropes could, on the one hand, be read as a deconstruction of
stereotypes. Their use, after all, is remarkably blatant. However, she
never fully, or even partially, problematizes these terms. As a result,
their function is more in accordance with Morrison's analysis than representative of a new direction in fiction taken by a white writer.

The attempt by Gurganus and Brasil to take whiteness seriously
both as a racial category and as a theme is indicative, I believe, of
some inroads to social change. The fact that both texts have central
characters who exhibit considerable insecurity about what it means to
be white is a distinctly post–civil rights phenomenon. Race anxiety is
not a new topic for white authors of American fiction; however, the
traditional focus has been on loss of supremacy as a result of misce-
genation rather than the white characters' personal doubts about their
own whiteness. Do these texts present formidable challenges to white
supremacy? Probably not. As I have stated earlier, the act of situating whiteness either on the part of the critic or on the part of the
author does not lead to a quick reshuffling of power relations. Nonetheless, I believe that a critical reading of these texts does contribute
to our understanding of the complexities associated with whiteness as
a racial category and thereby challenges a monolithic notion of whiteness and a construction of whiteness as the ordinary and inevitable
way of being human.

Conclusion

In this essay I have argued for the study of race and literature to include a focus on whiteness as race. This inclusion necessarily involves
a disruption of whiteness as the racially neutral category in much of
American fiction by white authors. I have advocated two kinds of readings. The first examines texts in which the characters are assumed by
both the author and the reader to be white. Only characters of color
in these texts are racially marked, leaving the white characters unraced and thus reinforcing whiteness as the assumed norm. The second reading examines texts by white writers that do racially mark the

white characters and take whiteness as a primary theme. The texts I have chosen to examine in this essay span a period of seventy-five years; like all texts they are products of the historical and regional cultures in which they were written. While the reading I offer of Chopin's *Awakening* is one that I believe is applicable to a text written at almost any point in U.S. history because the representation of whiteness as racially neutral on the part of white writers has largely been a constant, I am not arguing for an ahistorical reading practice. The political beliefs and investments of and the historical and regional influences on white authors ultimately inform the representation of whiteness in their texts. For instance, Chopin's particular milieu as well as her conscious or unconscious views on race inevitably shaped the construction of whiteness in her novels and short stories.[33] My readings of the Gurganus and Brasil texts highlight the historical period in which they were written because the practice of marking whiteness as a racial category is directly linked to the post–civil rights racial climate.

Between the time that this essay was originally conceived and written and the time of going to press there has been growing interest in the critical analysis of whiteness. This blossoming of interest will hopefully continue to push us to see the ways that "race" is an ever present component in American literature—even when all the characters are white. An expanded critical analysis of our literature not only provides a new avenue to the study of American fiction but also gives readers and writers alike another tool with which to challenge that which all too often passes as the norm, whether it be in terms of race, class, or sexuality.

Notes

My thanks to Carolyn Allen, Ruth Frankenberg, Nancy Hartsock, Susan Jeffords, Tamara Kaplan, Diana Paulin, F. Winddance Twine, Yvonne Yarbro-Bejarano, and Kevin Aanerud for their thoughtful readings and helpful comments on earlier versions of this essay.

1   Kate Chopin, *The Awakening*, in *The Complete Works of Kate Chopin*, 2 vols., ed. Per Seyersted (Baton Rouge: Louisiana State University Press, 1969), 1000. Further references in the text are cited as *KC*.

2   Henry Louis Gates Jr., "Editor's Introduction: Writing 'Race' and the Difference It Makes," *Critical Inquiry* 12 (Autumn 1985): 2.

3   Kobena Mercer, "Skin Head Sex Thing and the Homoerotic Imaginary," in *How Do I Look? Queer Film and Video*, ed. Bad Object-Choices (Seattle: Bay Press, 1991), 206.

4   Teresa de Lauretis, "Film and the Visible," in *How Do I Look? Queer Film and Video*, ed. Bad Object-Choices (Seattle: Bay Press), 268.

58 Rebecca Aanerud

5   For a full discussion and analysis of this point see Ruth Frankenberg, *White Women, Race Matters: The Social Construction of Whiteness* (Minneapolis: University of Minnesota Press, 1993).

6   Richard Dyer, "White," *Screen* 29, no. 4 (1983): 44.

7   Toni Morrison, *Playing in the Dark: Whiteness and the Literary Imagination* (Cambridge: Harvard University Press, 1992), xii.

8   Ibid., 72.

9   Dyer, "White," 44.

10 Ibid., 45.

11 Morrison, *Playing in the Dark,* 9.

12 See essays in *Kate Chopin Reconsidered: Beyond the Bayou,* ed. Lynda S. Boren and Sara deSassaure Davis (Baton Rouge: Louisiana State University Press, 1992); Bernard Koloski, *Approaches to Teaching Chopin's "The Awakening"* (New York: MLA, 1988); Wendy Martin, *New Essays on "The Awakening"* (Cambridge: Cambridge University Press, 1992).

13 Vron Ware, *Beyond the Pale: White Women, Racism and History* (New York: Verso, 1992), xii.

14 I would draw readers' attention to Michele A. Birnbaum's "'Alien Hands': Kate Chopin and the Colonialization of Race," *American Literature* 66, no. 2 (1994): 301–23. Birnbaum's excellent reading of the functions played by the characters of color in Chopin's novel brings into sharp relief the centrality of Edna's whiteness. However, Birnbaum's claim that "there is no racial or ethnic presence in the final scene on the beach" (316)—a claim presumably made because only Edna is present—in effect reinscribes the racially neutral position of whiteness in American literature. It is this very neutrality of whiteness that my reading calls into question and disrupts.

15 See Barbara Welter, "The Cult of True Womanhood: 1820–1860," *American Quarterly* (Summer 1966): 152; and Linda M. Perkins, "The Impact of the 'Cult of True Womanhood' on the Education of Black Women," *Journal of Social Issues* 39, no. 3 (1983): 18.

16 Hazel Carby, *Reconstructing Womanhood: The Emergence of the Afro-American Novelist* (New York: Oxford University Press, 1987), 26.

17 For discussions on the status of motherhood for black women in the nineteenth-century United States, see Carby, *Reconstructing Womanhood;* Hortense J. Spillers, "Mama's Baby, Papa's Maybe: An American Grammar Book," *Diacritics* (Summer 1987): 65–81; Deborah Gray White, *Ar'n't I a Woman? Female Slaves in the Plantation South* (New York: Norton, 1985).

18 Patricia Hill Collins writes of the debilitating effects of this stereotype for black women in *Black Feminist Thought* (New York: Routledge, 1991). Angela Davis, *Women, Race and Class* (New York: Random House, 1981); and White, *Ar'n't I a Woman?* engage similar discussions and include analyses of the resulting hostility and envy of white women toward black women.

19 Barbara H. Solomon, "Characters as Foils to Edna," in *Approaches to Teaching Chopin's "The Awakening,"* ed. Bernard Koloski (New York: MLA, 1988), 116.

20 Anna Shannon Elfenbein, *Women on the Color Line: Evolving Stereotypes and the Writings of George Washington Cable, Grace King, and Kate Chopin* (Charlottesville: University Press of Virginia, 1989), 147.

21 Ware, *Beyond the Pale,* 182.

22 Because the Gurganus and Brasil texts are not as well known as *The Awakening,* the following analyses include more extensive background and plot information.

23 Allan Gurganus, "Blessed Assurance: A Morality Tale," in *White People* (New York: Ivy Books, 1990). Further references in the text are cited as *BA*.

24 Gurganus, "Blessed Assurance," 10.

25 Henry Louis Gates Jr., "Art and Ardor," *Nation,* 493.

26 Michel Foucault, *The History of Sexuality,* vol. 1: *An Introduction* (New York: Random House, 1978), 59.

27 Joanne Brasil, *Escape from Billy's Bar-B-Que* (Navarro, Calif.: Wild Trees, 1985). Further references in the text are cited as *EBB*.

28 For a discussion of the often uncertain and ambiguous position Irish Americans occupied in terms of whiteness, see David R. Roediger, "Irish-American Workers and the White Racial Formation in the Antebellum United States," in *The Wages of Whiteness: Race and the Making of the American Working Class* (New York: Verso, 1991); and Theodore W. Allen, *The Invention of the White Race: Racial Oppression and Social Control* (New York: Verso, 1994).

29 Vron Ware, *Beyond the Pale,* 232.

30 Writers Avery Gordon and Christopher Newfield refer to this shift as the phenomenon within liberal racial thinking to go "beyond race" in their article "White Philosophy," *Critical Inquiry* 20 (Summer 1994): 737–57. See also Bob Blauner, "White Radicals, White Liberals, and White People: Rebuilding the Anti-Racist Coalition," in *Racism and Anti-Racism in World Perspective,* ed. Benjamin P. Bowser (London: Sage, 1995).

31 Morrison, *Playing in the Dark,* viii.

32 Ibid., x.

33 Given that her husband was a member of the White League, a prowhite organization, it is unlikely that she had not considered her own position on questions of race.

Rereading *Gandhi*

T. Muraleedharan

AVID Lloyd says that "the racism of culture is not a question of certain contingent racist observations by its major theoreticians nor of the still incomplete dissemination of its goods but an ineradicable effect of its fundamental structures."[1] The continuing proliferation of racism as a violent and fanatic sentiment is still too powerful to be ignored, as has been proved most recently by the incidents that led to the Los Angeles riots of 1992. Such violent lessons emphasize the need for organized resistance and opposition to racism at a social level but also the necessity for enhancing investigations of the structural complexities of various cultural products that subtly camouflage and sustain the racist foundations of the dominant orders, and thereby aid the proliferation of discriminatory feelings in an apparently invisible and subsequently more alarming way. It is the scarcely visible stain of such a diffused racism ambushed in the narrative of one of the most famous films of the 1980s, *Gandhi,* that this essay proposes to explore.

An important feature of race studies in recent times, especially those related to cinema, is their predominant concern with the presentation of the racially nondominant people. The major impulse for such work lies in the sense that how such groups are represented is part of the process of their oppression. At the same time there is another reason for this constant focusing of the critical gaze on the images of the racially subordinated people: the general invisibility of whites as an ethnic category. For example, in cinema, most frequently, the category white replaces the universal, subsequently rendering its racial identity invisible. Richard Dyer explains this invisibility of whites as being the result of their dominance, which enables them to be nothing in particular. Whiteness colonizes the definition of the normal and subsequently achieves a complete disavowal of ethnic categorization. Any instance of white representation is immediately looked on as something more specific. Thus *Brief Encounters* is never studied as a film about white people, but rather as a film about English middle-class people; similarly, *The Godfather* is mostly studied as a film about Italian American people. By contrast, *The Color Purple* is not studied as a film about poor southern U.S. people but about black people.[2]

Yet, whiteness is not always invisible in aesthetic representations. Skin color emerges as a significant factor defining identity when its difference from blackness is inescapable and at issue. In other words, whiteness becomes visible only with reference to that which is not white—as if only nonwhiteness can give whiteness substance. This is what can be seen in *Gandhi:* the film begins with nonwhiteness, only to attempt a definition of *white* that is then cleverly camouflaged as the universal. The function of India in this film is to represent the nonwhiteness that makes white visible. The film begins with "brownness": Gandhi begins as a brown man, and the narrative explores the gradual washing away of this brown pigmentation. This is the contribution of the Indian experience to the life of the protagonist. The narrative cycle is complete when Gandhi's brownness is completely washed away and he becomes shining white.

The narrative construction of whiteness attempted in *Gandhi* gains further significance when we take into account the sociohistorical context in which the film was made. *Gandhi* is just one among a series of films and television programs about India produced in Britain during the 1980s generally described as the Raj revival in British cinema. The genre of Raj-nostalgia films also includes such well-known films as *A Passage to India* (1984), *Heat and Dust* (1982), *Staying On* (1984), and *The Jewel in the Crown* (1984). According to the British Film Institute, more than ten films and several television programs on India, especially India under British rule, were produced in Britain in the first half of the 1980s. Several novels and other literary works on India were published during this period as well. In short, the period was marked by a general resurgence of British interest in India, and this must be seen as something more than the continuing interest of the colonizer in the former colony. Especially since these recent films, television programs, and literary works differ in content and approach from similar works produced when India was under British rule, the consolidation and propagation of imperialism in a purely political sense is no longer the major concern in them. This once again points out the need to analyze the Raj revival in the context of the sociohistorical situation in which it took place.

The late 1970s and early 1980s, which saw the revival of Raj nostalgia in a big way, were difficult years for Britain, as they were for many other countries. The social basis of the postwar settlement had already become fragile by the late 1960s. Growing poverty and unemployment were causing great anxiety in Britain, which resulted in much unrest and occasional violence. By 1981 unemployment was reported to have clambered toward three million and there were widespread riots. Large-scale migrations from the "darker" zones of the world and the emergence of Asiatic and black communities as comparatively powerful social forces in Britain made race an important issue in social discourses. Racism once again gained prominence in the social scene, and racial riots became common. And dominating all these problems was the continuing trauma of the loss of the empire and the financial problems and identity crisis that entailed.

Meanwhile, the social scene was also going through significant transitions. Trade unionism was continuing to gather strength, as proved by the well-known miners' strike. The increasing involvement of women in such activities and the emergence of single-parent families and alternate ways of pairing and cohabitation all gave severe jolts to the conservative sections of the society. The already deteriorating self-image of the nation was being further damaged or at least disturbed by the proliferation of the critiques of imperialism and colonialism initiated by both the former colonies and radical sections within Britain itself. All these, along with several other factors, led the right wing in Britain to evolve a cultural offensive which later came to be known by the name Thatcherism.[3]

Although named after the then prime minister, Mrs. Margaret Thatcher, Thatcherism was in fact a political and ideological project that owed more to the conservative and right wings of the society in general than to any single person. According to Stuart Hall, who coined the term, "Just as Stalinism is not attributable to Stalin alone, so Thatcherism, as a political formation, is not limited to the person of the prime minister. One uses it in order to insist on the specific and distinct character of the new Right as a political formation."[4] One important feature of Thatcherism pointed out by Marxist critics is its much publicized link with modernism. Though a political project, its modus operandi was different from the usual repressive political machineries. Associating itself generally with progress and modernism, Thatcherism was intent on seducing the people to constitute themselves in accordance with the dominant ideologies of the right. It was essentially an ideological project that survived by eliciting consent, thereby enjoying a dialectic relationship with the masses. Stuart Hall describes it as an "authoritarian populist" project, and describes "authoritarian populism" as a form of hegemonic politics that involved an attempt to impose a new form of social regulation and authority from "above." What is distinctive about the project is the fact that regulations and authority were rooted in the fears and anxieties of those "below." In other words, the project was intent on imposing social discipline while at the same time retaining intact the paraphernalia of the Liberal Democratic state. Thus it was simultaneously authoritarian and populist.

As might be expected, culture was a principal domain of this disciplinary project. Its supporters often described Thatcherism as a cultural critique of the lawlessness of the 1970s. The crucial terrain of the ideological offensive was its "moral agenda," which was preoccupied with issues such as crime, law and order, abortion and sexuality, the position and social role of women, sex education, social and moral respectability, and homosexuality. Simultaneous with all these was the search for an "enemy within" onto whom was projected the entire responsibility for all the problems the nation was facing. There was also a rhetorical shift in emphasis from society or people as a whole to the individual. In speech after speech during her rule, Mrs. Thatcher emphasized the importance of the individual, with whom, she claimed, her government was principally concerned. But who was this individual who mattered most? According to the various discourses of Thatcherism, not everybody who lived within the geographical boundaries of Britain, and not even all British citizens, could claim this status. In fact, one of the prominent strains in the Thatcherite project was the attempt to define the individual who could actually claim "Englishness." As we shall see, this involved defining several groups who fell outside the scope of legitimate citizenship. These groups included new immigrants but also pensioners and the increasing number of unemployed.

History and *tradition* are two important terms that found widespread redeployment in the discourses of Thatcherism. Stuart Hall says that "the moral discourse of Thatcherism was the site for the mobilisation of social identities." By appropriating tradition, Thatcherism put down deep roots in the traditional, conventional, social culture of English society."[5] Thus, Britain in the 1980s was marked by a search for a sense of continuity with the past, "a sense of identity and stability to secure (the people) as (they) plunge into the future."[6] Bob Jessop and his colleagues see Thatcherism as "merely the latest form in which the peculiarities of British capitalism have been expressed in conservative politics."[7] Thus, in short, Thatcherism was merely the modified reenactment of certain older tendencies in British society; at the same time, its source of inspiration and model was a version of the past modified to suit the current concerns.

In this essay I will consider the implications of the Raj revival in British cinema in its specific sociohistorical context with special reference to *Gandhi,* which has been considered the most significant British film of the 1980s. A detailed study of the film is beyond the scope of this essay. I shall examine only the ways in which imperialist and patriarchal notions interact in the film text, declaring a covert loyalty to the Thatcherite cultural project. Of special interest to me is the manipulation of gender and race attempted in this film and the way these are streamlined to accomplish a redefinition of whiteness as an achievement attainable only through sacrifice and suffering. Since the crucial issue I address is the function of cinema in the rewriting of history and the recasting of cultural and national identities, I shall draw insights from some of the recent debates in film and cultural studies pertaining to this issue. Of particular interest here are the theories of Althusser, Jacques Lacan, Colin MacCabe, Stephen Heath, and Michael Ryan, as these help me discuss cinema as both an ideological apparatus and a cultural practice intimately connected to sociopolitical contingencies.[8]

The Picaresque Hero

The narrative structure of *Gandhi* conforms to the pattern of the bildungsroman tradition. The term *bildungsroman* generally refers to the genre of fictions that record the development of a young hero from discordance with his immediate environment to maturity and harmony. The term was first used by Karl Morgenstern in 1820 in his study of a genre of fiction that described the adventures of an antisocial hero, culminating in his final acceptance into the secure folds of his society. Wilhem Dilthey uses the term to describe German novels in which "a regulated development within the life of the individual is observed;

each of its stages has its own intrinsic value and is at the same time the basis for a higher stage. The dissonances and conflicts of life appear as the necessary growth points through which the individual must pass on his way to maturity and harmony."[9] This description suits the structure of *Gandhi:* in the film we see a young hero, obviously ill at ease in his environment, slowly developing through a series of conflicts to maturity, self-realization, and finally harmony with his environment. Thus Gandhi is more or less a picaro, though the picaresque structure is diffused and not immediately visible in the film. The young protagonist in black suit who is presented at the beginning of the main narrative of *Gandhi* does not have the explicit features of a picaro, yet his subsequent journey has almost all the elements of a spiritual bildungsroman.

The story of *Gandhi* begins with the protagonist's journey to southern Africa, although the film itself begins with a prologue comprising Gandhi's assassination and the spectacular funeral sequence. Gandhi in the train scene is represented as a young man seemingly unaware of the racial discrimination that he soon will suffer. In other words, he appears as a man who has not acquainted himself with the felt realities of the world he inhabits. He responds to the racial discrimination and violence to which he is subjected during the journey with indignation and revolt, but also with utter surprise. The scene gives no indication that Gandhi is expecting the treatment that he eventually will receive, even though he is introduced as a barrister who studied law in London. On the other hand, the viewer is given sufficient warning of the incidents to come, initially by the behavior of the uneasy black porter and later by the reactions of the indignant whites. The initial naïveté and the subsequent defiance and protest that Gandhi demonstrates in this scene are markedly similar to the tradition of the picaresque heroes. Incidentally, this train journey is the first of a series of journeys that Gandhi takes in the film, another allegiance to the picaresque tradition, in which the main narrative is about the journey of the protagonist.

The rest of the film narrates how Gandhi organizes protests against racial discrimination in South Africa, meets Charlie Andrews, serves a prison term, and establishes an ashram. Later, he returns to India to join the independence movement. On Gokhale's advice he travels all over India, slowly becoming the most important figure in the nationalist movement. After India achieves independence, violence breaks out as a result of the partition of India from Pakistan. Gandhi's hunger strike succeeds in putting an end to communal riots. Later, he is assassinated by Godse and the nation pays a tearful homage to its departed leader. The assassination scene with which the film begins is repeated at the end.

The journey motif recurs throughout the film. Gandhi is on the move almost all the time. He travels from continent to continent and from city to city. Trains appear several times in the film; there are also tongas, ships, and cars. When Gandhi is not traveling in any of these vehicles he is taking long walks—the vitriolic stride down the seashore with the journalist, Walker, and the spectacular march to Dhandi are examples. The protagonist goes through a gradual transformation as part of his long journey. From the naive train passenger in southern Africa he slowly develops into a self aware of its mission and its relationship with the rest of the world; a person who manages to save a nation from various crises and also earns enough confidence to talk to journalists like Walker and Margaret Bourke-White about his own life and philosophy. The Gandhi who appears in the last scene before the final assassination is a person who has discovered his own identity and has proved himself superior in wit, intelligence, and moral values to the rest of the world. The spectacular funeral procession demonstrates his successful integration into and acceptance by society. Thus Gandhi's long journey has indeed been a spiritual bildungsroman.

The Nation in Need of Help

Complementing the picaresque image of the protagonist in this film is the image of India. India in *Gandhi* is a complex geographical entity— a nation colonized and suffering from acute poverty. Moreover, it is a nation facing a crisis and in need of help, help that the protagonist provides. The narrative explores the changes that occur in the protagonist as he performs this service of redeeming his nation.

The nation that Gandhi saves from crisis is a curious country of absolute contrasts. This is suggested from the moment when Gandhi lands in Bombay after his South African experiences. After the welcome given by the Congress party, the tonga in which Gandhi and Patel sit moves down the streets of Bombay. While Patel is talking about the future activities of the party, Gandhi's eyes turn toward the sights on both the sides of the street. From Gandhi's perspective, the moving camera captures in vivid detail a grand panorama of poverty: half-naked children begging, dissipated-looking women with forlorn expressions and sick children on their laps, weary and fatigued old people, dilapidated hutments and chawls, and above all, the hopeless expression on each and every face. The entire scene is shot in dull light with slow Indian music in the background, reinforcing the pathos. From here, a straight cut takes Gandhi to the party organized by Congress. The scene is set in a lush green garden with beautiful lawns, flowers, and bright sunlight. It is a space inhabited by Indians belonging to the upper class. The dress of the men and the general ambience of the party suggest their imitation of the European lifestyle. The scene opens with a shot of Nehru's mother telling a guest: "I leave political matters to my husband and revolution to my son"—a statement suggestive of upper-class indifference.

Similar direct shifts from scenes of acute poverty to rampant luxury are repeated several times in the film. The spaces where the Congress leaders meet are always ornate and posh, with European decor. Mohammed Ali Jinnah is the archetypal representative of the Europeanized upper class in the film. Most of the Congress meetings take place in his bungalow, which is done up in Western style. A direct contrast to this world of luxury is the India that Gandhi discovers during his all-India tour. From the window of the train, the camera captures images of village life. The picture of India that emerges from these moving shots is one of acute poverty. At least one shot from every Indian province is included in the cartography of India attempted by this film, and each of these shots is about poverty and hard labor, whether that of the paddy workers of Kerala or the tea plantation workers in Assam. This image is further reinforced by the Champaran episode, which once again draws attention to the terrible poverty existing in the villages. What is absent from the India this film imagines, with its images of shocking poverty and alluring, exotic luxury, is a middle class. There is no middle space between the European costumes and the sweaty brown bodies. Gandhi's mission in the film is to fill this gap: the ashram he establishes and the ethnic lifestyle it advertises serve exactly this purpose by constituting a middle stratum in between the two extreme economic positions. This world is also inhabited by people such as Herman Kallenbach and Mira Behn. Thus an association is made between the Western middle class and the world that Gandhi creates in India. Apart from indicating the contrast in economic positions, the direct cuts from pictures of poverty to those of abundance have another function: they suggest a pervading violence. The quick change from images of dissipated faces, ragged clothes, and ramshackle huts to well-groomed, smiling visages, European costumes, and posh interiors creates an identity for India as a space of moral violence. It is a country in which one section of the population enjoys all the luxuries yet is indifferent to the suffering of the other sections. The responsibility of British colonialism for this contrast is just mildly suggested during the Champaran episode, and only through dialogue. By and large, the rampant poverty is portrayed as an empirical, ahistorical reality which fails to evoke any response from upper-class Indians, except Gandhi. In other words, Gandhi is an exception in India, which is otherwise a land of moral violence.

Gandhi is an alienated figure in India. He has an easy rapport with people like Kallenbach, Baker, and Bourke-White, who understand him without any difficulty. But the same cannot be said about the Indians in the film. The Congress leaders are always finding it difficult to understand him. Their initial responses to his ideas are always disbelief and opposition, though eventually they are converted to his faith. Even when Gandhi is seen with the masses, he stands apart — mostly due to his skin color, thanks to the selection of a fair-skinned, biracial actor to play the role. These Indian crowds always worship him as a god; he is not one of them. There is always a gap between the deity and the devotees. By contrast, when Gandhi visits the Glasgow workers, he is comfortably at home; the black-and-white sequence presents him as part of the crowd, who treat him as an equal by hugging and kissing him instead of worshipping him.

The violence that pervades India extends beyond the realm of morality, and the film portrays in vivid detail its physical manifestations. The incident of Chaurichaura and the communal riots following the partition are examples of this. The Chaurichaura incident begins with the beating of a demonstrator by the police. The brown, sweaty faces of the policemen are specially lit in these frames so as to emphasize the national/racial identity of the Indian policemen. The retaliation of the demonstrators is recorded in a rapid montage, with various shots of the group of torch-wielding crowd members indulging in various forms of assault and destruction. The climax of the scene is the lethal blow given to the policeman by one of the rioters, captured in a low-angled close shot taken from the perspective of the victim that transfers the impact of the violence with all its strength onto the viewer. The Calcutta riots are presented as a spectacle. The climax to the entire narrative, this episode is extended over numerous scenes of mutual assaults by the crowd, arson, murder, and so on. In both sequences the Indian crowd appears like an uncontrollable evil force with only a group identity. The comment made by Lord Irwin during his conversation with the Congress leaders—that India will be reduced to chaos if the British leave—is proved by these two scenes. Compared with these violent crowds, the white men in India are apostles of peace. Even when recording the violence inflicted by the colonial government on the Indians (e.g., Jalian Wala Bagh and the assault in front of Darsana Salt Works), the camera repeatedly calls attention to the Indian policemen and soldiers who act as the instruments of violence. It is the Gurkha regiment that opens fire on the mob in Jalian Wala Bagh, and it is Indian policemen who break the heads and shoulders of the salt workers. All these scenes are streamlined to foreground and celebrate the values of peace, patience, and nonviolence that Gandhi personifies; at the same time they construct India as a land of violence. Gandhi is the only exception to the rule; but then the film begins with the assassination of Gandhi, and the Indian face of his assailant is almost celebrated in the shots preceding the assassination. The image of India is confirmed as a land that crucifies the only ray of hope it ever had. From the shot of the falling Gandhi, a dissolve takes the viewer to a close shot of military boots treading on flower petals—another indication that the land this film is going to describe is one that is violent toward its own past glory—one that crushes its own fallen flowers. It is such a country—violent both morally and physically—that is redeemed by Gandhi, who achieves saintliness in the process.

Moral and physical violence, poverty, internal and external threats, and so on are thus the important factors constituting the image of the nation facing a crisis that appears in *Gandhi*. The picaresque hero is developed mainly through his actions to help this nation through its crisis. But apart from providing a platform for the protagonist to perform his redeeming act, this type of representation of the nation can also be read as an instance of what Michael Ryan calls "transcoding." According to Ryan, film discourse transcodes social discourses. He uses the term "material circuits" to name the real, concrete linkages that conduct ideas, issues, and meanings as well as tensions, fears, and desires from society to film. He points out that "the notion of material circuit implies that there is no exteriority of the referent, no objective ground to the signifier. Rather the two are part of one system, or a multiplicity of interconnected systems that relay social ideas and feelings from extra cinematic culture to film and back into culture, where they circulate further." [10]

Edward Guerrero has demonstrated such transcoding of social anxieties and fears into cinematic discourse in his study of Hollywood science fiction and horror cinema. According to Guerrero, *The Thing* (1982) and *The Fly* (1986) can be read as allegories of the epidemiological spread of AIDS through society.[11] In the case of *Gandhi* the references are even more evident: the nation that is facing a crisis in this film reflects without much distortion the contemporary social anxieties in Britain, which was itself going through a crisis in the 1980s that featured general economic breakdown, breakup of the conventional family and moral codes, widespread street violence, and so on. It was the awareness of that earlier crisis that helped to revive the racist ideologies that became an important component of the Thatcherite offensive in the 1980s. At the same time, the reflection of the social anxieties transcoded in *Gandhi* has another important narrative function: it helps define the protagonist, who goes through a symbolic transformation from brown to white as he is engaged in the task of redeeming the nation.

Rewriting Race

I have already discussed the structure of bildungsroman that orders the narrative in *Gandhi*. The bildungsroman records the progress of a militant hero from protest to relative maturity and harmony with his environment. But in *Gandhi*, the change of color from brown to white adds an additional dimension to the "progress" of the protagonist. This change also has a quasi-spiritual dimension in the film. When we consider the recent transformations in racist notions, such a change becomes a curious instance of "rewriting the race." Errol Lawrence has pointed out that "the current racist ideologues are concerned to distance themselves from the notion of racial superiority, which, though implied, are seldom explicit in their arguments. At one level, this is because such talk is not necessary."[12] This is what we see in *Gandhi*. The actual racial identity of the protagonist remains relatively ambiguous while his superiority is defined in qualitative terms that conceal the commonsense norms of whiteness. On the other hand, this also becomes an instance of social policing in which the whites are interpellated to redefine them according to these "qualities" which might equip them to become ideal citizens and the saviors of their endangered nation. Moreover, the qualities that Gandhi acquires and the

narrative celebrates can be seen as falling into two prominent traditions: Christian morality and a patronizing patriarchy. It is through
the regular demonstration of these virtues that Gandhi proves himself
superior to the whites.

Gandhi's response to the racial discrimination that he encounters
in South Africa is inspired by his awareness of the Christian doctrines
that consider all people as children of God. His surprised response
to apartheid is, "It is not Christian." There are recurring references to
Christian morality in Gandhi's conversations with Charlie, the rowdy
boys on the street, and Mr. Baker, the sympathetic white man. Back in
India, Gandhi's quarrel with British colonialism is motivated primarily
by his encounter with the acute poverty of the masses. In short, he
is the biblical Good Samaritan, whose thought and action reverberate
with his love for his neighbor. His philosophy is that of sacrifice and
suffering. In short, Gandhi is constructed in this film as the personifi-
cation of Christian virtues.

At the same time, Gandhi is also a patronizing patriarch. Always
poised in public, the only person with whom he ever expresses his
anger is his wife, Kasturba. The Kasturba-Gandhi relationship is portrayed as the ideal heterosexual relationship desired by patriarchy. He
is the leader and she is the follower; he is the lord and she is his subject. This unequal relationship is another "ideal" celebrated in the film.
The well-known quarrel between Kasturba and Gandhi over the clean-
ing of toilets is used in the film to reinforce this point. The scene ends
with Kasturba shouting at Gandhi, "I am your wife!" and a suddenly
repentant Gandhi asking himself: "What has happened to me?" This
is followed by an impressive close-up in which the reconciled couple
face each other. The scene is shot in soft light, and both look at each
other with tenderness. Subsequently, the man realizes his duty to be
protective and patronizing toward his wife, while the woman happily
acknowledges her duty to obey the command of her husband—in this
case, to clean and cover the toilets. The scene thus defines Gandhi as
a patronizing male who realizes his role as the natural leader but also
his duty as the protector and savior. This gender role assignment is
defined as the "norm" by Kasturba's statement: "You are just human."
The pattern established in this scene is reinforced several times in the
film, with Kasturba acting as the prominent mouthpiece of these glorified patriarchal values. The narrative seduction here is in the transfer-
ence of the responsibility for this system to the cultural identity of the

protagonists, so that attention is diverted from the explicit patriarchal framework of their relationship. Kasturba says: "As an Indian woman, my duty is to follow my husband."

The major part of the narrative in *Gandhi* is structured in a cause-effect-response pattern. For example, the South African train episode begins with a reference to Christian values, which is immediately followed by white officers throwing Gandhi off the train. The cause of their uncharitable behavior is thus their loss of Christian values—an indication given by the earlier reference—and its effect is, of course, the violence inflicted on Gandhi. Gandhi's response is the realization that dawns on him as he watches the poor Indian couple in the shadows of the railway station carrying a crying child. This also is the first instance of Gandhi demonstrating his moral superiority to the people around him—whether they are whites or Indians. Gandhi is constantly surprising the rest of the world, which earns him the respect and adoration of the millions. The function of most of the other characters in the film is to provide this response, which in turn conditions the viewers to respond in a similar manner. They are more or less like a chorus responding to the actions of the hero. Incidentally, the first character to appear as chorus in the film is the black train porter in South Africa. In the train sequence he is a passive onlooker. He is at the same time both Gandhi's alter identity and his "other." He is black, and thus has a racial identity akin to that of the protagonist; yet he obeys the racist system and refuses to protest. This makes him the other. He is also the onlooker whose emotional response the viewer is invited to identify with. Gandhi's refusal to submit to the system is foregrounded by the porter's apparent agreement with the system. The function of this character is also to prove Gandhi's superior merit, which differentiates him from the ordinary and qualifies him for his subsequent transformation to whiteness. Thus, Gandhi is a brown man who finally achieves whiteness but also one predestined to do so—the chosen one. What makes Gandhi the chosen one? The answer is given by his dress and by the claim he makes in the scene. Gandhi, in this scene dressed like an Englishman—in dark suit and tie—declares that he has been educated in London, thus subtly establishing the value of an English education.

If *Gandhi* is a film about a brown man's evolution to whiteness through suffering and sacrifice, then the film also makes it clear that not all brown men can attain this position. From the very beginning the film presents Gandhi as the chosen one—the one who is different from everybody else. In the train in South Africa, Gandhi reacts to the apartheid, but the black porter does not. Later, when he discusses racial discrimination with other Indians, they are by and large indifferent. In the meeting that is subsequently organized, most of the Asians propose violence against racial oppression but Gandhi recommends passive resistance. Later, in India, Gandhi very often suggests an option exactly contrary to what the other leaders of the Congress propose. All these scenes project Gandhi as basically different in perspective and intelligence. And he is the only one who manages to prove himself superior to the whites. Thus, once again, this film reverses its own apparent ideology and suggests that whiteness is a state to be attained only by unique human beings. Moreover, the narrative of *Gandhi* portrays the protagonist's change of color as occurring simultaneously with his progress to self-awareness. At the same time, the change is also synchronized with his success in saving his endangered nation. Gandhi goes through immense sacrifice and suffering in his effort to save the nation. What makes him capable of these actions is obviously his "difference" from the rest of the characters. Thus the film celebrates Gandhi as a unique personality.

As mentioned earlier, the assassination and the spectacular funeral procession with which *Gandhi* begins have the function of a prologue that gives the viewer hints about what to expect in the rest of the film. The panorama of the long shots that record the sea of humanity that comprises the mourners and the shots (taken from a top right angle) showing Gandhi's body decked with flowers celebrate the epic personality of the historical figure whose story the rest of the film is going to explore. But Gandhi as he appears in the beginning of the film and encounters racial discrimination is pronouncedly a brown man, race being the prominent factor defining his identity. Through sacrifice and suffering, he "progresses" through the film until he proves himself greater than the whites. In other words, he finally attains the status of an ideal, which washes away the brownness of his skin. Considering that the film is based on a historical figure, this elevation of the protagonist to the status of a moral value system is also a recasting of his personality and a rewriting of history. If the moral qualities of Gandhi are celebrated in the earlier scenes, in a later scene he is also projected as unconventional and liberal. It cannot be mere coincidence that this scene precedes Gandhi's meeting with Mr. Walker, the American journalist. Walker comes to know about Gandhi from General Jan Christian Smuts, who is in charge of the prison in South Africa. Gandhi confronts Gen. Smuts in his office when he is summoned there in connection with his release from the prison. The scene presents a different picture of Gandhi: with his humorous and unconventional behavior, he comes off in this scene as the archetypal American. General Smuts's announcement of his release does not produce any significant emotion in him. Instead of being pleasantly surprised by this news, he manages to astonish Smuts by asking him for some money to pay for a taxi. The general is "zapped," and so is Mr. Danube, who is eventually asked to lend the money to Gandhi. Coming as a prelude to Gandhi's meeting with Mr. Walker, this scene presents the typically "American uncon-ventionality" of the protagonist; at the same time, it also suggests the complexity of Gandhi's identity—an identity in which all national and racial identities converge. Moreover, this scene is also an indicator of Gandhi's capability to treat even an antagonist like a friend and an equal. Much later in the film, we are also shown Gandhi's love for animals: he considers the treatment of a goat's sprained leg as impor-tant as discussing the nation's political future. He addresses the herd of sheep with a warm hello and is busy feeding them when he talks to Nehru about a cultural offensive against the British. Together these scenes precipitate Gandhi as "the friend of all the world."

The most important contribution to the definition of Gandhi's personality is provided by the "nice" whites such as Walker, Mira Behn, and Margaret Bourke-White. These men and women are the real heroes and heroines of the film, for *Gandhi* is essentially about such people and their discovery and subsequent acceptance of Gandhi. It is with these people that viewers are made to identify and whose emo-tions they come to share. The prominence of these people in the nar-rative is established from the very beginning of the film. It starts with the funeral procession when the camera lingers over the mourners in a series of close-ups. Most of these shots have a similar composition: a white face in the center of the frame surrounded by a few brown (Indian) faces. The shots are composed in such a way that the viewer's immediate attention falls on these white faces. The shots are too brief for the viewer's attention to spread to the other faces. It is the expres-sion of gloom reflected on these white faces that defines the tragic loss that opens the narrative and sets it in motion.

Later in the film we recognize some of these same faces among the "good" white men and women who are shown as recognizing and appreciating Gandhi's greatness. What makes them different from the colonial authorities is their populist identity. These white men and women—Herman Kallenbach, Charlie Andrews, Mira Behn, Mr.

Walker, Margaret Bourke-White, and even the sympathetic Mr. Baker, whom Gandhi meets in South Africa—are the common people, the archetypal ordinary men. While the representatives of the colonial mission are always in formal dress and always inside highly ornate interiors of European decor, these ordinary men and women are frequently seen in casual dress, mostly moving about outdoors. Herman Kallenbach, for example, is always outdoors and actively engaged in physical labor. Even when he comes to Jinnah's house, he refuses to go inside but prefers to stay in the garden. The first meeting of Charlie and Gandhi takes place outside the house, and in the rest of the film he also is mostly seen in outdoor spaces. Mira Behn, who has a larger role in the film, is seen in various spaces, but never in conventional interiors. The same can be said about the journalist Mr. Walker. Though Margaret Bourke-White visits Gandhi when he is imprisoned in the Aga Khan's palace, most of her conversations with Gandhi take place in the shade of a tree in the prison compound. These outdoor sites, the domain of the "good" whites, are most of the time brightly lit and without shadows.

These heroes and heroines of the film have an important function: they are not merely Gandhi's followers but also the ones who instantly recognize his messiah status. The grim-faced Indian leaders who surround Gandhi often fail to understand him, or at least take a long time to do so, whereas people like Kallenbach and Mira Behn have an instant rapport with him. By recognizing his greatness, these people construct Gandhi; in other words, the glory of Gandhi is their creation. They are the apostles of this new messiah. It is Charlie Andrews who first takes the gospel of Gandhi to the public (read "whites") through his preaching in the church. Later this duty is taken up by the American journalist, Walker, who gives international exposure to the glory of the sacrifice and suffering performed in front of the Darsana Salt Works in connection with the salt tax. At the end of his frantic telephonic reporting, he declares: "Any claim of moral superiority that the West had, has been lost; India is free." Mira Behn becomes the spokeswoman of the people "back home" when she tells Gandhi that "they understand, they really do." Ultimately, it is Margaret Bourke-White who records Gandhi for posterity, through her repeated clicking of the camera. England also appears in the film for a brief while; it appears in black and white as an idyllic country full of open spaces and cheerful, smiling people. The sequence includes shots of Gandhi shaking hands with the prime minister and of the Glasgow industrial workers—mostly women—welcoming and pampering him. The voice-over commentary mentions Gandhi's meeting with Einstein, Charlie Chaplin, and the archbishop of Canterbury.

While Gandhi's transformation from a brown man to whiteness is by and large figurative, there are also some literal suggestions of it. Gandhi's moral and spiritual superiority is celebrated in the scene in which the Calcutta rioters surrender their weapons. The highlight of this episode is Gandhi's dramatic encounter with the repentant Hindu rioter. The almost hysterical rioter throws a piece of bread on Gandhi and screams at him to eat it. He is a sinner, yet he doesn't want to go to hell with the sin of Gandhi's death on his head. When he confesses that he killed a Muslim child to avenge the killing of his own child, Gandhi suggests, "Adopt a Muslim child who has lost his parents and bring him up as your own. Only remember that he is a Muslim, and bring him up as a good Muslim." This emotionally charged episode comes immediately after the noisy, chaotic scenes of the Calcutta riots. During this scene, both the rioter and Gandhi appear in separate shots. The close-ups of Gandhi are particularly significant. They show just his face toward the right half of the frame brightly lit from the left side. The actor playing the role has almost completely abandoned his brown makeup by now, so that in the bright light, Gandhi appears completely white. The light reflects off his bald head, giving him the aura of a saint. This is also the culmination of his spiritual journey. The white-ness that he had been gradually acquiring during his bildungsroman is now complete. At the same time, the scene is also the culmination of the crises that India has been facing (according to the film). What is now left is the consolidation of the protagonist's saintliness, which, according to history, is best accomplished through martyrdom. More-over, this brings to a logical culmination the motif of Christianity that is kept up throughout the narrative and declares Gandhi to be a Christ figure. This function is fulfilled by the final assassination.

The image of Gandhi portrayed in the film, a man one who de-velops from brownness to whiteness through his superior moral quali-ties, is clearly connected to the dominant thought patterns of the film's historical context. In a period when "colored races" were being regularly constructed as the major threat to social security and the civil society, the development of the protagonist from brownness to whiteness reinforced the myth of white superiority. At the same time, the moral superiority of Gandhi is equated directly with his patience and passive resistance toward violence. The celebration of Gandhi's

patience and passive resistance inevitably exhorts viewers to internalize such qualities. When this invitation comes in a social context in
which police brutality and the militaristic oppression of mass revolts
have become the order of the day, it can be read as a conscious effort
to "police" the sense of revolt expressed by the masses by advertising
qualities such as patience, suffering, and sacrifice. Moreover, the model
who demonstrates these cultural products of Christian morality—suffering, sacrifice, and patience—is a brown man, a member of one of
the racially nondominant groups. The dehistoricized celebration of a
colored man who achieved a great deal—the liberation of a nation and
the elevation of himself to saintliness—through passive resistance and
patience, when performed in the context of continuing racial discrimination, hatred, and violence, also has the function of soliciting a similar response from the colored races who are engaged in other forms of
protest. The moral lesson of this film is simple and clear: nonviolence
makes successful revolutions. The function of such a moral lesson ad-
ministered in a society in which most of the unprivileged sections are
driven to various forms of protest is predominantly the interpolation
of these groups (blacks, women, laborers, gays, ethnic minorities, and
migrants) into more controllable and less threatening forms of resistance—which, given the changed context, could be a great advantage
to those policing them.

Apart from his capacity for adventure, sacrifice, and suffering
there is another important feature that defines the character of Gandhi.
Although he is the representative of a patronizing patriarchy, Gandhi
is portrayed as predominantly asexual. He is a married man, but his
relationship with his wife is presented as platonic. Apart from the significant absence of physicality in the Gandhi-Kasturba relationship, the
several references in the latter part of the film to Gandhi's celebrated
abstinence from sex also define him as asexual. Once again, Kasturba
is made the mouthpiece of this redefining of "masculinity" as she talks
to Margaret Bourke-White about how her husband trained himself to a
life of celibacy. The scene depicts Kasturba blushing and smiling, like
a coy young woman confiding to a close friend about her first time.

Thus, if Gandhi represents the "masculine," then he also accom-
plishes a rewriting of it. According to Ginette Vincendeau, this sort of
conceptual shift in the representation of masculinity can be seen in
several "male community films": "The (new) male paradigm is male ex-
cess male rather than male/female (or, to be precise, male/non-male).
Against the excessive values embodied by his friends and accomplices,

the hero . . . stands as a norm. It is not so much that they are weaker, inferior versions of himself, but that their embodiment of certain values (positive or negative) allows him to represent, by comparison, an equilibrium."[13] Vincendeau calls this the "degree zero" of masculinity and points out that such a depiction of masculine has another significant narrative function: "By allowing a different male/female division to cut across its central hero, whose masculinity is thus truly at a 'degree zero,' the films also allow him to be a powerful figure of identification for both male and female spectators. And as far as the male spectator is concerned, the anxieties that might have been aroused by an all powerful hero are mitigated."[14]

The "degree zero" masculinity of its protagonist is extremely significant in the case of *Gandhi*. As has been mentioned earlier, the prominent strain in the narrative of the film is the construction of a certain subjectivity, which in turn strives to recast the white British identity in a specific historical context. Subsequently, the degree zero masculinity of the protagonist equips him as a figure for general identification—for both the male and female spectators—and thus makes him a powerful weapon in the effort to rewrite national identity. By trespassing the limits of gender and sex, this protagonist represents a universal humanism that is prescribed as the antidote for all the maladies that the nation/society has been facing.

The shift in the position of subject sought by the narrative is prominent in *Gandhi,* and this can be easily seen if we compare the assassination sequence as it appears at the beginning of the film with the sequence at the end. The film begins with a long shot of a red morning in New Delhi. From the resplendent golden waters of Ganga and the rising sun, a dissolve shifts the scene to a close-up of Godse. He wears a gray suit and has a powerful, fixed gaze. The camera follows him from close quarters as he moves and merges with the moving people. The first glimpse of Gandhi is as a tiny stooping figure leaving a white building—the ashram—far away, observed from Godse's point of view. The shot captures Godse from the back, looming large in a medium close-up occupying the entire left side of the frame while a glimpse of Gandhi's tiny figure—almost invisible—appears on the right side. During the entire sequence, the camera takes the position of someone who is at Godse's side, sometimes taking his perspective. This is followed by shots of Gandhi walking toward the camera, the people gathering around him, and then the assassination.

Though this scene is repeated at the end with the same incidental details, the point of view is shifted. This sequence begins with Gandhi getting ready to leave the ashram after chatting with Margaret Bourke-White and Mira Behn. The camera follows him from behind as he comes out, observing the gathering crowd from his point of view: in the crowd can be seen the face of Godse. He is now "the enemy within" whom one has to recognize in the crowd.

Taken together the two assassination sequences summarize the shift in subject position that the narrative of *Gandhi* proposes. In the initial sequence the viewer is positioned with the young Godse—cool, controlled, and composed. Yet he represents violence; he is the aggressor with a fixed gaze. In the sequence at the end of the film, the viewer is shifted to the position of the victim, Gandhi. The violator has now become an alien figure, the antagonist whom the helpless viewer recognizes as one among the crowd—as the enemy within (Godse looks straight into the camera in a manner that can be described as a "castrating gaze," whereas Gandhi in these sequences has an averted gaze, which posits him as the vulnerable, the Victim). Thus the shift is from the violator to the victim, but also from direct action to passive resistance.

The invitation to identify with the victim that the film extends to its viewers is simultaneously a solicitation to dissociate from the aggressor, the one who engages in violence. The victim has already earned not just the sympathy but also the love, respect, and even devotion of the viewer by his gradual self-elevation to saintliness; hence the identification solicited is a pleasurable one. In addition, the victim here has rescued his country from a severe crisis through sacrifice and suffering. As a result, allegiance to him and his way of life gives viewers the hope of rescuing their own country, which is also going through a crisis, though not exactly of the same type. This, in brief, is the structure of the interpellation to which the viewer is subjected, clearly indicating the political significance of *Gandhi* in the context of Thatcherism. The relative prominence the film gives to the question of race in the redefining of the national identity has a distinctly political dimension. By negating race as a biological factor and defining it in terms of spiritual progress and moral values, and also as an achievement, *Gandhi* manages a seeming disavowal and at the same time a covert reactivation of racism. Thus the film also makes a significant yet anonymous contribution to the reconfiguration of racist sentiments that occurred during the period of Thatcherism.

On the other hand, the motif of a nation facing a crisis can also be read as the reflection of the general anxiety that had been emerging in England since the 1960s. By presenting the protagonist as someone able to grow beyond his immediate environment and rescue his nation in the process, this film offers a pleasurable dream that can both satisfy its viewers and at the same time solicit them to construct themselves on similar lines. Thus *Gandhi* is suggesting a solution to the "crisis" that the country is supposed to be facing—a solution that unconditionally celebrates spiritual values, Christian virtues, and liberal humanism.

Translating the Empire

Much has already been written about the injury inflicted on British national pride by the process of decolonization, especially the "independence" of India, long considered the most precious jewel in the Crown. The end of the empire called for a significant rewriting and reconceptualization of the imperial ideology. Thus, what emerged along with the process of decolonization was a new set of discourses that translated the colonial adventure into a modified language of paternalism. According to Errol Lawrence, "The whole debate about the 'end of the empire' was suffused with this general attitude of paternal superiority; the talk was all of 'trusteeship,' 'standards,' 'conditions,' 'building up,' 'guidance,' 'responsibility' and 'granting.'"[15] It must be presumed that the postcolonial polemics that proliferated from the colonies and ex-colonies persuaded the colonizer to search for possible solutions and explanations for the blatantly "negative" aspects of imperial domination. But the ever resourceful imperial ideology came up with easy resolutions to such problems: "The strength of Imperialist ideology is not only that it includes the idea of natural superiority but also that it can absorb almost any attack on its power. It can absorb the decline of Empire while avoiding the notion that it is a defeat."[16]

In *Gandhi,* the well-known evils of colonialism are translated as being the result of the loss of Christian values, thereby using the film as another space for the redeployment of the moral agenda. This is evident from the very first scene, in which Gandhi is thrown off the train by the white policeman in South Africa. The scene begins with a close side shot of Gandhi reading a book. Though the book is not properly seen, there is a suggestion that it could be the Bible. Raising his head from the book, Gandhi asks the black porter whether he ever thinks of Heaven and Hell. It is this conversation that is interrupted by the intruding white men who finally throw Gandhi out. A low-angled frontal shot of the policeman records his act of throwing out Gandhi's luggage along with the book Gandhi was reading. It is the same book that had provoked Gandhi to talk about Heaven, thus presumably a Bible. Hence, the white policeman who throws it out is rejecting Christian values. It is white men such as this one who are at the receiving end of Gandhi's moral lessons throughout the film. Similarly, the policeman in the pass-burning sequence is more an incarnation of violence than a representation of the white regime. His defining characteristic is the violence he represents. (Incidentally, he is wearing a black uniform.) In contrast to him is Gandhi, whose passive resistance in this scene becomes a celebration not merely of his perseverance but also of his sacrifice and suffering—the values cherished by Christian doctrine. Such a pattern helps the narrative to negate the racial or national identity of the whites who are presented as "bad" by replacing it with the loss of Christian values.

By beginning the spiritual bildungsroman of Gandhi with a briefing on Christian values and perhaps a reading of the Bible, the film translates Gandhi's spiritual journey as his initiation into Christian values. The Christian theme in the film is further reinforced by the presence of Charlie Andrews throughout the first half of the film. References to the Bible and Christianity come up repeatedly in Gandhi's various conversations with Charlie. The association of the values that Gandhi represents with the ideals of Christianity later becomes the topic of Charlie's sermon in the church. In this scene, there are several close-ups of Charlie preaching that present him as speaking straight to the camera. Referring to the activities of Gandhi, Charlie tells the faithful assembled in the church: "As Christians we have to question ourselves." This, considering the direct address to the camera, has to be considered as direct preaching to the viewers. In between the close-ups there are shots of the audience in the church; most are attentive, but a few irritated ones walk out. Thus a suggestion is made that those who reject the values that Gandhi represents are also those who reject Christian duties. In other words, the white identity of these antagonists is cast under a spell of mystification by projecting them prominently as "unworthy Christians."

The film's celebration of Gandhi's liberal humanism has another important function; it is used as a trope to lament the loss of such moral values in a broader context. A very good example of this is the scene of the massacre at Jalian Wala Bagh, which defines General Dyer as an incarnation of inhumanity. The court-martial scene that follows begins with a close shot of Dyer's profile with a flag of Britain in the background. Dyer is a blot on the national pride. In the court-martial itself, he is further projected as both an incarnation of evil and at the same time the representation of guilt. He accepts full responsibility for the massacre and justifies it, yet his voice breaks as he admits that there were children and women in the crowd. During the course of the trial, the image of Dyer is gradually redefined. The entire scene is composed of shots of Dyer appearing alone in the frame and shots of the jurors appearing together. The presence of an Indian among the jurors is prominently stated. At the beginning of the court-martial, Dyer's answers defend his actions, but the expression on his face is one of remorse and intense mental strain. He appears to be a person going through a severe inner crisis rather than a dictatorial military officer. Yet he becomes speechless only when the issue of women and children comes up. At this point, the sin of colonial and racial oppression and violence is replaced by the sin of having forsaken the values of a patronizing patriarchy. His crime is having used force and violence on "helpless" women and children; thus he is a man who has failed to fulfill his masculine responsibility of protecting women and children. He has gone against his duty by inflicting violence on these helpless beings. Thus in effect he has betrayed masculinity. This point has already been emphasized in the earlier spectacular massacre scene, in which the camera lingers on the panic-stricken crowd, with women and children appearing center frame. There are several shots of mothers carrying children, running desperately for their lives, and even jumping into a well to escape the violence. A clichéd shot of a child crying near a woman's dead body surrounded by the frantic crowd adds further dimension to the tragedy and threat the child faces. Thus General Dyer is portrayed as one who has betrayed both Christian values and masculine responsibilities—once again, the "other" to Gandhi. Immediately after the court-martial sequence there is a shot of Gandhi, an expression of agony on his face, looking down the well into which many mothers had jumped. Yet there is only agony. The absence of indignation once again defines the massacre as a human tragedy and not an expression of colonial oppression. Incidentally, the honor of knighthood conferred on General Dyer on his return to England is a detail conveniently forgotten by this film.

The translation of colonial and racial violence as being the result of the lack or loss of moral values is repeated throughout the film, and this has to be recognized as another instance of narrative seduction. It negates the racial or colonizer identity of the oppressor and also the subsequent transformation of him into a black sheep, the prodigal son who must be reformed and accepted back into the fold. In other words, characters such as Dyer are also the "enemies within" who undermine the national honor and must be located and reformed. The function of Gandhi in such a context is to provide the catechism necessary to produce the desired change in these prodigal sons. This is exactly what he does when he faces the rowdy youth in the South African street; Gandhi counters the violent motivations of the young boys who want to "clean up the neighborhood" with references to the New Testament and the parable of the Good Samaritan. The mounted African police who confront Gandhi's peaceful march are made ashamed of their inhumanity by their own horses, which evince a "human" response in refusing to tread on the human bodies. Later, in India, Lord Irwin and his officials, who deliberately attempt to provoke violence, are frustrated by the absolute refusal of the crowds to engage in any form of violence as per Gandhi's instructions. But these white men are not "ordinary" people; except for the rowdy youth in Africa, they are all representatives of the upper, ruling class. Trapped in gray or dark formal suits, their personalities are defined by the offices they bear or the "duties" they perform. They do not represent the masses. In other words, the common people are relieved of the sin of this empire. Instead, they are represented by the "nice" whites like Walker, Mira Behn, and so on—the whites who construct Gandhi.

In this essay I have not made value judgments on the aesthetic competence or technical excellence of the film *Gandhi*. Neither have I tried to see whether the film is "truthful" to the life of the historical figure it portrays. My intention has been merely to point out that this film, when studied in the specific sociohistorical context in which it was made, can be seen as reflecting the rearticulation of a cultural racism capable of providing a satisfactory explanation to the contemporary socioeconomic problems in Britain. This is in spite of the film's overt disapproval of racism and colonialism. The questions that a film like *Gandhi* evokes might seem to be of little social or political relevance unless we see them as part of an ongoing effort on the part of the racist and imperialist nations and communities to salvage and consolidate their shaky cultural and political hegemony. Asserting the need to produce counterdiscourses that quarrel with these efforts, Salman Rushdie says: "We are left with a fairly straightforward choice. Either we agree to delude ourselves, to lose ourselves in fantasy . . . [or] we can make the very devil of a racket. Certainly when we cry . . . we cry to affirm ourselves, to say, here I am, I matter too—you are going to reckon with me."[17] For films such as *Gandhi* and the revival of imperialism initiated by Thatcherism are making use of our history—manipulating our past and our identities to propagate ideologies that help consolidate their power.

Notes

1   David Lloyd, "Race under Representation," *Oxford Literary Review* 18, nos. 1–2 (1991): 63.
2   Richard Dyer, "White," *Screen* 29, no. 4 (Autumn 1988): 46.
3   Centre for Contemporary Cultural Studies, University of Birmingham, *The Empire Strikes Back: Race and Racism in 70s Britain* (London: Hutchinson, 1982).
4   Stuart Hall, "Faith, Hope or Clarity," *Marxism Today* 20, no. 1 (January 1985): 16.
5   Stuart Hall, "No Light at the End of the Tunnel," *Marxism Today* 21, no. 12 (December 1986): 16.
6   Charlie Leadbeater, "Back to the Future," *Marxism Today* 24, no. 5 (May 1989): 14.
7   Bob Jessop, Kevin Bonnett, and Simon Bromley, "Farewell to Thatcherism? Neoliberalism and 'New Times,'" *New Left Review* 179 (January–February 1990): 89.
8   Drawing inspiration from Jacques Lacan's psychoanalytical theories on the formation of subject and Louis Althusser's adaptation of this in the discussion of the ideological apparatus, Stephen Heath argues that popular cinema shares a dialectical relationship with the viewing subject. Signification in cinema is a "dialectic of the subject," in which the subject is as much constituting as constituted. In other words, cinematic signification is a "subject production"—a production both by and of the subject; Stephen Heath, *Questions of Cinema* (Bloomington: Indiana University Press, 1981). Colin MacCabe also argues that realism (in cinema) is merely a textual organization whose effect is to position the reader. The narratives employ a variety of strategies to induce the reader to identify with certain characters or with a certain point of view. See Colin MacCabe, *Theoretical Essays: Film, Linguistics, Literature* (Manchester: Manchester University Press, 1985). Michael Ryan makes use of the concepts in the object-relations theory of psychology to theorize on cinema's intimate relation to sociopolitical contingencies. According to him, cinema represents the collectively felt "frustrations, fears and anxieties" in a society. He imagines cinema as an articulation of the broader systems of significance that make up a society and also an object of collective identification that can help recode prevailing social valorizations. See Michael Ryan, "The Politics of Film: Discourse, Psychoanalysis, Ideology," in *Marxism and Interpretation of Culture,* ed. Cary Nelson and Larry Grossberg (Urbana: University of Illinois Press 1988), 477–86.
9   William Dilthey, *Das Erlebnis und die Dishtung,* quoted by Martin Swales in *The German Bildungsroman from Wieland to Hesse* (Princeton: Princeton University Press, 1978), 10.
10   Ryan, "The Politics of Film," 479–80.
11   Edward Guerrero, "AIDS as Monster in Science Fiction and Horror Cinema," *Journal of Popular Film and Television* 18, no. 3 (Fall 1990): 86–93.

12 Errol Lawrence, "Just Plain Commonsense: The 'Roots' of Racism," in *The Empire Strikes Back,* 81–82.

13 Ginette Vincendeau, "Community, Nostalgia and the Spectacle of Masculinity," *Screen* 6, no. 26 (November–December 1985): 32.

14 Ibid., 32–33.

15 Lawrence, "Just Plain Commonsense," 66.

16 Richard Allen, "Empire, Imperialism and Literature," block 5, sec. 2, p. 19 (unpublished manuscript).

17 Salman Rushdie, "Outside the Whale," *Granta* 2 (1984): 136.

Theorizing White Consciousness for
a Post-Empire World: Barthes, Fanon,
and the Rhetoric of Love

Chéla Sandoval

FRANZ Fanon's 1951 book *Black Skin, White Masks* is well known for ruthlessly detailing the wounded forms of consciousness developed by colonized peoples of color living under white supremacist rule. Not so well known is that six years later Roland Barthes paralleled Fanon's effort—but with a difference. Barthes's 1957 *Mythologies* poses the question of how "innocent" or well-intentioned citizens can enact the forms-of-being tied to racist colonialism. The answer Barthes provides is in the form of an inventory of the psychosocial forms around which consciousness becomes constituted as "white," middle class, and, above all else, supremacist. The result is a "rhetoric" of supremacy comprised of seven figures, or poses, for the performance and dispersal of a legitimate, human, and racialized consciousness; a language, Barthes thinks, that structures and naturalizes the unjust relations of exchange that arise within and between colonizer and colonized communities.[1] It is crucial to realize that for Barthes, such poses are experienced by their practitioners as natural, normal, and neutral categories of being. Indeed, these poses call up the possibilities and prohibitions for thought and behavior that typify the "good citizen/subject" capable of functioning well under the imperatives of nationalist state formation. The danger of these categories for identity is that they encourage the development of authoritarianism, domination, supremacism—and even fascism. At the same time they construct the most innocuous forms of personal and everyday life—of subjectivity, of citizenship itself.

This rhetoric of supremacism, writes Barthes, is a "set of fixed, regulated, insistent figures, according to which the varied forms" that comprise ideology and its signifiers are arranged. Citizen/subjects take up and utilize any unit of this rhetoric, and differently, for "each of us can fill in" a specific figure "according to" our own particular history, no matter what its national, race, ethnic, sex, gender, or class inflections (150). What must be recognized over any historical content is that certain forms-of-being operate together to comprise the rhetoric of figures that orders and regulates Western social space and consciousness. Barthes wanted to reveal this rhetoric as animating the great ideological perversions that permit citizen/subjects to faultlessly consume ideology and guilelessly reproduce supremacist forms of speech, consciousness, morality, values, law, family life, and personal relations (as well as racial, language, nation, gender, sex, and class identities). Regardless of the historical basis of such supremacy,[2] this rhetoric arranges and disperses consciousness to call up and naturalize as the real— as history itself—a "dream," writes Barthes; a dream that, once lived out, becomes a contemporary global culture that insinuates domination into personal, family, cultural, and political relations.

During the 1950s and 1960s, Roland Barthes hoped that the methodology he had developed and called "semiology" would provide an apparatus for challenging supremacism in all its forms—that it would challenge identity itself as it energized the Western colonial project.[3] It was this methodology that enabled Barthes to identify the rhetoric and the figures through which the white middle classes of the 1950s became dispersed in a process that drew together, arranged, maintained, and regenerated consciousness-in-culture. To summarize Barthes's hope, semiology challenges supremacism in all its modes insofar as it is an approach that operates through (1) the recognition of differences and their inescapable consequences; (2) the reconnection of history to objects; (3) the disallowal of pure identification; (4) the self-conscious relocation of the practitioner of semiology in transits of meaning and power; (5) the undermining of authority, objectivity, fact, and science insofar as it seeks to reconnect each of these processes to the history, power, and systems of meaning that create them; and (6) the constant reconstruction of the consciousness of the semiotic practitioner, along with the method itself, as both mutually interact to call up—something else.

This essay outlines Barthes's methodical encodation of the rhetorical forms that he believed would shape middle-class and dominating forms of consciousness during the late twentieth century. My examination of Barthes's early work views him as one of the first white Western critical theorists to develop an analytical apparatus for theorizing white consciousness in a postempire world. I then reread Barthes's propositions against and in the context of another theorist of supremacism, Franz Fanon. I argue that Barthes's work and Fanon's are both driven by what I call the "methodology of the oppressed." The questions we will consider in comparing Barthes and Fanon are these: Why have Barthes's fundamental contributions to anticolonial resistance, to a quite contemporary and utopian postcolonial theory, and particularly his work on the rhetoric of white consciousness been elided in contemporary cultural, critical, and literary theory, even by those scholars who are also concerned with identifying such "poses" for consciousness? Indeed, many of Barthes's anticolonial and utopian formulations, though still read, are submerged in academic discourse—ironically, in a manner similar to the way Barthes's own work utilizes but submerges what I call the methodology of the oppressed. What are the connections between these two different kinds of academic submersions? More important, what are the profound similarities between the new and unexplored mode of consciousness Barthes proposes—the "something else" he hopes semiology can release—and Franz Fanon's call for "the open door of every consciousness"? How can this shared but untraditional configuration of consciousness be incited? What are its modes and methods of agency? How can the new forms of human being it summons end supremacism for the twenty-first century?

Roland Barthes and the Rhetoric of Supremacism

Each figure, or pose, for consciousness in the rhetoric that follows is easily recognizable; they emerge in every population. What hails this rhetoric into the real is difference; once enacted, however, each figure becomes a machine, a deputy for the real that works to erase difference. Under present cultural conditions, the following figures are called on to shape and inhabit not only the most obedient and deserving citizen/subject, but also even the most rebellious agent of social change.

1. THE INOCULATION
The first figure in this rhetoric of supremacy is fundamental to the construction of Western identity, as it is through the figure Barthes calls inoculation that consciousness surrounds, limits, and protects itself against invasion by difference. Barthes describes inoculation as if it

works homeopathically, for it provides cautious injections—in modest doses only—of dissimilarity (the affirmative action approach). By incorporating a small, tidy portion of difference, the good citizen/subject does not have to accept its depth or enormity and thus can remain as is. Middle-class, liberal, and Western citizen/subjects do admirably express a "tolerance" of difference, Barthes insists, but such tolerance is only a means to control its final impact. Difference is recognized, taken in, tamed, and domesticated. Indeed, this form of consciousness keeps its practitioners safe yet stimulated, for difference is treated as a controlled substance: to be enjoyed in small doses, always under conditions of moderation and restraint.

Inoculation, warns Barthes, is not only capable of immunizing individual consciousness; its force extends to immunize "the collective imagination" as well. The inoculating figure, for example, encourages general recognition of "the accidental evil of a class-bound institution," but only so as to better "conceal its principle evil" (150). This figure, pose, or habit of consciousness, Barthes believes, thus protects not just the psyche, but culture as well against any threatening difference capable of causing the "generalized subversion" of what-is. The inoculation performs as a preventative, securely buffering consciousness, providing a sanitary precaution against the contamination of the same by difference.

2. THE PRIVATION OF HISTORY

The second of the seven figures in Barthes's rhetoric works by estranging all objects in culture from what has made them what they are—an estrangement, Barthes insists, that deprives (Western) consciousness of any responsibility for what has and will become. The tragedy for the good citizen/subject is that this estrangement also creates and encourages a type of passivity-in-consciousness. This is because any dominant ideological system serves its population as a kind of "ideal servant," he writes. "It prepares all things, brings them, lays them out, the master arrives, it silently disappears: all that is left for one to do is to enjoy this beautiful object without wondering where it comes from." What happens, worries Barthes, to the colonizing and white consciousness after it accepts and submits to this work of ideology, this estrangement and privation of history, this luxury-at-a-price? For the rhetoric of supremacy now colonizes the colonizers' consciousness as well.

Barthes's insistence on decolonization, for colonized *and* colonizer, emerges in his example of the privation of History at work. His analysis is of a tour book designed to guide the first world consumer through third world countries by providing photos of exotic "primitives" preparing dances, food, clothing, and so on, seemingly for the camera's pleasure. In these photos the intricate and profound differences (in both historical trajectories and present conditions) of the peoples depicted dissolve under their primary appearance as festive objects for Western consumption as entertainment.

The privation of History is "felicitous," a happy but ignorant figure. Inoculating consciousness, procuring a little tantalizing difference — but not too much — the privation of History protects and tames the colonizer's imagination as viewer. But if this pose for consciousness happily turns its practitioners away from the very production of contemporary and past histories, it also distances the citizen/subject from recognizing its ability to intervene in that which ever rages: the possibility of shaping one's own destiny. Under the imperatives of the privation of History, all the participating citizen/subject must do is perceive, reach out, and "possess these new objects from which all soiling trace of origin and choice have been removed" (151). Barthes believes that this "miraculous evaporation" of history covers the world with pleasurable magic and is one of the most determining figures in the rhetoric of supremacy that enlivens, shapes, and (neo)colonizes most white bourgeois forms of consciousness (151).[4]

3. IDENTIFICATION

Identification is the third figure in Barthes's rhetoric of supremacy. When enacting this third pose, consciousness must draw itself up, comfort, and "identify" itself (or, as Fanon writes, constitute itself as "Human") through a comparing and weighing operation that seeks to equate all varying differences with itself, the better then to either brush them aside as unimportant or to assimilate them. This figure thus calls up a colonizing consciousness incapable of conceiving how real differences in others can actually exist, for everything can be seen only as the self — but in other guises. Locations, Barthes warns, where "the Other threatens to appear in full view," such as the "spectacle" or the "courthouse" are transformed through the figure of identification into mirrors in which the good citizen/subject can see refracted only more versions of itself, though gone astray. Should the good citizen/subject inadvertently find itself face-to-face with what is sublimely and horrifically other, Barthes predicts one of the four following responses. The citizen/subject can either blind himself, ignore the other, deny the other, or transform the other into himself (152). In Barthes's view, possibilities for confrontation are thus undone and sabotaged, and perceptions of otherness are "reduced to sameness." Under the imperatives of the first world cultural order Barthes inhabits, the other can at best be recognized only as a deceptive snare, a lure threatening to ambush with its duplicity the sense of self on which the citizen/subject secures its own forms of humanity. Barthes warns that from the point of view that becomes dominating in any culture, what is truly "other" becomes perceived as "a scandal which threatens" the very essence-of-being when, under the rhetorical pose of identification, that being has become supremacist in function.

Barthes warns that there are emergency conditions when the other cannot help but appear in all its sublime dissimilarity. In such an emergency another figure related to identification can comfort and save dominant forms of subjectivity from the horror of confronting the abyss of absolute difference. Identification extends as a dependable emergency figure to become "exoticism," so that the exoticized other can be perceived as pure "object," "spectacle," or "clown," Barthes writes. Difference is then relegated to the limits of humanity and can no longer threaten "the security of the home" (152). Supremacism seduces perception of difference.

These figures permit the citizen/subject to situate and "identify" itself as living at the center and best of all that yet is. The privation of History extracts the colonizing consciousness from the imperatives of any history that might say differently. And the citizen/subject can be painlessly, effectively, and pleasurably inoculated against incorporating any unlikeness that might transform or subvert what-is. Hope and faith draw the converted to inhabit and live out these figures; they provide entry to the first-world promised land, that 1950s Camelot of consciousness.

4. TAUTOLOGY

Barthes's list continues with tautology, his term for the metaphoric device that defines like by like. This figure defines the fourth principal pose around which Western consciousness is formulated, as demonstrated in the way tautology activates the previous three figures. The figures of inoculation, the privation of History, and identification, Barthes explains, are united insofar as they operate by defining the dominant tautologically: what is other is itself dominant, but in other forms. It is tautological reasoning that enables citizen/subjects to believe that Western knowledge can be understood and justified as such: "History is History," "Truth is Truth," and even, "That's just the way it is, that's all." Tautology operates behind a badge of authority, where its rationality is hidden. The favorite tautological answer to a challenging question is: "Because I said so, that's why!" This figure of supremacy, Barthes thinks, works like a magic act. The magic it produces? A "dead motionless" world (153). This redundant, superficial figure depends for its influence on power itself,[5] which it uses to freeze meaning into place, thereby protecting and legitimizing what-is. Any citizen/subject in a state of crisis can turn to tautology for protection. It acts as a stop-gap. Is one speechless? Powerless? At a loss? In need of a quick answer or explanation for what-is? Then take refuge in tautology, Barthes recommends, in the same way one takes refuge in fear, anger, or sadness.

5. NEITHER-NORISM

Neither-norism is the pose for enabling an independent "neutrality" in consciousness. It generates the kind of noncommitted, detached, moderate, and nonextreme mode of being that is so highly valued in the West. According to Barthes, this figure is exemplified in the phrase "I want *neither* this *nor* that" (153).[6] Here the citizen/subject reduces reality to two or more formal opposites, and each is relieved of its historically produced differences. Neither-norism thus enables a "final equilibrium" for being that immobilizes "values, life, and destiny." The performer of neither-norism no longer has to choose between contending realities, but only to endorse what already is (108). Choosing between contending realities means judging what already is as intolerable, Barthes thinks. But under the influence of neither-norism one can appear to take a "higher" moral ground and make no commitment to move in any alternative direction. This seeming neutrality encourages an inflexibility-of-being, however, that supports the order of the dominant rather than some other moral or political order.

6. THE QUANTIFICATION OF QUALITY

The sixth figure in Barthes's rhetoric of supremacy values all images—indeed, reality itself—according to the quantity of effects produced. The more, the better: more tears, increased emotion, added travel, hyperexperience, accumulated commodities, amassing garage sales, heaps of money, greater distances, collections, values, multiple dwellings, rooms, books, articles—the measure is never finally enough. Hyperaccrual, more flamboyant effects are understood to be the measure, degree, depth, and magnitude of goodness achieved. The search for increase becomes recognized generally as one with the search for a higher, more noble existence. The *inexpressible goodness of quality,* however, is reduced to quantity. Barthes thinks that this valuing of quality through the quantity of effects it produces is a social and psychological dynamic that is not well studied or analyzed in the academy, for the quantification of quality economizes scholarly intelligence itself, and even academic knowledge "understands reality more cheaply" (153).[7]

7. STATEMENT OF FACT

The final figure, statement of fact, supports all those that came before. Under this last pose for consciousness the citizen/subject is encouraged to speak and know with certainty and is trained to assert its own reality as if there is no other. Barthes explains that this performance operates through two central devices: the aphorism and the maxim. These stand in resistance to a fourth way of speaking and knowing with certainty, the proverb, which, unlike the others, allows humans to express the "revolutionary truth" of knowledge and power (154).

What distinguishes the proverb and bestows this radical possibility is the experimental and active engagement that it fashions between its speaker and some aspect of everyday life. Enacting its meaning as it is spoken, the proverb is transitively completed only by human encounter with the world. Insofar as the proverb expresses and demands human engagement with its surroundings, Barthes stresses that it represents a form of emancipatory speech, as opposed to the ideologically circumscribed forms of speech generated by the seven figures defined above. Barthes's example of proverbial speech in action is the statement "the weather is fine." When spoken by a hopeful farmer concerned with the crops, this statement is not meant to direct others how to view or feel about the weather. Rather, it is meant to be a "technological statement," meaning that farmers must draw today's weather into their farming labor every hour, through speech, in order to successfully farm and cultivate their crops and livestock. This kind of technological statement represents the innovative side of the proverb, which sends forth speech as (uncompleted) action—the results of which are hoped for, but still unknown.

The innovative activity of a technological statement such as this differs profoundly from the activity produced by the other ways of knowing and speaking with certainty, the aphorism and the maxim.

The aphorism represents language gathered up with the expressed purpose of dividing and marking off boundaries and horizons of being: it is a speech act devised to make reality "hold." The essence and power of the aphorism are expressed fully only when it is extended and transfigured to become an allied but different speech act called the maxim. The maxim is the language device that asserts the greatest authority insofar as its meanings appear to rise out of some fundamental kind of philosophical or religious premise. Together the aphorism and the maxim are tools for communication that support the ideological pose of the speaker who "knows for sure." The costs of this form of knowledge and its powers are high, for the statement of fact is "no longer directed towards a world to be made; it must overlay one which is already made, bury the traces of this production under a self-evident appearance of eternity: it is a counter-explanation, the decorous equivalent of a *tautology,* of this preemptory BECAUSE which parents in need of knowledge hang above the heads of their children" (155). The statement of fact is a form of authority supported by the structure of the dominant social order, but its confidence and knowledge are not spoken, heard, or experienced by its users as socially constructed but rather as rising out of the nature of how-things-are-and-should-be. Thus, this figure for knowing and power creates a peculiar certainty-of-being felt by its practitioners to be only the honest, straightforward expression of what-is, of common sense. The term *common sense* as used here should be defined, Barthes points out, as "truth when it stops on the arbitrary order of him who speaks it" (153). This is why the statement of fact and its devices, the aphorism and the maxim, wielded as though they are the most innocuous, innocent, and straightforward containers for common sense, contain all the force of supremacism.

The confidence, security, and structured arrogances of the statement of fact imbue and empower each of the six forms of colonial ideology outlined so far: the inoculation, which takes in quite small, controlled portions of difference, the better to assert essential truths; the privation of history and neither-norism, both of which entertain and solidify the self and social reality by overlooking specific situated histories (reality is already well under control!); identification, through which all differences can appear only as varying or deviant units of oneself; tautology, in which all knowledge necessary for living is circuited through some authoritative and centralizing power; and the quantification of quality, wherein differences are counted, added up, cataloged, and hierarchically displayed in order to demonstrate the depth and quality of existence as it already is.

Together, these seven figures comprise Barthes's 1957 postulation for a rhetoric that catalogs the poses possible for inhabiting white consciousness in its colonizing mode. This structured rhetoric for dominant ideology circulates in innocuous yet (I have argued) supremacist modes. Barthes warns that this rhetoric of supremacism installs a phony nature as the real, and prohibits humans from "inventing" themselves (155). This prohibition is central to the horror of the process of Western ideological formation, he thinks, and of the imperialist, racist, and colonial project, for it stubbornly "cannot rest until it has obscured the ceaseless making of the world, fixated this world into an object which can be forever possessed, catalogued its riches, embalmed it, and injected into reality some purifying essence which will stop its transformation, its flight towards other forms of existence" (155).

This rhetoric of supremacy immobilizes the world, for, Barthes argues, it nurtures and constructs a consciousness and culture that desires "a universal order that has fixated once and for all the hierarchy of possessions," of selfhood, of passion, of being (155). This order is even computed, according to Barthes, for white morality becomes "a weighing operation," constructed essences are "placed in scales," and the successful, middle-class, colonizing citizen/subject in its illusion of power becomes "the motionless beam." The final computation in the rhetoric of supremacism freezes the world, for essentializing and weighing incapacitate difference and the unknown, so that culture arrives, after all is said and done, at what-is-the-same.

Barthes's *Mythologies* represents one of the first efforts to critique and outline "white" forms of consciousness by a member of the colonizing class responding to the decolonizing processes going on at the time he was writing. His was the first critique of white consciousness to emerge from the imperatives of what was fast becoming a postempire history.[8] In this sense Barthes's early work can be seen as equivalent to the work on "white consciousness" now being accomplished, forty years later, most powerfully in work generated by the volatile relations between the white and U.S. women of color feminisms of the 1960s, 1970s, and 1980s by thinkers such as Ruth Frankenberg, Vron Ware, Bernice Johnson Reagon, bell hooks, and Cherríe Moraga.[9] But investigations of "white" forms of consciousness are also being generated by other scholars of culture in disciplines ranging from biology, anthropology, and sociology to ethnic studies, cultural studies, and postmodernism. Thinkers from every vantage point are interested in the attempt to graph the various subject positions that are unconsciously structured, categories of psychosocial formation that comprise Barthes's poses (or masks, as Fanon earlier called them) that structure supremacist forms of consciousness. Strangely, however, Barthes's attempt to theorize the structure of colonial and "middle-class" consciousness has been taken up by only a few contemporary theorists of culture. And this is so despite Barthes's reliance on a quite contemporary and decolonial critical criticism.

In finding the dominant social rhetoric that functions in the mode of a language, the poses for subjectivity available to dominating classes, Barthes hoped to undo the effects of being a citizen/subject in Euro-American Western culture; to undermine the subject positions of legitimate, "bourgeois" citizens; to cite these poses and their languages as comfortable masquerades for identity. Barthes's horror was that the innocent usage, consumption, acceptance, or production of these rhetorical figures consigned citizen/subjects to generating and accepting a multilevel, profound alienation-in-consciousness as a natural state of being. Barthes's pain over the recognition of this profound alienation as it determined psychic and social life brought him face-to-face with the languages and idioms of survival spoken by colonized peoples, and into contact with the methodology of the oppressed, which he at once affirms and asserts while blinding himself to its ongoing practices and practitioners. I am suggesting that the erasure from academic scholarship of Barthes's important contributions on the topic of supremacist and/or white consciousness is in part due to his own simultaneous recognition and repression of the methodology of the oppressed, a methodology that had been accounted for by Franz Fanon six years earlier, in 1951.

Franz Fanon and the Methodology of the Oppressed

In comparing Barthes's *Mythologies* with Fanon's *Black Skin, White Masks* (1951),[10] both published in France, one discovers more than either book can disclose on its own. What emerges is the authors' shared commitment to a method that enables the findings of both, the enactment of which I call the methodology of the oppressed. This methodology comprises five interrelated technologies: (1) semiotics, the semiotic reading of signs in culture as structured meanings that carry power (a basic survival skill necessary to subordinated and oppressed citizenry); (2) the deconstruction of dominant sign signification; (3) meta-ideologizing, the creation of new meta-meanings that appropriate and build on dominant sign systems; (4) democratics, the accomplishment of these previous technologies under the guidance of an ethical commitment to egalitarian and democratic redistributions of power; and (5) differential movement, in which each previous technology is activated by "differential" movement through consciousness, signs, social order, and meaning. (Indeed, this last, differential, technology can itself also comprise not only its own form of oppositional consciousness but also a type of postmodern social movement, described in contemporary critical and cultural theory by such terms as "fragmented," "hybrid" "mobile," "flexible," "radical democratic politics," "the lines of flight of minority discourse," "eccentric subjectivity," "diasporic movement," "U.S. third world feminism," "the critical apparatus of mestizaje," and "*la conciencia de la mestiza*.") When guided, however, as one technology within this five-technology machine of the methodology of the oppressed, it is differential movement that breaks up the kind of objectification and embalming of the world that Barthes warns can end all difference, all "flight toward other forms of existence" (155).

In 1957, Barthes was not yet capable of fully linking his academicized "science" of semiology—the method that enabled him to disclose the rhetoric of middle-class consciousness in the West—with methods developed within the very populations on whose behalf he spoke, those his book calls "the colonized," "the excluded," or the "oppressed," who might have been for him a community of allies. Without recognizing those links, Barthes experienced himself as alone in his commitments to anticolonial social change, abandoned, and in despair. The very methods and principles of semiology that Barthes proposes in *Mythologies* and that, once applied, can intervene in the rhetoric of colonizing consciousness, will only banish him from the very world he occupies. He fears he will be excluded, cut off from his peers, estranged from his entire community, and condemned to live in isolation from citizens of like stature (157). Semiology, he believes, is a method that will exile and sever him from dominant "reality" and its pleasures. The alternative is to live as a solitary, principled, and heroic figure, yet paradoxically, in lucid agony, Barthes continues to long for connection and community with the same dominant culture that he has committed himself to transform.

Ironically, during the very decade that Barthes recognized himself as exiled from history through his commitment to semiology as method, people of color engaged in anticolonial struggle were being released into a realm of possibility, reentering history as what Fanon calls "mutated" citizen/subjects of social orders undergoing metamorphosis. Just as Barthes's (self) study of colonial psychology as it was effected in white middle-class consciousness was designed to reveal the horrifying effects of racism and colonialism on the perpetrators themselves, Fanon's book *Black Skin, White Masks* had been written to point out the "various attitudes" and forms of consciousness that colonized peoples of color "adopt in contact with white civilization" (12). Like Barthes, who methodically encodes semiology in *Myth Today,* thus discovering the "rhetorical figures" that organize Western consciousness, Fanon too begins his book by recognizing sign reading (or semiology) as a central technology in a five-technology methodology of the oppressed. The following analysis sketches Fanon's narrative in *Black Skin, White Masks* in order to demonstrate (1) how his argument depends on and unfolds across the methodology of the oppressed; (2) that Fanon's work, written seven years before Barthes's, prefigures and replicates many dimensions of Barthes's theorization of white forms of colonized consciousness; and (3) how Fanon's use of method provides and enables him to reach a radically different conclusion.

Fanon's book begins by insisting that "every dialect," whether spoken by the "white man" or by the "oppressed," should be recognized semiotically: all idioms develop selective meanings and alternative "ways of thinking" (25). Dominant Euro-American ways of thinking are not ordered, he continues, with any intention to hurt or anger the colonized. The peculiarity, however, of their order for making meaning is that "it is just this *absence* of wish, this lack of interest, this indifference, this automatic manner" of "classifying," "imprisoning," and "primitivizing" that injures colonized and colonizer alike (32). Fanon explains that the damage to the colonized is this: Intentions (good or bad) aside, the structured rhetoric of colonizing consciousness and its forms of speech stubbornly "fasten" those who are different to an "effigy" of themselves. Like Barthes, Fanon believes that this rhetoric creates a consciousness and speech that "snare" and "imprison" the colonized in a dream, "eternal victims" of an "essence" for which they are not responsible (35). Fanon warns that this naturalized rhetoric of supremacy damages and enslaves the colonizer as well, for the good citizen/subject is given legitimate entrance to a dominant society that in return provides rigidification "in predetermined forms, forbidding all evolution, all gains, all progress, all discovery" of difference (224). Fanon's assertion is that legitimized citizen/subjects of this dominant society, those "allowed to assume the attitude of a master," are unwitting "slaves" to a dominating and structured process of "cultural imposition" (117).

Indeed, he continues, any society that freezes social hierarchies into place is a society where equality and justice between humans will be impossible to achieve, for justice in a world that naturalizes hierarchy-through-domination will always be defined in a manner that serves the needs of the dominating order. From time to time colonized peoples of color have been asked by members of a white colonizing class to fight "for Liberty and Justice, but these were always white liberty and white justice." Such forms of liberty and justice should be recognized as "values secreted" by those good citizen/subjects who live according to the meanings of the dominating order. This is why, Fanon explains, former slaves watch "unmoved before" those young white men singing and dancing on the tightrope of existence who yearn for the kind of liberty and justice defined by the white philosopher Kierkegaard (221). Their forms of liberty and justice, formulated within the cultural matrix of the colonizers, Fanon insists, are not the same justice and liberty that must be constructed by subordinated and revolutionary peoples.

Revolutionary justice is difficult to imagine for those legitimized citizen/subjects shaped by the social and psychic categories of a (nation/class/gender/race) colonizing state, Fanon believes, insofar as these categories also call up an innocuous but everyday craving for supremacy. Though such cravings, knowledges, and powers are "cultural, which means acquired" and thus transformable, the colonizing Euro-American white mind desires what-is and feels certain forms of supremacy to be natural. Fanon's example is of the great white Western thinker of his time, Carl Jung, who asserted that the "collective unconscious" of the dominating class, "its mythologies and archetypes," are "permanent engrams of the race" of humans and rooted in "spirit" itself (188). Fanon, however, insists that Jung's collective unconscious, when understood as dependent on biological heredity regardless of culture, represents only Jung's naturalization of his own particular dominant order. Fanon reiterates that any so-called collective unconscious discovered by science is a product—like consciousness itself—a result of the "unreflected imposition of culture." And mind formed through the imperatives of culture is transformable through self-conscious reflection. It is this possibility of transformation and self-formation that makes the hope for sharing a definition and practice of liberty and justice possible between differing categories of the human (191).

How does one go about resisting the dominant rhetoric of supremacy and its forms of cultural imposition, thus making individual and social transformation possible? Fanon's suggestion is this: "White society—which is based on myths of progress, civilization, liberalism, education, enlightenment, refinement"—will be transformed precisely by forces, skills, methods, and techniques that are organized to oppose "the expansion and the triumph" of those Western colonial ideologies that are tainted with supremacy (194). When such oppositional forces are not mobilized, Fanon warns, then the rhetoric of supremacy, its signs and meanings, "the movements, the attitudes, the glances" of the legitimized citizen/subject, "fix" those who are different, the world as well as the citizen/subject practitioner itself, "in the sense in which a chemical solution is fixed by a dye" (109). This is the danger of the rhetoric of supremacism: it works to "fix" all peoples into images that support and rigidify its own forms of being.[11]

This situation propels Fanon to exhort every enslaved consciousness (those who have become dominant image) to "burst apart" all they have become—an eruption that fragments the self, he warns. But these fragments can be put together again when another kind of transformative self arises (109). This self can liberate citizen/subjects from Jung's "archetypes," free them from the dominant poses and figures that comprise the rhetoric of "civilized" consciousness. This liberty requires citizen/subjects to "incarnate a new type" of subjectivity, which can occur only through a process Fanon describes as a slow, painful, re-"composition of my self in an ongoing process of mutation" (111, 23, 51). The choice for Fanon is to speak in and along with "the white world (that is to say the real world," he adds ironically, to become its consciousness by embodying its rhetoric), or to found a new, unhabituated real with its own concomitant language forms, meanings, psychic terrains, and countrypeople. Fanon claims to have made this shift: "In the world in which I travel," he writes, "I am endlessly creating" and re-creating myself (229).

It is not only the individual psyche that must undergo reformation and mutation; the categories by which the human becomes human must also be re-formed. Fanon warns, for example, that as long as whiteness remains a mythology, a set of learned behaviors called up within a specific rhetoric and its categories, any race can come to inhabit the supremacist imperatives of whiteness. He explains that "the Negro problem does not resolve itself into the problem of Negroes living among white men," but "rather of Negros exploited, enslaved, despised by a colonialist, capitalist society that is *only accidentally white*." This colonialist, capitalist society creates a liberal form of naturalized supremacism that binds (in varying forms) *all* citizen/subjects, including the white man, who has become "enslaved" by his own forms of "superiority" (60). Thus, using Barthes's terms now, the rhetoric and the figures of the dominant order, as well as the human beings who inhabit and enact this order, must be transformed to free all from what both Fanon and Barthes agree is a predetermined, rigidified, and immobilized state of being. Unlike Barthes, Fanon is hopeful about the consequences of becoming an agent for these transformations. One who "takes a stand against" the death-of-being in supremacism, he writes, joins a new, original, revolutionary cadre that is cross-racial, cross-class, and cross-nation: an alliance of countrypeople of the same psychic terrain (225).

What are the strategies and tactics that guide the transformative agency of this original alliance of revolutionaries? The preceding pages sketched the outlines of a methodology shared by Fanon and Barthes. Their decolonizing method guides the transfiguring movement proposed by Fanon according to five interwoven technologies that include (1) reading signs of power; (2) deconstructing them when necessary; (3) remaking signs in the interests of renegotiating power; (4) commitment to an ethical position through which all signs and their meanings are organized in order to bring about egalitarian power relations; and (5) the focused mobilization of the four previous technologies in differential movement through mind, body, social body, sign, and meaning. This last flexible, improvisational, "differential" technology permits the technologies of semiotic reading, deconstruction, meta-ideologizing, and ethical commitment to occur as powers of reapportionment and boundary change. The ethical technology also guides the enactment of each technology according to a commitment to social justice through egalitarian redistributions of power across differences encoded as race, gender, sex, nation, culture, or class distinctions. Together, these five technologies comprise the methodology of the oppressed, the method embedded in the writings of both Fanon and Barthes, and the compass that guides their work. Fanon's recognition of the new routes of hope provided through the differential form of social movement and consciousness provides an exemplary link, a hypermodern point of connection between his own constituencies and those of allies such as Barthes. This innovative point of connection, however, is one Barthes is unable to perceive.

The Neo-rhetoric of Love

How can cultural, critical, and literary theorists of whiteness use, learn from, and build on Barthes, Fanon, and the lessons of their juxtapositioning? Have scholars genericized Barthes, taking him up only as a critic of the "human" condition in its drive-to-signify (also known as the unmarked-dominant-posing-as-universal) while ignoring his substantial contributions toward undoing colonial, middle-class, white, and supremacist forms of consciousness? Have we marginalized Fanon by reading him only as a critic of the subjecthood of the colonized and oppressed while failing to engage him as a critic of dominant subject formation? Are these tendencies symptoms of an apartheid of theoretical domains that keeps knowledge in the academy developing separate versions of the methodology of the oppressed—under varying terminologies—while at the same time seeking a method for transdisciplinarity that works?

I have argued that the 1951 work by Fanon and the 1957 work by Barthes parallel one another. Inspired by the anticolonial revolutionary activities of their times, each author provides methods for comprehending raced consciousness in the colonizer and colonized alike. Both represent "whiteness" as integral to the standards by which identity, confidence, humanity, gender, knowledge, and academic values are constructed in the West; and both sought to agitate these categories by revealing them as constructs of the white imaginary, as a set of mythologies.[12] Fanon's book was written to point out the "various attitudes that the Negro adopts in contact with white civilization" (12), while Barthes' self-study of colonial psychology as it is effected in white middle-class consciousness reveals the horrifying effects of racism and colonialism on the perpetrators themselves. Both books comprise an exposé of the rhetorics of being, the poses for consciousness produced by the demands of a particular economic, political, and cultural order. Both thinkers acknowledge that this rhetoric for dominant identity generates its own pleasures and comforts; that is why it is enlisted, though it calls up supremacist exchanges of power. And each believes that undermining the constitution of this rhetoric means challenging any final hope for an integrated, whole self capable of warding off the polluting effects of differences based on color, physiology, race, gender, sex, culture, or nation. Both Fanon and Barthes labored as diagnosticians of the psychopathology of Western culture, each driven by the expectation that a different kind of rhetoric-for-being could emerge that would divide and figure consciousness differently than the current order did, and thereby generate new individual, collective, and political imaginations.

Fanon and Barthes differ, however, insofar as Barthes's solitary sense of self seduces him into representing semiology as a method fathomable and applicable only should its practitioner be able to live as lone hero. This understanding is reasonable insofar as Barthes's own sense of self as exile comes from his dis-location from the ruling class and its sex and gender legitimacies; and from this dislocation comes his sense of otherness as one whose consciousness is at odds with dominant class, gender, sex, and even race positionings, which nevertheless always beckon to him. But Barthes's felt exile also derives from a kind of white solipsism, a sense of aloneness in the world, which means that Barthes is able to draw examples from colonized peoples, situations, and knowledges—indeed, from the methodology of the oppressed itself (without recognizing how doing so inflects his theoretical apparatus)—bringing him, without knowing it, into close proximity with a world of potential allies, even friends. The isolation Barthes feels as activist, knower, semiologist, and theorist functions, then, to make his overall argument more pessimistic and static than that of Fanon. Conversely, Fanon sees himself in elective affinity with a revolutionary community, as another member of a cadre of actors and potential actors similarly committed to transforming the dominant according to principles derived from the methodology of the oppressed. Both end their books with an invitation to a new world pried open by the tools of this method: semiotics, deconstruction—and reconstruction—of signs, the ethical commitment to justice, and the differential movement that keeps all aspects of being in motion and mutation.

This comparison of Barthes and Fanon draws our attention to a permeable boundary—between psyche and the rhetoric of dominant citizenship, between socially reinforced poses-for-being and new configurations of order and consciousness, between colored skins and figurations of "white masks." This vulnerable borderland is entered through a new kind of interfacing: the ability to tell another story, to find a differing version while facing the difference of degree between renditions and interpretations, to recognize the function that recurs in spite of all disparities.[13] In this essay I have suggested that the methodology of the oppressed renders that necessary interface. It devises the recovery of meaning-through-movement called for by Fanon in the bursting of the self and its reformation through mutation; it allows the differential intervention of that new self into social and ideological categories for the sake of their reapportionment and conversion; it develops a stubborn differential function that thrives on correlations, shifts, conversions, and transfers of meaning. Previous categories of race; the rhetoric of supremacy and its necessary colonizations of nation, color, sex, gender, class, and identity; and older strategies of interpretation transform under the instruments of this method. And from its activities rises the differential mode of social movement that is bent on coalition between subordinated constituencies, that is capable of transforming the politics of power. The methodology of the oppressed and its practices constitute a new hermeneutic that spins new forms and contents. In Barthes's terms, these forms and contents can be recognized as another kind of rhetoric—a neo-rhetoric of love in the postmodern world.

What Barthes forgot to encode in his 1957 theories of oppositional consciousness is what Fanon had asserted seven years before when he concluded *Black Skin, White Masks* by saying: "I want the world to recognize, with me, the open door of every consciousness" (123). Fanon's "open door of consciousness" refers not only to a location of access and departure, but to a site of crossing, transition, translocation, and metamorphosis where identity alters and is mutated. At this threshold meanings are recovered and dispersed through another rhetoric that transfigures all others, and whose movement is its nature. The consciousness called up by this rhetoric operates differentially because, guided by the methodology of the oppressed, it reads variables of meaning, it apprehends and caresses their differences, it shuffles their continual rearrangement, while its own parameters shift queerly *according to necessity, power, and ethical positioning.* Contemporary cultural, literary, and critical theory posits motion as a primary element in theorizing a coalitional consciousness under postmodern conditions. Terms such as "oppositional movement," "flexibility," "diaspora," "mobility," and "differential" are being coded under U.S. postmodern and postcolonial discourses, under U.S. women of color and hegemonic feminist theories, and under queer theory as varying types of theory-in-resistance, but all these conceptions are part and parcel of the methodology of the oppressed—what has been identified in this essay as a neo-rhetoric of love in the postmodern world.

Notes

This essay is dedicated to Hayden White, who many years ago lent me his copy of *Black Skin, White Masks,* and who taught me to love the work of Roland Barthes; to the 1969–76 imaginations of liberty proposed by the Black Panther party, the Wounded Knee Rebellion, the Blow outs and Chicano Moratorium against Vietnam, and the I-Hotel protests; and for Huey Newton, Marge Frantz, Elena Flores, Susana Montaña, Catherine Angel, Timothy Leary, the Sisters from Another Planet, and Mé Shell Ndegeocello . . . peace beyond passion.

1   Roland Barthes, *Mythologies* (Paris: Seuil, 1957), *Mythologies,* trans. Annette Lavers (New York: Hill and Wang, 1976). Barthes sketches the rhetoric that he believes structures middle-class ideologies and that defines the "dream of the contemporary" Western world on pages 150–55. In opposition to this rhetoric, he thinks, stands the social rhetoric of peoples of color in colonial status. In 1957 Barthes wrote, "Today it is the colonized peoples who assume to the full the ethical and political conditions described by Marx as being that of the proletariat" (148n). This rhetoric comprises one of the earliest attempts to define and theorize white consciousness in a postempire world. Further references are cited in the text by page number.

2   Whether it be race, gender, culture, class, sexuality, nation, or something else.

3   The roots of semiotic thought extend far back into history, but contemporary academic studies in semiotics developed primarily from two sources: the work of the Swiss linguist Ferdinand de Saussure and the writings of the American logician Charles Sanders Peirce, who independently formulated theories of signs and their functioning that came to serve as the basis for specialists in numerous disciplines. Saussure's term *semiology* was taken up by Roland Barthes in 1957. See Charles Sanders Peirce, *Collected Papers* (Cambridge: Harvard University Press, 1931), 58; Ferdinand de Saussure, *Course in General Linguistics,* ed. Charles Bally and Albert Sechehaye, trans. Roy Harris (La Salle, Ill.: Open Court, 1986); Roland Barthes, *Elements of Semiology,* trans. Annette Lavers and Colin Smith (New York: Hill and Wang, 1967); Barthes, *Image Music Text,* trans. Stephen Heath (New York: Hill and Wang, 1977).

4   Thus the original *neocolonization* of consciousness occurring under postmodern cultural conditions as suggestively theorized by Fredric Jameson in *Postmodernism, or, The Cultural Logic of Late Capitalism* (Durham: Duke University Press, 1991).

5   Which it can never admit; all finally depends on the effectiveness of ideology/naturalization.

6   As reflected in the anti–affirmative action position that states: We want neither white nor people of color, we only want the "best."

7   Donna Haraway pointed out to me that the quantification of quality also is crucial to the affect of postmodernism—the subject immersed in sensation, in stimulation, in the hyperreal. The quantification of quality is not only a liberal, figural pose,

then, as it was in Barthes's time, but also a figure of the "new world" postmodern order in its neocolonial mode. The larger project suggested here is to make the postmodern de- and postcolonial.

8   Western thinkers such as Hegel (1770–1831), Marx (1818–1883), Nietzsche (1844–1900), Saussure (1857–1913), and Freud (1856–1939), of course, considered consciousness in its supremacist forms. Their clarity of insight was very well generated through their ability to compare Western forms of being with those that insistently appeared as profoundly "other" during the imperialist expansion of the West, but none of these thinkers explicitly drew on the survival techniques of colonized and oppressed classes by turning those techniques into a "science," as Barthes attempts to do. Barthes does refer to statements by both Marx and Gorki in order to guide his own definition of the rhetoric of supremacy. He quotes Marx as saying: "What makes [people] representative of the petit-bourgeois class, is that their minds, their consciousnesses do not extend beyond the limits which this class has set to its activities" (Eighteenth Brumaire). And, from Gorki: "The petit-bourgeois is the man who has preferred himself to all else" (151).

9   Ruth Frankenberg, *White Women, Race Matters: The Social Construction of Whiteness* (Minneapolis: University of Minnesota Press, 1993, and London: Routledge, 1993); Bernice Johnson Reagon, "Coalition Politics, Turning the Century," in *Home Girls: A Black Feminist Anthology,* ed. Barbara Smith (New York: Kitchen Table Women of Color Press, 1983), 356–69; bell hooks, "Representing Whiteness in the Black Imagination," in *Black Looks: Race and Representation* (Boston: South End Press, 1992), 165–79; Vron Ware, *Beyond the Pale: White Women, Racism and History* (London: Verso, 1992); Gloria Anzaldúa, "Haciendo Caras, Una Entrada, an Introduction," in *Making Face, Making Soul/Haciendo Caras: Creative and Critical Perspectives by Women of Color,* ed. Gloria Anzaldúa (San Francisco: Aunt Lute, 1990), xv–xxvii.

10   Franz Fanon, *Black Skin, White Masks* (New York: Grove Press, 1982). All further references are cited in the text by page number. For recent literary and critical analyses of Fanon's contributions, see Henry Louis Gates Jr., "Critical Fanonism," *Critical Inquiry* 17, no. 3 (Spring 1991): 457–70; and Barbara Harlow, "Narratives of Resistance," *New Formations* 1 (Spring 1987): 131–35.

11   The supremacism analyzed here is capable of making a black African soldier saluting the French national flag in 1955, in Barthes's famous example, an example of the goodness of colonialism; or, in Fanon's famous 1951 example, of modifying "black skin" to signify only through a "white mask:" what is seen, or enacted, is a white mask—in blackface.

12   It should be emphasized that Fanon's work preceded Barthes's by seven years. Both men lived and worked in France during the 1940s and 1950s, each knew and was intellectually influenced by Sartre. Fanon's *Black Skin, White Masks* achieved international fame immediately after publication. It is hard to imagine Barthes as uninfluenced by Fanon's work in 1957, a point I argue in *Oppositional Consciousness in the Postmodern World,* forthcoming from the University of Minnesota Press.

13   This "recurring function" also depends on correlations, conversions, and transfers of meaning, and represents another praxis and form of being that even under postmodern, neocolonial, and postcolonial conditions is still not yet comfortably named. Derrida calls it "différance"; I call it "differential consciousness."

On the Social Construction of Whiteness
within Selected Chicana/o Discourses
Angie Chabram-Dernersesian

Posing the Necessary Question: Why Study
Whiteness Anyway?

THE decline of an essentialist brand of identity politics within the alternative sector has been punctuated by the eruption of increasingly complex social and political identities, generated by shifting transnational and ethnic movements across disparate geographical, political, cultural, and linguistic spaces. Chicana/o cultural practitioners have come to terms with this plethora of social identities by negotiating the hyphen between Chicana/o and Latina/o and by attending to the gender linkages that are inscribed in this transnational movement through the Americas. Within Chicana/o discourse, much less attention has been paid to examining how Chicanas/os have pursued an ongoing construction of whiteness with the end of positioning alternative and even oppositional identities within a conflicted social arena that is local.

In fact, the very idea that Chicana/o cultural practitioners have produced a construction of whiteness (even a counterdiscourse that appropriates whiteness as a way of contesting it from the location of another political imaginary) is an embarrassment to some, particularly to those who follow a supernationalist inclination to shadow all traces of the dominant culture and its preferred ethnicity under an overarching brown umbrella.

And, if this were not enough, on the surface it would appear that not even the emergence of a new critical discourse within Chicana/o studies—informed by feminism, Marxism, and cultural studies and bent on consciously inscribing multiple identities and subject positions in the face of formidable pressures "to do the opposite" from various sectors that seek a less complex grounding of social processes—has resulted in a sustained inquiry into the social construction of whiteness within the Chicana/o critical discourse.

What might be construed as a general reluctance to inquire cannot be explained in these simplistic terms. First, studies involving the social identities and thematic clusters generally linked to whiteness exist within Chicana/o critical discourse—it could even be said that they abound. Notwithstanding this fact, they cannot be "contained" within fashionable representations of whiteness, which offer a particular delimitation of this field, because these studies within Chicana/o critical discourse span not only various intellectual fields and modes of cultural production, but also historical periods and sociopolitical camps.[1]

Second, it could also be said that in these cases the examination of whiteness is not only intentionally diffused but, more important, it is not always privileged through the type of selective "racialization" of social and/or intellectual fields that such a representation often suggests. None of which precludes the fact that there *are* important political questions at stake when approaching this thematic whiteness "head-on," questions not easily ignored for those whose daily practice involves not only crossing borders but also setting territorial limits that sanction a public space for progressive action and self-reflection within an increasingly hostile and inhumane environment.

Some of these questions are revisited here from the ideological purview of different intellectual and political imaginaries, as a way of recovering the significant pre-texts that mediate the intellectual territory, beginning with the following:

Why focus on whiteness and dominant white identities within a social formation that privileges them on a daily basis and does so to the detriment of other social and political identities? Why threaten to reenact the colonial position of seeing yourself through a construction of the other when that other has multiplied itself to your detriment and to the detriment of your original nation-state and nationality? Why engage in such an inquiry when you have already developed a full-blown counterdiscourse that decenters whiteness? Doesn't this type of inquiry fall prey to a reinvention of Eurocentrism and U.S. chauvinism precisely at a time when they are being contested on the streets and in our scholarship, and fortified in public policy and the media?

Doesn't an inquiry into whiteness by Chicanas/os smack a little of assimilationist posturing or at least confirm a trace of the dominant culture's menacing grip *acá*/over here? Wouldn't the dominant culture benefit from this type of inquiry and thus release itself from the social obligation of diversifying representation? Aren't you on dangerous territory studying whiteness within Chicana/o discourse when the new conservative backlash in the humanities seems to be attaching a particular self-serving construction of a generic white male to you, without looking at how you have constructed yourself through multiple mediations and a new Chicana/o center that is transnational and socially nuanced? Whose interests are served by examining whiteness?

Isn't whiteness something that other people should "acknowledge" and scrutinize in order to convince themselves of the fact that they too have a race, and that this race offers certain privileges that "matter"? Isn't whiteness a terrain for examining how essentialism functions "over there," within a state-sanctioned discourse or within someone else's social body—a body that has been universally privileged as "the body" of Americans on a continent that is also and always will be Nuestra América? Is the study of whiteness just another untapped arena of investigation that we can now mine—without recrimination—successfully applying the body of our situated knowledges through a kind of naive and opportunistic theoretical travel? Is studying whiteness within Chicana/o discourse a dangerous waste of time?

Examining whiteness can also be seen as being intellectually regressive. Chicana/o critical practitioners have critiqued the tendencies of nationalists to subsume social processes into ideal forms of subjectivity/identity that hypostatize social relations in a reactive fashion. For this reason, many cultural practitioners have left behind brownness, the counterdiscourse to whiteness, because in and of itself, brownness clouds other social categories that construct our social identities and explain social inequalities and transformations.

So, the question becomes: Why regress to examining the social construction of whiteness when most of us agree that our social bodies are racialized in any number of ways and through any number of categories? Why go around the corner, so to speak? Why not articulate the multiple identities in their plurality, address the social inequalities, name the social formation, and, yes, avoid the risk of essentializing all over again—from someone else's towering backyard?

Why risk a mistaken impression that you are promoting whiteness? After all, notwithstanding current efforts to revise the field, whiteness is generally understood as the study of socially and ethnically dominant white identities. Dominant culture has assisted in this type of definition because it favors a construction of whiteness that is the exclusive territory not only of ethnically dominant white identities and subjectivities but of politically dominant ones too—the ones for whom and about whom a rendition of whiteness is selectively rendered.

Unfortunately, there is no avoiding this type of vulgar equation in a society as racialized as our own, where affirming/identifying whiteness is still linked with racism and social privilege (including the privilege to name others), where the historical memories of people of color are replete with associations that link whiteness with terror, pillage, conquest, exile, repatriation, and the loss of identity and national autonomy.

Dominant constructions of whiteness prevail, and this is true no matter how cognizant we are of the fact that Chicanas/os and other people of color have rendered a counterdiscourse that turns a dominant construction of whiteness on its head and is spoken with the end of renarrativizing hidden her/histories from another "standpoint."[2]

As a practitioner of Chicana/o studies, I must confess that I too question the validity of correcting the intellectual project surrounding whiteness, the validity of giving it what might be construed as a necessary face-lift: a class, race, and gender accent. That is to say, I question the validity of providing a Chicana/o variant/construction of whiteness that can then be ushered into a mainstream Euro-American or pluralistic construction and take the jagged edge off the kinds of social practices and material effects that have traditionally been associated with whiteness within the dominant social formation. There is always the danger that somewhere, somebody down the line will say, here we have it: a Chicana/o rendition of whiteness! See how important we are, we are everywhere! Even at the margins! The imperialist gaze of whiteness couldn't be more solidly anchored and my intent more seriously distorted.

Notwithstanding the dangers of navigating this admittedly slippery territory within an alternative discourse that is always subject to misappropriation and forced deterritorialization, dangers now compounded by the way whiteness is being newly interpellated by a conservative agenda that has targeted it as the invisible-but-yet-visible haven for American identities and nationalities seeking to escape a perceived influx of "illegal brown others" and "welfare mothers" and the unkind squeeze of a transnational global economy; and notwithstanding the fact that I continue to reject the idea that whiteness[3] is or should ever be a category of social analysis in the way that race, class, and gender or other social categories are, I was inspired to write this essay.[4]

I took the intellectual plunge into this territory with this highly "partial" representation of the subject matter because, like it or not, Chicanas/os have nourished their own counterdiscourse around whiteness as a way to navigate the social text; name social relations; negotiate a political identity—Chicana/o; think about racism, domination, colonization, heterosexism, gender oppression, and cultural imperialism; and imagine a different kind of social location for themselves as well as for others, including different types of "white identities and subjectivities."

I do not, of course, mean to suggest that this is the only way Chicanas/os have inscribed social relations and social processes. Such a proposal, aside from being reductive, conveniently fails to consider the variety of ways in which the social text has made its appearance within Chicana/o discourse through a different type of native vernacular. Nor do I suggest that Chicanas/os have recentered whiteness in the way dominant culture does. There are multiple constructions of whiteness that must be apprehended within Chicana/o discourse, some of them concern dominant identities and others marginalized social identities, and even the language with which to designate diverse forms of whiteness is radically different in its multiple, and oftentimes contradictory, significations.

Finally, the fact that the social construction of whiteness within Chicana/o discourse is generally rendered as a counterdiscourse, that it assumes particular forms that set it apart from dominant ones, does not mean that this native construction of whiteness shouldn't be scrutinized for inherent limitations—for the way that it is often wedded to the binaries of an internally generated nationalist discourse and the way it is often engendered in culturally specific ways.[5] On the contrary, this type of scrutiny furnishes a compelling reason to study the social construction of whiteness within Chicana/o cultural discourse.

Given this backdrop, this essay examines very "select" gendered representations of whiteness as a way of (1) further generating a critical dialogue around this thematic within Chicana/o discourse, (2) mapping a small segment of this highly complex terrain, (3) familiarizing the reader with descriptive snapshots of literary and cultural practices that incorporate native constructions of whiteness as a way to reconfigure social relations and identities, and (4) examining some of the limitations of these constructions in terms of the way they reference systems of differentiation (various forms of social privilege, difference) as a means to target and obliterate them.

Before I outline the conceptual framework for my discussion, it is necessary to highlight my particular "take" on whiteness in terms of some of the concerns I raise in the queries listed above. In this essay, whiteness does not stand alone—it is framed within Chicana/o discourse, and this framing matters.[6] Whiteness is approached as a social construction (not an affirmative reflection)—there is an acknowledged difference here between the social identity that is being interpellated and the speaking subject who enunciates it by way of an independent construction. This construction interprets dominant renditions of whiteness by "marking" formerly unmarked social identities within a Chicana/o discourse and by "naming" an alternative political identity that "interrupts" the kind of compulsory assimilation that is directed to those occupying the category of nonwhite other within racist and classist discourses featuring national identity.

Within the scope of this essay, I view the social construction of whiteness within Chicana/o discourse through Stuart Hall's notion of identity as "positionality." I am referring here to a social construction of whiteness that has emerged as a by-product of *one* of the ways we have positioned ourselves within one of the discourses of history, culture, and society in response to the manner in which we have been positioned therein.[7] But I extend this much quoted and still valuable notion of identity as a way of foregrounding an "interrupted" territorial movement that implicates different constructions of whiteness that are rendered within Chicana/o discourse and that are followed in this essay. I am referring to the movement from "whiteness on the outside" (a native rendition of whiteness that targets dominant social identities and ethnicities) to "whiteness on the inside" (a native rendition of whiteness that is internally directed).[8]

I hope to activate this notion of whiteness as an interrupted territorial movement through my presentation and criticism of selected literary and cultural practices that construct whiteness across different social registers, transnational contexts, social identities, literary genres, cultural rhetorics, and sociopolitical horizons. I have privileged the native constructions of "whiteness on the inside" because these renditions are prevalent and they implicate other social identities (dominant and marginalized) that are then taken up, modified, and addressed through various alternative self-representations.

I very intentionally "detain" my overview of these native constructions of whiteness within a section entitled "Engendering Whiteness on the Inside: Nationalism's Drama of Assimilation through the Brown Female Other." Here I offer a lengthy analysis of "Los Vendidos," because this cultural performance/political action was so influential in divulging "whiteness on the inside" that it furnished an archetypal representation and a nationalist blueprint for social change.

The section entitled "Mexico's Brown Other: Pocho," examines how a social construction of whiteness is activated as a way of defining "generic" in-group Chicano Mexicano relations within the border zone. This paves the way for an incipient Chicana feminist critique—"I Am Not a Pochita/Your/Their Brown Other"—that disrupts the kinds of paradigmatic representations widely circulated at the height of the Chicano movement because it contests internal constructions of whiteness on the in/other side and writes some of the necessary social categories into a narrative of Chicana/o liberation.

While this narrative is not without need for further scrutiny, I end by suggesting that this type of practice—rewriting the social categories—will help us work through many of the social mythologies promoted by nationalism, an ideological and political orientation that leads the way in reconstructing whiteness in an effort to ward off the effects of conquest and racial and ethnic domination.

In advance I caution my reader that these movements through the interrupted and disputed territories of whiteness within Chicana/o discourse incorporate many thematic ruptures that I have very deliberately not glossed over because, within the scope of this essay, whiteness is tantamount to particular types of discursive formations that are primarily rendered within a grouping of literary practices. These practices are not identical and do not form an insular artistic field, as is often proposed within traditional "literary" representations that project an overriding aesthetic mode and organization, thereby dulling the vibrant relationship between the literary and the cultural, the literary and the political, the literary and the experiential, the literary and the (extratextual) symbolic. By shifting my attention to literary *practices,* I highlight the type of productive social and artistic agency that is present in the disarticulation and rearticulation of heterogeneous social identities within Chicana/o discourse.

I also alert my reader to the fact that I do not hide the seams that mark the end of one set of practices (and the movements they generate) and the beginning of others. I interweave and transition

these practices and movements, which incorporate disparate constructions of whiteness that are not easily reconciled within social reality
or literary/cultural practices, and which present different types of aesthetic and ideological opportunities for further description and analysis. Because this collection of essays is fundamentally concerned with
"locating" whiteness, I begin by pinpointing one such location with a
discussion of works that situate whiteness on the other side.

It should be noted however, that this construction of whiteness
is spoken from "the inside"—it is internally generated, even though
it refers to "other" social identities and processes that are positioned
"outside." Historically, this type of construction is paradigmatic within
Chicana/o cultural productions, incorporating a wide range of critical discourses that aim to reconfigure social relations and identities—
to talk back—and that often seek to explain why, as José de Molina
suggests in the song "Chicano" and the album *Manifesto,* "Vivo en los
Estados Unidos, no me siento anglosajón" (I live in the United States,
but I do not feel like an Anglo-Saxon).

*Whiteness on the Other Side: From Domination
to Assimilation to Cultural Nationalism*

Within the context of this section, "whiteness on the other side" refers
to native constructions of various forms of structured domination that
adversely affect Chicanas/os within the social formation, or to earlier
social formations in which a colonial legacy is identified and contested. In this case whiteness is often an overarching sign for the culturally, politically, racially, and economically dominant; whiteness is
generally linked to specific agents of domination—imperialist masculinities, dominant masculinities—the capitalist boss who lives off the
labor of his workers, the *patrón* (boss) who exploits the poor in the
fields or on the job, the career politician who orchestrates tokenism to
avoid inclusion. The colonizer generally prevails as the quintessential
agent who is named and often vilified through a barrage of linguistic denominations: the Anglo, the Gringo,[9] the Patrón, the Gabacho,
the Anglo-Saxon, the White Man, the Bolillo, the Norteamericano, the
North American, the Americano, and so on.[10]

Within this construction of whiteness, social processes and racial
identities are often fused within archetypal representations. Whiteness
is partnered both with structures of domination and with the effects
of domination. Such effects include different types of loss: of one's

nation of origin, one's territory, one's barrio, one's social location, as well as a "perceived threat" to one's national ethnic or regional identity and economic well-being. In addition, whiteness is often a metaphor for assimilation—here, forced participation in the language, traditions, institutions, and beliefs of the economically, racially, and politically dominant group.

It can be said that the social construction of whiteness within these types of Chicana/o discourses is the result of a complex process of encoding and decoding of hegemonic definitions and practices. As part of the process of communication, these hegemonic definitions of whiteness render a classification of the sociopolitical order; they form part of what Stuart Hall has referred to as a "structure produced and sustained" through the articulation of linked but distinctive movements—production, circulation, distribution, consumption, reproduction. This process is described as a "complex structure in dominance." [11]

Viewed from this perspective, this native construction of whiteness involves a kind of "decoding" position that is at odds with the preferred meanings that are encoded in hegemonic renditions of whiteness, which make it coterminous with that which is legitimate and "natural" about the social order.[12] To follow Hall's logic, then, within this native discourse whiteness and its meanings are "detotalized" in order to "retotalize" the message within an alternative framework. It is in this sense that the social construction of whiteness within Chicana/o discourse often involves various interrupted movements that narrate whiteness in other discursive maps.

These maps interrogate the legitimacy of its official sociopolitical mapping in addition to rendering a series of contrary definitions of whiteness that foreground sociopolitical conflicts among different social actors. Aside from contesting the hegemonic definitions and practices surrounding whiteness, this kind of discursive repositioning of knowledge around whiteness has reproduced the limitations of critical paradigms that inherit a "totalizing" impulse (certainly not the same type of impulse as the dominant culture). Thus, even within the alternative sector, a great part of "the mental horizon," the "universe of possible meanings," a "whole sector of relations in a society or culture," are globally subsumed within these types of superarchetypal representations—the ones that are positioned on the other side of the social and ethnic divide. This makes it difficult to distinguish between different types of social processes that extend "over here" too and to envision how they intersect to structure dominance. This type of recoding of whiteness has also resulted in a superracialization of the social order—disparate social processes are decoded through a racial formation and/or identity that is privileged as *the* lens from which to view, interpret, and transform them.

However problematic these native constructions are, and however difficult they have made it to offer a more complex vision of social relations, it is important to remember that these constructions are socially marked by a context in which social phenomena and discursive knowledge are racialized at the level of theory and practice to the extent that when social problems are acknowledged, they are generally viewed as the singular product of racism. It is also important to note that although these counternarratives re-totalize the larger social formation in ways that are often limited by a particular construction of whiteness, in this construction whiteness itself does not appear in the same form;[13] on the contrary, it is intentionally deterritorialized from the center of Chicana/o identities, subjectivities, and political geographies.

In this sense, the hegemonic quality of whiteness is bracketed. But, most important, whiteness is subordinated to another political imaginary and historical narrative, one in which social phenomena are not fully contained by the overarching language of whiteness promoted by the dominant culture. The question is, how is its hegemonic quality bracketed from the cultural-ideological and linguistic spaces of authoritative discourses featuring Chicano?

El Plan Espiritual de Aztlán (The Spiritual Manifesto of Aztlán, 1969),[14] which articulates the case for Chicano self-determination and nationhood, furnishes a poignant example. This powerful manifesto is replete with references to whiteness that activate a memory of armed clashes, dispossession, conquest, and open hostility to Anglo-American elements (social processes and archetypal identities) in an effort to "reclaim" that which was lost through colonization and sustained occupation. El Plan is a call to arms—it aims to restore not only cultural and national sovereignty, but also land rights through an appeal to unity that stresses similarity.

It is *within* this discursive context (a public declaration of intentions, opinions, and motives) that a social construction of whiteness is activated through cryptic references to larger social processes that are strategically contained through the articulation of another set of national principles and a narrative of liberation that embraces an ascendant geopolitical community: Chicanos. Interestingly enough, el

Plan names the political identity to be reconciled with its historic community before raising the violent specter of whiteness. From the start, however, the social identities, which are depicted as subjects in armed and political combat, are polarized through contrasting *racial* formations in this manner: "In the spirit of a people/'race' that is conscious not only of its proud historical heritage, but also the brutal *"gringo"* invasion of our territories, we the Chicano inhabitants . . ." El Plan imagines a scenario that militates against all that this decoded rendition of whiteness (as a brutal conquest and colonization) implied during the period after the takeover, and attributes this political consciousness to a social identity, Chicano. However, within the confines of el Plan, the decoding of whiteness implies not only the articulation of another racial and political community but also the articulation of another form of national sovereignty which draws from *lo popular*. Thus, in a discursive sweep and without concern for what is officially legislated, el Plan declares: "We are free and sovereign to determine those tasks which are justly called for by our house, our land, the sweat of our brows and by our hearts."

If this were not enough, el Plan redefines the national community through a particular class identity (which is also racialized by way of context) that contrasts with official forms on suggesting that "Aztlán belongs to those that plant the seeds, water the fields, and gather the crops." Notwithstanding the fact that typical formulas that define the national community are abandoned with this emphasis on social location, nativity is factored into the equation because this national patrimony is flatly denied to the foreigner. In this context, the foreigner is the European(s) extranjero gabacho, the usurper and colonizer. It is understood that it is he who owns but does not work the land, and that it is he who does not stand with his heart in his hands and his hands in the soil. In the final segment, the foreigner gabacho is directly faulted with exploiting "our riches" and destroying "our culture."

Within el Plan there is nothing legitimate or natural about the hegemonic quality assigned to whiteness "outside." For this reason, its hegemonic quality is bracketed through discursive maps featuring an economy of language that is intended to minimize the importance of whiteness within the alternative political narrative, and through an ideological framework in which whiteness is foreign not only because it is aligned to competing political forces but because it is spiritually counterposed to all that is held to be Chicano. Ultimately whiteness is supplanted by another imaginary racial order with popular overtones that is symbolically wedded to Chicanismo and extends the national space into a continental one. Thus el Plan imagines an independent "mestizo" nation comprising a bronze people, a bronze culture, and a bronze continent. Finally, a symbolic linkage to pre-Conquest times is established at the discursive level.

El Plan invites a utopian vision—one of total separatism—that fails to factor in the competing realities and social identities that frame Chicanas/os within the transnational, multiethnic border region. El Plan appeals to racial binaries (raza Chicanos and gringos/europeos, gabachos) and formations. "El Plan" also fails to attend to those (of us/*nosotros*) who are not free to determine those tasks which are justly called for by "our" (read, "my/your") house or those (aztlánenses) who make it impossible to do so. Within el Plan, social processes appear as unidimensional racial formations interpellated through unflattering epithets and stock characters who are often "faceless and nameless," more an idea than someone in particular.[15] Thus it is the case that an Anglo-American presence may be implied even when an Anglo-American identity is not openly interpellated.

The problem with this vision of whiteness is that social identities are neither nameless nor faceless—and neither are the social processes to which this vision of whiteness is linked. The contemporary addressee of this manifesto who is not ignorant of the way social and historical events are racialized on this side of the ethnic border can certainly counter as follows after reading el Plan outside the nationalist purview: Just who is the gabacho? the gringo? What particular social identities, institutions, historical events, interests, material infrastructures, relations of production and domination, cultural logics, gender dynamics, public policies, representational powers lurk therein? lurk outside? Can disparate social identities and historical processes be contained within these unchanging semantic representations that invite easy identifications? Does a "brown" racial order and political formation (homeland) always denote reterritorialization and the articulation of collective liberation?

As Rafael Pérez-Torres suggests, "What this Nation consists of—beyond the essentializing and vague vision of a 'Bronze People' with a 'Bronze Culture' forming a 'Union of free pueblos'—remains unspoken."[16] Further, it is not enough to suggest, as these native constructions of whiteness do, that whiteness is partnered to conquest, domination, and racism, and that whiteness is scattered into multiple domains through the extensive power of what appear to be larger-than-life archetypal figures whose presence is seemingly everywhere.

Within a society in which whiteness is mystified and legitimated as the normative without mention of its competing social moorings or of other social identities, it is important to demystify whiteness by divesting it not only of its normative qualities but also of the singular racial dimensions attached to it. However, such an enterprise is made difficult from the purview of a political imaginary that proposes that the call—here, the *political* call: *grito*—of our blood is our power, our responsibility, and our inevitable destiny.

Following Pérez-Torres, I do not seek to diminish the historical significance of el Plan. I seek only to reevaluate its counterhegemonic value, especially insofar as this pertains to a particular decoding of whiteness and to the notably patriarchal and spiritual basis for this reclamation, not to mention its lack of attention to "the diverse indigenous past of actual Chicanos." [17] While Pérez-Torres has provided one of the best and most interesting discussions of el Plan, I do take issue with his assertion that el Plan serves to highlight the role of history—"the brutal 'Gringo' invasion of our territories"—for it is through this type of construction that histories are obfuscated and an essentialist view of identity is reinstated from the purview of another ideological standpoint.

This discussion of el Plan illuminates one of the major problems that is confronted when seemingly invisible social identities are marked with the intent of factoring race into the sociopolitical horizon. While an important step forward is registered when the myth of a free, colorless society is contested by the identification of a form of social inequality with racial overtones and social privileges, this progressive movement is compromised by a naming practice that is spoken from the "prison house" of nationalist discourses on whiteness. In what can only be seen as a supreme ironic twist, within these nationalist discourses whiteness is magnified to encompass an unwarranted social value and social function in terms of its ability to affect the destiny of the nation and its people.

Although many of the limitations associated with whiteness here can be found in other Chicano movement discourses that feature an identity formation, it is important to keep in mind that native constructions of whiteness "on the other side" offer different semantic and political horizons that cannot be reduced to what we see recovered in el Plan. It is also important to remember that the native construction of whiteness is affected by the particular cultural form which it assumes, the sociohistorical period which it frames, and the ideological orientation that it articulates.

For example, many early folk songs offer constructions of whiteness that nuance the above-noted significations within narratives featuring border conflicts in which there is a vivid memory of the Mexican nation. Here there is a polarization of Mexican and white identities that favors Mexicans and incorporates a negative definition of dominant white identities (here the usurpers and aggressors) as "Americans." Such is the case, for example, with "El Corrido de Joaquín Murrieta,"[18] which recounts in testimonial style a border hero's attempt to defend his rights amid the personal injustices that followed the takeover.

Unlike later Chicanos who often partnered the Mexican with the American through various means, the speaker in this folk song defines himself in marked opposition to "Americans" by beginning his identity narrative with a negation: "Yo no soy americano" (I am not an American). He couples this negation with another strategic one that appears later: "Yo no soy gringo" (I am not a white man). This contrast in national and racial identities is wedded to native constructions of whiteness that link the gringo to a colonial legacy of foreign domination, for the second negation is followed by the explicative phrase "ni extraño / en este suelo en que piso" (nor a foreigner / on this land on which I stand).

In addition to the fact that this representation of whiteness is greatly affected by its framing in relation to a particular national community and its utterance within an individual life history that does not intend to provide a collective platform for action, whiteness is interpellated in relation to a local transnational conflict and the reclaiming of a particular "Mexican" region. The poetic subject offers this interpretation by instructing his listeners that *California* belongs to *Mexico*. While it says little to suggest how California will become Mexican once again (other than through the power of scattered armed skirmishes like the one the hero wages), the poem does offer a counternarrative to whiteness and its preferred nationality. This occurs in an affirmative verse in which the hero identifies with the persecuted and subjugated nationality: "Yo soy aquel Mexicano" (I am that Mexican). And according to his particular differential logic, to be that Mexican (Joaquín Murrieta) is not to be a gringo or an americano or a foreigner who usurps. In this way, both the dominant racial identity and its preferred national affiliation are countered through poetic verses that remember the integrity of the Mexican nation even while drawing racial and political distances by the coupling of gringo/americano/extranjero.

If "El Corrido de Joaquín Murrieta" chronicles the conflicts that were synonymous with the invasion and deterritorialization of Mexicans, Gloria Anzaldúa's introductory chapter in *Borderlands, la Frontera* (1987) [19] offers an autobioethnographic reflection of life on the borderlands through an imaginary reconstruction of the conquest, viewed from the perspective of its aftermath. Within her narrative the national space, Mexico, is already divided by a steel curtain: a "1,950 mile-long open wound," which not only divides a "pueblo" and a "culture" but also "runs down the body" of its inhabitants, splitting Mexican subjects and nationalities, and creating an unnatural boundary that militates against all that is natural and human. [20]

As others have already suggested, Anzaldúa's introductory chapter, "The Homeland," is an unconventional blend of poetry, ethnography, personal testimony, memories, and social history that is voiced within an admittedly untamed bilingual tongue. However, this highly unconventional narrative also draws from native constructions of whiteness that link whiteness to a history of conquest and colonization. In fact, it could be said that here Anzaldúa offers one of the most dramatic articulations of whiteness as *destierro* (loss of land, separation from the place of one's origin), *exilio* (exile, banishment), and terror ever published. *Borderlands* also intersects with earlier movimiento constructions of whiteness on other counts, for Anzaldúa narrates a counterhistory that strategically names the unofficial Mexican nation on this side (Aztlán), that targets a political and racial formation that is indisputably white/gringo for its loss, and that later imagines a time in which Aztlán will be Mexican and Indian once again. [21]

To be sure, whiteness itself appears in many forms in *Borderlands*. In the introductory poem it is the *white* man's arrogance that comes between Mexicans and their historic community and national destiny; in the essayistic narrative, it is the *gringos* in the U.S. Southwest who reproduce a social logic that partners "normal" with "white," and casts others (Chicanos, Indians, and blacks) into the category of illegal nonwhite. Whiteness also incorporates socially relevant power relations, for as Anzaldúa explains, "the only legitimate inhabitants are those in power, the whites and those who align themselves with the whites." Whiteness is not only linked to hierarchical power relations, it is also associated with a particular type of racial positioning—white supremacy—that is enacted by the white man/gringo: "The Gringo, locked into the fiction of white superiority, seized complete political power, stripping Indians and Mexicans of their land while their feet were still rooted in it."

In this sentence, Anzaldúa consciously doubles up a bilingual discourse of whiteness and disrupts dominant constructions that "naturalize" and sanction it. She scripts the linguistic partnership between gringo and white superiority that accompanies one particular manifestation of this native construction of whiteness "on the other side." Anzaldúa substitutes the familiar term, Anglo-American (white), with the harsh-sounding Spanish variant, Gringo, which is capitalized. With this she draws an unequivocal semantic and ideological difference between "him (the Gringo) and us" (the Mexicans and Indians) that identifies the Gringo with the foreigner, the invader, and the enemy— the indisputable Colonizer, the Man. This masculine characterization is enhanced by the following description, which expands the meanings of destierro and exilio to incorporate various types of loss: "Con el destierro y el exilio fuimos desuñados, destroncados, destripados—we were jerked out by the roots, truncated, disemboweled, dispossessed, and separated from our identity and our history." [22]

Within Anzaldúa's text, whiteness is interpellated as a way of foregrounding a vivid memory of the unmistakably racial tensions in the Southwest and the racial overtones of social domination during the conquest and after. Without a doubt Anzaldúa draws from native archetypal representations that script dominance in her autobiographical narrative and incorporates some of their attendant limitations. However, it is important to note that in her narrative, whiteness does not always have the same type of archetypal value—it can also be a marker that racializes socially dominant ethnic identities or formations. Insofar as the archetypal value of whiteness is concerned, this value is tempered in Anzaldúa's first chapter by the presence of a competing social and ethnographic history. In this multilayered history whiteness is partnered with a variety of historical and personal events that are individual, local, familial, national, and continental, and it is contested. Whiteness is linked to such concrete manifestations as conquest, dispossession, immigration, repatriation, employment, and specific corporate enterprises, attaching an abstract value to these social elements that threatens to reinstate the kinds of problematic dimensions viewed before.

Notwithstanding this fact, Anzaldúa disrupts the kind of binary (Mexican white) that is evident in the gringo/Mexican Indian split by peopling the borderlands with other social identities (sexual, ethnic, gender), by contemplating the complicity of the natives in their oppression, and by suggesting a third space of ethnic identification that overwrites whiteness.[23] In later chapters Anzaldúa offers another dramatic break with identity narratives that develop an identity formation in strict opposition to all that is white by acknowledging that she has to reckon with this dimension of herself by way of her own mestizaje, which incorporates a form of whiteness. In addition, she openly contrasts her perspective with that of those "who do not want to have any dealings with white people."

Anzaldúa raises the possibility of a coalition with whites, something unheard of in nationalist discourses that cast the white as the quintessential and immortal political and racial other. However, this desired relationship is a conditional one—Anzaldúa proposes that we (Chicanos) should voice our needs to *white* society, and that we do this both as individuals and as "*racial* entities," that as a collective "we need to say to white society":

> We need you to accept the fact that Chicanos are different, to acknowledge your rejection and negation of us. We need you to own the fact that you looked upon us as less than human, that you stole our lands, our personhood, our self-respect. We need you to make public restitution: to say that, to compensate for your own sense of defectiveness, you strive for power over us, you erase our history and our experience. . . . To say that you've split yourself from minority groups, that you disown us, that your dual consciousness splits off parts of yourself, transferring the "negative" parts onto us. . . . To say that you are afraid of us, that to put distance between us, you wear the mask of contempt. Admit that Mexico is your double, that she exists in the shadow of this country, that we are irrevocably tied to her. Gringo, accept the doppel-ganger in your psyche. By taking back your collective shadow the intercultural split will heal.[24]

Interestingly enough, this is among the *least*-quoted sections of *Borderlands, la Frontera,* even though it clearly dictates that the movements of *traversía y rebeldía* (Anzaldúa's construction of the undocumented border crossings of officially legislated racial, cultural, political, sexual, and gender identities) require specific types of *political* commitments and restitutions. This involves reckoning with unpleasant territorial racial and geopolitical legacies. Significantly, Anzaldúa reminds "white people" that "race matters," providing an exemplary lesson in strategic essentialism of the old style, uncut but filled with a political conviction that is no less powerful than that seen in el Plan.

Anzaldúa's particular recasting of social relations between Chica-

nas/os and whites is the product of a conscious desire to go beyond
blocking with a counterstance. When evaluating her seemingly contradictory decoding of whiteness (she revisits earlier representations of
whiteness, reframes them, repositions them, destabilizes some of their
discursive positions, and at times abandons them), it is important to
remember that within its particular historical context, *Borderlands* is a
highly innovative and transitional work in which the tensions between
earlier forms of scripting Chicano liberation and oppression and the
new ones (Chicana/o) are evident.

She admits that she is participating in the creation of yet another
culture, "a new story to explain the world and our participation in
it, a new value system with images and symbols." She does this in
many ways, taking us light years ahead of the patriarchal nationalist
narratives that plot Chicano histories of expropriation along a unidimensional racial line and a collective epic legacy full of traditional
cultural bliss, compulsory heterosexuality, and singularly racial trau-
mas. In what can only be evaluated as a dramatic gesture away from
paradigmatic representations of conquest, the speaking subject not
only imagines the nation from the fractured margins but strategically
moves across the racial and national borders, "across the hole" under
the fence, into the undocumented gender and sexual territory.

If it is true that within authoritative discourses the hegemonic
value of whiteness is contested by a political imaginary featuring
brownness, here it is contested by a feminist political imaginary with
disparate social interests and largely novel native antecedents.[25] It begins with a political imaginary that aims to dislocate whiteness (here
not only racism but also sexism and homophobia), and in so doing,
also destabilizes the authoritative discourse featuring Chicano and its
investments in a nationalist project that steers clear of multiple internal contradictions.

In order to see how in *Borderlands* the authoritative discourses are
not only transformed but often destabilized, it is necessary to briefly
re-review its point of entry. For instance, Anzaldúa's opening chapter
begins with a brief musical and essayistic reconstruction of Aztlán in
a verse from Los Tigres de Norte that redefines the Mexican nation as
the product of a particular construction — the effort of those who have
known how to progress. Then the native dimensions of Aztlán, here
the other Mexico, are reaffirmed by the assignment of a particular indigenous legacy, that of the "Aztecas del Norte." This provides *the* geopolitical link to the contemporary inhabitants of Aztlán and their spe-

cific naming practices. She declares: "Some call themselves Chicanos and see themselves as a people whose true homeland is in Aztlán."[26]

These narrative markers (what I see as traces of the authoritative discourse) could be extracted from any conventional Chicano history book. However, Anzaldúa's poetic reflection destabilizes them with a mestiza speaking subject who is cast as the subject of the borderlands and also stands at the edge, looking across the border to Mexico. She thematizes the movements of resistance and rebeldía by walking through the hole on the other side of the fence (the symbolic articulation of whiteness); by decoupling nationhood from home with the violent suggestion of home as a barbed wire; and by imagining *herself* as the one who embodies the bridge to the undocumented world. Finally, she assumes the identity formation of a Mexicana—but not just any Mexicana—she is an embodied and contested Mestiza-Chicana. Within this identity formation the plight of other women of color, other Mexicanas, and other exiles is factored into a common position through a broadening of the undocumented category that has raised some eyebrows.

Anzaldúa's entry into "the other Mexico" doesn't just open with a mujer's poetic narrative and essayistic chronicle and testimony of conquest and dispossession; it also closes with an allusion to *la mujer indocumentada*—a Mexican woman immigrant undocumented in the literal sense. While the Mexicanas who cross the frontera from different sides do not occupy the same discursive or social position, their destinies are linked in this chapter because they provide the symbolic passageway to the other side of the other nation. Finally, they both enact the textual passage from *país* (country) to *cultura* (culture), from one type of oppression to another, after the broad, sweeping social history where national and territorial spaces are redefined through the kinds of innovations seen here. This is the other narrative; it features another kind of wounding and exile, exposes and contests gender relations and the patriarchal traditions of Mexican culture, and imagines a socially nuanced lesbian identity.

The strategic movements away from the authoritative discourse do not occur without contradictions or lapses, and for this reason it is necessary to view *Borderlands* as part "of a collective Chican[a]/o negotiation around the meanings of historical and cultural hybridity."[27] There are traces of this negotiation throughout the text, and the influence of the past (authoritative nationalist discourses) is not limited to the paradigmatic representations of race or social relations. Many collective characterizations and claims about our "people" (Chicanos) are spoken within a movimiento language that is viewed with great suspicion by contemporary cultural and feminist critics seeking to re-fashion a native feminist architecture and another type of critical discourse around race, and who are cognizant of the fact that they can be assisted by the critical insights of *Borderlands* on other counts.[28] While narrative traces of earlier Chicano movement discourses make themselves felt throughout *Borderlands,* there are other places in this book where another voice prevails that does not interconnect with the authoritative movimiento legacy but does connect with other marginalized communal legacies. This is not surprising; Anzaldúa admits to being guided by "a creative motion that keeps breaking down the unitary aspects of each paradigm."[29] Suffice it to say that this movement needs to be further explored in ways that do not deracinate the text.[30] Beyond this, *Borderlands* provides a marked contrast to other native representations of whiteness that link colonialism to imperialist "white" masculinities and a critique of racism without critiquing the patriarchal dimensions of conquest or incorporating the social histories of Mexicanas/Chicanas.

This type of nuancing of social relations and identities is not unique to *Borderlands, la Frontera;* in other creative works Anzaldúa also breaks with narratives of the deterritorialized Mexican that offer paradigmatic constructions of whiteness along a unidimensional racial axis. In "We Called Them Greasers" (1987),[31] for example, she describes through poetic verse how white imperialist masculinities dominated Mexicans through a "drama" of racial, gender, and sexual conquest in which Mexicanas were the targets and the vehicles of political contest. Interestingly enough, in the poem whiteness is interpellated not through the naming of the archetypal gringo but through the behavior and attitudes that have been associated with the gringo/rinche as he has been characterized within the native vernacular. While this literary rendition of whiteness "over there" is not marked in the way we have seen in other examples, the power relations that are often attributed to the gringo are supplied through this narrative in which the usurper is the speaking subject. For it is he who directs discourse as he imagines dispossessing Mexicans, and it is he who speaks directly to the reader without mediation, reinforcing all that has been associated with the gringo identity within paradigmatic representations through a horrific account of his contempt for Mexicans, his systematic expropriation of Mexican lands, and his intimidation of Mexican subjects.

The poem is effective because Anzaldúa gets inside the psychology of the oppressor and chronicles how his perceived victory is realized through the way he imagines the "ethnographic gaze" of the other (the subjugated and enslaved male of color) and through his repetition of racist stereotypes of women, which he activates even as he rapes and murders one of them as a prelude to lynching her partner. This segment of the poem, which records the patriarchal imperialist's voice, confirms how his guilt is staged through a conscious repetition of the conqueror's "I" and a voyeuristic impulse, directed toward the imprisoned male:

> .   .   .   .
>
> I plowed into her hard
> kept thrusting and thrusting
> felt him watching me from the mesquite tree
> heard him keening like a wild animal
> in that instant I felt such contempt for her
> round face and beady black eyes like an Indian's.[32]

This narrative of conquest forecasts the subordinate position of Mexican women in U.S. society, for as the colonizer explains in a crude and vivid passage: "I sat on her face until her arms stopped flailing, / didn't want to waste a bullet on her." Perhaps it is because Anzaldúa sidesteps the all too common paradigmatic representations of the gringo here—giving him a specific body, identity (that of the "I"), and voiced agency—that the poem succeeds in concretizing social domination.

In "We Called Them Greasers" Anzaldúa also demonstrates how the terror that accompanied "Anglo-American proprietorship of the land" is linked to a notion of white supremacy that casts the Mexican as inferior and incorporates gender and sexuality as a way of dividing and subordinating. In addition, the poem affirms that Texas wasn't secured by enterprise, redemption, feats of heroism, or superior attributes of Anglo-American blood, as a poem by William H. Wharton that Anzaldúa quotes in her opening chapter of *Borderlands* suggests,[33] but by brute force, violence, and intimidation of Mexican women and Mexican men.

White supremacy is also revisited in "To Live in the Borderlands Means You" (1987) within the context of the border conflicts that involve the border subject "who carries five races on her back."[34] In this case the mestiza is subjected to a racial logic that seeks to dismember

social elements and artificially reconfigure them according to its hegemonic mold, producing drastic results:

> To live in the Borderlands means
>   the mill with the razor white teeth wants to shred off
> your olive-red skin
> crush out the kernel, your heart
> pound you, pinch you roll you out
> smelling like white bread but dead;

In the poem "Immigrants" (1986), Pat Mora reveals how whiteness is forcibly directed toward Mexican nationals as a group through
the melting pot — a notion of American identity that privileges socially
dominant white identities to the exclusion of others and requires those
who have been assigned to the position of "nonwhite other" to submit to this type of positionality. "Immigrants" demonstrates how this
mode of legislating national identity operates through fear. We see this
through the practices of recently arrived parents who are instructed in
this ideology, and who acquiesce. Thus they sadly "wrap their babies
in the American flag / feed them mashed hot dogs and apple pie, . . .
buy them blonde dolls that blink blue . . . speak to them in thick English," all because of "that dark parent fear" that they like "our fine
American boy, our fine American girl." [35]

In contrast, "A Middle-Class Mexican American" articulates this
notion of American identity with respect to the ethnic identities of
those who are expected to assimilate in order to succeed. Whereas in
"Immigrants" we do not see the price of succumbing to this mode of
forced entry into America and its dominant nationality, in "A Middle
Class Mexican American" we do — the speaker literally fades into the
background as all traces of a native culture are systematically erased
through a particular construction of whiteness that bespeaks an American identity. In this case, culture loss is the expression of a particular
class and economic advancement. Ironically, middle-class status signals a spiral movement downward, a fading into "nothingness" that is
graphically described in this autobiographical narrative:

> My education coats my
> tongue with
> clichés,
> my reasoning is rational,
> my Latin temperament

has been
controlled . . .

. . . I have a vision:
Las Conchas y
Los Panchos
have disintegrated
barrios have vanished,
The world is blending into
a pale color.[36]

These two poems highlight the compulsory nature of whiteness by staging its effects through a symbolic reconstruction of loss of self, life, and culture, thereby magnifying how whiteness on the "outside" affects and permeates the "inside" through a movement that is always officially legislated and implies a kind of violent end. These constructions of whiteness are often generic—the naming of whiteness (its effects and agents) often precludes the naming of the varied social interests, agents, processes, and structures that propagate it.

In contrast to what we see in these verses, which record a social dynamic that was strategically linked to "Anglification," other poems symbolically halt this movement by enacting a nationalist counterstance that turns whiteness on its head with poetic expressions featuring brownness. Among them is "Poesía Aztlán," a poem attributed to Ruth Nuñez that cries: "Viva la raza. . . . Be proud of your color / Brown, Brown, Brown."[37] At the same time, Chicano essays attached a negative connotation to assimilation and white culture, as can be seen in Armando Rendón's, *Chicano Manifesto* (1971), in which he admits:

Consistently I place quotation marks around the word culture when it is preceded by the word Anglo because America has yet to develop a culture worth emulating and passing on to posterity. . . . The North American culture is not worth copying; it is destructive of personal dignity; is callous, vindictive, arrogant, militaristic, self-deceiving, and greedy; it is a gold-plated ball-point pen; it is James Eastland and Richard Nixon; it is Strom Thurmond and Lyndon Johnson; it is a Mustang and old folk's homes; it is Medicare and OEO; it is an 80 billion defense budget and $75 a month welfare; it is a cultural cesspool and a social and spiritual vacuum for the Chicano.[38]

In response to the commonly circulated notions that to "be non-Anglo is to be inferior; to speak other than English is to be inferior; to be brown or black or yellow is to be inferior,"[39] Chicano essays frequently argued that Chicanos were naturally superior, and that this superiority was based on racial, linguistic, national, and indigenous differences. But contesting whiteness within the political imaginary of nationalism also meant renegotiating a common stock of racial and national symbols, interrupting the black/white binary with a border race: "brown," and celebrating primarily masculine Mexican cultural symbols and national identities. Most important, it meant rejecting externally generated definitions of Chicano identity—terms such as Hispanic, Spanish, and Spanish American—and European identities that recentered whiteness through a colonial narrative that was reissued through a U.S. affiliation.[40] Finally, this meant targeting a widely divulged Mexican American identity that saw Mexican culture as an unproblematic extension of U.S. culture, an extension that privileged the ethnically dominant U.S. American through an appeal to melting-potism. This Mexican American identity was also to be rejected because it favored the political ideology of assimilation instead of separatism and because it failed to mark the racial differences between Mexicans and Americans (read "dominant white identities") and to promote a coalition of la raza (the race) based on race and nationality.

A Brief Interlude. Whiteness on the Inside: Profile of the Brown Anglo

Key to such coalition building was the development of an internal system of differentiation that could separate la raza from those Mexicans who did buy into the U.S. government's mode of hyphenating identities and legislating whiteness, and who did accept assimilation. This system of differentiation was generated through the appearance of a new raced identity: the "brown Anglos," who were described as being traitors to their race.[41] Unfortunately, by way of symbolic association, Chicanas were frequently cast into the role of the Mexican American other,[42] the one who has become "agringado (Anglicized—assimilated, in sociologists' jargon), like the Anglo in almost every respect."[43]

According to Rendón, agringado Mexican Americans comply with "el plan" of the gringo (the white man); they would "have us remade in his image and likeness: materialistic, cultureless, colorless, monolingual and racist." These Mexican Americans are also portrayed as *vendidos,* sellouts, because they have assimilated and "they accept the educational, economic and prestige opportunities that activists have opened up, and turn their backs on la raza."

Chicanas are symbolically affiliated with this group because this type of Mexican American was feminized by way of a symbolic association with la Malinche, the embodiment of race betrayal, as Rendón's description confirms: "We Chicanos have our own share of Malinches, which is what we call traitors to la raza who are of la raza, after the example of an Aztec woman of that name who became Cortez' concubine under the name of Doña Marina."[44]

Here the feminine rendition of race betrayal is viewed as being worse than other gendered forms because it attacks Chicano manhood, whose essence is associated with machismo—for Rendón, machismo is the symbolic principle of the Chicano revolt, the guideline for the conduct of family life, and the manifestation of nationhood. He elaborates on this vision of betrayal: "The Malinches are worse characters and more dangerous than the Tío Tacos, the Chicano euphemism for an Uncle Tom. The Tío Taco may stand in the way of progress only out of fear or misplaced self-importance. In the service of the gringo, Malinches attack their own brothers, betray our dignity and manhood . . . and actually seek to retard the advance of the Chicanos, it benefits themselves—while the gringo watches."[45]

Already in *The Chicano Manifesto* there is an inversion of power (race) relations (a suggestion of an "internal form of racial domination")[46] linked to women and strategically embodied by them that argues against Rendón's later point that the revolt is not a mortal struggle (between women and men) or a divisive one. Aside from coating gender conflicts with racial conflicts and failing to apprehend how the advance of Chicanos is retarded from the outside, this framing of domination does target Chicanas through the figure of la Malinche and a ranking of betrayal that favors the male gender.

It would be wrong to single out Rendón for representing "whiteness on the inside" in a way that symbolically affiliates Chicana women with a brown Anglo: a Mexican American female. Other representations also promoted this figure during the same period and further nuanced his vision with their own aesthetic and ideological dimensions. Perhaps one of the most popular representations can be found in Luis Valdez's play *Los Vendidos* (1967),[47] which stages nationalism's drama of assimilation through a female embodiment of whiteness and race betrayal.

Engendering Whiteness on the Inside:
Staging Nationalism's Drama of Assimilation
through the Brown Female Other

It is significant that even before the film rendition of *Los Vendidos* (The sellouts) actually begins, Miss JIM-enez is identified with the much vilified Mexican American, the brown female other (Anglo). This occurs in the brief introduction, in which the social philosophy, function, and dramatic principles of the Teatro Campesino (Farmworker Theater)[48] are described and the narrator explains that the members of the troop are Chicanos who attack "racist schools," white-washed Mexican Americans," "police brutality," and the "war in Viet Nam." When the narrator mentions "Mexican Americans" in the plural, the camera zooms in on Miss JIM-enez, who will protagonize "nationalism's drama of assimilation." She is dressed in professional clothes and a blonde wig, and is striking the contemplative, elitist pose that she will strike in the play every time she confronts Mexican types in Honest Sancho's Used Mexican Shop.

As the play unfolds, this characterization of Miss JIM-enez as the brown female Mexican American other becomes complete. She is so invested in the way dominant culture translates Chicana/o identities that she "insists" that Honest Sancho speak English because she is from the governor's office. Her distance from the rest of the Mexican prototypes is evident at other levels as well. She appears at the door as a visitor, a potential client at Honest Sancho's Shop, where Mexican identities are "sold" to government officials needing tokens for their race politics (tokenism). Unlike the Chicana/o Mexicana identities (the farmworker family, the pachuco, the low rider, the revolucionario, the campus militant, the boxer, the india/o) who share the stage and "represent" a community of social actors, Miss JIM-enez is an outsider, even a foreigner. She is unfamiliar with the language spoken in the shop—variants of Spanish—and is ignorant of the social types who form part of her racial and ethnic community, ones she has obviously left behind and which have been targeted by the governor, who has assigned her the job of securing a respectable "Mexican type" ("brown face") for his luncheon. Her social status (she is middle class) and close links with the upper echelons of the state's government, in addition to her elitist attitude (she continuously turns up her nose at all the Mexican types) and discursive connection to their political project (she continuously reiterates that we need a Mexican that . . .), set her apart from the other

Mexican types, who are either alienated from official representatives of social institutions, consumed with making a living in labor-intensive industries, or operating outside the law.

By contrast, Miss JIM-enez is privileged. Not only is she a professional, her labor is primarily "intellectual": she takes copious notes throughout the play and sports dark-rimmed preppy glasses. Unlike the other Mexican types in Honest Sancho's Used Mexican Shop, who must respond immediately to Honest Sancho's request for an assembly-line type of labor (a performance), Miss JIM-enez is relatively independent. That is to say, while she translates the governor's vision of an ideal White Mexican type, she also interjects her own set of biases, thus crucially affecting the outcome. Without a doubt she is assigned the role of the native bourgeoisie that upholds colonial relations by translating a politically dominant vision of marginalized social identities. It is clear that she has been selected for the role because she is somewhat an insider—her skin is brown and her name carries traces of Spanish when it is pronounced correctly.

The only other Mexican whose labor involves this type of cultural and ethnic translation is Honest Sancho, the former contractor and dealer of the Mexican lot who receives monetary compensation for his "sales pitch" on the marketability of certain Mexican types. Ideologically speaking, both he and Miss JIM-enez are the sellouts featured in the title, *Los Vendidos*—he sells Mexican types to the governor's office for a price, living off the transactions, and she sells out her people by actively contributing to a form of token representation that places the government's interests above theirs. Notwithstanding this fact, Miss JIM-enez occupies a position superior to Honest Sancho's. While he is a former contractor and the one in charge at the lot, it is he who must "sell" his product to Miss JIM-enez, who functions as the government's quintessential consumer.

By staging racial and political identities through an exchange of commodities (Mexican types who are analogous to cars), Luis Valdez underscores how the production of whiteness is realized through a complex web of social relations within a capitalist framework. Within this framework the Mexican types who occupy Honest Sancho's Shop as if they were cars or museum displays are objects for consumption; they have no control over how their labor will be expended (in the governor's office), and they are subject to the whims of Honest Sancho, who arbitrarily brings them to life by shaping his fingers—a gesture that inaugurates an en-vivo display of Mexican types. From the very beginning it is clear that their economic value is low—in fact, much of Honest Sancho's sales pitch is directed at underscoring this point and the idea that they require little maintenance and housing. This economic value is underscored by Miss JIM-enez, who is miffed at having to pay "15,000" for a "Mexican."

In contrast to the Mexican prototypes, who alternate between being puppets, machines, and lifeless dummies, and who are the objects of consumption in the political marketplace, Miss JIM-enez freely wanders around the room, examining and sampling the merchandise, and delivering her own opinions on the Mexican types presented to her. Finally, it is Miss JIM-enez who negotiates the preferred Mexican identity—rendition of whiteness, after she meets and rejects the pachuco, the vato loco, the zoot-suiter, and the revolutionary. Her choice is Eric, the "1970 Mexican-American" model.

In the published version of the play Eric is described as a clean-shaven middle-class type wearing a business suit and glasses. Without a doubt Eric is the perfect assimilationist. Honest Sancho even brags to Miss JIM-enez that Eric is "built exactly like our Anglo models, except that he comes in a variety of darker shades: naugahide, leather or leatherette"; that Eric "accelerates when he hears the word 'acculturate'"; that he represents "the apex of American engineering"; that he is "bilingual, college educated, and ambitious"; that he is "intelligent, well-mannered, and clean"; that he functions on "parole boards, draft boards, school boards"; that he is kept running on "dry Martinis" and "Langendorf bread"; and that "he is also programmed to eat Mexican food at ceremonial functions."[49]

Unlike the witless Miss JIM-enez, whose verbal abilities are seriously lacking, Eric is a sophisticated type and a "political machine" who can deliver political speeches filled with patriotism, and in addition complies with the requirement of speaking English without an accent and being "native"-born in the USA. (American) Eric is programmed to enter into the inner circle of the governor's political sanctum because of his questionable racial authority and his contempt for Mexicans, as his address confirms: "Mr. Congressman, Mr. Chairman, members of the board, honored guests, ladies and gentlemen. . . . I come before you as a Mexican-American to tell you about the problems of the Mexican. The problems of the Mexican stem from one thing and one thing only: he's stupid. He's uneducated. He needs to stay in school. He needs to be ambitious, forward-looking, harder working.

He needs to think American, American, American, American, American! God bless America! God Bless America! God Bless America!"[50]

While Eric "supersedes" Miss JIM-enez as the ideal assimilationist because he offers a political articulation of whiteness for the administration, both characters construct a dominant rendition of whiteness by attaching a negative value to the Mexican, a value that nourishes disinformation and racial prejudice. In the case of Eric, the disinformation involves faulting the victim for her/his condition and circulating pejorative stereotypes about Mexicans as well as the flawed notion (much in vogue today) that patriotism alone can cure all social ills. Eric's speech reproduces the biases of those social science theories that attempted to explain the inequality of Mexicans through a supposed culture of poverty, exaggerated family ties, or lack of contact with Western value systems.

Miss JIM-enez complements Eric's political speech with a variety of stereotypes which she activates in the movie while selecting the premier Mexican American. Concretely, she refuses the Mexican peon because she thinks he looks lazy, the farmworker family because she thinks they are always so defeated, the Mexican revolutionary because he's foreign born and she thinks he's too savage (he eats raw horsemeat and drinks tequila), the urban models (the pachuco, the vato loco, and the zoot-suiter) for not upholding the law.

Miss JIM-enez applies a double standard when she says that the urban types won't do because we "cannot have any more thieves in the State Capitol" (unwittingly airing the government's dirty laundry) and then insists that the ideal Mexican American must uphold the judicial and economic systems. It is for this reason that she rejects the farmworkers when she finds out that they are programmed to strike. She angrily retorts: "We can't strike in the State Capitol." Thus, at every level, the preferred Mexican "American" identity is the identity that is legislated and mandated and ultimately indebted to the state. The function of this identity is clearly a political one—to assist upper-level governmental officials in their quest to block the political representation of Mexicans and maintain the status quo.

On the surface Eric seems an excellent candidate for the position, not only because of his ideology but also because he lives up to the compulsory heterosexual orientation that is required for the job—he's the perfect Latin lover, according to Honest Sancho. However, in the film *Los Vendidos* things are not what they appear to be. After Miss

JIM-enez leaves with Eric on her arm, the camera focuses on the other characters in the room, and Honest Sancho's hand freezes. The Spanish conquistador reaches over and picks up the money, and an actor tells all the raza to relax. Then the actors celebrate tricking Miss JIM-enez by selling her Eric, a Chicano who only masqueraded as a Mexican American. Next, Luis Valdez, author, character, and director, emerges to center stage and reveals to the public that the performance (in this context, a production that makes whiteness into a spectacle) was intended to allow la raza to infiltrate urban centers all over the world.

Thus the performance of this Mexican drama of assimilation is a strategy, a mode of entry into positions that will enable Mexicans to actively contest the government's identity politics and mode of regulating social identities in political representations. The real social drama here is the one that isn't performed in the presence of Miss JIM-enez, Honest Sancho, or the governmental agency—it is the drama that represents whiteness as a means of contesting it, that relies on sarcasm and humor, disguise, and guerrilla tactics as a means of teaching its public not to imitate the behavior of the sellouts, both of whom are ridiculed and outsmarted in the end by the actors who demonstrate their one-upmanship and use the money from Eric's sale to launch another alternative production.

In stepping outside their preordained slots, the characters invite the spectators to reflect on their agency. As they tell us, they are not the objects—robots, puppets, machines—others think they are. They are motivated by the mission described by the actor-director, who states: "God help us to be human beings."

Within the play the contestation of whiteness/whitening is artistically rendered through an appeal to the principle of self-determination, a value that was divulged through the Chicana/o movement and is enlisted in the production of an alternative identity produced by, for, and about Chicanas/os. As the ending of the film version demonstrates, this type of production is not a public spectacle in the way that the production of whiteness is. This point is made when one of the characters notices the camera zeroing in on the group and alerts the actors, "Nos están güachando" (They are looking at us). The actor-director steps up to the camera and is followed by the others, who join him in defiantly gazing out the window of Honest Sancho's Shop, meeting the eyes of the spectator-public one on one. Then the director yells, "Honest Sancho's is closed," thus officially ending the spectacle, and pulls down a screen. The group then begins its victory celebration "behind closed doors."

By engaging the camera and public in this way, the actors promote an aesthetic vision of the principle of self-determination—they can decide how and when they'll be seen; they can refuse to circulate alternative identities; and they can look directly into the camera without their mediating social prototypes or an externally generated facade of whiteness. It would appear that they have the ability to affect the play's content and the relations of representation that were laid out in the preface through their dramatic gestures and political insights and activism. However, there are serious problems with the way representation is staged in the play at the political level and within the group. These stem from the way gender relations are inverted and distorted within nationalism's drama of assimilation. Here the Chicana female character (who is admittedly a middle-class Mexican American) is symbolically associated not only with the race but also with the gender privilege of politically dominant masculinities.[51]

It is not an accident that at the beginning of the play she corrects Honest Sancho and asks him to call her Miss JIM-enez, a name that suggests her identification with this group and its identity politics that recenters whiteness. As the play ends, she completes this identification as she tells the Mexican American to "just call me Jimmy," dropping the "Miss" altogether. In the complete absence of the real symbol of authority and power, the governor, Miss JIM-enez becomes his symbolic replacement. Through her translation of his preferred Mexican American identity, she is not only the governor's voice, she is also the embodiment of the dominant rendition of whiteness that he aims to circulate at the political level. She activates dominant notions of Mexican whiteness through her speech, appearance (blonde wig), allegiance to the governor's office, stereotypical views of Mexican national identity, and apparent ignorance about Chicana/o culture.

While Honest Sancho also sells his people for profit, at least he possesses the linguistic and cultural capital that qualifies him as a Mexican, notwithstanding his parasitical behavior. In the end, he is disassociated from the assimilationist designs of the governor's office because he is not an authentic social identity—he is just a computerized puppet being directed by a theater troupe as a way of exposing how Mexican identities are manipulated to ensure a political outcome that maintains the status quo. The same type of ethnic and political disidentification takes place with respect to Eric, the prized Mexican American model. His connection to whiteness is solely at the performance level. He is masquerading whiteness for a larger political goal: organizing and representing Chicanos. His character is thus not wedded to a particular notion of whiteness, as is evident at the end of the play when the characters argue over which of them will get to play the part of the Mexican American and trade their prototypes for the premium role solicited by the government.

The only character fully wedded to whiteness is Miss JIM-enez,[52] who does not appear in the alternative drama that takes place at the end of the performance. At the ideological level, there appears to be no difference between who she performs and who she is. Because she is the embodiment of whiteness and its structures of domination, it is not surprising that in the published version of the play, it is she who is the target when the Chicano actors take up arms to defend themselves against "gabachos" following Eric's speech urging them to do so. A pachuco lunges at her and threatens her with the cry, "I am going to get you baby," against the backdrop of shouts of "Chicano power" and Eric's own "¡Viva la Raza!" Afterward, three Chicano models join together and advance toward her as she runs out of the shop screaming.[53]

Los Vendidos follows Chicano movement productions that engender and racialize domination through representations of the brown female other, a figure who bears the brunt of nationalism's misogyny once she is targeted as la Malinche, who purportedly betrays her race and works with the oppressor. This type of gender warfare (physical abuse) directed toward the middle-class Mexican American woman is not unique to this play. In "El Corrido de Jesús Pelado Rasquachi," the campesino named in the title puts the noose around his campesina wife's neck as a symbolic gesture of the chain of oppression (*patrón, patroncito, y tú*/the big boss, the little boss, and you) that farmworkers are subjected to. He beats her because he sees her as forming a privileged part of the chain (as the patroncito) by limiting his freedom, although he has fathered a multitude of their children. Ironically, his battery of his wife is not interrupted by the divine intervention of la Virgen María de Guadalupe, as later occurs when he picks a fight with another Mexican male in frustration over his plight. Thus the battery of women seems to be an acceptable way to counterdomination, and in *Los Vendidos* this line of masculinist thinking becomes an acceptable part of resistance given that Miss JIM-enez has already become wedded in the play to Uncle Sam/Jim.

This type of symbolic identification with Uncle Sam can be disputed by reexamining the play from another vantage point. To begin with, there are notable differences between Miss JIM-enez and the governor, and these are not only racial, they are gender based as well. Her body and skin color separate her from those in power, and so does her marital status. While she represents the governor's office and performs the function of the native bourgeoisie, she is still the target of gender stereotypes—she plays the role of the dumb blonde—and her normal position is secretary, a type of work that is negatively marked by the female gender in U.S. society as being lower level, and which lacks the kind of symbolic capital associated with the high-level political go-between.[54]

Miss JIM-enez's gender identity also conflicts with the kind of social relations with which she is symbolically affiliated in the play. Although she is a sellout, she is not the premier sellout. On the contrary, she needs to secure a "masculine" model—someone who can sit at the governor's banquet and show his brown face, not just work behind the scenes "doing the shopping." The premier Mexican American is obviously not a brown woman. Miss JIM-enez thus occupies a lower position on the governor's hierarchy than her male cohort, no matter how white either of them appears to be at the level of language, culture, and politics, or how antagonistic either appears to be toward Mexicans.

However, Eric's gender privilege is downplayed in the production as the audience is made to sympathize with the Chicano models who are featured in the play and must subject themselves to Miss JIM-enez's "drama of assimilation." The Chicanas in the play are either silent or they whisper, often "echoing" the words of their partners. They also are stuck in traditional roles—we see them serving the dinner, accompanying their boyfriends or husbands, and we hear one of them respond in a flash to her husband's request to work harder. In the film version of Los Vendidos, we do not see the Chicana militant, the wide range of Chicana urban identities, the Chicana athlete, the Chicana politician on center stage. They are truly objectified—they are not performed. The Chicana prototypes who appear do so only for an instant, and never through individual en-vivo representations. In the published version of the play, things are even worse—there are no female characters other than Miss JIM-enez.

While this representation of women reflects the way Chicana women are often edited out of collective portraits staging *comunidad* (community), this positioning of women is instructive on other counts because it unwittingly displays their secondary, and therefore unprivileged, position within the greater political culture. They are so undervalued within this culture that they cannot enter into its competitive marketplace of politics and compete alongside their Chicano cohorts. However, their social condition does not elicit adequate attention within this "alternative political drama" that reinscribes racial difference through its projected mode of resistance and silences the differences between Mexicans by privileging race over class and gender. The way is paved for this type of scenario once Miss JIM-enez is symbolically cast as the brown/white other, once she is remanded to the other side: the male gender and an assimilationist viewpoint. At that point the differences between the Mexican protagonists of the play, who are united in their antiassimilationist stance, disappear, and so does the need to further nuance social inequality and to factor other types of difference (structural privilege) into the political imaginary of Viva la Causa or into nuanced conceptions of Chicano, that is Chicana/o, Power!

The consequences of this type of positioning are not limited to Miss JIM-enez, because she not only represents dominant white masculinity, she also embodies raced Chicana subjects at the level of her flesh and blood. Without a doubt, she is the speaking subject, and her identity politics and social location also mark the Chicana's brown body as a site for colonization and political contention (here, physical attack and a refutation of whiteness). Chicanas who don't identify with her position are not provided with a leading voice. While we catch a glance of the Adelita, the Mexican *revolucionaria* (revolutionary), at the beginning, the camera "zooms" by her and focuses on Miss JIM-enez instead, a female character who is privileged because she comes to life throughout the entire performance. However, she is identified as "una chicana" by Honest Sancho at the beginning of the play.

The reversal of gender and ethnic relations that defines the social hierarchy within *Los Vendidos* makes it impossible to examine the impact of gender oppression on Chicana/o communities, the way gender intersects with race and class at both ends of the social hierarchy, and, more specifically, the way Chicanas bear the burden of their oppression and must struggle to lift this burden through coalitions. In addition, while the play attacks racial privilege, it reinscribes a masculine gender and sanctions a patriarchal vision that cuts across racial and ethnic differences, dominant and alternative identities. Not only is the governor free from having to hear the contestatory voices of those who combat whiteness, but Chicano males have dibs on the part of the Mexican American, as is evident when Eric leaves and another male immediately volunteers for the part.

Playing the part of the Mexican American means having the potential to exercise another type of political leadership and to affect public policy, and Chicanas are denied this opportunity because of the types of identities that are privileged in the mainstream arena and then restaged in the alternative arena. Since Chicanas are not cast in the role, they cannot affect the political life of the state by interjecting their own gender interests, interests that crisscross race and class interests too.

While their voices are intermittently heard at the end in the alternative drama of Chicano liberation, it is the staged director of the play, Luis Valdez, who is centered in the final performance when he once again renders its social motivation. He "looks back" with his "defiant" gesture of self-determination. Resistance to racial, ethnic, and political domination is embodied in Chicano masculinity through Valdez, who directs the alternative drama on the stage, and Eric, who will stage it in the political arena now that he has a seat at the governor's luncheon.

In the early days of El Teatro Campesino it was not uncommon for workers to be staged in the dreaded role of patrones and to reluctantly assume these roles as a way of promoting social consciousness, particularly class consciousness. One can only imagine what effect this type of role reversal would have on the play's outcome if Miss JIM-enez had been staged by a male patrona in this fantastic drama of assimilation, where those who occupy the lowest position in society and those who occupy the highest are enjoined through a brown female at the discursive, physical, and political levels. While seeing Miss JIM-enez as a male cross-dresser might seem far-fetched to those who have not focused on the way she also masquerades a dominant masculinity in this play without any break in her performance, this type of role reversal also serves to underscore the preposterous nature of Luis Valdez's alternative drama, which inverts power relations at the level of gender (and by extension, class and race) while reinscribing pejorative views of Chicana women, views that are nourished by their bodies and subordinate position in U.S. society.

It could be argued that there are middle-class Chicana types like Miss JIM-enez who have sold out and now assist the dominant culture in its misrepresentation of Chicana/o subjects, and that these types work against a progressive movement for social justice. However, this view does not consider the fact that within this play, assimilation is exclusively the territory of brown females. Brown male subjects, who historically have had greater access to political leadership, particularly within the higher echelons of politics, are let off the hook. They do not visualize or experience themselves through mimesis as cultural traitors or as mute display models. This view does not consider the fact that the play also misrepresents social hierarchies by staging assimilation as primarily an "in-group" drama that is polarized along gender lines, and by removing masculine gender privilege from ethnic, political, and racial domination.

Apart from the affirmation of a Chicano political identity, the play's ultimate message is that of the salvation of the race (from Chicana Malinches who bear and suffer the burden of the white man's guilt) by Chicano masculinities (who also envelop women and symbolically restore the cultural and ethnic and political order that is temporarily threatened by the specter of a native female rendition of whiteness). For contemporary readers who are currently bombarded with a conservative discourse that recenters a patriarchal model of whiteness through a cultural politics targeting the civil rights gains of the 1960s, this "native" return of the father is problematic,[55] not because the return of the brown man is the same as the return of the white man (this would reproduce the distortions inherent in Los Vendidos from another location) but because this gender politics ultimately absolves dominant culture and its identities by failing to name, confront, embody, present, and contest those who have the power and the means to legislate whiteness by contracting brown go-betweens.[56] In the same way that Chicana issues were largely deferred for the "good" of racial unity, this all-important contestation is also deferred.

While Los Vendidos does target the ways government agencies, universities, and political organizations obstruct representation by staging ethnic minorities and women who work against the interests of these groups as a way of capitalizing on "ethnic authority," it also provides a vivid example of how the early forms of nationalism contributed to obfuscating a clear understanding of social relations by ranking oppressions through restrictive theories of intersection that postulated that "we are oppressed first because we are Chicanos, because our skin is dark. But we are exploited as workers by a system which feeds like a vulture off the work of our people only to enrich a few who own and control this entire country. We suffer a double oppression. We catch a double hell."[57]

In a country where numbers of "our people" are female workers of color who catch a "triple" hell, who are increasingly the single heads of households and are frequently targeted for political and domestic abuse; in a country where political leadership is increasingly synonymous with socially privileged masculinities, the type of collective political articulation that also informs *Los Vendidos* is seriously lacking.

Early on, Chicana feminists offered a counterdiscourse to this type of construction. Today there is a growing body of theories of social intersection that go beyond "the atomistic and essentialist logic" of "identity politics" that we see in *Los Vendidos*.[58] Notwithstanding this fact, the ideological orientation of the play—nationalism—continues to thrive and multiply in the 1990s, buttressed by the renewed polarization of social identities along racial lines.

In Chicano studies classes and theater classes, for example, *Los Vendidos* is a classic—it is often studied because it stages Chicano identity and rejects assimilation. But the play's problematic representation of Chicana women and social inequality needs to be further scrutinized so that the systems of differentiation that articulate whiteness can be apprehended and debunked.

It goes without saying that Chicana women are unfairly targeted within this "internal" drama of Mexican assimilation, which features a brown female other who masquerades for politically dominant masculinities, whose social condition is foreign to a majority of Chicanas, and who lacks any political agency of her own. The nationalist strategy of bracketing the hegemonic quality of whiteness by relocating whiteness onto the Chicana's body (here the body of a gendered and a classed other) ultimately fails, however, because of its inherent limitations and because there are other "native" Mexican representations of whiteness that are internally directed and are embodied in Chicano/Mexicano male prototypes universally associated with the greater collective. These representations tend to be less specific in terms of their references to social dynamics other than "Americanization," and they often engage transnational issues from various culturalist and linguistic viewpoints.

To encounter this variant of whiteness "on the inside" it is necessary to cross over to the other side of the border (the other Mexico), to move beyond those nationalist constructions of identity that suppress differences between Chicanas/os and Mexicanas/os by postulating that we were all the same (nation/body/color) within the political imaginary of Chicano, and to examine a trans/national identity—the pocho.

The Trans/National Context: Encountering Whiteness on the In/Other Side: Mexico's Brown Other: Pocho

Within Chicana/o discourse, *pocho* (half-breed) is the site of a series of complex ethnic and national identifications and disidentifications that are generated through contrary trans/national movements.[59] These contrary movements are central to the definition of pocho, which refers to a native construction of whiteness that is simultaneously "on the inside" (because it refers to Mexicans) and "on the other side" (because it commonly identifies Mexicanos who live outside the officially recognized Mexican nation, generally in the United States; socially acceptable notions of Mexican nationality; and politically charged constructions of the term *Chicano*).

Within popular discourse, pocho is often a Mexican construction of assimilation that targets "gringoized Mexicans," who are perceived to be ashamed of their origins and to have lost their cultural identity as Mexicans, and who are scorned because they are perceived as unable to control the standard dialect of Mexican Spanish. Dictionaries of the Spanish language often define the term *pocho* in relation to a "pale or faded color," and this definition is often rearticulated through an expression of fractured national identity—or the loss of a national identity—within the context of geographical and historical displacement from the nation of one's origin.

This framing of Chicano identity was widely disseminated by Octavio Paz in his classic essay *The Labyrinth of Solitude* (1961), which opens with a Mexican national's description of the pachuco. Significantly, the pachuco has lost all traces of Mexicanness: his language, culture, and religion. For the much acclaimed Mexican writer, the pachuco is not only the deterritorialized Mexican, he is the Mexican who voluntarily and arbitrarily chooses not to be Mexican—the one who flaunts his difference by defiantly adopting a different language and sporting an unconventional form of dress.[60]

While Octavio Paz captures many of the characteristics typically associated with the pocho through this representation of Chicano youth in California, it is important to recognize that pocho became a generalized term to refer to those Mexicans "de aca—de este lado" (from this side—the United States) "whose Mexicanness was suspect."[61] In his seminal essay on the topic, "Pochos, the Different Mexicans," Arturo Madrid-Barela proposes that "it [pocho] was not an affectionate apodo (nickname). To be a pocho was only slightly worse than being a pinche gringo. . . . Our accommodations to American society were traiciones (betrayals) in their eyes, era agringarse" (it was to become white).[62] Madrid explains that the pocho identity was fluid because it could also incorporate Mexicans who came to the north "to swell the numbers of mexicanos de acá—de este lado" (Mexicans from here—from this side). He is referring to those who would "eventually become Chicanos" and "share in our disgrace."[63]

Contrary to what most dictionaries of Spanish and Chicana/o slang suggest, Madrid-Barela proposes that "to be a pocho was a complicated matter, with cultural, linguistic, class, social, regional, geographical, temporal, and national implications." In other words, the pocho was defined according to the social position of the definer:

> To Spanish-speakers those of us whose Spanish was deficient were pochos. To working class mexicanos middle class Mexican Americans were pochos. To la gente del barrio (the people of the barrio) those of us who no longer lived there were pochos. To rural raza, urban dwellers were pochos. To the residents of the border areas, especially to our tejano relations, those of us who lived north of the frontera/border were pochos. To the newly arrived all those previously here were pochos. And of course to our hermanos mexicanos (Mexican brothers) all of us on this side of the border were pochos.[64]

Quoting Ernesto Galarza to substantiate his claim that another social location is paramount, Madrid elaborates that it was not the nature of our relationship to Mexico and Mexicans that basically defined pochos, since *who we were* had to do with *where we were*": "Turning pocho was a halfstep toward turning American. And America was all around us, in and out of the barrio."[65]

To further complicate the matter, Américo Paredes explains in "The Pocho Appears"[66] that the discursive and geopolitical positions articulated through pocho were not always identical, for the border Mexican often drew on the convention of assuming the identity of a newcomer from "el interior" (of Mexico) in this type of critique, although such a critique rendered a Mexican American rather than Mexican point of view.

The fluidity of this type of identity is in part explained by the interaction between what Paredes calls the "México de Afuera" (Out-side/Aztlán) and the "México de Adentro" (the Mexican Republic). In this interaction, discursive exchanges between Mexicans do not recognize political boundaries, as Paredes observes with respect to folklore: "Not only is there a continuing influence by Mexican oral tradition on Mexican-American folklore but influences may also move in the opposite direction." [67]

Because of the types of cultural movements on the border, it is not surprising that many of the negative cultural attributes associated with Chicanas/os, including hybridism and language loss, were also used to characterize Mexicans residing in northern Mexico. Miguel Méndez describes the conflation of Mexican identities in his introductory notes to *De la vida y el folclore de la frontera* (1986) in my translation of this section: "That the border lacks culture is a stereotype that has already been coined. According to one classic criterion, 'outside Mexico City, everything is Cautitlán.' The Northern Mexican is a brute and the Mexican American is a pocho." [68] As Méndez suggests, both prototypes cancel out any possibility of an elevated cultural manifestation, be it intellectual or artistic.

It would be a mistake to assume that all Mexicans universally associate Chicana/o or northern identities with this negative definition—for instance, the album *Las Reinas del Pueblo,* by Selena and Marcela, features a song entitled "Morena y Delgadita" in which the female affirms that she is a pochita as a way of describing a Mexican regional identity without negative consequences.[69] However, the negative definition is prevalent, especially within cultural productions that associate the pocho with the renegade—he who betrays his fatherland, prefers English, or speaks a variant of Spanish that is affected by English or bilingualism.

This figure can be found in a song called "El renegado," [70] which is linked to the 1920s and criticizes the Mexican show-off who has crossed the border; he engages in a conspicuous display of his economic prowess, consciously "forgets" his ethnic roots, and looks down on those he left behind in Mexico. The function of the poem is to impart a lesson: this happens to many when "they learn a little American." The poem aims not only to expose but also to critique this Mexican prototype, for according to its moral register, "there is nothing in the world so vile as he." The poem also aims to orient its Mexican public in the United States toward an alternative path—the path of a patriarchal rendition of Mexican nationalism—through the example of the speaking subject, who has also been cast out by revolutions but is a "good Mexican" because he "never disowns / the dear fatherland / of his affections."

As can be inferred through this brief review, pocho is a border identity that cannot be apprehended through an unproblematic border crossing, a celebratory multiculturalism, or a specific political program or social identity. The pocho identity is the site where the relations between nation-states (Mexico and the United States) are negotiated, where their conflicts are reinscribed over disparate Mexican bodies, and where contrary interpretations of national identities vie for attention. The pocho identity is the site where engendered geopolitical borders are newly drawn in an effort to reckon with competing social interests and historical movements within a transnational context; where there are two Mexicos engraved in the popular imagination, often superimposed on one another; and where a Mexican national identity is disputed in different ways and often in relation to different types of political interests.

The pocho identity often frames social relations through blanket references to assimilation or acculturation that do not promote further social analysis. Perhaps it is for this reason that Arturo Madrid remarked that "nobody ever rallied to the cry of Pocho Power."[71] However, the pocho identity is also a contested identity—contested from the political imaginary of the term Chicano,[72] contested in literary practices that disputed the vision of Chicano = pocho as a renegade or an assimilationist.

For example, in the poem "Alma Pocha" (Pocho soul, 1936),[73] also written by Américo Paredes, the pocho is he who has lost his territory/nation, not an assimilated Mexican or a Mexican who arbitrarily "chooses" to sport a mix of unacceptable cultural differences, including hybridity. "Alma Pocha" chronicles the social and historical realities that were endured in Mexico after the invasion and loss of Mexican territory (what is now Texas), and forfeits the negative judgments that normally accompany characterizations of the Mexican to the north. "Alma Pocha" can be seen as responding to those representations of Chicano identity that "could never understand why" Chicanas/os had altered the language of their mothers and fathers,[74] or why they were differentially affected by the dominant U.S. culture in ways that were not reproduced in the homeland. "Alma Pocha" is a tribute to the Mexicans on this side, the forgotten ones who have suffered at the hands of the invaders and who continue to lament Mexico's shame—her defeat at the hands of the foreigners who colonized her territory.

Mexicans on this side of the border are characterized as noble and enduring. It is significant that Paredes chose to entitle and frame his introduction to this group with a description of the pocho's soul, here a disembodied as well as deterritorialized Mexican. With this strategy Paredes reverses popular misconceptions of the U.S. Mexican that associate this new Mexican identity and sociocultural condition with a lack of moral fortitude—the inability to maintain loyalty to the homeland or to an original culture. In fact, in the poem this Mexican historical figure is not addressed by the name "pocho," which carries a negative connotation, but rather through the familiar *tú* (you). Unlike many other native constructions of the pocho, this figure is characterized as the victim and the witness of the conquest, the one who has lost his territory/nation and a nationality, the one who has suffered unjustly and is condemned to live without pride and with bitter memories of all that was once owned (the fields, the skies, the birds, the flowers) but is now the booty of the invading colonizers.

Through the voice of destiny, "Alma Pocha" foreshadows the effects of the invasion of Mexican territory by the United States with its opening and closing stanza, which is the heart of the poem: "In your own land you'll be a stranger / by the law of the gun and the law of steal" (En tu propio terruño serás extranjero / por la ley del fusil y la ley delacero). These effects include the price of armed combat (the victim of conquest will see his father shot to death for defending that which he earned by the sweat of his brow), and racial contention (the victim will see his brother hanging from a tree for "the moral crime of having been born brown"). The conquered Mexican will also lose his social position—where he was once the master, now he will be the servant.

With this poetic tribute Américo Paredes bypasses the familiar scapegoating of northern/border Mexicans that condemns them for a purported lack of national allegiance without any regard for the larger social processes that shaped Mexican culture and identity on both sides of the international border. In contrast to widely divulged representations of U.S. Mexicans which suggest that this group acquiesced to domination or assimilation, Paredes suggests that this Mexican is not defeated, that while he is long-suffering, he does not totally acquiesce—he waits.

Decades would pass before a new sociopolitical rendition of Mexican identity appeared to give this bloodied and forgotten Mexican rebel "without a sword" an arm with which to wage the struggle to reclaim the land, combat white supremacy, and shed the yoke of the slave. The Chicano movement did this by giving this Mexican a different political identity that remembered the tragic consequences of the invasion and takeover and underscored the point made earlier by Paredes in "Alma Pocha"—that Mexicans have often borne the brunt of the conflictive relations between Mexico and the United States at the level of their flesh and blood.

From the margins of a political movement that was intent on forever banishing the pocho legacy from the annals of Chicano history, the more bold-spirited among Chicanas/os also took up the linguistic challenge by insisting that the educational objectives of the movement should include promoting the use of "pocho" (a mixture of Spanish, English, and some unique elements). While many avoided this characterization because of the cultural and political connotations associated with the pocho, the more courageous went so far as to reaffirm in 1971 that Pocho was a "truly artistic and expressive bastard tongue." Without apologies, it was even proposed by Macías that "pocho" was the native tongue of Chicanos, that it expressed "Chicanos better than Spanish or English" and that it "should be preserved and expanded."[75] The attitude was *pocho, y qué!* (and so what!)

The limitations of Paredes's own poetic tribute were not, however, fully addressed by the authoritative discourse of the Chicano movement, which featured male resistance and commonly silenced the unique ways in which impoverished brown women "bore the brunt" of U.S.-Mexican relations during and after the takeover. Significantly, "Alma Pocha" does not capture the rape of Mexican women seen in Anzaldúa's "We Call Them Greasers," or their condition in society. Paredes's visionary portrait of the effects of domination (where you were once a master, now you shall be a slave) does not incorporate the plight of Chicana/Mexicana subjects—they are outside the social and linguistic parameters of dominance as it is featured in Spanish here through the masculine *amo*, "master," which refers to a gendered condition of ownership associated with the life of a socially privileged Mexican before the conquest.

This is not to say that women have been excluded from group characterizations of unflattering pocho identities—more often than not they are interpolated within these constructions in gender-specific ways. In an early *canción* (song) from New Mexico, "Los pochis de California,"[76] for example, a Mexican national residing in the United States simultaneously describes how the pochis from California don't know how to eat tortillas because they only use bread and butter on their table, and how he married a "pochi" (a Mexican woman from this side) so he could learn English. He ends by stating that after "three days" he was "already telling her yes."

This image of the domineering women predates the one that is staged in the film and theatrical renditions of *Los Vendidos*, which also invert social relations and link Mexican women to the process of Americanization/domination through stereotypical portraits. In the case of the canción, this inversion takes place in the domestic sphere, where female rather than male privilege is targeted, and from where commonly circulated stereotypes of Chicana *and* white women arise (that they have greater independence simply because they live in the United States) as a way of preserving traditional (patriarchal) Mexican values and practices on both sides of the international border.

Ironically, it is a Chicana from New Mexico, a Nuevo Mexicana named Erlinda Gonzales-Berry, who offers one of the most powerful critiques of the Chicano Mexicano representation of the Chicana as the brown female other, the pochis/pochita. She achieves this in her unconventional travel narrative and female confessional, *Paletitas de Guayaba,* published in 1991.[77] Whereas the voices and lived experiences of mujeres aren't heard in "Los pochis de California," *Los Vendidos,* and "Alma Pocha," in this novel a Chicana takes control of the discourse and doesn't let go—she says "any damn thing she wants." She tells her-story, and her story explodes the social mythology of the brown female other.

I Am Not a Pochita/Your/Their Brown Female Other: Resisting Nationalism's Malinche Syndrome

The Chicana transnational identity that resists the Malinche syndrome in *Paletitas* is negotiated by way of a deconstructive gesture by an autobiographical subject: Mari, who talks back and assures the population on both sides of the international border (and the gender divide) that she is *not* a pochita. Implicit in her critical intervention is the notion that the production of identity involves not only the way in which we position ourselves within the discourses of *our* history, culture, and society, but also the way we are positioned therein by *nos otros* ("us others": a fractured and plural "we").[78]

It is thus not an accident that the novel is composed of a series of conversations—here, discourse is the selected place of contestation, resistance, and conscious revision of disparate Chicana/o Mexican identities.[79] *Paletitas* also transgresses the borders of authoritative nationalist formations by speaking the Chicana/o discourse in the other Mexico, by rooting the Chicana/o nation in the other Mexico (Casa Aztlán), and by challenging the patriarchal transnational alliance that figures Chicanas as *agringadas* (whitened women).

Paletitas not only crosses the discursive and geopolitical borders into contemporary Mexico, it also allows a variety of tensions between Chicanas/os and Mexicans to emerge. As I have pointed out elsewhere, in *Paletitas,* the scene of the multicultural encounter is there, in Mexico, and "the protagonist does not leave her baggage behind once she arrives—she does not instantaneously receive a new fictitious identity and it isn't presumed that she'll be nourished in spirit automatically. She negotiates from the inside of a Chicana [Nuevo Mexicana] representation and these negotiations are often painful, ironic, sarcastic, and humorous. She travels through layers of contestation, this . . . means confronting the discourse of the brown female other: 'pochita' at the very point of origin."[80] This is also the point where she is susceptible to insult, the point where she is disrupting another hegemonic construction of national identity, from the inside, as someone who carries different traces of Mexicanness that are foreign to accepted notions of mestizaje.

In addition to marking these tensions that are obscured in the authoritative identity narratives of the movimiento such as *I Am Joaquín,*[81] *Paletitas* also incorporates uncharacteristic regional differences (Mari is motivated to go to Mexico as a way of contending with her "New Mexican" experience) as well as sexual and political differences. *Paletitas* follows disparate transnational movements (across nations, nationalities, regions, and genders) that implicate the Chicana's body: one movement appropriates her body through the lens of a hegemonic national identity (the brown female other/pochita), and another "reclaims" her body through a mujer-centered Chicana autobiography that counters the pochita identity, which is uttered in the public sphere with a series of affirmations. These affirmations extend into different social, political, and sexual arenas and further nuance and contest earlier notions of "pocha/o."

In order to reclaim her identity as a Chicana Nuevo Mexicana, Mari must come to terms with the way her Mexican national "pochita identity" is overwritten by a public heterosexist discourse that renders her a sexual object, readily available for any masculine advance. Through her imaginary conversations, she repeatedly offers scathing critiques of disgusting public spectacles that are set into motion by married men who eyeball her on the street. But her critique of hetero-sexism is not limited to the Mexican; it is also directed at Chicanos (at Casa Aztlán), who are likened to their Mexican cohorts in terms of their attitudes and behavior toward women. Through her counter-discourse Mari not only responds to the way she is treated, she talks back to the way other women are treated in Mexico, including a white woman who is racially constructed as a hypersexual other available to anyone wanting a sexual encounter and a Chicana lesbian who is sub-jected to homophobic comments by the Chicanos at Casa Aztlán.

Mari's rejection of the pochita identity extends far beyond the U.S.-Mexican dyad—it enlists a coalition with other women who are generally left out of transnational coalitions featuring Chicano and Mexicano identities. However, Mari's distance from the pochita iden-tity is not complete until she confronts and comes to terms with male-centered discourses of national identity that "stage" her exile through native constructions of whiteness that target Chicana subjects.

In the novel this takes place in the context of her arrival at El Centro, a place for foreign language study in the Distrito Federal. Mari arrives in Mexico with nationalist dreams of being a born-again Mexi-can, but she is placed into a beginners' Spanish class to take away her pocho accent, even though she is a native speaker of Spanish. The symbolic exile from Mexican national identity is complete when she finds out that the Mexican families who house students prefer not to house pocho students such as herself.

Mari finds refuge in Casa Aztlán, a haven from hostility and a political affiliate of the Mexican nation; however, there she is also singled out for being a New Mexican, which within the political dis-course of the leadership of Casa Aztlán means conservative, Euro-centric, and prone to assimilation. Once again the Chicana subject is constructed as the brown female other, but this time it is by her own national and ethnic cohorts, Chicanos as well as Mexicanos, who label her as a means of shocking her into their mode of political or cultural consciousness. She responds to the challenge. She immerses herself in their movimiento histories, but it is *her* travel narrative (a collec-tion of notes, memories, and the like) that provides her with the space for analyzing the realities and complexities of her life as she remem-bers instances of national, racial, and gender oppression and comes to terms with this type of positioning across trans/national and regional contexts through what is ultimately her own brand of consciousness raising and counterdiscourse.

She talks back to Mexican nationals for their prejudiced view of Chicanos as pochos and enunciates the social conditions that are repressed when Chicanas/os are accused of betraying their Mexican culture and language through Mexican constructions of pochos/pochas/pochis: "I don't know why they [Mexicans] can't give us any credit. For a hundred years we've lived under the North American flag where English is the dominant language and every attempt has been made to eradicate Spanish." [82] She further disputes stereotypical representations of pochos—the fact that Chicanas/os can't speak Spanish—with her wonderfully orchestrated Spanish-language autobiography, which flaunts a variety of dialects that are not subsumed into standard Mexican and Castilian Spanish. In addition, she obliges the reader and her selected Mexican addressee to reflect on the fact that within the United States, Spanish is stigmatized because the people who speak it are stigmatized—second-class citizens. Mari explains that in the United States "they put down our culture and language" and "treat us like animals." If this were not enough, she links this type of discrimination to class, adding that Chicanas/os aren't put into the ovens only because their labor is needed.

Mari also disputes Chicano claims of New Mexican whiteness that link this regional identity to a far-fetched Spanish heritage: she intentionally reclaims a Mexican national identity, makes the connection to her regional identity, and rejects the idea that New Mexicans have to assimilate a Spanish-centered Eurocentric identity in order to be accepted into U.S. society on the basis that assimilation is a myth: "When will we understand that they will never accept us as equals? And it is not only a question of brown skin. . . . If they accepted us as equals . . . who would be the beasts of burden? . . . harvest the crops . . . wash the dirty dishes . . . who?" [83]

Like the flesh-and-blood autobiographies examined by Lourdes Torres,[84] this Chicana narrative constructs a politics of personal and collective transformation that is built on the strength of difference and seeks to disentangle the contradictions that form part of her multiple Chicana/o and Mexicana/o identities. In each case this means deterritorializing whiteness as featured through the brown female other, removing it from the Chicana's body and encountering it through social categories that are enlisted through a political register as a way of challenging domination across interethnic, regional, sexual, and trans/national borders. Finally, this means providing the connection to the subaltern woman, here the "flesh-and-blood woman" beyond the

U.S.-Mexican dyad and beyond conventional representations of la Malinche.

Thus *Paletitas* interrupts discourses of Chicano and Mexicano national identity that locate whiteness in Chicana bodies as a way of counteracting and describing larger social processes that involve the presence of the United States in both Mexicos. *Paletitas* offers a counterdiscourse to these native constructions of whiteness by reappropriating the Chicana body (and Chicana sexuality) and by naming disparate instances of social inequality. *Paletitas* articulates in rudimentary form the social processes (racism and classism, gender oppression, imperialism) that adversely affect Chicanas/os and Mexicanas/os, and opens up a space for an incipient Chicana political discourse that must attend to various competing languages of whiteness that are rendered in different cultural and geopolitical locations.

While this incipient political discourse is not without its own set of problems—including the fact that it draws from dated models of Chicano identity and political consciousness—it nonetheless invites its reader to go beyond paradigmatic framings of domination (whiteness) that associate it with monocausality, and to move toward further specifying the "other" cartographies of our oppression and liberation, those that are often shadowed under our/their constructions of whiteness within discourse and are enunciated in other cultural languages. These languages need to be translated, encountered, and engaged with another Chicana/o political imaginary if we are to contest whiteness "over there," within the social formation, and "over here," within our overwritten social bodies.[85]

Conclusion: Revisiting Whiteness

I began this essay with a question: Why study whiteness? I end with a cautionary note. We are living in a period in which whiteness is being recentered through the voices and public policies of the politically dominant—we need to recognize and critique these constructions, which aim to reessentialize and homogenize U.S. national identity, and do so with the assistance of legal venues and a well-orchestrated political campaign, and without naming the privileged (racialized) social identities of those whose interests are being served.

There is a danger of falling into a trap, of assuming that because domination is racialized, it can be apprehended only through a nationalist register, even though this nationalist register is being enlisted through a discourse that is supposedly "ours," not "theirs." It goes without saying that we need to examine how locally produced nationalist discourses are activated in response to changing social conditions and to critique them for their insufficiencies. The cautionary note applies not only to the discursive arena, it extends to the political one as well.

Chicanas/os have furnished an organized response to this type of recentering by mobilizing and challenging Proposition 187[86] and the affirmative action backlash, and by creating broad-based coalitions between "Chicanos and Latinos" or "Latinos." The tactic of strategic essentialism (unity based on race and national origin) has rendered a positive result because it inscribed "resistance" onto the social text and the popular imagination in a period when social conditions have deteriorated and the public sphere has been targeted for the budget ax. However, if uncritically extended and nourished by authoritative discourses, strategic essentialism can also be a justification for a return to an earlier nationalist politics that privileges and essentializes race, takes gender out of class and race—or engenders brown masculinities in a patriarchal fashion, thus wrenching mujeres/women out of the political imaginary of resistance and contestation. Through their counterdiscourses, las mujeres remind us, Chicanas/os, that we need to be weary of internal constructions of whiteness that cloud and engender social and political relations in this problematic manner. I end this essay by recalling an event narrated to me in testimonial form in the San Gabriel Valley that confirms this fact.

At one point a Chicana, who is now a single parent with several children to support and a lifetime of experience working in a factory and the domestic arena, was told that she should dye her hair blonde so that she would be more appealing to her Latino husband. She didn't get mad, she said, in fact, she giggled a bit as she recounted the story. She simply answered, "You can change the color of my hair, but you'll never, you hear me, you'll never change the color of my skin." With a lot of spice and gusto, she added that the subject was dropped—she was never asked to dye her hair again (it was understood: never asked to be white again). She explained that of course she would have refused to do this in the first place—she was proud that her hair (and by implication, skin) shone dark. Beyond that, she was proud that she had not paid that price to keep a husband, thus making the connection between racial and patriarchal structures that promote dominance through a particular encoding of whiteness.

Testimonies such as these lead us to consider how it is possible to simultaneously decode dominant and "native" constructions of whiteness from outside the intended limits of the political imaginary of authoritative discourses that are radically different in their social and political expressions and objectives. In addition, this *testimonio de sobrevivencia y valentía* (strength and survival), which was rendered by a community theorist, invites us to reconsider how internally directed constructions of whiteness intrude on the resistance project and threaten to implicate this alternative discourse in dominant culture's pervasive social mythology and political scapegoating.

In a country in which Mexican women can be charged with being unfit parents because they speak to their children in Spanish,[87] where speaking Spanish to one's offspring can be misconstrued as "abuse," and where massive deportations of Mexicans (women and men) are once again viewed as a cure to the nation's ills—as well as being a springboard for conservative political agendas that aim to further impoverish one of the most impoverished social identities—the perils of this type of coimplication are multiplied. By relocating the social and political registers that have been traditionally subsumed and displaced by authoritative constructions of whiteness, we can bracket its hegemonic quality, notwithstanding the fact that this quality is engendered in ways that implicate gender differentially, notwithstanding the fact that this quality is not only transnational but also global in its extensions, and notwithstanding the fact that this quality is activated through scattered hegemonies that variously interpellate and obfuscate the social body. If it is true, as Robert Young has suggested elsewhere in a different context, that "the fundamental problem concerns the way in which knowledge [for my purposes, social knowledge] is constituted through the comprehension and incorporation of the other,"[88] then it behooves us to reexamine these native constructions of whiteness within Chicana/o discourse wherever they mark a social divide, assume a social body and identity, imagine the sociohistorical, or seek to interrupt the movements associated with this highly contested territory "outside."

Notes

A las reinas del pueblo, las de carne y hueso que pisan la tierra y luchan y merecen más que esa terrible otredad, and with special thanks to the volume editor, Ruth Frankenberg, for everything. To those writers whose works are registered here: gracias for initiating diálogo across the page, the stage, and the screen.

1   Studies that address whiteness directly generally focus on assimilation, "Anglo" attitudes and speech patterns, and identity formation. Studies concerning the Anglo-American are too numerous to quote here, but a representative example includes the following: Américo Paredes, "The Anglo-American in Mexican Folklore," in *New Voices in American Studies,* ed. Ray Browne et al. (West Lafayette: Purdue University Press, 1965), 113–28. Paredes also writes about the internal forms of whiteness in "The Pocho Appears," in *A Texas-Mexican Cancionero* (Urbana: University of Illinois Press, 1976), 153–61. José Limón targets the discursive structure of this internal form in "Agringado Joking in Texas Mexican Society," *New Scholar* 6 (1977): 33–50. Yolanda Broyles-Gonzalez examines theatrical representations of whiteness in "Zoot-Suit" and "Corridos"; see her book *El Teatro Campesino: Theater in the Chicano Movement* (Austin: University of Texas Press, 1994), and her essay "What Price Mainstream," *Cultural Studies* 4, no. 3 (October 1990): 281–93, for examples of the ways whiteness is engendered in these representations. Studies of Chicana feminism form another important body of criticism that incorporates an examination of Malinche/Malinztin, who is negatively associated with a form of race betrayal and/or assimilation in authoritative discourse. Although these now abound, two examples are Norma Alarcón, "Traddutora, Traidora: A Paradigmatic Figure of Chicana Feminism," *Cultural Critique* (Fall 1989): 57–87; and Tey Diana Rebolledo, *Women Singing in the Snow* (Tucson: University of Arizona Press, 1995). Chicana cultural critics have also delved into the territory of whiteness through their critique of mainstream feminism and heterosexism.

2   This is an alternative standpoint to the one Frankenberg describes in her groundbreaking introduction to this volume.

3   Following the insights of Ian F. Hanley López, I see "whiteness as a complex, falsely homogenizing term." In many of the Chicano representations reviewed here, *white* denotes "a rigidly defined, congeneric group of indistinguishable individuals." I concur with Hanley López that the term *white* "gains its meaning only through social relations," relations that "encompass a profoundly diverse set of persons" (xiv). For a fuller account of his perspectives on whiteness and the law, see Hanley López, *White by Law: The Legal Construction of Race* (New York: New York University Press, 1996).

4   I was inspired to write this essay after reading bell hooks, "Representing Whiteness in the Black Imagination," in *Cultural Studies,* ed. Lawrence Grossberg, Cary Nelson, and Paula Treichler (New York: Routledge, 1992); and Ruth Frankenberg's *White Women, Race Matters: The Social Construction of Whiteness* (Minneapolis: University of Minnesota Press, 1993). They prompted me to reconsider how whiteness is constructed within another transnational and racial context.

5   Or for the way these binaries often favor particular types of problematic racial constructions.

6   I am recasting Frankenberg here to suit the requirements of the context.

7   I am referring here to a discourse that targets American culture and identity. In "Cultural Identity and Diaspora," Stuart Hall refers to identities as "the names we give to the different ways we are positioned by, and position ourselves within, the narratives of the past" (225). This essay appears in *Identity, Community, Cultural Difference,* ed. Jonathan Rutherford (London: Lawrence and Wishart, 1990).

8   There are so many representations of whiteness within Chicana/o productions that

any sampling seems arbitrary, so I once again warn my reader to steer clear of thinking that these examples "represent" the field. I have selected native examples of whiteness that are paradigmatic in each "movement" selected for analysis, or which critique the paradigms under consideration. It should be noted, however, that there are many interrupted movements of whiteness within Chicana/o discourse that register whiteness in manners that are not examined here, such as those that disassociate whiteness from structures of domination or view dominant representations of whiteness through the lens of sexuality. Within paradigmatic representations of whiteness, there is an important body of poetry that targets the Spanish Conquistador and the White Man. There are also other representations of white identities and subjectivities that are so sympathetic that they appear to be paternalistic. For an examination of these variants, see Yolanda Broyles-Gonzalez's work on Chicana/o corridos and stage productions. Cherríe Moraga's "La Güera," in *This Bridge Called My Back*, ed. Moraga and Gloria Anzaldúa (New York: Kitchen Table, 1981), 27–40, offers a conscious disarticulation of dominant forms of whiteness through the counterdiscourse of a mixed ethnicity and a feminist standpoint. For purposes of clarity, I would like to underscore that this essay does not attempt to offer a genealogy of whiteness within Chicana/o discourse, nor does it attempt to provide a complete study of the Chicana/o literary construction of whiteness. As the title suggests, in this work I offer an examination of selected Chicana/o discourses.

9   Speaking of some of these terms, Américo Paredes suggests:

> If one is to judge by names and epithets little attention was paid to the Anglo-American as a person in the folklore of central Mexico during the days of conflict between Mexico and the United States. Even the occupation of Mexico City by Scott's forces seems to have produced no dirtier name for the invaders than "yanqui (Yankee)." Meanwhile along the Río Grande, where cultural conflict was a vivid and personal thing, names like "gringo" (foreigner), "patón" (bigfoot), and "gademe" (goddam) are reported by the time of the Mier Expedition. "Gringo" and "patón" appear in the folklore of central Mexico near the end of the Díaz regime. Resentment in Mexico seems to have been much stronger originally against the French troops that supported Maximilian. Names like "güero" (fair-haired) and "bolillo" (French bread), now used by Mexican-Americans and northern Mexicans for the Anglo-American, originally were used in Mexico for the French. Most interesting is "gabacho," said to come from gave, a torrent in the Pyrenees. The name was first used by the Spanish against the troops of Napoleon I who occupied Spain during the Peninsular War. Mexicans applied the same epithet to the troops of Napoleon III supporting Maximilian in Mexico during the 1860's. In the 1930's gabacho reappeared, not in Mexico or Spain but among urban Mexican-Americans and applied not to Frenchmen but to Anglo-Americans. ("The Anglo-American in Mexican Folklore," 114)

10   I do not attempt to provide a complete inventory of the taxonomical practices of Chicanas/os around whiteness, nor do I mean to suggest that these terms are equivalent or that the definitions provided above are themselves stable. As I suggest later, native definitions of whiteness depend on context for meaning.

11   Stuart Hall, "Encoding/Decoding," in *Culture, Media, Language,* ed. Hall et al. (Birmingham: Center for Contemporary Cultural Studies, 1980), 10.

12   I am reframing some of Hall's ideas on the hegemonic viewpoint here to suit my context; see ibid., 137.

13   This furnishes a mode of decoding that is contrary to that which is intended. For Hall's viewpoint on "intended" meanings, see ibid., 138.

14   In *Literatura Chicana: Texto y Contexto,* ed. Antonia Castañeda et al. (Englewood Cliffs, N.J.: Prentice-Hall, 1982), 83–84. From this point onward I refer to El Plan Espiritual de Aztlan as "el Plan."

15   I am influenced here by Américo Paredes's discussion of whiteness as an idea in "The Anglo-American in Mexican-American Folklore," 115. He makes this point in another context that does not incorporate the type of critique I make here.

16   Rafael Pérez-Torres, *Movements in Chicano Poetry: Against Myths, Against Margins* (Cambridge: Cambridge University Press, 1995), 60.

17   Pérez-Torres discusses the masculine legacy of the plan, its lack of diversity, and its problematic indigenous antecedents in ibid., 62.

18   Author unknown, "El Corrido de Joaquín Murrieta," in *Literatura Chicana,* 66–67. José Limón elaborates on the legendary history of Joaquín Murrieta: "Joaquín Murrieta was an honest Mexican miner in Northern California in the early 1850's, just as Anglo-Americans were coming into newly acquired California to exploit its recently discovered gold. Murrieta turned to social banditry against the Americans, because again, according to legend, he had been oppressed, robbed and persecuted by the Americans . . . had been insulted and grossly maltreated without justice— had been flogged—and was determined to be avenged for his wrong four-fold" (*Mexican Ballads,* 116–17). Here Limón quotes from a section of the *San Francisco Daily Herald* (April 18, 1893) reprinted by Pedro Castillo and Alberto Camarillo in *Furia y Muerte: Los Bandidos Chicanos,* Aztlán Publication no. 4 (Los Angeles: Aztlan Publications, 1973), 47.

19   For this discussion I focus primarily but not exclusively on "The Homeland, Aztlan, El Otro Mexico," in *Borderlands/la Frontera, the New Mestiza* (San Francisco: Aunt Lute, 1987), 1–13.

20   I am recasting Anzaldúa here since these words are spoken from the perspective of la mestiza (ibid., 1).

21   For a description of how these elements are reclaimed and renegotiated by the mestiza, see Yvonne Yarbro-Bejarano, "*Borderlands/la Frontera:* Cultural Studies, 'Difference' and the Non-Unitary Subject," *Cultural Critique* 28 (1994): 24.

22   This quoted material featuring the gringo is in *Borderlands,* 7.

23   Yvonne Yarbro-Bejarano relates this space to the formation of a plural subject in "*Borderlands,*" 11.

24   Anzaldúa, *Borderlands,* 85–86.

25   I am stressing the way she revises Mexican female icons and deities. I am astonished by the number of people who take her invention of indigenous female deities and legacies literally and then proceed to query Chicanos about them as if these elements were a part of everyone's lived experience, as if they were passed down like this, in unadulterated form, from one's parents. Suffice it to say that Chicana spirituality is not homogeneous; there are Chicana materialists who don't subscribe to a native Chicana spirituality.

26   Anzaldúa, *Borderlands,* 1.

27   Yarbro-Bejarano, "*Borderlands,*" 8.

28 I include myself among them while making it clear that this is *my* critique. I am cognizant of the conceptual difficulties of speaking through multiple identities and different social locations. While it is true that Anzaldúa often slides from the "I" to the "we" to the "they" in a manner that is jarring to cultural critics, those who react in this way must also contend with how to move from the individual to the collective—from this collective to that one—without falling into problematic legacies associated with these collectives. Having said that, I also note that precisely by speaking the "I," by having the courage to utter this (engendered) I, Anzaldúa broke with the nationalistic dictum that postulated that individual histories were of secondary importance to the monumental epic histories of peoples, which, ironically, were held to stand above them. Many have unjustly suffered and have been censored in the name of the collective and it goes without saying that Anzaldúa's work also militates against this silencing, this taming of the wild tongue, and gives us an unforgettable example of just how wild it can be. For an important contribution to the feminist work regarding *Borderlands,* see Inderpal Grewal, "Autobiographic Subjects, Diasporic Locations," in *Scattered Hegemonies* (Minneapolis: University of Minnesota Press, 1994), 231–51.

29 Anzaldúa, *Borderlands,* 80.

30 I am drawing on Yarbro-Bejarano's critique of the way this text is deracinated.

31 "We Called Them Greasers," in *Borderlands,* 194–95. Soñia Saldívar Hull offers important insights on this poem in her wonderful essay "Feminism on the Border: From Gender Politics to Geopolitics," in *Criticism on the Borderlands,* 203–10.

32 Anzaldúa, *Borderlands,* 194–95.

33 Ibid., 7.

34 Ibid., 194–95.

35 Pat Mora, "Immigrants," in *Borders* (Houston: Arte Público, 1986), 15.

36 David Monreal, "A Middle-Class Mexican American," *In Sighs and Songs of Aztlan,* ed. F. E. Alibi and Jesús de Otero (Bakersfield: Universal Press, 1975), 59–60.

37 The entire poem is reprinted in Armando Rendón, *The Chicano Manifesto* (New York: Collier Books, 1971), 169.

38 Ibid., 177. To his credit, Rendón points out that the victims of this culture aren't only the minority peoples but the dominant white group as well.

39 Ibid., 178.

40 For an account of the way the term *Chicano* superseded these identities, see Angie Chabram and Rosa Linda Fregoso, "Introduction," *Cultural Studies* 4, no. 3 (October 1990): 205.

41 Although Rendón infers this category in the case of Chicanos by way of association, he actually uses the term *black anglo* to refer to African Americans; see *Chicano Manifesto* 15.

42 I make this point in "I Throw Punches for My Race," in *Cultural Studies,* ed. Lawrence Grossberg, Cary Nelson, and Paula Treichler (New York: Routledge, 1992), 93.

43 This sentence references quotation from Rendón, *Chicano Manifesto,* 46.

44 Ibid., 96.

45 Ibid., 96–97.

46 Ibid., 47.

47 By most estimations *Los Vendidos* was created in 1967. It was published by Luis

Valdez in *Actos* (San Juan Bautista: Cucaracha Press, 1971), and reappeared in Luis Valdez, *Early Works* (Houston: Arte Público, 1990), 40–53. The movie version was created and directed by Luis Valdez and produced by George Paul. According to Jorge Huerta, *Los Vendidos* was videotaped by KNBC in Los Angeles for broadcast in 1973. For his perspective on the play, see "How to Buy a Used Mexican: *Los Vendidos*," in *Chicano Theater* (Ypsilanti: Bilingual Press, 1982), 60–68. According to the information that precedes the published version in *Early Works*, the first performance of *Los Vendidos* was at a Brown Beret junta at Elysian Park, East Los Angeles.

48 For a discussion of El Teatro Campesino, see Yolanda Broyles, "Women in El Teatro Campesino: ¿a poco estaba molacha la Virgen de Guadalupe?" in *Chicana Voices: Intersections of Class, Race, and Gender*, ed. Ricardo Romo (Austin: Center for Mexican American Studies Publications, 19), 162–87.

49 While many of the observations here center on the film, I also quote from the play, drawing from *Los Vendidos*, in *Early Works*, 40–53.

50 *Los Vendidos*, 49.

51 This is true even though Honest Sancho reasserts a socially privileged masculine temperament in the play as he teases, outwits, and invites her to succumb to a heterosexual appetite that is circulated in patriarchal-capitalist social formations.

52 Significantly, in the play Miss JIM-enez loves beating the Zoot-Suiter and loves squeezing and sexually attacking Eric. It is not far-fetched to assume that she enacts the patriarchal behavior circulated in capitalist formations, including police brutality and sexual harassment, even though in the play this behavior is given a comedic effect. It's as if she is "squeezing the Charmin."

53 *Los Vendidos*, 51.

54 In the published version of *Los Vendidos* Miss JIM-enez's occupation as a secretary is emphasized through the dialogue, but this doesn't alter the facts that she is wedded to dominant white masculinities and represents them, and that she is targeted in the race war of the Chicanos against Anglos. Significantly, in one performance of the play Miss JIM-enez was played by Jane Fonda, and all brownness disappeared and the link to the white man was made stronger.

55 I would like to acknowledge my fruitful conversations with Judy Newton in our cultural studies group.

56 In the filmed play we assume that Eric will confront the white man once he's gotten his foot into the political sanctum, but we never see this; we only see him mumbling subversive words to Miss JIM-enez.

57 Rendón, *Chicano Manifesto*, 180.

58 The early feminist critique is covered by Alma García in "The Development of Chicana Feminist Discourse, 1970–1980," in *Unequal Sisters: A Multicultural Reader in U.S. Women's History*, ed. Ellen Carol DuBois and Vicki L. Ruiz (New York: Routledge, 1990), 418–31. For a cultural studies perspective, see Kobena Mercer, "1968: Periodizing Politics and Identity," in *Cultural Studies*, ed. Lawrence Grossberg, Cary Nelson, and Paula Treichler (New York: Routledge, 1992), 424–37.

59 Although I have entitled this section "The Trans/National Context," the division between this section and the first one is a false one to the extent that the term *gringo* is also a transnational one and to the extent that the problematics that are targeted in the first section are the product of transnational movements. I term this section "Trans/National" as a way of describing movements between the two

Mexicos and their imagined communities. In this sense, "Mexico" refers to las dos caras de México.

60 Paz stresses that what is most significant is the pachuco's "stubborn desire to be different," not examining the causes of his conflicts or, by extension, the nature of his differences, in *The Labyrinth of Solitude,* trans. Lysander Kemp (New York: Grove Press, 1961), 15.

61 Arturo Madrid-Barela, "Pochos: The Different Mexicans, an Interpretative Essay, Part I," *Aztlan* 7, no. 1 (Spring 1976): 52.

62 Ibid., 52.

63 Ibid.

64 Ibid. In an early work on immigration, Manuel Gamio elaborates on some of the attitudes that go into the fashioning of pocho identities by immigrants, which I supply here. It should be noted, however, that the attitudes he identifies are not limited to this group, and that they need to be seriously scrutinized, particularly for their essentialist dimensions and gender connotations. He summarizes these attitudes as follows:

The immigrant, on his part, considers the American of Mexican origin as a man without a country. He reminds him frequently of the inferior position to which he is relegated by the white American. He criticizes, as well, certain details of American material culture, above all the "Americanized" Mexican women who dress like Americans and have the customs and habits of American women. The American of Mexican origin is known as a pocho.

The American of Mexican race is really, so far as nationality is concerned, in a difficult and unfortunate position. Such a person, when he goes to Mexico, wearing American clothes and speaking Spanish with a foreign accent, calls himself a Mexican because he is accustomed to being called a Mexican in the United States. Nevertheless, Mexicans in Mexico, knowing nothing of this, become indignant at the idea of such a person being a Mexican, while on the other hand, Americans find it strange that he call himself an American, since in the United States he is always a Mexican or a Spanish-American.

Notwithstanding these differences in point of view between the Mexican immigrant and the Mexican-Americans—differences which in reality are of a purely superficial and formal nature—both groups consider themselves as together composing that body called by them "The Race"; both are called Mexicans by white Americans. (*Mexican Immigration to the United States* [New York: Dover, 1971], 129)

David Maciel offers another perspective:

Specifically, the label pocho was placed on Chicanos whom Mexicans believed consciously attempted to assimilate into U.S. society at the expense of their Mexican roots. This term signifies a negative view of lo mexicano. Many Mexicans alleged that Chicanos also have a condescending attitude toward the homeland. Later, class biases were incorporated into the stereotypes: most Chicanos were thought to be descendants of the lower classes, since it was widely believed in Mexico that only the poor, the unskilled, and the illiterate emigrated to the United States. Between the 1940's and the late 1960's, pocho was the most-employed Mexican label for Chicanos. It is not surprising then, that between 1922 and 1970, Chicano characters in Mexican cinema were, with very few exceptions, portrayed as stereotypical pochos. ("Pochos and Other Extremes: Mexican Cinema . . . ," in, *Chicanos and Film,* ed. Chon A. Noriega [Minneapolis: University of Minnesota Press, 1992], 103)

Américo Paredes also describes the pocho phenomenon:

The pocho, however, does not really appear until the time of the Revolution in Mexico, when great numbers of Mexican refugees of all social classes settled in cities like Los Angeles and San Antonio. During this period the "Mexiquitos" in the larger cities of the Southwest exhibited two contrasting states of mind. One was a truly refugee state of mind. . . . Another state of mind was found among the younger people of the barrios, who were being forced to adapt to the environment of Anglo cities and who found acculturation an inevitable product of their fight for survival. It was the barrios that produced the pocho, the early version of the Chicano. And it was in contemptuous reference to the young Mexican-American of East Los Angeles, children of migrants workers and middle-class revolutionary refugees alike, that José Vasconcelos is said to have first used the term pocho. But whatever his degree of Americanization, the average Mexican-American of this period continued to think of himself as possessing a "pure" Mexican culture. It was always the other fellow who was an agringado, not him. . . . (*A Texas-Mexican Cancionero,* 154)

65   Madrid-Barela, "Pochos," 53, quoting Ernesto Galarza's *Barrio Boy* (New York: Ballantine Books, 1972), 203.

66   Paredes, "The Pocho Appears," 153–66.

67   Paredes, "The Anglo-American in Mexican Folklore," 113.

68   The quote is my translation of the Spanish; Miguel Méndez, *De la Vida y el Folclore de la Frontera* (Tucson: Mexican-American Studies Research Center, 1986), 4.

69   See the compact disc, *Las Reinas del Pueblo,* Capitol Records, Inc., 1995; in particular, "Morena y Delgadita," sung by Graciela and written by Pedro Rivera.

70   Author unknown, in Gamio, *Mexican Immigration,* 93.

71   I am not suggesting that pocho cannot promote social analysis if rendered within different types of social imaginaries and not merely a vague and pejorative language of cultural or social difference. In fact, within their art and cultural works many Chicana/o cultural practitioners have reclaimed pocho as a productive political space, moving beyond these traditional representations of whiteness. In my own case I am particularly attracted to the kinds of linguistic directions that are anticipated in the construction of pocho as a third space of linguistic and cultural identification that refutes whiteness and inscribes hybridity.

72   Chicanas/os contested pocho by reclaiming Mexicanness, by refuting the ideas that Chicanas/os were ashamed of their Mexican heritage and that they didn't want to speak Spanish or couldn't speak it.

73   The quoted translations of Spanish are mine; Américo Paredes, "Alma Pocha," in *Between Two Worlds* (Houston: Arte Público, 1991), 35–36.

74   I am recasting Madrid here.

75   Ysidro Ramón Macías, "The Chicano Movement," in *A Documentary History of Mexican-Americans,* ed. Wayne Moquin with Charles Van Doren (New York: Praeger, 1971), 501–2.

76   Author unknown, in Arthur Campa, *Spanish Folk-Poetry in New Mexico* (Albuquerque: University of New Mexico Press, 1946), 214.

77 Erlinda Gonzales-Berry, *Paletitas de Guayba* (Albuquerque: El Norte, 1991). All quoted materials are my translations from Spanish, which have been approved by the author.

78 This is normally written *nosotros*, but I divide it in order to tag contested split identities.

79 I am revisiting Hall's notion of identity here through a notion of identity that targets contested Chicana/o subjects.

80 Angie Chabram-Dernersesian, "Chicana! Riqueña . . . ," in *Multiculturalism: A Critical Reader*, ed. David T. Goldberg (Oxford: Blackwell, 1994), 281. I have written a longer essay on Erlinda Gonzales-Berry for a forthcoming volume of the *Dictionary of Literary Biography*, ed. Francisco Lomelí and Carl Shirley. Some of the points made here are revisited there in different form. However, in that essay I emphasize the links between whiteness and sexuality.

81 Rodolfo Gonzales, *I Am Joaquín* (Denver: El Gallo, 1967).

82 Gonzales-Berry, *Paletitas*, 14.

83 Ibid., 30.

84 Lourdes Torres, "The Construction of the Self in U.S. Latina Autobiographies," in *Third World Women and the Politics of Feminism*, ed. Chandra Talpade Mohanty et al. (Bloomington: Indiana University Press, 1991).

85 I am not suggesting that we abandon all of our native vernacular around whiteness, but rather that we critically revisit its national and gender connotations within specific contexts, and that we reassess its potential for fostering critical perspectives that do not promote the kinds of nationalist scenarios examined here.

86 This California proposition, directed primarily at Mexicans and Central Americans, was recently passed in a wave of anti-immigrant sentiment. The proposition denies medical and educational benefits and other social services to the undocumented and their children. Since the passage of this proposition there have been similar efforts in other states and in the national arena, plus efforts to take away benefits from "legal aliens." Nowhere in the propaganda denouncing Mexican immigrants, and especially Mexican women, was there ever mention of the fact that this land was once Mexico and that these Mexicans contribute in a positive way to the economy and the life of the state, often doing menial jobs that others won't do. Proposition 187 is especially contradictory given that undocumented workers are periodically granted free entry when economic demands require their cheap labor.

87 This happened to a Chicana from Texas who was threatened with losing custody of her child if she didn't speak to her in English. This mentality has permeated far more than the legal sphere — across the nation, English-only movements and legislation are thriving.

88 I have modified his initial quote to suit the requirements of my argument. His original text is part of a section entitled "The Philosophical Allegory," which reads, "As we have seen, the fundamental problem concerns the way in which knowledge — and therefore theory or history, is constituted through the comprehension and incorporation of the other." Here I stress social knowledge versus theory and history because this knowledge activates both theories and histories within Chicana/o discourse. See Robert Young, *White Mythologies: Writing History and the West* (London: Routledge, 1990), 12.

Representing Whiteness in
the Black Imagination
bell hooks

ALTHOUGH there has never been any official body of black people in the United States who have gathered as anthropologists and/or enthnographers whose central critical project is the study of whiteness, black folks have, from slavery on, shared with one another in conversations "special" knowledge of whiteness gleaned from close scrutiny of white people. Deemed special because it was not a way of knowing that has been recorded fully in written material, its purpose was to help black folks cope and survive in a white supremacist society. For years black domestic servants, working in white homes, acted as informants who brought knowledge back to segregated communities—details, facts, observations, psychoanalytic readings of the white "Other."

Sharing, in a similar way, the fascination with difference and the different that white people have collectively expressed openly (and at times vulgarly) as they have traveled around the world in pursuit of the other and otherness, black people, especially those living during the historical period of racial apartheid and legal segregation, have maintained steadfast and ongoing curiosity about the "ghosts," "the barbarians," these strange apparitions they were forced to serve. In the chapter on "Wildness" in *Shamanism, Colonialism, and the Wild Man,* Michael Taussig urges a stretching of our imagination and understanding of the Other to include inscriptions "on the edge of official history." Naming his critical project, identifying the passion he brings to the quest to know more deeply *you who are not ourselves,* Taussig explains:

I am trying to reproduce a mode of perception—a way of seeing through a way of talking—figuring the world through dialogue that comes alive with sudden transformative force in the crannies of everyday life's pauses and juxtapositions, as in the kitchens of the Putumayo or in the streets around the church in the Nina Maria. It is always a way of representing the world in the round-about "speech" of the collage of things. . . . It is a mode of perception that catches on the debris of history.[1]

I, too, am in search of the debris of history, am wiping the dust from past conversations to remember some of what was shared in the old days, when black folks had little intimate contact with whites, when we were much more open about the way we connected whiteness with the mysterious, the strange, the terrible. Of course, everything has changed. Now many black people live in the "bush of ghosts" and do not know themselves separate from whiteness, do not know this thing we call "difference." Though systems of domination, imperialism, colonialism, racism, actively coerce black folks to internalize negative perceptions of blackness, to be self-hating, and many of us succumb, blacks who imitate whites (adopting their values, speech, habits of being, etc.) continue to regard whiteness with suspicion, fear, and even hatred. This contradictory longing to possess the reality of the Other, even though that reality is one that wounds and negates, is expressive of the desire to understand the mystery, to know intimately through imitation, as though such knowing worn like an amulet, a mask, will ward away the evil, the terror.

Searching the critical work of postcolonial critics, I found much writing that bespeaks the continued fascination with the way white minds, particularly the colonial imperialist traveler, perceive blackness, and very little expressed interest in representations of whiteness in the black imagination. Black cultural and social critics allude to such rep-resentations in their writing, yet only a few have dared to make explicit those perceptions of whiteness that they think will discomfort or an-tagonize readers. James Baldwin's collection of essays *Notes of a Native Son* (1955) explores these issues with a clarity and frankness that are no longer fashionable in a world where evocations of pluralism and di-versity act to obscure differences arbitrarily imposed and maintained by white racist domination. Writing about being the first black person to visit a Swiss village with only white inhabitants, who had a yearly ritual of painting individuals black who were then positioned as slaves and bought, so that the villagers could celebrate their concern with converting the souls of the "natives," Baldwin responded:

> I thought of white men arriving for the first time in an African village, strangers there, as I am a stranger here, and tried to imagine the astounded populace touching their hair and marveling at the color of their skin. But there is a great difference between being the first white man to be seen by Africans and being the first black man to be seen by whites. The white man takes the astonishment as tribute, for he arrives to conquer and to convert the natives, whose inferiority in relation to himself is not even to be questioned, whereas I, without a thought of conquest, find myself among a people whose culture controls me, has even in a sense, created me, people who have cost me more in anguish and rage than they will ever know, who yet do not even know of my existence. The astonishment with which I might have greeted them, should they have stumbled into my African village a few hundred years ago, might have rejoiced their hearts. But the astonishment with which they greet me today can only poison mine.[2]

Addressing the way in which whiteness exists without knowledge of blackness even as it collectively asserts control, Baldwin links issues of recognition to the practice of imperialist racial domination.

My thinking about representations of whiteness in the black imagination has been stimulated by classroom discussions about the way in which the absence of recognition is a strategy that facilitates making a group "the Other." In these classrooms there have been heated debates among students when white students respond with disbelief, shock, and rage, as they listen to black students talk about whiteness, when they are compelled to hear observations, stereotypes, etc., that are offered as "data" gleaned from close scrutiny and study. Usually, white students respond with naive amazement that black people critically assess white people from a standpoint where "whiteness" is the privileged signifier. Their amazement that black people watch white people with a critical "ethnographic" gaze, is itself an expression of racism. Often their rage erupts because they believe that all ways of looking that highlight difference subvert the liberal conviction that it is the assertion of universal subjectivity (we are all just people) that will make racism disappear. They have a deep emotional investment in the myth of "sameness" even as their actions reflect the primacy of whiteness as a sign informing who they are and how they think. Many of them are shocked that black people think critically about whiteness because racist thinking perpetuates the fantasy that the Other who is subjugated, who is subhuman, lacks the ability to comprehend, to understand, to see the working of the powerful. Even though the majority of these students politically consider themselves liberals, who are antiracist, they too unwittingly invest in the sense of whiteness as mystery.

In white supremacist society, white people can "safely" imagine that they are invisible to black people since the power they have historically asserted, and even now collectively assert over black people accorded them the right to control the black gaze. As fantastic as it may seem, racist white people find it easy to imagine that black people cannot see them if within their desire they do not want to be seen by the dark Other. One mark of oppression was that black folks were compelled to assume the mantle of invisibility, to erase all traces of their subjectivity during slavery and the long years of racial apartheid, so that they could be better—less threatening—servants. An effective strategy of white supremacist terror and dehumanization during slavery centered on white control of the black gaze. Black slaves, and later manumitted servants, could be brutally punished for looking, for appearing to observe the whites they were serving as only a subject can observe, or see. To be fully an object, then, was to lack the capacity to see or recognize reality. These looking relations were reinforced as whites cultivated the practice of denying the subjectivity of blacks (the better to dehumanize and oppress), of relegating them to the realm of the invisible. Growing up in a Kentucky household where black servants lived in the same dwelling with her white family who employed them, newspaper heiress Sallie Bingham recalls, in her autobiography *Passion and Prejudice* (1989), "Blacks, I realized, were simply invisible to most white people, except as a pair of hands offering a drink on a silver tray."[3] Reduced to the machinery of bodily physical labor, black people learned to appear before whites as though they were zombies, cultivating the habit of casting the gaze downward so as not to appear uppity. To look directly was an assertion of subjectivity, equality. Safety resided in the pretense of invisibility.

Even though legal racial apartheid no longer is a norm in the United States, the habits of being cultivated to uphold and maintain institutionalized white supremacy linger. Since most white people do not have to "see" black people (constantly appearing on billboards, television, movies, in magazines, etc.) and they do not need to be ever on guard, observing black people, to be "safe," they can live as though black people are invisible and can imagine that they are also invisible to blacks. Some white people may even imagine there is no representation of whiteness in the black imagination, especially one that is based on concrete observation or mythic conjecture; they think they are seen by black folks only as they want to appear. Ideologically, the rhetoric of white supremacy supplies a fantasy of whiteness. Described in Richard Dyer's 1988 essay "White" this fantasy makes whiteness synonymous with goodness:

> Power in contemporary society habitually passes itself off as embodied in the normal as opposed to the superior. This is common to all forms of power, but it works in a peculiarly seductive way with whiteness, because of the way it seems rooted, in commonsense thought, in things other than ethnic difference. . . . Thus it is said (even in liberal textbooks) that there are inevitable associations of white with light and therefore safety, and black with dark and therefore danger, and that this explains racism (whereas one might well argue about the safety of the cover of darkness, and the danger of exposure to the light); again, and with more justice, people point to the Judaeo-Christian use of white and black to symbolize good and evil, as carried still in such expressions as "a black mark," "white magic," "to blacken the character," and so on.[4]

Socialized to believe the fantasy, that whiteness represents goodness and all that is benign and nonthreatening, many white people assume this is the way black people conceptualize whiteness. They do not imagine that the way whiteness makes its presence felt in black life, most often as terrorizing imposition, a power that wounds, hurts, tortures, is a reality that disrupts the fantasy of whiteness as representing goodness.

Collectively, black people remain rather silent about representations of whiteness in the black imagination. As in the old days of racial segregation where black folks learned to "wear the mask," many of us pretend to be comfortable in the face of whiteness only to turn our backs and give expression to intense levels of discomfort. Especially talked about is the representation of whiteness as terrorizing. Without evoking a simplistic, essentialist "us and them" dichotomy that suggests black folks merely invert stereotypical racist interpretations, so that black becomes synonymous with goodness and white with evil, I want to focus on that representation of whiteness that is not formed in reaction to stereotypes but emerges as a response to the traumatic pain and anguish that remain a consequence of white racist domination, a psychic state that informs and shapes the way black folks "see" whiteness. Stereotypes black folks maintain about white folks are not the only representations of whiteness in the black imagination. They emerge primarily as responses to white stereotypes of blackness. Speaking about white stereotypes of blackness as engendering a trickle-down process, where there is the projection onto an Other of all that we deny about ourselves, Lorraine Hansberry in *To Be Young, Gifted, and Black* (1969) identifies particular stereotypes about white people that are commonly cited in black communities and urges us not to "celebrate this madness in any direction":

> Is it not "known" in the ghetto that white people, as an entity, are "dirty" (especially white women—who never seem to do their own cleaning); inherently "cruel" (the cold, fierce roots of Europe; who else could put all those people into ovens *scientifically*); "smart" (you really have to hand it to the m.f.'s); and anything *but* cold and passionless (because look who has had to live with little else than their passions in the guise of love and hatred all these centuries)? And so on.[5]

Stereotypes, however inaccurate, are one form of representation. Like fictions, they are created to serve as substitutions, standing in for what is real. They are there not to tell it like it is but to invite and encourage pretense. They are a fantasy, a projection onto the Other that makes them less threatening. Stereotypes abound when there is distance. They are an invention, a pretense that one knows when the steps that would make real knowing possible cannot be taken—are not allowed.

Looking past stereotypes to consider various representations of whiteness in the black imagination, I appeal to memory, to my earliest recollections of ways these issues were raised in black life. Returning to memories of growing up in the social circumstances created by racial apartheid, to all-black spaces on the edges of town, I reinhabit a location where black folks associated whiteness with the terrible, the terrifying, the terrorizing. White people were regarded as terrorists, especially those who dared to enter that segregated space of blackness. As a child I did not know any white people. They were strangers, rarely seen in our neighborhoods. The "official" white men who came across the tracks were there to sell products, Bibles, insurance. They terrorized by economic exploitation. What did I see in the gazes of those white men who crossed our thresholds that made me afraid, that made black children unable to speak? Did they understand at all how strange their whiteness appeared in our living rooms, how threatening? Did they journey across the tracks with the same "adventurous" spirit that other white men carried to Africa, Asia, to those mysterious places they would one day call the third world? Did they come to our houses to meet the Other face to face and enact the colonizer role, dominating us on our own turf? Their presence terrified me. Whatever their mission they looked too much like the unofficial white men who came to enact rituals of terror and torture. As a child, I did not know how to tell them apart, how to ask the "real white people to please stand up." The terror that I felt is one black people have shared. Whites learn about it secondhand. Confessing in *Soul Sister* (1969) that she too began to feel this terror after changing her skin to appear "black" and going to live in the South, Grace Halsell described her altered sense of whiteness:

> Caught in this climate of hate, I am totally terror-stricken, and I search my mind to know why I am fearful of my own people. Yet they no longer seem my people, but rather the "enemy" arrayed in large numbers against me in some hostile territory. . . . My wild heartbeat is a secondhand kind of terror I know that I cannot possibly experience what *they,* the black people experience.[6]

Black folks raised in the North do not escape this sense of terror. In her autobiography, *Every Good-bye Ain't Gone* (1990), Itabari Njeri begins the narrative of her northern childhood with a memory of southern roots. Traveling south as an adult to investigate the long-ago murder of her grandfather by white youths who were drag racing and ran him down in the streets, killing him, Njeri recalls that for many years "the distant and accidental violence that took my grandfather's life could not compete with the psychological terror that had begun to engulf my own." Ultimately, she begins to link that terror with the history of black people in the United States, seeing it as an imprint carried from the past to the present:

> As I grew older, my grandfather assumed mythic proportions in my imagination. Even in absence, he filled my room like music and watched over me when I was fearful. His fantasized presence diverted thoughts of my father's drunken rages. With age, my fantasizing ceased, the image of my grandfather faded. What lingered

was the memory of his caress, the pain of something missing in my life, wrenched away by reckless white youths. I had a growing sense—the beginning of an inevitable comprehension—that this society deals blacks a disproportionate share of pain and denial.[7]

Njeri's journey takes her through the pain and terror of the past, only the memories do not fade. They linger, as do the pain and bitterness: "Against a backdrop of personal loss, against the evidence of history that fills me with a knowledge of the hateful behavior of whites toward blacks, I see the people of Bainbridge. And I cannot trust them. I cannot absolve them." If it is possible to conquer terror through ritual reenactment, that is what Njeri does. She goes back to the scene of the crime, dares to face the enemy. It is this confrontation that forces the terror of history to loosen its grip.

To name that whiteness in the black imagination is often a representation of terror: one must face a palimpsest of written histories that erase and deny, that reinvent the past to make the present vision of racial harmony and pluralism more plausible. To bear the burden of memory one must willingly journey to places long uninhabited, searching the debris of history for traces of the unforgettable, all knowledge of which has been suppressed. Njeri laments in her Prelude that "nobody really knows us"; "So institutionalized is the ignorance of our history, our culture, our everyday existence that, often, we do not even know ourselves." Theorizing black experience, we seek to uncover, restore, as well as to deconstruct, so that new paths, different journeys are possible. Indeed, Edward Said (1983) in "Traveling Theory" argues that theory can "threaten reification, as well as the entire bourgeoise system on which reification depends, with destruction." The call to theorize black experience is constantly challenged and subverted by conservative voices reluctant to move from fixed locations. Said reminds us:

> Theory, in fine, is won as the result of a process that begins when consciousness first experiences its own terrible ossification in the general reification of all things under capitalism; then when consciousness generalizes (or classes) itself as something opposed to other objects, and feels itself as contradiction to (or crisis within) objectification, there emerges a consciousness of change in the status quo; finally, moving toward freedom and fulfillment, consciousness looks ahead to complete self-realization, which is of course the revolutionary process stretching forward in time, perceivable now only as theory or projection.[8]

Traveling, moving into the past, Njeri pieces together fragments. Who does she see staring into the face of a southern white man who was said to be the one? Does the terror in his face mirror the look of the unsuspected black man whose dying history does not name or record? Baldwin wrote that "people are trapped in history and history is trapped in them." There is then only the fantasy of escape, or the promise that what is lost will be found, rediscovered, returned. For black folks, reconstructing an archaeology of memory makes return possible, the journey to a place we can never call home even as we re-inhabit it to make sense of present locations. Such journeying cannot be fully encompassed by conventional notions of travel.

Spinning off from Said's essay, James Clifford in "Notes on Travel and Theory" celebrates the idea of journeying, asserting that

> this sense of worldly, "mapped" movement is also why it may be worth holding on to the term "travel," despite its connotations of middle-class "literary," or recreational, journeying, spatial prac-tices long associated with male experiences and virtues. "Travel" suggests, at least, profane activity, following public routes and beaten tracks. How do different populations, classes, and genders travel? What kinds of knowledges, stories, and theories do they produce? A crucial research agenda opens up.[9]

Reading this piece and listening to Clifford talk about theory and travel, I appreciated his efforts to expand the travel/theoretical frontier so that it might be more inclusive, even as I considered that to answer the questions he poses is to propose a deconstruction of the conven-tional sense of travel, and put alongside it or in its place a theory of the journey that would expose the extent to which holding on to the concept of "travel" as we know it is also a way to hold on to imperial-ism. For some individuals, clinging to the conventional sense of travel allows them to remain fascinated with imperialism, to write about it seductively, evoking what Renato Rosaldo (1988) aptly calls in *Culture and Truth* "imperialist nostalgia."[10] Significantly, he reminds readers that "even politically progressive North American audiences have en-joyed the elegance of manners governing relations of dominance and subordination between the 'races.'" Theories of travel produced out-side conventional borders might want the Journey to become the rubric within which travel as a starting point for discourse is associated with different headings—rites of passage, immigration, enforced migration, relocation, enslavement, homelessness. Travel is not a word that can be easily evoked to talk about the Middle Passage, the Trail of Tears,

the landing of Chinese immigrants at Ellis Island, the forced relocation of Japanese Americans, the plight of the homeless. Theorizing
diverse journeying is crucial to our understanding of any politics of
location. As Clifford asserts at the end of his essay: "Theory is always
written from some 'where,' and that 'where' is less a place than itiner-
aries: different, concrete histories of dwelling, immigration, exile, migration. These include the migration of third world intellectuals into
the metropolitan universities, to pass through or to remain, changed
by their travel but marked by places of origin, by peculiar allegiances
and alienations."

Listening to Clifford "playfully" evoke a sense of travel, I felt such
an evocation would always make it difficult for there to be recognition
of an experience of travel that is not about play but is an encounter
with terrorism. And it is crucial that we recognize that the hegemony
of one experience of travel can make it impossible to articulate another
experience and be heard. From certain standpoints, to travel is to encounter the terrorizing force of white supremacy. To tell my "travel"
stories, I must name the movement from a racially segregated southern community, from a rural black Baptist origin, to prestigious white
university settings, etc. I must be able to speak about what it is like
to be leaving Italy after I have given a talk on racism and feminism,
hosted by the parliament, only to stand for hours while I am interrogated by white officials who do not have to respond when I inquire as
to why the questions they ask me are different from those asked the
white people in line before me. Thinking only that I must endure this
public questioning, the stares of those around me, because my skin
is black, I am startled when I am asked if I speak Arabic, when I am
told that women like me receive presents from men without knowing
what those presents are. Reminded of another time when I was strip-
searched by French officials, who were stopping black people to make
sure we were not illegal immigrants and/or terrorists, I think that one
fantasy of whiteness is that the threatening Other is always a terrorist. This projection enables many white people to imagine there is no
representation of whiteness as terror, as terrorizing. Yet it is this representation of whiteness in the black imagination, first learned in the
narrow confines of the poor black rural community, that is sustained
by my travels to many different locations.

To travel, I must always move through fear, confront terror. It
helps to be able to link this individual experience to the collective journeying of black people, to the Middle Passage, to the mass migration

of southern black folks to northern cities in the early part of the twentieth century. Michel Foucault posits memory as a site of resistance suggesting (as Jonathan Arac puts it in his introduction to *Postmodernism and Politics*) that the process of remembering can be a practice which "transforms history from a judgment on the past in the name of a present truth to a 'counter-memory' that combats our current modes of truth and justice, helping us to understand and change the present by placing it in a new relation to the past."[11] It is useful when theorizing black experience to examine the way the concept of "terror" is linked to representations of whiteness.

In the absence of the reality of whiteness, I learned as a child that to be "safe" it was important to recognize the power of whiteness, even to fear it, and to avoid encountering it. There was nothing terrifying about the sharing of this knowledge as survival strategy; the terror was made real only when I journeyed from the black side of town to a predominantly white area near my grandmother's house. I had to pass through this area to reach her place. Describing these journeys "across town" in the essay "Homeplace: A Site of Resistance" I remembered:

> It was a movement away from the segregated blackness of our community into a poor white neighborhood. I remember the fear, being scared to walk to Baba's, our grandmother's house, because we would have to pass that terrifying whiteness — those white faces on the porches staring us down with hate. Even when empty or vacant those porches seemed to say *danger,* you do not belong here, you are not safe.
>
> Oh! that feeling of safety, of arrival, of homecoming when we finally reached the edges of her yard, when we could see the soot black face of our grandfather, Daddy Gus, sitting in his chair on the porch, smell his cigar, and rest on his lap. Such a contrast, that feeling of arrival, of homecoming — this sweetness and the bitterness of that journey, that constant reminder of white power and control.[12]

Even though it was a long time ago that I made this journey, associations of whiteness with terror and the terrorizing remain. Even though I live and move in spaces where I am surrounded by whiteness, surrounded, there is no comfort that makes the terrorism disappear. All black people in the United States, irrespective of their class status or politics, live with the possibility that they will be terrorized by whiteness.

This terror is most vividly described in fiction writing by black authors, particularly the recent novel by Toni Morrison (1987), *Beloved*. Baby Suggs, the black prophet, who is most vocal about representations of whiteness, dies because she suffers an absence of color. Surrounded by a lack, an empty space, taken over by whiteness, she remembers: "Those white things have taken all I had or dreamed and broke my heartstrings too. There is no bad luck in the world but white folks." [13] If the mask of whiteness, the pretense, represents it as always benign, benevolent, then what this representation obscures is the representation of danger, the sense of threat. During the period of racial apartheid, still known by many folks as Jim Crow, it was more difficult for black people to internalize this pretense, hard for us not to know that the shapes under white sheets had a mission to threaten, to terrorize. That representation of whiteness, and its association with innocence, which engulfed and murdered Emmett Till was a sign; it was meant to torture with the reminder of possible future terror. In Morrison's *Beloved* the memory of terror is so deeply inscribed on the body of Sethe and in her consciousness, and the association of terror with whiteness is so intense, that she kills her young so that they will never know the terror. Explaining her actions to Paul D. she tells him that it is her job "to keep them away from what I know is terrible." Of course Sethe's attempt to end the historical anguish of black people only reproduces it in a different form. She conquers the terror through perverse reenactment, through resistance, using violence as a means of fleeing from a history that is a burden too great to bear. It is the telling of that history that makes possible political self-recovery.

In contemporary society, white and black people alike believe that racism no longer exists. This erasure, however mythic, diffuses the representation of whiteness as terror in the black imagination. It allows for assimilation and forgetfulness. The eagerness with which contemporary society does away with racism, replacing this recognition with evocations of pluralism and diversity that further mask reality, is a response to the terror, but it has also become a way to perpetuate the terror by providing a cover, a hiding place. Black people still feel the terror, still associate it with whiteness, but are rarely able to articulate the varied ways we are terrorized because it is easy to silence by accusations of reverse racism or by suggesting that black folks who talk about the ways we are terrorized by whites are merely evoking victimization to demand special treatment.

Attending a recent conference on cultural studies, I was reminded of the way in which the discourse of race is increasingly divorced from any recognition of the politics of racism. I went there because I was confident that I would be in the company of like-minded, progressive, "aware" intellectuals; instead, I was disturbed when the usual arrangements of white supremacist hierarchy were mirrored in terms of who was speaking, of how bodies were arranged on the stage, of who was in the audience, of what voices were deemed worthy to speak and be heard. As the conference progressed I began to feel afraid. If progressive people, most of whom were white, could so blindly reproduce a version of the status quo and not "see" it, the thought of how racial politics would be played out "outside" this arena was horrifying. That feeling of terror that I had known so intimately in my childhood surfaced. Without even considering whether the audience was able to shift from the prevailing standpoint and hear another perspective, I talked openly about that sense of terror. Later, I heard stories of white women joking about how ludicrous it was for me (in their eyes I suppose I represent the "bad" tough black woman) to say I felt terrorized. Their inability to conceive that my terror, like that of Sethe, is a response to the legacy of white domination and the contemporary expression of white supremacy is an indication of how little this culture really understands the profound psychological impact of white racist domination.

At this same conference I bonded with a progressive black woman and white man who, like me, were troubled by the extent to which folks chose to ignore the way white supremacy was informing the structure of the conference. Talking with the black woman, I asked her: "What do you do, when you are tired of confronting white racism, tired of the day-to-day incidental acts of racial terrorism? I mean, how do you deal with coming home to a white person?" Laughing, she said, "Oh, you mean when I am suffering from White People Fatigue Syndrome. He gets that more than I do." After we finished our laughter, we talked about the way white people who shift locations, as her companion has done, begin to see the world differently. Understanding how racism works, he can see the way in which whiteness acts to terrorize without seeing himself as bad, or all white people as bad, and black people as good. Repudiating "us and them" dichotomies does not mean that we should *never* speak of the ways observing the world from the standpoint of "whiteness" may indeed distort perception, impede understanding of the way racism works both in the larger world as well as the world of our intimate interactions. Calling for a shift in locations in "the intervention interview" published with the collection *The Post-*

Colonial Critic (1990), Gayatri Spivak clarifies the radical possibilities that surface when positionality is problematized, explaining that "what we are asking for is that the hegemonic discourses, the holders of hegemonic discourse should de-hegemonize their position and themselves learn how to occupy the subject position of the other."[14] Generally, this process of repositioning has the power to deconstruct practices of racism and make possible the disassociation of whiteness with terror in the black imagination. As critical intervention, it allows for the recognition that progressive white people who are antiracist might be able to understand the way in which their cultural practice reinscribes white supremacy without promoting paralyzing guilt or denial. Without the capacity to inspire terror, whiteness no longer signifies the right to dominate. It truly becomes a benevolent absence. Baldwin ends his essay "Stranger in the Village" with the declaration: "This world is white no longer, and it will never be white again." Critically examining the association of whiteness as terror in the black imagination, deconstructing it, we both name racism's impact and help to break its hold. We decolonize our minds and our imaginations.

Notes

This essay was first printed in *Cultural Studies,* ed. Lawrence Grossberg; Cary Nelson, and Paula Treichler (New York: Routledge, 1992).

1   Michael Taussig, *Shamanism, Colonialism and the Wild Man: A Study in Terror and Healing* (Chicago: University of Chicago Press, 1987).

2   James Baldwin, "Stranger in the Village," in *Notes of a Native Son* (1955; reprint, Boston: Beacon Press, 1984).

3   Sallie Bingham, *Passion and Prejudice* (New York: Knopf, 1989).

4   Richard Dyer, "White," *Screen* 29, no. 4 (1988): 44–64.

5   Lorraine Hansberry, *To Be Young, Gifted, and Black* (Englewood Cliffs, N.J.: Prentice-Hall, 1969).

6   Grace Halsell, *Soul Sister* (New York: World, 1969).

7   Itabari Njeri, *Every Good-bye Ain't Gone* (New York: Random House, 1990).

8   Edward Said, "Traveling Theory," in *The World, the Text, and the Critic* (Cambridge: Harvard University Press, 1983).

9   James Clifford, "Notes on Travel and Theory," in *Traveling Theory, Traveling Theorists, Inscriptions,* ed. James Clifford and Vivek Dhareshwar (Santa Cruz: University of California Santa Cruz, 1986).

10   Renato Rosaldo, *Culture and Truth: The Remaking of Social Analysis* (Boston: Beacon Press, 1988).

11   Jonathan Arac, ed., *Postmodernism and Politics* (Minneapolis: University of Minnesota Press, 1986).

12   bell hooks, "Homeplace: A Site of Resistance," in *Yearning: Race, Gender and Cultural Politics* (Boston: South End Press, 1990).

13   Toni Morrison, *Beloved* (New York: Knopf, 1987).

14   Gayatri Chakravorty Spivak, *The Post-Colonial Critic: Interviews, Strategies, Dialogues,* ed. Sarah Harasym (New York: Routledge, 1990).

Locating White Detroit

John Hartigan Jr.

WHERE does whiteness end, where do whites begin? At its core, this question highlights the problematic issue of scale when regarding racial matters. This shift between singular and plural orders (whiteness and whites) materializes differently depending on the domain in which it is located. While whiteness may be fixed as a unified or unifying phenomenon when regarded ideologically at the national level, "on the ground" that unity quickly becomes illusory. Instead of one firm "ground," there is a shifting series of domains (local, regional, national, transnational) across which whiteness materializes according to distinct centers of significance, assimilating or effacing a varying array of internal differences, and projecting or excluding a host of corporal others. Each level displays a certain intermittency of effects. Whiteness may be inhabited and active at each, but the order of replication in each domain is not absolutely determined by the domains "above" or "below." The intervals and gaps between domains create an irregular and unpredictable basis for the cultural reproduction of this racial category, white.

The interminable difference and distance between whiteness and whites became apparent to me while conducting fieldwork in Detroit, Michigan. Over a twenty-month period I worked in three distinct class communities: two inner-city neighborhoods—one "gentrifying" and the other "underclass"—and a working-class neighborhood on the city's far west side.[1] Initially, I assumed that by studying the everyday lives of whites in this city, at the end, I would be able to abstract out some order of solidarity or cultural coherence that was identifiably whiteness which linked them all. What I found, though, was that articulations of the significance of white racialness varied widely between these class zones. The differences between these whites were amplified further when I shifted geographical focus from these neighborhoods to the city and region as political entities, and when I attempted to draw on national forms of discourse on whiteness as a means of providing an overarching context. Whiteness, which can be ideologically and discursively distinct when viewed from a national or global perspective, appeared "on the ground" in Detroit to be inundated with heterogeneous social materials that were not abstractable into one racial category. The differences between whites were magnified across the distinct geographical orders of the neighborhood, the city, the region (southeastern Michigan), and the nation.[2]

In grappling with the cultural complexity revealed by shifting scales of reference in relation to whiteness, I found Marilyn Strathern's reassessment of cross-cultural comparisons quite useful.[3] Strathern suggests that interdisciplinary and comparative projects should model the scaling of cultural phenomena on the chaotic nature of the transmission of information and the "not quite replication" of fractals, which generate patterned irregularities. This approach focuses on the gaps between levels and the new backgrounds of significance that emerge as one analytically shifts attention between distinct domains. Strathern contrasts this theoretical tack with a "segmentary model," which assumes that levels are "generated by the division of a pre-existing entity into discrete parts through distinction or opposition like a unit dividing or doubling itself."[4] Considered through a segmentary model, whiteness appears to be a top-down version of ideology. Rather than assuming an intrinsic order of connections, Strathern asserts that the emphasis should be placed on drawing out "partial connections" that link the distinct domains across which the phenomenon in question—in this case, whiteness—replicates in increasingly irregular yet relentlessly connected patterns.

This essay will illustrate the complexity of whiteness by elaborating the partial connections that exist between distinct domains and conditions of whites. The significance of whiteness is inconsistent across the variety of levels at which whites may be examined collectively: the terms of inclusion and exclusion by which racial decorums and conventions are maintained or contested among whites involve a specificity according to place and time.[5] Toward this end, I examine whiteness as something akin to a message or transmission in which varying occurrences of errors repeat their irregularities at each increasingly minute level of attention to the content of the message/error. The *gap* between whiteness and whites generates numerous locations, which, like points on an initial line scored by intermittency, may be interrupted infinitely, forming increasingly distinct positions while retaining a patterned similarity across escalating irregular extensions. "The result is that, however numerous, the points never exceed the quantity contained in the initial level. And however sparse, they never lose the complexity that the initial level was capable of conveying, for each point is capable of further interruptions. For every piece of information lost, information is gained."[6]

In this regard, a thorough objectification of whiteness requires a recognition, first, of the provisional or relational character of racial matters, and, second, the deployment of an analytic mode of attention that facilitates shifts between incomparable orders of phenomena. The question of scale is never resolved into a final ground of comprehension and understanding, but is replicated at each level, where each answer produces more questions and each insight leads into more tangled quantifications and instances.

Applying Strathern's method for analyzing gaps and partial connections to the study of whiteness in the field helpfully recasts the orientation of established analyses of racial orders. In my fieldwork, for instance, I relied on the notion of racial formation developed by Michael Omi and Howard Winant. While I certainly confirmed their finding that racial meanings are never static or absolute, the singular order of focus implied by racial *formation* delimited my ability to detail the linked but divergent articulations of whiteness in Detroit.[7] Omi and Winant define racial formation in the following manner: "The meaning of race is defined and contested throughout society, in both collective action and personal practice. In the process, racial categories themselves are formed, transformed, destroyed, and re-formed. We use the term racial formation to refer to the process by which social, economic and political forces determine the content and importance of racial categories, and by which they are in turn shaped by racial meanings. Crucial to this formulation is the treatment of race as a central axis of social relations subsumed under or reduced to some broader category."[8]

The broad frame of reference, the national scale of attention Omi and Winant deploy in rendering historical and political versions of racial categories and their meanings, can obscure the nuanced modes of differentiation that obtain in distinct geographical zones within the nation. Detroit, rather than simply providing an instantiation of national discourses on race, is a location in which the significance of racial categories is contested and negotiated in situations quite distinct from those assumed to be the norm in the United States. In order to detail the local dynamics through which the significance of racial matters was interpreted, I began to consider Detroit as a particular "racial formation." In this regard, I found it more relevant to think in terms of plural ("racial formations") rather than singular orders.

Shifting attention from singular to plural forms extends the scope of the analytic perspective articulated by Omi and Winant in three key regards, each of which elaborates on rather than criticizes their project. The first elaboration entails a recognition of multiple racial formations within the United States instead of one unified formation; this draws attention to the level of regional specificity wherein distinct operations that maintain or transform racial categories can be seen as functioning simultaneously across the nation.[9] The social, economic, and political forces they refer to have differential effects across the United States; regions emerge from and, in turn, shape the uneven consequences and determinations of these forces. So too, the contours and scope of the connection between whiteness and positions of privilege vary distinctly by region, continually being reconfigured and reasserted in relation to local pressures and challenges. The clearest instance of the regional variations of whiteness is glimpsed in the demographic revolution now under way in the United States. Already in this country's largest cities whites have lost their majority status. This same shift is occurring as well in the nation's most populous states, including California and Texas, with others like Florida sure to follow. In locations such as Detroit, Chicago, Miami, San Jose, and Atlanta, the contours of whiteness have rapidly mutated and reformulated; the background of significance against which whiteness is articulated, the gaps that have emerged between whites in these locales and those in the nation at large, have generated new "racial meanings" too heterogeneous to be summarized into one abstract racial order of significance.[10]

A second elaboration follows from this last point. Omi and Winant's articulation of racial formation divides levels of analysis too rigorously between the abstract individual and the social collective: "At the micro-level, race is a matter of individuality. . . . At the macro-level, race is a matter of collectivity. . . . The racial order is organized and enforced by the continuity and reciprocity between these two levels of social relations."[11] In between these levels is perhaps the most critical site for the generation and reproduction of racial formations—the family.[12] The "meaning" of race depends to a large degree on whether particular families reproduce homogeneous or heterogeneous racial categories. Families process social relations (friendships, animosities, kin networks) in addition to reproducing cultural subjects.[13] As I will explain below, the family is a distended and nebulous location, a scale of reference between individuals and the broader society that generates a great degree of variation in how racial categories gain and lose their significance.[14]

The third elaboration required by the notion of racial formation involves Omi and Winant's insistence that race is "a central axis of social relations." The problem with this formulation is that it requires that race be a unified phenomenon, not reducible to or subsumed by other orders. Such a requirement results in interminable debates over how to prioritize race with competing "central" axes, such as class, and undermines a recognition of the fundamental heterogeneity of objects produced simultaneously by class and racial systems of domination.[15] In this elaboration, as in the other two, the key shift in attention is from the implicit assumption that racial categories are homogeneous orders to the recognition that they are relentlessly heterogeneous constructs.[16] Even at the level of greatest abstraction, the nation or the globe, racial categories are rarely so rigorously delimited as to produce a consistently homogeneous content. With whiteness, gaps continually emerge between whites in different regions, in distinct families, and in various class positions. These gaps reveal distinct backgrounds of significance against which whites varyingly articulate and interpret the scope of their racialness.[17] The extent of this heterogeneity in racial categories becomes clearer with increasing attention to specific locations.

"Welcome to Detroit . . ."

As a racial formation, Detroit is quite opposite of the United States at large.[18] Whiteness may be hegemonic nationally, but that condition is bracketed in this city where blacks form 76 percent of the population.[19] Within the city's boundaries, "blackness" is hegemonic in terms of politics and culture.[20] This black hegemony has limits, of course. The surrounding suburbs are vastly white, and the inhabitants are quite interested in asserting regional mastery over certain operations of the city's infrastructure. At this level, the metropolitan Detroit area

mirrors or mimicks aspects of the seemingly absolute social divide between blacks and whites in the United States.[21] Yet, within the city
proper this mirror is shattered, leaving whites and blacks to negotiate
the significance of their racial markings in contexts that are quite unfamiliar to most Americans.

As a racial formation, Detroit provides a context in which the
meaning of race generally, and of whiteness and blackness in particular,
diverges from national assumptions and understandings. The most important difference is that whiteness, here, is rarely an unmarked or normative condition. In fact, whiteness is often read as being out of place
in this "black metropolis." A primary form of this reading of whiteness
involves critiques of the racial interests of white suburban politicians
who are striving to "regionalize" certain operations of the city's infrastructure. White suburbanites who make incursions into the city for
entertainment and recreation also provide instances for reading whiteness as out of place in Detroit. Since the 1984 World Series victory-
celebration-turned-riot, Detroiters have been quick to note that white
suburbanites are responsible for some of the most notorious instances
of havoc that are read nationally as evidence of the lack of discipline
among blacks in the city. The national media that covered the chaos
following the World Series in 1984 reported that once again Detroiters
were destroying their own city. But a more thorough examination of
the "rioters" by the local media revealed that they were predominantly
white suburbanites who had come into the city for the Series.

Such forays by whites into the city are often read popularly as
moments of contamination. This connection between white incursions
into the city and pollution is illuminated by Mary Douglas's continually relevant insight that cultural boundaries are ratified through an
obsessive marking (as dirt or trash) of matter that is out of place.[22] Illegal dumping is a huge problem in Detroit. By conservative estimates,
discarded tires piled in vacant lots and in abandoned buildings out-
number city residents by more than two to one.[23] And most of this
dumping seems to be carried out by city residents. This issue, though,
garners little attention or symbolic charge unless the matter can be cast
in racial terms. The city hosts an annual hydroplane race in the Detroit
River off Belle Isle, a city park. In the summer of 1993, the crowd on
the island was, as usual, vastly white, and they left behind mounds of
trash, some of which were spectacularly burned in their wake. The next
day's headline of the *Detroit Free Press* read: "Boat Race Fans Trash Belle
Isle."[24] The article reported that "some Thunderfest revelers went too

far this year, torching piles of trash and discarded couches which forced city parks crews to work overtime to clean up the mess." The article highlighted, in an accompanying frame, a quote from the city parks director, Alonzo Bates: "Most of the folks who came in were whites. . . . They feel that this is a black city and we don't care. They think they can leave dirt and destruction behind and nobody will do anything about it. . . . They go wild and we look bad, but it's not Detroiters doing it."

The article highlighted a debate over the accuracy of this racial assessment, and the matter was also fiercely discussed and featured in subsequent letters to the editor.[25] Suburbanites who took offense at being lumped together and read in reductively racialized terms charged Bates with making "racist comments." One resident of affluent Grosse Pointe Woods complained: "Why is he assuming all Thunderfest fans were non-Detroiters? Simply because the majority of them were white? How can you be so sure some of those fans weren't Detroiters?" A Detroit resident put the blame for the problem on city officials and police who grant suburbanites "carte blanche" when they come into Detroit. Others insisted that race was irrelevant because the offending fans were simply "slobs." But what stands out in the collection of statements is the simultaneous ease and explosiveness with which whites are considered out of place in Detroit.

While the connection between whiteness and pollution in Detroit is quite active at one level, the matter appears to provide scant direct significance to the operation of racial categories in particular locations within the city, such as the neighborhood where I did the majority of my fieldwork—a blighted, "extreme-poverty" area adjacent to Tiger Stadium and within a mile of the city's downtown.[26] Residents here are ambivalent about the vastly white crowds that appear for the baseball games. The suburbanites do leave behind their garbage and frustrate some of the few remaining homeowners by urinating on lawns and in empty lots before and after the game, but most people in the area welcome the crowds because of the money they bring. Some residents make cash off these spectators by selling them parking spots, game tickets, and drugs. During the time I lived in this neighborhood, I never heard black residents racialize these incursions by white suburbanites.

The crowds at the Tigers' games illustrate one of the complexities involved with assessing the "content" of racial formations. While the broader characterization of Detroit as black and the suburbs as white may be accurate, certain locations within these orders are subject to periodic fluctuations that disrupt the clarity and stability of such characterizations. Residentially, this census tract is 54 percent black, which, it might be assumed, establishes a certain order of racial dominance in this neighborhood. But the frequent appearance of these massively white crowds (98 to 96 percent of spectators at the stadium are white)[27] for the eighty-one home games each year undermines the facile equation of residential demographics with a certain racial balance. As well, the fluctuation in racial composition points to a crucial connection between local and national racial dynamics: the economic advantage of the visiting white suburbanites is a facet of the privileged mobility that distinguishes them from the impoverished residents of this zone, white and black.

While the racial reading of these periodic reversals might seem the most obvious, for white residents the class component of the baseball crowds was a more compelling issue. I heard local whites expressing anxious discomfort about these visitors, emphasizing the fact that they were wealthy, and hence arrogant and contemptuous. Local whites reported hearing snide comments from these suburbanites as they parked their cars in the vacant lots where houses once stood or purchased tickets from local scalpers. Such exchanges distinguished whites who seamlessly manipulated the privileges associated with their racial position from whites whose very racialness accentuated the degraded coding of their class standing.[28]

Over the course of my fieldwork, I often observed acquaintances among the white residents working in the lots parking cars before the games. Their difference from the suburban white visitors involved a complex of class distinctions—not just their occupational differences, but the fact of their particular location ("poor whites" in Detroit) mattered greatly.[29] Whites in this neighborhood did not participate in the same order of racial privilege and power with which whiteness is typically associated. For suburban whites, their racialness was an advantage; for the poor whites in this neighborhood, their racialness was a matter of shifting, everyday contexts; their whiteness might mark them as vulnerable to a host of "black" reactions, or leave them open to contemptuous sneers from suburban whites, sparked by their lack of shared position or status that a common order of whiteness should have assured.

The position of "poor whites" in Detroit points to an aspect of racial meanings that may or may not vary from formation to formation: the significance of race fluctuates in relation to other modes of interest.[30] While racial meanings are often quickly rendered and asserted in

Detroit, there are also many situations in which they are suspended, held in abeyance, or simply do not come to mind. Any analysis of racial categories and meanings must be able to take into account the play between active and passive articulations of racial identity. The distinction between active and passive does not imply alternate modes of presence or absence such that, at times, a person's racialness might be simply not present. Rather, the value of this distinction is that it points to an interpretive continuum according to which the racial aspect of an event or situation is either significant or not to the participants. This type of analytic alternation involves an ability to understand how racial readings are prioritized among a host of other interpretive interests and concerns that assemble the cultural complexity of social subjects. In other words, locating whiteness is not simply a matter of specifying certain sites and determining how they shape and contour racial categories; it also entails locating whiteness among a host of concerns and values that occupy the realm of a person's consciousness in everyday or ritualistic registers. The meaning of race varies from location to location, but it also depends on the set of concerns against which it is prioritized and the other forms of consciousness or modes of reading with which it is ranked and arranged.

This aspect of locating whiteness is suggested by the complex situation presented by another periodic event that temporarily shifts the racial content of this zone: the annual Saint Patrick's Day parade. The southern portion of the area is known as Corktown, after the county in Ireland that offered up many of the first Irish immigrants to settle in Detroit. Though the ethnic content of the area has shifted with the changing generations, becoming inhabited subsequently by Mexicans and Maltese, the neighborhood's Irish identity remains quite visible, supported largely by the "Irish" bars along Michigan Avenue. As well, the parish of Most Holy Trinity remains "home" to the Irish Americans who grew up here, and to their children raised in the suburbs. They return annually during the "high holy days" surrounding Saint Patrick's Day. The central event of their return is the Irish parade down Michigan Avenue, past Tiger Stadium.

As a slice of the racial formation of Detroit, the parade presents a stunning picture: Its content is only partially ethnic; in between the line of floats featuring scenes of Irish history or demonstrations of Irish culture march all-black bands from the city's high schools and junior highs.[31] On one frigid day in March, I stood with the other huddled spectators, white and black, watching the "ethnic" parade as it rolled down Michigan Avenue with its dozen or so bands from the city schools. For the white spectators I spoke with, the presence of black high school bands presented no disruption of the ethnic nature of the event, even if only one of the bands performed a traditional tune such as "Danny Boy." These whites seemed to be intrigued by the seamless-ness with which blacks moved in this performance of "ethnicity," as if it confirmed the fundamentally ironic nature of ethnic identity in the United States.[32] Nor were the black spectators that I talked with per-turbed by the presence of whites in this "black metropolis." People of both races were fascinated by the ability of this parade to unfold yearly with its heterogeneous racial content.

Inside the Gaelic League, a huge "Irish-American Club" located along the parade route, a more traditional performance of ethnic heri-tage and identity ensued. The bands played an onslaught of standard jigs, reels, and waltzes; ballads and patriotic songs were thrown in to give the grandparents whirling their excited grandchildren across the floor a few moments' rest. On one stage the microphone was opened to those who wanted to come up and sing their favorite songs from Ireland, and the kitchen ran full bore late into the night. Here, all the participants were white, and yet in the most public performance of Irish ethnicity, the parade down one of Detroit's main avenues, the order of participants was racially heterogeneous. The racialness of all present at the parade was never absolved, but simply remained in a passive modality, paused on the cusp of some unarticulated threshold, waiting for something to be made out of it.

The significance of racial materiality in this particular zone de-pends largely on alternating active and passive modalities. There are thresholds across which race matters absolutely, but they compete with a diverse array of other thresholds that individuals rely on to determine when other abstractions matter more, such as "crime" or "violence" or "poverty." On the streets and in social spaces—on front porches and in corner bars—whites and blacks move alongside each other continu-ally, mutually inhabiting the same blighted zone where the poverty rate runs at 48 percent. Few people actually own their own homes; most are on welfare or currently unemployed. Yet, with all this in com-mon, everyone here is an obviously racial being. They all notice and are marked by race; they think and talk about race; they recognize it as a substance that inexorably links and divides them. While race never materializes as exclusive residential zones within this "hood," neither is it simply a matter of individual attitudes; it depends on the context and on the significance people are interested in making out of racial difference.[33]

Family, Race, Class

JERRY

The family I lived next door to in the neighborhood was a group of "hillbillies" centered on the relations of three brothers: Jerry, Sam, and David. They were one family among many who came to Detroit from West Virginia, Kentucky, and Tennessee. Such Appalachian migrant families form an "invisible minority" of inner-city whites in cities throughout the Midwest.[34] In the case of Jerry and his brothers, their parents were both born in the South and met and married in the North. The brothers used "hillbilly" as a term of self-identification, but with a great deal of ambivalence. The designation marked their difference from the older generation of white native Detroiters who remained in the neighborhood in the wake of the mass exodus of whites from the city that began in the early 1950s.[35] "Hillbilly" was also used to distinguish them from other southern whites who had achieved more financial security and assimilated into the suburbs.[36] Whenever "hillbilly" was used, it carried a volatile charge of social contempt—a contempt these brothers alternately reveled in or rejected—inscribing a particular class difference that divided the whites in the neighborhood. Objectifications of a collective order among these whites were quite rare, and "hillbilly" operated as the most salient common identity recognized by whites here.

One afternoon, I joined the brothers around David's Ford LTD, watching and sometimes helping Jerry tinker with the failing water pump. David was trying to decide which problem was more critical: the transmission, the brakes, or the water pump; he could afford to repair only one. I had been moved in for a couple of days, and the brothers were still sizing me up. Sam wanted to know why I had not gone "to school" yesterday. I went over again how I was doing a study of the neighborhood rather than taking classes or literally "going to school." Jerry asked, "What is it you're studying again?"

"Race relations," I replied.

They exploded, laughing. David said, "Oh you come to the right place for that. Just keep going to the bars with us, you'll learn all you need to know about race relations."

Sam offered, "I'll take you over to them bars on Third, and you'll sure learn something."

David: "Naw man, you want to learn about race relations, you just walk from here through them projects over to the freeway on the other side. That's an education! 'Cause I'll tell you what, you won't come out the other side. You walk in there and you're gonna learn more than you can handle what race relations is. You won't come out the other side."

Sam: "Yeah, go in there at night, you won't get a hundred yards."

They giggled over this, then their talk turned back to more concrete matters involving the LTD. The bars on Third Avenue, I later found out, had been their stomping ground as slightly younger, rowdier men, when Third Avenue was the spine of the concentration of "hillbillies" in Detroit. They now visited them only occasionally in part because increasing age had made the brothers less adept at negotiating the dangerous contexts of such places. They preferred O'Leary's, around the corner, which was frequented by somewhat more whites than blacks and featured a mix of honky-tonk and rhythm and blues tunes on the jukebox. The "projects" were directly across the broad, three-way intersection from our house. When a graduate student from nearby Wayne State University was shot to death by a thirteen-year-old boy on the street in front of the projects, the brothers were all quick to point out that this proved their assessment: "See, I told you. That's what happens to researchers." [37]

It was not until many months later, when I began to wrap up my fieldwork, that this exchange came back to me as quite striking. The brothers immediately connected the abstraction "race relations" with the absolute racial zone of "the projects," not simply for the degree of blackness of that demographic site, but because if they entered or passed by it they would be out of place and read as absolute racial objects—whites. The basis for their sense of direction stemmed from an awareness of place and location. In this neighborhood, they were one family among many, white and black, who held elaborate and lengthy knowledge of each other reaching back over the tumultuous past three decades. But across the intersection, they were simply "whites," partly for their skin color, but also in terms of location and being out of place.[38]

What I found fascinating in their response was the way that it ignored their immediate setting, which they obviously did not regard as "racial," Jerry maintained the three remaining houses on this corner for their Maltese landlord. He, his wife, Jessi Rae, and his brother Sam, his wife, and their two children lived in the first house. There were three black men living in the other rental rooms in that house; this number varied, as one black tenant took in fluctuating numbers of

friends from off the street. The middle house was a two-family flat—I
lived in the bottom flat, and David lived upstairs with his wife and their
son. Two black couples, one white couple, and a single white man lived
in the third house. One of the black couples in this house, Marvin and
Charlotte, had a long friendship with Jerry and Jessi Rae. They celebrated birthdays together at O'Leary's and collaborated on some mean
barbecues in the yard. Marvin and Jerry had worked together for at
least the past two years, using Marvin's truck for various hauling and
towing jobs. Jerry enjoyed waxing on about the past bad winters, and
how if it had not been for Marvin and him working together they all
would have gone hungry.

     Yet this relationship and the general living situation did not spring
to mind when I asked them about "race relations." They shared their
houses with blacks and faced similar economic dilemmas with their
black neighbors, but they did not feel that met the criteria of the academic abstraction I had posed regarding race relations. The problem of
whiteness arose for them when they ventured out of their place in the
"hood," but it did not starkly matter in the immediate context of their
homes. This is not to say that they did not recognize themselves, or
understand the ways their black neighbors regarded them, as whites.
But whiteness preeminently gained active significance as a feature of
their identity when they were challenged in biracial contexts.[39]

     As social aggregates, whites and blacks in this neighborhood are
diverse and distended associations, but they do not materialize into
reified, spatial orders. Instead, race is a matter of scattered instances
and inexorable histories. Both whites and blacks resisted narrating the
conflicts that arose between neighbors as being of racial origin. The
most consistent generalizing phrase I heard from people of both races
was that "there's good and bad in everybody." Or as Bill, a black man
in his sixties, explained to me, "Peoples is like dogs: there some you
get along with, and there some you're born to fight. Can't change
that." Such distinctions between people "you get along with" and those
"you're born to fight" often fall within racial categories rather than
characterizing the difference between two collectives, which leaves
the significance of race open to varying interpretations. Such benign
renderings would evaporate, on occasion, in conflicts that had become racialized by one or both parties, but racial polarization was not
sustainable for long because the social worlds and economic circumstances of whites and blacks in this area were too intermeshed.

     The members of this "hillbilly" family showed no consistent attitude concerning blacks. Just distinguishing between and explaining the range of understandings and experiences of each of the three brothers regarding blacks would require more space than this essay allows. David was aloof from the rest of the family. He was going to school to get a cosmetology degree, and he made a point of emphasizing his disgust and distrust of his brothers whenever possible. He was also usually quite emphatic in his contempt for blacks. Sam, while at times quite suspicious of blacks generally, and prone to bitter racial sentiments, was the one brother who most emphasized the importance of moments of racial transcendence when they occurred. He cared, too, about specifying how he developed a sense racial animosity, rather than have me think that he was just raised that way.

Late one night, Sam and I were sitting out in the yard. In the few weeks that I had known him, he had dissected for me the roots of his suspicion toward blacks. It began in elementary school with being shaken down daily for his lunch money by black kids who controlled the bridge over the freeway that led to their school. Other childhood recollections centered on trying to get back home from Tiger Stadium and being chased by black kids through these very streets. "Every year we'd go up there on Bat Day, and not once did we make it back to Canfield with those bats. When they caught us, they'd beat us up and take them bats." He had a number of tales of being "jumped" by black youths, which resonated with those told by his brothers and other whites who grew up in that neighborhood. But that night what came to mind for him was a warning to me, a prediction drenched in memories, a past that continued to return. He began explaining to me the formula that produced racial violence, describing how he had been caught up in its inexorably arbitrary logic. The times he had been "jumped" were mainly on those hot summer nights when people are irritable and reckless. "It's quiet now," he noted, looking down Martin Luther King Jr. Avenue. "But one of these nights, it's gonna be too hot to sleep. A bunch of them are gonna come down that street looking to kick your ass. They don't know you, but they're looking for you. It's happened to me, it'll happen to you too if you stay here long enough. One of these hot nights, they're gonna come right down that street." Sam's wariness developed from his particular past rather than drawing on an essentialized sense of otherized difference. For Sam, racial antagonism was a contextual order; individual relations did little to obviate the relentlessly volatile nature of arbitrary racial violence; all one could do was "watch out."[40]

As vulnerable as they were to sporadic racial violence, I was surprised to find that this induced no general sense of solidarity between whites in the area. In fact, these "hillbillies" were more animatedly detached from other whites than they were from many black families. One afternoon a couple of weeks later, while we were sitting out on the porch, I asked Jerry about a white family that lived around the corner. He disgustedly snarled, "They're a bunch of assholes. Well, Tommy's alright, and so is Billy if he ain't drunk. They all hang out at O'Leary's some, but they just go down there looking to fight. They get stupid and make trouble. They're a bunch of assholes. The grandfather, old man Johnson, he's all right; he'd talk to you. But watch out for the rest of them." I almost laughed when I heard Jerry's response. Since I had moved in, other whites had warned me about Jerry's family, and in particular, told me, "Don't trust Jerry." While unknown blacks might present a degree of uncertainty for Jerry and his brother, the depth of distrust or contempt reserved for fellow whites was typically profound and intense.

During the course of my fieldwork I realized that conflicts in this zone tended to follow family divides: the largest embroilments were produced when family members were drawn into conflicts in defense or support of their relatives. The repercussion of such conflicts produced elaborate fractures and rifts among residents in the neighborhood, such as that between Jerry and his brothers and the white family that lived around the corner. What this dynamic reveals is that the strength of family solidarity, here, problematizes any stable, collective notion of racial allegiance. The "family" is ostensibly a racial site, and yet it erodes any certain larger sense of racial commonality because it demands a sense of allegiance that is much more compelling than any notion of a shared whiteness. The many differences generated by past conflicts prevented whites from finding a basis for enacting a solidarity that might have provided the basis for a collective identity. Along with the fact that they resided with and among blacks, their preference for responding to conflicts as family members was yet another reason why whiteness was rarely objectified as a shared racial order in this zone.

This is not to say that there were no similarities among the white residents. The sense of a displaced regional identity was strong among the whites with connections to the South. Some traveled "back home" to register their cars and to visit families with regularity; they also received visiting family members who came north for a weekend or longer. But another common condition for these white families was the extent to which they were divided from their own family members by the city's boundaries. I had expected the city limits to uniquely signify a racial divide separating black from white, but for these inner-city whites, the borders of Detroit predominantly indicated a stark class division. Detroit's population peaked around 1952; its hemorrhaging of people has been largely steady since then.[41] Over time, as the city limits have been increasingly racialized, those who left have grown more estranged from both their old neighborhoods and their own family members who still reside here. Broadly speaking, class mobility marks the difference between whites who stayed in this zone and those who left, but an interesting racial significance has developed as well regarding this relocation of whites.

Late one evening, after it had become too dark for Jerry to keep working on the ruptured fuel line on his Gremlin, we slipped into a long conversation about family. At the moment, he was furious with his brother Sam, who was living in the house rent free. The landlord had finally realized that Jerry had allowed Sam and his family to live there on the sly. Though Jerry had bought him several free months by fooling the landlord, now, when the game was up, Sam was still refusing to any gesture toward paying rent. This conflict played out over the next month and a half, but that night it got Jerry and Jessi Rae, who joined us in the yard, talking about raising kids and strained family relations. On the matter of discipline, Jerry was proud of the restraint he had shown with their kids.

> *Jerry:* Those kids got only five whippings between 'em their whole lives. That's it. Just five. That was enough. After that I could just raise my voice and they listened.
> *Jessi Rae:* Well kids know, if you don't raise your voice you don't really mean it.
> *Jerry:* Just five whippings. I never beat them up or slapped them around cause that ain't right. And they minded, too. And my brothers and sisters were all the time giving me shit, saying they were gonna grow up all fucked up cause we lived in Detroit. Barry was the worst of them. He was saying, "Your boys gonna be in the pen, and your daughter's gonna be a nigger lover." [Jerry's face drew into a sneer as he repeated his brother's predictions.]
> *Jessi Rae:* That's right, he said she'd grow up to be a nigger lovin' whore.
> *Jerry:* That's what he said. And every one of them have given us

shit about staying here. They all live in the suburbs and they shit
on us because we never left. We never left the inner city of Detroit.
We never tried to, either. We've never lived any more than a few
blocks from where we grew up. Those kids grew up between here
and Third and Alexandrine. We never left this city. And those kids
all went to the Detroit schools, and they all turned out fine.

For Jerry's brothers who left Detroit, his position challenged notions of racial allegiance that might have been based on family ties.
The term "nigger lover" makes their offended sense of racialness clear.
With one exception, the only time I heard this term used in Detroit was
in the context of midst of arguments between local whites and those
from beyond the city's boundaries. To whites like Jerry, the term was
no more offensive, it seemed, than a host of other insults that could
be applied: if he was ready to fight anyway, then any mode of name-
calling offered sufficient cause. But "nigger lover" points to a reservoir
of anger and confusion felt strongly by whites who left the city toward
those who stayed behind. While his brothers' fears of (and disgust
for) blacks were so great that they left the city, Jerry stayed because
he loved the area, David stayed because it was cheap, and Sam came
and went ambivalently. The three brothers remained for reasons that
are not "racial," but their brothers left for reasons that predominantly
involve race and the felt need to reestablish a sense of whiteness in a
more homogeneous zone.[42]

While whites' motivation for leaving the city significantly involves
race, it also complexly and inextricably involves a sense of class division. While the range of sentiment among Jerry and his brothers regarding race is interesting, Jerry was far more concerned with the great
degree of class variation that had developed within his family. When
Jerry recounted Barry's predictions, it was the classed tones of contempt his brother articulated that bothered him deeply. While Jerry
survived on various hustles, government checks, and his work as a
"bouncer" at the corner grocery store; Sam was regularly out of work;
Sam's wife was a cook at a fast food restaurant in Taylor, a thirteen-
mile drive each way. But several of the other brothers had "made
good." Barry had taken a job training program while he was on welfare, started in a maintenance job for a large hotel firm, and worked his
way up to being in charge of maintenance for the company in this region. Another brother supposedly held a management-level position at
a large brewing company. Barry stopped by Jerry's when he needed his

cars worked on; the only other times I saw the suburban brothers were when their mother, who still lived in Detroit, was either sick or celebrating a birthday. What kept the other brothers away was not simply a contempt for the racial order in the city, but also Jerry's generally degraded class position, which recalled their own meager beginnings.

I heard from many other whites in the neighborhood that, for them, the city limits form a class divide that sunders their ties with family members who have "moved up in the world." Betty, a white woman in her late fifties, lives with her brother in one of the old worker's cottages that were thrown up all over this area in the 1880s to meet the city's burgeoning demands for "affordable housing" in the last century. Aside from her brother, the rest of her family lives in the suburbs, "Way out there. They never come to visit us. They've got their noses up in the air, y'know what I mean. They won't come down here anymore." One afternoon I was helping her put signs up on the abandoned houses, warning that "This house is being watched"; Devil's Night was approaching.[43] She reeled off stories about the past occupants of each of the houses that now stood vacant and ruined. Between the mostly burnt abandoned houses and the hundreds of lots now turned to prairie grass, the "old neighborhood" has changed drastically since the rest of her family left. "They never want to come down here, anymore. They just can't stand it. 'It's gross,'" she mimicked. "'It's gross.' They're terrible." She cannot understand her sisters' attitudes because they were all raised in this neighborhood. "They even went to school here, too." But they refuse to come back, apparently not wanting to be reminded of their humble beginnings.

Now, she only sees the family on rare occasions, "like weddings." The last time had been at the funeral for one of her sisters. "See, we don't have a car, so we can't get out there. And they won't come and visit us." Betty said that at the funeral, "We wanted to leave, cause we couldn't take anymore. So we asked if somebody could give us a ride. Well, my brother-in-law tells someone to tell us that he'll give us the money to take a cab. Can you believe that? I just told them to tell him 'We don't need your money,' then we just left." They never returned any of Betty's calls. "I believe my sister always made him call before, but now he just doesn't want to talk to us."

These instances demonstrate that family and kin groups are more than little social factories, where ideological orders are homogeneously reproduced or replicated. The content and function of this *site* varies depending on its location and position.[44] Perhaps in more homogeneous racial zones, this site generates social units with little variation, and the children inherit their parents' belief structure fairly intact. But even in such zones, the family is also the site in which social relations are magnified and changing experiences are examined, manipulated, and contested collectively. The family is never a static entity; members are typically added and lost over time, through birth and death, but also through various social relationships such as adoption, friendship, and marriage. What makes this site continually mutable is the variety of shifting social relationships that it grounds.

An interesting aspect of the role of families in constituting racial formations is that they fuse temporal and spatial orders. The racial materiality that composes a family is distended across a given past that cannot be perfectly replicated, a present in which members synthesize copious social relations and experiences as a group, and a future into which their given social materiality is refracted and extended through births, adoptions, and marriages. In other words, family is as much a process as it is an abstract cultural site. This essay cannot provide an exhaustive account of family; this site is too volatile and mutable. But I do want to stress the critical basis that family provides for racial formations, even if this site is inconsistently racially homogeneous in terms of past, present, or future relations. With this in mind, I turn now to a brief discussion of the role that adoption plays for families in this zone. Partly because of the general economic instability, families here dissolve, leaving younger members either to fend for themselves or to be (legally or informally) adopted into extant families. This process is a generative source for the racial heterogeneity of this zone.

ESTHER

One of the first people Jerry introduced me to at O'Leary's was Esther, a white woman in her late forties. Jerry affectionately referred to her as "mom." She was a well-regarded regular at the bar, with an elaborate network of social relations that she developed over a lifetime spent in this neighborhood. I later interviewed her on a hot and miserable day while she was on vacation from her job of cooking and washing dishes at a west-side club.

Esther embodies many of the dynamics involving adoption in the "hood." She told me her father "sold" her to a family moving to Florida when she was a child. In Florida, she got pregnant at age thirteen. When her adopted mother took her baby and gave it up for adoption, Esther left in a fury and came back to her family in Detroit. She has never seen that child or her adopted family since. Though several of her siblings live a few blocks away and even frequent the same bar, she tries to avoid them. "They only live right there on Butternut, but I only see them twice a year. Because, I mean, it's just gossip all the time: Who did this and who did that, and 'They ain't no good,' when they [her family] ain't no damn better." Although Esther remains disgusted with "living in the ghetto," she considers her family "is used to living like that. My family wouldn't give a shit if there was a roof over their heads or not."

Esther had eight children, three stillborn, and she adopted one of her brother's daughters after he and his wife gave up on raising the child. She was raising her "black" grandson, Jason, because her adopted daughter became "too wild" to care for him. Esther stays generally detached from her children. Only one son "got away" from the life that she hates so much. The others terrify or disgust her to varying degrees; she said they were too involved with drugs and crime.

"When it gets to the point that you start fearing your own kids, you don't need 'em around. And I wouldn't put nothing past them. My adopted daughter has been in prison three times for murder and got out of it; she got acquitted each time. They didn't believe that she could've done it—she's so small. But I knew she did it. I knew."

I asked her how she thought race mattered in this area.

"Down here? Well, there's a lot of mixed families—a lot. A lot of young girls . . . I think . . . to me, it has to be attention, it's got to do with attention. Because, a lot of times . . . because I've got it in my family, all my grandkids, most of them are all mixed. And it seems like it's their way of being noticed, if they're walking down the street with a black man. Because, it's just like my grandson, he's black. When we go somewhere and people hear him call me 'Ma,' they look. Y'know, cause he don't call me his grandmother, he calls me his ma. Y'know, people just look."

For Esther, in this case, race matters as a function of almost involuntary attention to an irreducible physical condition. Racial differences are accentuated in these couples that she sees as being drawn together because of race, not in spite of it. Race also mattered for Esther regarding her daughters' relations with black men, because the product of these unions had racialized her. The racial aspect of her reading is distinct, but it is subsumed within a more fundamental class logic of treating all social relations as manipulative.[45] As she continued, Esther described how her daughters' relationships had increasingly racialized her, largely against her will, it seemed. This surprised me, since I had noticed that her elaborate friendship network included many neighborhood blacks, mostly women.

> *Esther:* It just kinda makes you . . . Y'know, some of my best friends are black, but we don't get into all of that, y'know. It just irritates the shit out of me sometimes. It just makes me prejudiced in a way.
> *JH:* How so?
> *Esther:* It makes you kind of prejudiced against the black guy using the white girl. A lot of times the blacks use the whites.
> *JH:* In what way?
> *Esther:* A lot of black men use white women. Y'know, they just go . . . 'I got me a white bitch,' that's what the whole thing is about. They're useless to them, unless you're gonna go out and make him some money. That's about the way it goes.
> *JH:* Do you see that a lot?
> *Esther:* Oh yeah, with a lot of the young girls that hang out at the bar. I've got nothing against the races, its just, don't use people. And that's the way it goes. Like my one daughter, she won't go with nothing but a black man. It just irritates the shit out of me [she laughed].
> *JH:* Because you feel she's being used?
> *Esther:* No. She likes attention. My daughter thinks she's God's gift to man, y'know. She's got three kids and they all got three different black men for daddies.
> *JH:* That's Jason's mom?
> *Esther:* No, but she's got three kids too, all by different fathers. I've got eight grandchildren and none of them are by the same father. I'm talking about the girls, they're the ones having the babies, and each one has a different father. And then they give 'em all different last names; that's what irritates me too. If you're not married to him, why not at least give them the name you carry? These kids have got to go to school, and this one over here has got a different last name than this one, so how can we be brothers and sisters? And that irritates me.

For Esther, the "races" coming together did nothing to eliminate racial differences; the differences were only accentuated. But it is worth noting that when she considered the offspring of these relations, the confusion over family that bothered her was not that the grandchildren were different colors, but that they all had different names.[46] Her daughters' patronymic choices had left her disturbingly and legalistically estranged from the grandchildren that she was increasingly being called on to care for. In addition to the confusion of connections between the children, she also complained of bureaucratic problems arising when she had to sign their report cards or authorize any kind of medical care for them because she shared no family name with any of them. It was not the range of racial content that made their connection problematic, but that the familial basis that could process that range of difference had, from a bureaucratic perspective, been undermined.

Her "irritation," though, did involve race, just not so much in terms of personal opinion. While Esther was comfortable with her relations with blacks within the neighborhood, caring for her daughters' "black" children had put her into situations that not only racialized her, but racialized her perceptions involuntarily to the point that it became harder for her to have race not matter: "It makes you kind of prejudiced." She could will good relations with blacks her own age and her own gender, but other relations were outside her control.[47] Even though she was estranged from her parents and siblings, she encountered the racially productive site of family in another generation. The generational shift had taken her out of her place in the neighborhood and moved her into problematic institutional settings.

Esther described how she had to deal with the verbal taunts of blacks student whenever she went to one of the schools to deal with one of her grandkids. The Detroit public schools are even more racially absolute sites than is the city in general.[48] "No white person wants to go up to that school for their kid," she told me. "I've had problems up there before . . . Well, the kids, they call you names and all: 'You're all this. You're "snowflake,"' and me, I get pissed, and I say, 'Okay chocolate drop' [she laughed]. So, and then it starts confusion, so I try to stay away from it."

Relating to her grandchildren racialized her because it brought her into zones where only her racialness would be read; attending to her "black" grandchildren made her whiter even though she promoted no notion of racial superiority. It is notable that in such heterogeneous family sites, race retained an indelible content, no more diluted than if these members were in homogeneous family groups. This point is clear from the suspicion that Esther bore for both members of biracial couples. The issue of "attention" played both ways for her. She felt both sides were using the other race, though in unequal fashion based on gender differences. The fact of the racial union was not annoying, but the forms of manipulation she thought it embodied did "irritate" her.

> *JH:* The attention you mentioned before, where is that coming from mostly, other whites, other blacks?
> *Esther:* Well, no, it's . . . them theirselves. What it is, is they like to get noticed. So if you take a real fair-skinned white girl with bleached blonde hair and you stick her with a man that's black as tar, people are going to look! And they like this, they like this. The white girls like this! I mean, it's your choice, do whatever you're gonna do. Just don't do it for the wrong reasons.

For Esther, the complexity of their racialness (hers, her daughters', their children's) had expanded exponentially. Where as an individual she could efface the significance of race with her friends ("we don't get into that stuff"), as a family member she had become racialized in a manner outside her control or will, both by her nurturing role and by the positions in which it placed her. She was put into positions where she was out of place and subjected to the judgment: "You're all this." This was in stark contrast to social scenes in the bar, where black and white differences were more malleable matters and subject to discussion.

And in General?

In our efforts to analyze, dissect, and repudiate whiteness, it is critical that we keep in mind the problem of scale in relating to this racial construct. Jerry and Esther deal with and experience whiteness on a scale that is completely alien to most white Americans. This alienness is structured by their poverty, their social origins, and their position within the vastly black city of Detroit. Their modes of engagement with whiteness, in turn, differ in ways too numerous to adequately account. However, the phrases recounted here resonate with common tropes and discursive tacks of whites across the United States. Esther's phrase "some of my best friends are black" is the clearest example. But unlike most whites who speak this phrase, in addition to such friends Esther also has black grandchildren to tend to, and in the case of Jason, singly raise. For Esther, the fact of having "black friends" did not—as most often is the case when whites make this claim—assert that race is unimportant. Rather, it marked racialness as a mode of cultural significance that whites and blacks ineptly or deftly struggle with daily. Notably, it is not a point that Jerry was compelled to mention in our discussion of race relations. He did not reify his black friends and neighbors as a counterweight to his racial view of this zone. But this should not suggest that there is a qualitative distinction between his opinions on race and Esther's. It is not just the content and discursive character of her statement that matters, but the position and context in which it was articulated.

Esther noted of her black friends that "we don't get into all of that" about race. This phrase, like Bill's naturalizing comment comparing people's animosities to those of dogs, seems to be a form of avoiding race altogether—a discursive move that Ruth Frankenberg has shown is characteristic of white people's public assessments of race. But what do we make of the resonances between the comments of Bill, a black man, and Esther, a white woman? They are similar soundings of a domain in which race is every day in everybody's face. Race is something to be effaced in this inner-city zone where street violence is commonplace, where residents strive to find means of undermining motivating impulses that can polarize ambiguous or even accidental social exchanges. Where people find ample incitement to violence, "race" is just one excuse that black and white residents generally prefer to defuse, lest a conflict between individuals bleed into collective matters. Rather than a form of avoiding race, such comments are a means of restraining the significance of racialness from becoming too abstract and totalizing.

It is tempting to conclude with a sweeping point such as, "In a cultural regard, race is a materiality largely outside the control of individuals; its significance manifests in social relations and settings that an individual can attempt to manipulate, but are as often objects of others' manipulations." This would be an overly broad generalization. More to the point is that racial matters, like other social materials, are manipulable to varying degrees depending on a host of contexts and one's class position. What matters with race is as much a person's class position as his or her individual "opinions" and choices of whom to relate with. Locating class, geographically and in terms of structures of significance, is a simultaneous and overlapping function of locating racialness in general and whiteness in particular. The point of this essay is to offer a perspective on the ambiguous contexts and exchanges that are easily overwhelmed by modes of analysis that abstract the significance of racial matters too broadly.

My fieldwork convinced me that however whiteness may be regarded at the level of greatest expanse (ideology, for instance), no continuous motivating or informing impulse can be traced down through the various levels of increasing specificity with absolute consistency. Nor, in the obverse, can we compile a more or less thorough aggregate of whites, abstract out from them a common condition or an intrinsic set of connections, and have neatly defined by these efforts a succinct, abiding identity—whiteness. In each domain or level (nation, region, city, neighborhood, block, house, and yard) the material conditions of whites exhibit degrees of incomparability with those of other levels: the difference between whiteness and whites, in its continual repetition, assures an irregular terrain in which some whites always sit insecurely in the larger body of whiteness. At each level, the gap between whiteness and whites opens distinct horizons of social and political contexts. An attempt to map all of these would be stymied by the daunting task of proposing a unified means of mapping whites and whiteness into a range of domains in some standard, proportional relation to each other, and under consistent forms of magnification.

Instead of generating such a map, I will conclude by way of reinflecting a popular mythic image—the melting pot, that long-active paradigm of Americanization that envisioned a continuous stream of conventionalized, homogeneous products/citizens. In a sense, Detroit put the idea of the melting pot on the map of this nation's cultural imagination. The image, after all, is an industrial one. It was never simply an insidious ideology promoted by progressive business leaders and capitalists who required an efficient means for assimilating the great stream of foreign immigrants and black and white migrants from the rural South who poured into U.S. cities looking for work. The melting pot was a material, pervasive reality for those workers, and the very basis of the industrial order that drew them to the great northern cities. In the steel mills, coke plants, and smelting operations, they worked where the raw materials were melted, blended, pressed, forged, and produced into the infrastructure of the swelling consumer economy. For these workers, the image "made sense" at a more mundane level than could ever have been fully recognized or manipulated by publicists for the industrial order. Rather than an elusive object of desire, the melting pot was a livelihood, an unending argument and responsibility, a relentless, dangerous occupation.

The melting pot was largely a paradigm of ethnic rather than racial melding; its operations primarily involved smelting the array of cultures brought from across the Atlantic into one seamless body of efficient, unmarked labor. As the vicious conflicts that unfolded in plants and on shop floors in Detroit attest, blacks did not fit easily into this scheme of things.[49] The process of molding and fusing foreign workers' bodies into expendable components of the production process involved a mode of racial reproduction that required blackness to remain an indigestible embodiment of otherness. Through decades of struggle and conflict, though, the melting pot, in cities like Detroit, was grudgingly made to include and produce black workers as well.

Whatever is finally decided about the relative worth of that operation, whether the mode of assimilation that the melting pot provided was of positive or negative value to the Irish, Poles, Hungarians, Appalachians, and others who fell under its sway, the image is now defunct.[50] Detroit, once the symbol of America's industrial order, is now the image turned to by social commentators who want to demonstrate the tragic effects of deindustrialization.[51] In this desolate condition, Detroit remains charged mythic ground, symbolizing for whites in the nation at large both the unsalvageable refuse of the "underclass" left in the wake of the speeding new high-tech, "postindustrial" economy, and the shambles wrought by black civic self-rule. The future represented by Detroit differs distinctly from that of Los Angeles, a city similar in history and contemporary conflicts.[52] Where Los Angeles becomes the site for techno-conflicts by cyborgs in defense of humanity, as in *Terminator II*, the population of Detroit is subjected to the unrestrained lethal onslaught of the corporate cleansing agent, *Robo-Cop*. Aside from its mythic status as a playground for antipopulation technologies, deindustrialized Detroit can also be read figuratively, in the key of racial allegorizing, for a different emerging present and future. Detroit—in its deindustrialized condition, with the forges and furnaces shuttered and abandoned—also represents a current condition of racial material; it is no longer smelted or processed into homogeneous, purified metals, but remains heterogeneous, distended, and extractable from its location only at great cost.[53]

Notes

The research on which this essay is based was supported by a generous grant from the Social Science Research Council. I also thank the Guggenheim Foundation and the Smithsonian Institution for providing supporting grants while I was writing this essay. Many people helped me improve this essay through their engaging criticisms. Thanks to Donna Haraway, Susan Harding, Kathleen Stewart, Matt Wray, Marvette Perez, members of the Southeastern Michigan Study Group (particularly Charlie Bright, Andrea Sankar, and Deb Jackson), and Ruth Frankenberg, both for her research and for her insightful editing advice!

1   Each of these communities features largely white populations, though the census tract that encompasses the underclass neighborhood is predominantly black. In this essay I focus primarily on this underclass zone and its boundaries with the adjacent, gentrifying area. A fuller account of how the significance of whiteness is variously articulated in distinct class formations is detailed in my work, *Cultural Constructions of Whiteness,* (Princeton: Princeton University Press, forthcoming).

2   The notion of "region" for ethnography is hardly an objectively given unit. As Richard Fardon notes in *Localizing Strategies: The Regional Traditions of Ethnographic Writing* (Edinburgh: Scottish Academic Press, 1990), "the inscription of locality has been one of the more complex results of the history of ethnography." On the one hand, regions are political and economic constructs, following administrative delineations and academic divisions of labor. On the other hand, regions are areas that cohere according to "the terms on which members of a host culture allowed the ethnographer to know them" (22). Fardon argues that anthropological "research has not consisted of an encounter between a fieldworker and 'the Other,' but the nuanced continuation and modification of a relation between an approach delineating a region and the people who live within it" (25).

3   Marilyn Strathern, *Partial Connections* (Savage, Md.: Rowman and Littlefield, 1991).

4   Ibid., xxvii.

5   My stress on the uneven reproduction and experience of whiteness echoes that of Eric Lott in *Love and Theft: Blackface Minstrelsy and the American Working Class* (Oxford: Oxford University Press, 1993), who found in blackface minstrelsy a fractious white racial subjectivity that varied by region and was particularly animated and confused by transgressions of the color line in the urban centers of the North in the last century.

6   Strathern follows James Glick by invoking the model of Cantor's dust to describe scaling phenomena.

7   Michael Omi and Howard Winant, *Racial Formation in the United States: From the 1960's to the 1980's* (New York: Routledge, 1986).

8   Ibid., 61–62.

9   This notion of bringing greater regional specificity to racial analytics is not exactly novel, and it precedes social construction of race models. Anthropologist Stanley Garn delineates between "geographical," "local," and "micro" races in *Human Race* (Springfield, Ill.: Charles Thomas, 1961).

10   I examine the demographic basis of these transformations in urban settings in more detail in "When Whites Are a Minority," in *Cultural Diversity in the United States,* ed. Larry Naylor (Westport, Conn.: Bergin and Garvey, 1997), 103–15.

11   Omi and Winant, *Racial Formation,* 66–67.

12   While Omi and Winant's demarcation of micro- and macrolevels of racial orders are meant to be generally inclusive, and though the authors do not specifically exclude "family" from their definition of *collectivity,* I feel that family marks a level of phenomena between those they list that needs to be specified in this analysis.

13   Families have been a key analytical site for arguing about the significance of race

in American culture at least since the Moynihan Report (see Lee Rainwater and William Yancey, *The Moynihan Report and the Politics of Controversy* [Cambridge: MIT Press, 1967]). Following criticisms of ethnographic studies of this topic and critiques of notions such as the culture of poverty, anthropologists broke off their engagement with policy discussions concerning the "Negro family." But there are still important insights to be gained from fieldworkers' accounts of this critical site. David Schneider and Raymond Smith, in their study of poor Afro-American, southern white, and Spanish American families living in Chicago, make the case that kinship patterns are identical across these ethnoracial groupings. The fundamental aspect of their commonality as a lower-class culture emerges in contrast with kinship patterns of middle-class culture. See *Class Differences and Family Structure* (Englewood Cliffs, N.J.: Prentice-Hall, 1973).

14   Additionally, the location of the family in the home brings into focus another fundamental ground on which racial orders are constructed. One of the critical material inscriptions of race in the post–World War II era has been real estate. Though ostensibly geographic in nature, real estate conflates several distinct domains, such as family and economy. See the chapter "Homegrown Revolution" in Mike Davis, *City of Quartz: Excavating the Future in Los Angeles* (New York: Vintage Books, 1992).

15   Since my work is concentrated on the "underclass," I tend to follow William Julius Wilson in laying a primary stress on class and the increasing intraracial polarization along economic lines. See his works, *The Declining Significance of Race: Blacks and Changing American Institutions* (Chicago: University of Chicago Press, 1978), and *The Truly Disadvantaged: The Inner City, the Underclass, and Public Policy* (Chicago: University of Chicago Press, 1987). I address the political and theoretical issues of including whites in the urban underclass in "Green Ghettoes and the White Underclass," *Social Research* 64; no. 2 (1997).

16   Anthropologists are highlighting the heterogeneity of racial constructs from a number of critical perspectives. See Ann Stoler, "Making Empire Respectable: The Politics of Race and Sexual Morality in 20th Century Colonial Cultures," *American Ethnologist* 16, no. 4 (1989): 634–60; Winthrop Wright, *Cafe Con Leche: Race, Class, and National Image in Venezuela* (Austin: University of Texas Press, 1990); Brackette Williams, *Stains on My Name, War in My Veins: Guyana and the Politics of Cultural Struggle* (Durham: Duke University Press, 1991); Joel Streicker, "Policing Boundaries: Race, Class, and Gender in Cartagena, Colombia," *American Ethnologist* 22, no. 1 (1995): 54–74. I examine the complex tradition of ethnographers' engagements and avoidance of the issues surrounding whiteness in "Establishing the Fact of Whiteness," *American Anthropologist*. 99, no. 2 (June 1997).

17   I use the term *racialness* to indicate how race operates as a form of cultural materiality that is read in shifting contexts and against varying backgrounds of significance. In relation to both whiteness and blackness, racialness is a means of drawing attention to the possibilities of racially reading individuals when the collective character of distinct races in certain locales is mutable and unstable.

18   The title of this section is from the front of a T-shirt one of the white men I lived with wore occasionally. On the back, the shirt read: "now get yo' ass out of here."

19   My use of "black" here follows the local, preferred means of self-identification. A survey conducted by the *Detroit Free Press* (October 12, 1992) suggests a clear,

emerging generational divide concerning preferences for "African American" over "black": 46 percent of blacks in Detroit under age thirty-five preferred "African American," and 37 percent chose "black." Those over age thirty-five preferred "black" by a two-to-one margin (48 percent to 24 percent).

20   Though blackness is hegemonic in Detroit, its significance to or extension over all blacks is hardly a given. This was clear in the city's most recent mayoral election. The contest pitted two black opponents, Dennis Archer and Sharon McPhail, vying to replace the longtime, also black, mayor, Coleman Young. When Archer's blackness was called into question, first by Young and subsequently by McPhail and other civic leaders who tried to suggest that he was a pawn of white suburban interests, the local media referred to this tactic as "injecting race into the campaign," as if, before these comments, the unitary "color" of the campaigners precluded the presence or significance of race. McPhail's apparent strategy of trying to establish herself as "the black candidate" seemed to follow the contours of the mayoral race in Cleveland in 1989, when George Forbes tried to "out-black" his black opponent, Michael White, who was a state senator at the time. Like McPhail, Forbes lost that race.

21   See Douglass Massey and Nancy Denton, *American Apartheid: Segregation and the Making of the Underclass* (Cambridge: Harvard University Press, 1993).

22   Mary Douglas, *Purity and Danger: An Analysis of Concepts of Pollution and Taboo* (New York: Praeger, 1966).

23   This figure was reported in "City Caught in Trash Avalanche," *Detroit Free Press,* July 4, 1993.

24   *Detroit Free Press,* June 8, 1993.

25   *Detroit Free Press,* June 12, 1993, and June 14, 1993. In a related event, promoters of the Detroit Grand Prix held the following week on the island drew a storm of protests over a poster produced to announce the event. The poster was based on a painting by George Seurat that features a crowd of people taking in a sunny afternoon at a park. Over the image was a picture of the Detroit skyline, and in the foreground, a strip of roadway and several Formula One cars had been added. The *Detroit Free Press* for June 27, 1993, reported that "the creators of the poster were stunned when some black Detroiters objected to the poster for the Belle Isle event because it showed only white people."

26   The per capita income for white families ($7,132) was slightly less than for black families ($7,193) in this census tract, though the percentage of whites with incomes below the poverty line (39.5) was not as large as for blacks (52.1), according to the 1990 Census.

27   Reported by News Service, March 22, 1996.

28   The charged stigma of being both poor and white in the inner city is treated in detail by Jay MacLeod in *Ain't No Makin' It: Leveled Aspirations in a Low-Income Neighborhood* (Boulder: Westview Press, 1987). MacLeod studied two groups of youths in a low-income urban housing development, one white and the other black. The white group (the Hallway Hangers) was the central focus of his study because they so consistently expressed and enacted a near total sense of being forever mired at the bottom of this country's economic order. Just as consistently, the black teenagers (the Brothers) were animated by the achievement ideology operating broadly in the United States. Race played a multifaceted, critical role in these groups' divergent views and experiences. MacLeod summarizes this role as follows:

The Hallway Hangers reject the achievement ideology because most of them are white. Whereas poor blacks have racial discrimination to which they can point as a cause of their family's poverty, for the Hallway Hangers to accept the achievement ideology is to admit that their parents are lazy or stupid or both. Thus, the achievement ideology not only runs counter to the experiences of the Hallway Hangers, but is also a more serious assault on their self-esteem. Acceptance of the ideology on the part of the Brothers does not necessarily involve such harsh implications, for they can point to racial prejudice to explain their parents' defeats. The severe emotional toll that belief in the achievement ideology exacts on poor whites relative to poor blacks explains why the Hallway Hangers dismiss the ideology while the Brothers validate it. (129–30)

While the Brothers, too, are burdened with the "abnegations of the dominant society," "the achievement ideology represents a more potent assault on the Hallway Hangers because as white youths, they can point to no extenuating circumstances to account for their poverty. The subculture of the Hallway Hangers is in part a response to the stigma they feel as poor, white Americans" (133–34).

29   "Poor whites" derives from the confusion among researchers over whether class or race is more important for identifying these whites. As Michael Maloney asks: "What conceptual framework do we use in studying urban Appalachians: ethnicity, race, or class? The concept of 'poor white' implies both race and class, while the concept of 'working class' could imply an approach across racial and ethnic lines. The concept of 'Appalachian' ethnicity has been used for a combination of pragmatic and philosophical reasons too complex to discuss here, and the concept of 'minority group' has also been used by Appalachian advocates." Maloney's ambivalence regarding the suitability of all these terms is something we share. See his essay "A Decade in Review: The Development of the Ethnic Model in Urban Appalachian Studies," in *Too Few Tomorrows: Urban Appalachians in the 1980's*, ed. Phillip Obermiller and William Philliber (Boone, N.C.: Appalachian Consortium Press, 1987).

30   These modes of interest are linked to distinct traditions of name-calling. I deal with this range of attentions toward this strata of whites in "Name Calling: Objectifying 'Poor Whites' and 'White Trash' in Detroit," in *White Trash: Race and Class in America,* ed. Matt Wray and Annalee Newitz (New York: Routledge, 1997), 41–56.

31   The Irish are a key group through which the foundations and contours of developing constructions of whiteness can be traced historically. Irish parades in the United States are key sites for the performance and objectification of racial and ethnic consciousness. See Kenneth Moss, "St. Patrick's Day Celebrations and the Formation of Irish-American Identity, 1845–1875," *Journal of Social History* 29, no. 1 (1995): 125–48; "'Why Should We Care for a Little Trouble or a Walk through Mud': St. Patrick's and Columbus Day Parades in Worcester, Massachusetts," *New England Quarterly* 58, no. 1 (March 1985): 5–26; and Sallie Marston, "Public Rituals and Community Power, St. Patrick's Day Parade in Lowell, Massachusetts, 1841–1874," *Political Geography Quarterly* 8, no. 3 (July 1989): 255–69.

32   See Phyllis Chock, "The Irony of Stereotypes: Toward an Anthropology of Ethnicity," *Cultural Anthropology* 2 no. 3 (1987): 347–68.

33   The term *hood* was used by young blacks and some whites in this area. Whites like Jerry used it with playfully ironic inflections in referring to their neighborhood.

34   Urban Appalachians complicate a number of scholarly models and popular stereotypes of inner-city poverty. See *The Invisible Minority: Urban Appalachians,* ed.

William Philliber and Clyde McCoy (Lexington: University of Kentucky Press, 1981); William Philliber, *Appalachian Migrants in Urban America: Cultural Group or Ethnic Group Formation?* (New York: Praeger, 1981); *Too Few Tomorrows: Urban Appalachians in the 1980's,* ed. Phillip Obermiller and William Philliber (Boone, N.C.: Appalachian Consortium Press, 1987); *From Mountain to Metropolis: Appalachian Migrants in American Cities,* ed. Kathryn Borman and Phillip Obermiller (Westport, Conn.: Bergin and Garvey, 1994).

35   Between 1950 and 1990, Detroit's white population declined by approximately 1.3 million people.

36   I detail the complex usages of "hillbilly" in "Disgrace to the Race: 'Hillbillies' and the Color-Line in Detroit," *Downtown: Urban Appalachians Today,* ed. Phillip Obermiller (Dubuque: Kendall/Hunt, 1996), 55–72.

37   They seemed to be pointing to class differences as much as to being out of place in terms of race. In their later comments they stressed the occupational role, "researcher."

38   Other whites in the area who still walked past the projects while going toward Woodward, Detroit's central avenue, had many stories of being assaulted, verbally or physically, by blacks who lived there.

39   The distinctness of their class position in relation to whiteness is underscored by contrasting their sense of place with that of working-class whites. Sam and David talked about what would happen if they went over "there." They did not talk about blacks coming over "here," which is what sets off the defensive response that characterizes racial conflicts in cities like New York and Boston. This neighborhood in Detroit does not ground a sense of defensive racial community because it is too racially heterogeneous. The contrast is best demonstrated by drawing on Jonathan Rieder's ethnography, *Canarsie: The Jew and Italians of Brooklyn against Liberalism* (Cambridge: Harvard University Press, 1985).

40   I arrived in Detroit after the riots in Los Angeles, so I asked people why they thought there had been no outburst in Detroit, even though other cities around the nation had seen sympathetic outbursts of rage and frustration. In this zone, people in this neighborhood consistently replied that it wasn't hot enough. Michigan experienced its coldest summer on record that year, and whether true or not, the local estimation was that the weather had defused any potential upsurge in violence. Most of the whites in this area had lived through the 1967 riot, which devastated this neighborhood. Their accounts of this riot are featured in my forthcoming book, *Cultural Constructions of Whiteness.*

41   Though the popular narrative regarding Detroit's history is that the city was drained by "white flight," reasons for leaving Detroit were not exclusively racial. The trend of moving factories out of the city began during World War II. After Detroit's population peaked in 1952, the outflow of people followed jobs; this was years before the 1967 riot, which looms large in explanations of the city's depopulation. In 1948 Detroiters held 60.3 percent of the metropolitan area's manufacturing jobs, 72.6 percent of the area's retailing jobs, and 90.1 percent of the employment in the wholesale industry. By 1954, the percentage of these jobs held by Detroiters had already begun to decline noticeably. By 1982, the city had lost more than 185,000 jobs in these three sectors. The depopulation of Detroit and other "postindustrial" cities is as much a reflection of the mobility of capital as it is a function of racial

"flight." The statistics are from Joe Darden et al., *Detroit: Race and Uneven Development* (Philadelphia: Temple University Press, 1987), 19–26.

42   A key register through which the significance of racial categories materializes is through the use of statistics that reveal racial discrepancies in matters such as infant mortality rates, access to institutions, and the availability of mortgages. Opinion surveys generally produce an interesting version of racialness, in that the opinions of the races on particular issues evidence a fundamental heterogeneity along with whatever "significant" attitudes are demonstrated overall. In this regard, I want to call attention to a survey conducted by the University of Michigan in 1992 as part of the Detroit Area Study. One of the questions posed to white respondents involved a series of four residential scenarios. Each scenario presented a fifteen-house "block" with varying degrees of racial integration. The first scenario had only one of the fifteen houses occupied by a black family; the fourth had eight of the fifteen inhabited by blacks (which fairly closely resembles the demographics of this part of Detroit). White respondents were asked if they would feel comfortable in each "block," would they move in, or, if they lived there already, would they move out? Seventy percent of the whites said that they would not move into the area represented in the fourth scenario, and 52 percent responded that if they lived there already, they would move out. If whiteness is exemplified in the sentiments of the 70 percent of whites who were anxious about such living arrangements, then Jerry and the other whites in this neighborhood cannot be said to be participating in the "same" ideological construct or discursive order in any absolute manner.

43   In the 1980s, carrying through to today, Detroit received national attention for the huge number of houses that arsonists burned on Devil's Night. See Ze'ev Chafets, *Devil's Night and Other True Tales of Detroit* (New York: Vintage Press, 1990).

44   I follow Omi and Winant's usage of "site" as "a region of social life with a coherent set of constitutive relations" (*Racial Formation*, 67).

45   One day after I had apparently been ripped off by a friend of his, Jerry explained to me that I had to "watch out" for everybody. I replied, "I thought he was a friend of yours." And Jerry responded, "He is. But see, I only been knowing him five years now. You never know with people."

46   The class contempt of Esther's reflections on her daughters and her grandchildren emerges more clearly in Ruth Frankenberg's analysis of white women's discourses on interracial marriages in *White Women, Race Matters: The Social Construction of Whiteness* (Minneapolis: University of Minnesota Press, 1993). Frankenberg identifies a key aspect of middle- and working-class people's discourse on interracial couples as, instead of openly expressing concern over the union, articulating an anxiety about the social acceptance of the children's "mixed" racial identities. Esther, however, did not fret that her grandchildren would be "an affront to cultural belonging"; rather, she was distressed primarily by the bureaucratic challenges to her familial connections with the children. Also, she did not deploy the virulent images of black men as "primitive," "uncivilized," animalistic predators that Frankenberg found so common among middle-class white women. Another sense of the class difference entailed in this contrast involves the desire for "attention." Frankenberg points to the overwhelming dread on the part of her working-class informant, Sandy Alvarez, of drawing social attention by being part of an interracial couple. If Esther is right about her daughters' desire for attention, a desire perhaps

linked to the numerous "lacks" endured daily by members of the "underclass," then they seem even further removed from the social conditions of working-class white women.

47   Esther's sense of racialness is distinct from that of Jerry and his brothers. While a gendered reading of this difference seems apparent, there are many complexities that would require extensive elaboration for that difference to be established accurately.

48   Eighty-eight percent of Detroit public school students are black (*Detroit Free Press,* January 19, 1992).

49   This history of Detroit is recounted in many works; e.g., August Meirer and Elliot Ruwick, *Black Detroit and the Rise of the UAW* (New York: Oxford University Press, 1979); Dominic Capeci Jr., *Race Relations in Wartime Detroit: The Sojourner Truth Housing Controversy* (Philadelphia: Temple University Press, 1984); Steve Jefferies, "Matters of Mutual Interest: The Unionization Process at Dodge Main, 1933–1939," in *On the Line: Essays in the History of Autowork,* ed. Nelson Lichtenstein and Stephen Meyer (Urbana: University of Illinois Press, 1989).

50   It was, of course, Nathan Glazer and Daniel Moynihan in *Beyond the Melting Pot* (Cambridge: MIT Press, 1963) who first called attention to the "end" of this mythic image. They pointed to the stubborn maintenance of ethnic interests and identities in New York as proof that a homogeneous population was an elusive dream. My reading of the "end" of this myth differs by focusing on the irreducible basis of racialness as a continuing order of cultural significance in the United States, interpreted distinctly in changing and emergent social contexts. For an excellent account of how ethnic identities complicate the formation of a self-identified "working class" in this city, see Olivier Zunz, *The Changing Face of Inequality: Urbanization, Industrial Development, and Immigrants in Detroit, 1880–1920* (Chicago: University of Chicago Press, 1982). For accounts of the crucial transformation of class divisions within the black community in Detroit, see David Alan Levine, *Internal Combustion: The Races in Detroit, 1915–1926* (Westwood, Conn.: Greenwood Press, 1976); David Katzman, *Before the Ghetto: Black Detroit in the Nineteenth Century* (Urbana: University of Illinois Press, 1973); Richard Thomas, *Life for Us Is What We Make It: Building Black Community in Detroit, 1915–1945* (Bloomington: Indiana University Press, 1992).

51   See Camilo José Vergara, "Detroit Waits for the Millennium," *Nation,* May 18, 1992, 660–64; and Jerry Herron, *After Culture: Detroit and the Humiliation of History* (Detroit: Wayne State University Press, 1993).

52   I thank Roger Rouse for drawing my attention to the distinct futures that the two cities are used to envision in popular cultural productions in the United States today.

53   Rather than simply declare one myth dead and offer nothing in its stead, I turn to the real/fictional figure of the cyborg, particularly as elaborated by Donna Haraway in her essay "A Cyborg Manifesto: Science, Technology, and Socialist-Feminism in the Late Twentieth Century," in *Simians, Cyborgs, and Women: The Reinvention of the Nature* (New York: Routledge, 1991). This figure is compelling and irresistible in this context because, regarding race, it is important to rethink replication away from holistic models and more in synch with the new economic environment of biotechnical politics. "In relation to objects like biotic components, one must think

not in terms of essential properties, but in terms of design, boundary constraints, rates of flow, systems logics, costs of lowering constraints" (162).

Marilyn Strathern turns to the cyborg, as well, to help figure the future of ethnographic writing. In the disjointed realms of culture(s), she finds its figure useful, in part, because "it is a whole image, but not an image of a whole" (*Partial Connections,* 162). Like the racial formations I have sketched in this essay, "its internal connections comprise an integrated circuit, but not a single unit" (ibid.). But the segue from the melting pot to the cyborg occurs to Haraway also: "Our best machines are made of sunshine; they are all light and clean because they are nothing but signals, electromagnetic waves, a section of the spectrum, and these machines are eminently portable, mobile—a matter of immense human pain in Detroit and Singapore" (153).

Brown-Skinned White Girls: Class, Culture,

and the Construction of White Identity

in Suburban Communities

France Winddance Twine

Both what constitutes a race and how one recognizes a racial difference are culturally determined. Whether two individuals regard themselves as of the same or of different races depends not on the degree or similarity of their genetic material but on whether history, tradition and *personal training and experiences* have brought them to regard themselves as belonging to the same group or different groups. —J. C. King, *The Biology of Race*

THE empirical research generated by feminist scholars has provided little ethnographic data about the role of suburban residence in the acquisition of a racialized gender identity, particularly among U.S.-born women of African descent.[1] In this essay I will draw on material taken from ethnographic research to examine the importance of residence in middle-class suburban communities in the acquisition of a racially neutral identity among African-descent women. I first provide a specific case study of how *some* African-descent girls, in the absence of a politicized African American residential community, acquired a white cultural identity and not a black consciousness before leaving home to attend college. I then show how this identity shifted when it was challenged by a different residential and discursive milieu—that of the University of California at Berkeley.

I will analyze the social construction of identity among African-descent women who, as children, acquired white identities in their middle-class suburban communities. Feminist theorists have begun to address the social construction of whiteness and identity among women in the United States, but they have not yet addressed women who are not of exclusive or predominant European ancestry.[2] Biologically essentialist precepts that suggest one must be of exclusive European ancestry to have access to a white cultural identity can also be found in the works of cultural anthropologists interested in the social construction and enactment of whiteness.[3] Yet cultural anthropologists have been unable to explain the white identity claims and the "shifts" in racial consciousness that occur among African-descent women who have been "raised white."[4] Cultural anthropologists have assumed that a white identity that does not involve "passing" is not available to African-descent women who possess biological markers that place them in a nonwhite category. This essay departs from the previous scholarship on the construction of racialized gender identities by addressing the experiences of a neglected group of white women: women of mixed-race African descent. The experiences of African-descent women will highlight both the limits of "social constructionism" and the role that socioeconomic status plays in the construction of white identity in middle- and upper-class milieus.

In her book *Belonging in America: Reading between the Lines,* the cultural anthropologist Constance Perrin examines the meanings of kinship, friendship, privacy, and cultural belonging by examining how residents of middle-class suburban communities negotiate their relationships and maintain boundaries between themselves and their neighbors.[5] Although this book provides an excellent analysis and examination of the meaning of belonging to a suburban residential community, by choosing to interview only whites, whom she refers to as "Americans," Perrin reproduces the notion that middle-class suburban communities do not have any African-descent residents. She thus effectively erases all Americans of African, Asian, or multiracial descent in her discussion. Perrin defines her sample of suburban Americans as follows:

> I began by listening to suburbanites all around the country talk about their neighboring experiences. Wanting to hear "American ideas," I listened to men and women living in what is generally regarded as the "mainstream," those who have at least reached the suburban, single-family detached episode of the American Dream. The "American middle-class"; not knowing what it is any more precisely than anyone else, I've relied on this indigenous ideal of suburban residence and home ownership, which immediately implies another defining characteristic, namely white race. . . .

> I found that Americans see renters, blacks, children, the elderly, people with low incomes, together with signs of them in housing and geographical location, as being culturally unsettling.[6]

Any discussion of Americans of African and/or Asian descent living in suburban communities should include an analysis of the *historically specific* moment. Since 1960 the registered births to black-white couples in the United States have more than quintupled, from 9,600 in 1960 to 51,000 in 1988.[7] Although there are no accurate figures on the exact number of African-descent adolescents and young adults living in suburban communities, the significant increase in interracial marriages, particularly those involving a middle-class black spouse, means that an increasing number of African-descent children are growing up immersed in predominantly white, middle-class, suburban communities.

African-Descent Women and the Social Construction of Whiteness

A significant body of literature that interrogates the construction and enactment of whiteness and white identities has emerged since 1980.[8] However, this literature does not address the experiences of African-descent whites, assuming instead that Americans who claim and assert a white identity are exclusively of European descent. I am employing the term *white* to refer to a historically constituted identity that during other historical moments has excluded European Americans and non-Europeans who are *today* recognized by both Anglo-Americans and the U.S. government as unhyphenated whites.[9] I discuss the historical coconstruction of black and nonblack identities in the United States elsewhere.[10] As I will discuss later in this essay, the women I interviewed described their white identity as class-linked and restricted to *middle-* and *upper-middle-class* segments of the U.S. European American community.

This essay expands the analysis of racialized gender identities in middle-class suburban communities by examining how white identities are constructed and enacted by African-descent women. The central question I asked is, How do brown-skinned women of mixed African descent become socially constructed as white girls in the local context of a *middle-class* suburban community? In other words, what social conditions are necessary for the acquisition of a white identity by African-descent girls? My research is a response to the feminist scholarship on racialized gender identities and expands the discussion of racial identity and racial consciousness within the feminist literature on white women by addressing the experiences of a group of women who *shifted* their racial self-identifications from a white to a black or biracial identity during early adulthood.

Studies of suburban communities have not explicitly examined how adolescents and young adults of African descent negotiate their *cultural and racial identities*. The women interviewed in this study were the natural daughters of U.S.-born African American fathers and European American, European Jewish American, or Asian (born and raised outside the United States and later naturalized U.S. citizens as adults) mothers. By examining the construction and meaning of whiteness in the lives of African-descent women who became socially constructed as white prior to puberty and were subsequently reconstructed as black or biracial in a different geographical and cultural setting—the Berkeley campus of the University of California—this essay both expands on and departs from the previous literature on white identity and whiteness.

Research Methodology

My research is based on the transcripts of interviews I conducted with a nonrandom and nonclinical population of sixteen multiracial women of *known* African ancestry who self-identified as being of multiracial heritage, and were attending the Berkeley campus of the University of California during the 1990–91 academic year. I initially gained access to informants as a graduate student instructor of African and American Indian ancestry involved with a group of undergraduate students raised in multiracial families who established a campus student organization at the University of California at Berkeley in 1989. I recruited additional volunteers from introductory classes in the Departments of Anthropology and Sociology. Additional informants volunteered through a process of snowball sampling in which interviewees were asked to identify students from multiracial families who they believed might be interested in participating.[11]

I conducted audiotaped and videotaped interviews between October 1990 and November 1991 on the Berkeley campus. The interviews ranged from two to three hours per session and were structured by a series of preselected topics that included racial self-identification, childhood experiences, counteridentification in public settings, dating, ethnic affiliations, and shifts in ethnic and cultural identities.[12]

I interviewed a total of twenty-five female and male undergraduate students, but this essay draws on data only from my interviews with women of known African ancestry. These students had been raised by at least one white or Asian parent and had grown up in predominantly white middle-class suburban communities. My sample included individuals who were raised by both biological parents, one biological parent and a stepparent, or two adoptive parents. With one exception, all of the women I interviewed had U.S.-born black fathers. Three participants had Asian mothers who, at the time of their marriage to U.S. black men, were citizens of Korea, Japan, or Jamaica. The participants included ten women of European descent, three of Asian descent (Chinese, Korean, Japanese), and three of European Jewish descent. None of the women interviewed from this sample had an African American mother. The women had origins in fifteen different suburban communities in five states: California, Colorado, Hawaii, New York, and Texas.

"Raised White": The Middle-Class Suburban Experience

One social condition that *all* the women I interviewed identified as central to their experience of being "raised white" was their immersion in a family and social network that did not identify itself in *racial* terms. As children these women had been the culturally "unmarked" intimates of European American middle-class children; they had not been conscious of being perceived as culturally distinct from their peers. Not being distinguished from European American peers in everyday interactions was critical to the maintenance of a white cultural identity. I am *not* referring to physical distinctions in color, hair texture, or body type here. What I mean is that as children they experienced themselves as culturally neutral, as not deviating from their peer group. In other words, these African-descent women who acquired a white cultural identity did not position themselves, and were not positioned by those around them, as culturally distinct from their peers of no known African descent in terms of behavior, dress codes, speech patterns, leisure interests, or food preferences.

Whitney,[13] a female student who was adopted at birth, is the biological offspring of a U.S. black father and a European American white mother. She was raised in a racially exclusive middle-class suburban community in northern California in an all-white family, geographically and socially isolated from blacks and other nonwhites. Whitney was culturally indistinguishable from her monoracial adoptive sister, who shared the same communication style, clothing style, interests, friendship networks, and experience growing up in a European American family that embraced color-blindness as an ideal. When asked to describe her childhood and her family, Whitney described her family as white, her friends as white, and herself as culturally white.

> *FWT:* How would you describe the ethnic and racial background of your adoptive parents?
> *Whitney:* White. They are definitely white and had white culture . . . just the mainstream everyday. Now I am finding out this difference [between white and black culture] because of my boyfriend, who is black and has a black family. I get to see the difference between white—when people say white and black culture.[14]

Women of African descent who are socialized into a middle-class family network and a predominantly middle- or upper-middle-class suburban community may acquire a white identity as children despite possessing biological markers of African ancestry such as brown skin and dry, curly hair. Natasha, a young woman of African descent who was raised by her biological mother, a second-generation Russian Jewish woman, and her Anglo-American stepfather, described how she self-identified as an adolescent. Her parents separated when she was an infant, and Natasha had maintained no cultural ties and had no social contact with her biological father, whom she described as a "black American professional." Growing up, she had had no contact with any of her paternal relatives.

> *Natasha:* Until I got to high school I wouldn't tell people that I was black. I just told them that I was Caucasian. I mean I don't know if they believed me. I am Caucasian. . . . I didn't identify with [my black American father] at all. . . . My best friend would always have to tell people "she's Caucasian." She didn't know [about my African ancestry]. . . . I was assimilated not by choice but just by the way I was raised. I didn't try to fit into white culture. I *was* white culture. Both my parents were white.[15]

Note that Natasha is speaking from her present position as a self-identified "black Jew." She is interpreting her past experiences *as* a person who has recently acquired a black consciousness and identity.

In this discussion of her childhood, she says that she previously self-identified as "Caucasian," but her white friend had to "verify" her white identity for others when questions were raised by her olive-colored skin. What did it mean for Natasha to self-identify as Caucasian? She explained during the interview that she had identified as Caucasian on the basis of both her *cultural training* and *biological* factors. As the *daughter* of a white Jewish American mother and an Anglo-American father, she claimed a white identity. In other words, she relied on both her social location in a family of European descent and her biological relationship to a birth mother of second-generation Russian ancestry to name and claim a white cultural identity before puberty.

The acquisition of a white cultural identity begins in childhood and requires a confluence of factors. Being raised by a white parent is often a necessary but not a sufficient condition for the establishment of a white identity. Individuals with Asian parents (Chinese, Korean, and Japanese) were also able to acquire a white cultural identity in their predominantly white suburban milieu and white schools.

STRUCTURAL AND SOCIAL ISOLATION FROM NONWHITES
The important role that middle-class entitlement played in the shift of Jews from nonwhite to white, as a group, has been explored by the anthropologist Karen Brodkin Sacks. However, this inclusion of Jewish Americans into middle-class suburbia was not extended to African Americans before the Civil Rights movement. In their analysis and critique of perceptions of the suburbs, William Sharpe and Leonard Wallock argue that recent scholars of suburbia have emphasized the independence of the suburbs from the cities and claim that it represents a new "urban" environment.[16] The authors argue against recent characterizations of the suburbs and discuss the social exclusivity of the suburban environment, contending that despite the increasing diversity of suburban communities, "suburbia has remained an essentially exclusive domain. For example, in 1980, blacks constituted just 6.1% of suburbanites, as compared to 23.4% of city dwellers. That same year, only 8.2% of suburbanites reported incomes below the federal poverty line as compared to 17.2% of city residents. Minorities and the poor are still excluded from the suburbs."[17]

A cultural and social milieu dominated by consumerism continues to characterize many, though not all middle-class suburban communities. My participants described growing up in and feeling a sense of cultural belonging to an economically and racially exclusive environment where identity was based on middle-classdom and pur-chasing power. How do socioeconomic segregation and status gener-ate a social context in which African-descent adolescents who are *not* physically qualified for whiteness by virtue of their skin color, hair type, and other markers gain access to a white *cultural* experience as suburban residents?

Research suggests that gender division of reproductive labor in suburban communities has not changed radically, so, particularly in the event of divorce or separation, their African American fathers typically did assume the pivotal role in the socialization for the women I inter-viewed.[18] Furthermore like their middle-class peers of no known or visible African ancestry, these women grew up structurally and socially isolated from minority groups and working-class whites. Rebecca, a woman of European Jewish and African ancestry raised in a white sub-urban community in New York, described her social isolation from black students before her family moved from a white suburban com-munity to an urban area of New York City and she began attending a racially mixed junior high school.

> *Rebecca:* . . . so I was always isolated pretty much.
> *FWT:* Isolated from whom?
> *Rebecca:* From black kids. There were, like, two other black kids in my class.

The social segregation revealed in the above quote parallels the re-search findings of Ruth Frankenberg, who has provided scholars with a map of the "social geography" of white women's childhood. With few exceptions, the middle-class women I interviewed had had very lim-ited, if any, daily social contact with blacks or other nonwhites before attending college.

White Mothers and Their Daughters: Color-blindness and the Culture of Racial Neutrality

What do African-descent women learn from their mothers as children growing up in middle-class homes and communities? Recent and past feminist research on motherhood provides very little empirical data on how European American mothers transfer a white racial identity to their children.[19] Black feminist scholars have theorized more about the intersection of race and class on the transfer of identity between mothers and daughters, but this does not add to our understanding of transracial motherhood.[20] There is some ethnographic data on the attitudes of white adoptive mothers of African-descent women, and Ruth Frankenberg provides a model for understanding the ideological milieu inherited by African-descent women raised by middle-class mothers of European or Asian descent. The study described here did not involve interviews with any mothers, so I can discuss only daughters' discussion of their relationships with their mothers *after* they had constructed a "black" identity.

WHITENESS AS A POSITION OF RACIAL NEUTRALITY

In addition to being immersed in European American families living in residentially segregated communities of middle- and upper-middle class whites, some informants identified racial "neutrality" as an ideological condition necessary to acquiring a white identity. They defined racial "neutrality" as the childhood experience of seeing themselves as racially *invisible,* or racially neutral. Their Asian American and European American mothers played a critical role in providing an experience of racial neutrality in the home, and this enabled them to experience their class (and gender) identity as more primary than their African heritage. Racial visibility seemed linked to whether or not my participants felt stigmatized on the basis of being nonwhite in appearance. Angela, an eighteen-year-old woman who was raised by her biological mother and her stepfather, described how race or racial difference was never mentioned in her family.

> *Angela:* I look back at my family pictures and there's this white family and there's me in it. Like, wow, I never actually felt that I was [racially] different from my family. None of [my white relatives] actually said, "Why is your skin darker?" Never. I totally never thought about [skin color]. You know on my black side there's my brother who's mixed but looks white.[21]

Like her peers, Angela was not trained by her mother to a racially marked identity. She was not culturally trained to self-identify as racially visible, as children who grow up in poorer or more diverse communities are.[22]

Jessica, a twenty-one-year-old woman who was raised by her single Anglo-American mother and never lived with her African American father, described how she acquired a racially neutral identity in her suburban community. Her mother had never *racialized* her, had never told her that she belonged to the black racial category or any other racial group. Like many of her peers of no known African ancestry, she was *not* conscious of having a *racial* identity as a child, meaning that she did not acquire a black identity as a child.

> *Jessica:* Well, my mother is very idealistic. She was just. She would never use the word "race." She would never say I was black or white. She would just say "you're special." . . . She gave me a real sense of self but not a sense of a racial self.[23]

The African-descent women who claimed a white identity saw themselves as culturally and politically neutral and not targeted as members of a racial group until they were placed in an environment with a significant number of politicized people of color (African Americans/blacks, Mexican Americans/Chicanos). Mimi, the daughter of a Chinese American father and a mother of Chinese and African descent from the West Indies, described the "color-blind" and racially neutral analysis she was trained to embrace by her family.

> *Mimi:* [My family] is not racist. But they're very assimilated. They're not prejudiced, but in terms of their ideals, their standards, I think they've adopted white ideals and white standards. You know those sort of people who are "race neutral." . . . They don't see [racial identity] as defining them at all. . . . They try to ignore differences, and when I say to people "I'm black," I'm saying, "I am different and I want you to notice and not act like it's not an issue." And not to discriminate against me for it but to recognize and appreciate it.[24]

Although Mimi's mother is of African descent and chemically straightens her hair to emphasize her Asian heritage, she was forbidden by Mimi's father to discuss her African ancestry, and *never* discussed it with her children. Although Mimi identified herself as black and Asian at the time she was interviewed, she reported that prior to *leaving* her suburban community and prior to being integrated into the black campus community, she self-identified as culturally white.

In the context of a middle-class suburbia, being raised white involved having everyday social interactions and intimate contact with individuals who embraced a racially neutral identity. Having contact in which they were not differentiated or treated as culturally different from their peers or their family members enabled these African-descent children to experience the world as color-blind. They inhabited the same world as their middle-class peers. They were not excluded from any activities and were not aware of being perceived as different before puberty. Several women could not recall any situation in which they felt stigmatized or marked as different from their peers before adolescence (around twelve years of age).

The childhood experiences of my middle-class participants revealed that becoming culturally white required growing up immersed in a racially exclusive residential, academic, and social community and not being singled out as culturally distinct by white peers. Their mothers and peers had not called attention to markers of difference, thus they had not learned to experience themselves as racially *visible*. All described a childhood in which they had experienced a feeling of cultural belonging and acceptance. Individuals who had acquired their parents by birth or adoption were raised, as are many white children, to see themselves as "normal" or racially neutral. They were culturally trained not to see their skin color and physiognomy as relevant markers of cultural difference in the company of their siblings or peers.

Unconsciousness of racial position, a critical characteristic of the women who self-identified as white, was greatest among women who had been raised by white or Asian mothers. They saw themselves as racially neutral with regard to their membership in a middle-class suburban cultural community. However, this racial neutrality ceased being the primary interpretative framework through which these women described themselves prior to their attendance at the University of California at Berkeley, which appeared to provide an ideological milieu for these women as children.

WHITENESS AS A POSITION OF MIDDLE-CLASS PRIVILEGE

The women I interviewed identified their socioeconomic-economic status as one basis for their claim to a white cultural identity. In other words, they argued that they had been white because they had the same *material* privileges and socioeconomic-economic advantages as their suburban peers. Hence, white identity was inextricably linked to a middle-class economic position. For example, poor people of European descent did not represent whiteness to the middle-class women I interviewed. When they talked about whites, they referred *exclusively* to economically privileged European Americans. It was their access to material privileges as members of middle-class families that gave them access to a white cultural identity. Her status as the daughter of a professional psychologist enabled Angela to claim and name herself white. Angela's description of why she did not feel excluded from white social networks identifies her excellent grades, her interests, her friendships with whites, and her material privileges.

> *Angela:* I just remember filling out college applications. I'd [ask] my mother, "Mom what should I put? Should I put black or white?" "Put 'other.' Put 'biracial.' " My [white] counselor at school actually told me, "You have to put black because you're over whatever percentage." If it was 30 percent or 20 percent you're considered black. So I thought, "Okay," so I ended up listing myself as black.
> *FWT:* How did you feel about that?
> *Angela:* It was weird. I got lots of scholarships for being black, for being a minority. For my grades and stuff. I remember my best friend, Laurie, telling me, "Wow, you're really lucky that you're black and getting all of these privileges. I wish I was black." . . . I act white and everything. I kinda didn't really deserve them. People don't really consider me—black, like [economically] underprivileged, people who deserve this kind of scholarship because they are a minority. . . . I totally don't feel like one.[25]

In the above statement Angela's European American counselor imposes on her an *exclusive* definition of whiteness and an *inclusive* definition of blackness. Numerous scholars have argued that in the contemporary United States, as in the past, whiteness is constructed as a category that is restricted to non-African-descent people, while blackness continues to be culturally constructed as a category that can include people of a range of racial and ethnic backgrounds. In other words, while the white category in the United States has expanded to include previously excluded groups such as southern and eastern Europeans, it continues to exclude mixed-race African-descent people born in the United States.[26]

The importance of material consumption in conferring an identity that makes residents of any racial background culturally invisible and acceptable members of the community cannot be overstated. Sharpe and Wallock argue that the "culture of consumption merely reinforces the homogeneity it supposedly erodes. Consumer culture is built to conformist standards because it must appeal to many people to achieve commercial success. At the same time that it solidifies group identity, however, status-conscious consumerism also magnifies the social distinctions that mark off one group from another."[27] The women I interviewed had learned to link their ability to consume with a racially neutral identity. They had access to a racially neutral (read "culturally white") identity because of their purchasing power, their ability to consume the same products as their middle-class suburban peers of no known African ancestry. An example of this logic can be found in the following comments by a woman of Chinese and African ancestry:

> *Mimi:* My parents raised us in a very sheltered way. Both of them came from underprivileged backgrounds. My father is a doctor, though, and he was able to make it up the ladder. He is a big-time capitalist. He makes a lot of money and wants to keep it, so we had a lot of opportunities when we were younger. We didn't lack anything materially. . . . I think a lot of people of color in this country don't have the opportunities that money affords them. We did. None of us ever lacked anything [materially] that we saw white people [buying]. . . . That's why [racial privilege] is not an issue for them. And simply because it is not in the realm of their experience, they tend to discount [racial inequality]. It doesn't seem real to them. They're like "we have this and this and this, so what is this issue about color!"[28]

The above quote reveals the relationship between the ability to purchase material goods and the development of a class versus a racial allegiance. Mimi described being raised to see her *class* position, her position as a consumer, as more important than her color or racial heritage. In other words, she had been culturally trained by her parents to privilege her identity as a consumer, not as a member of a racial group. She described her sense of cultural belonging as a product of her material experiences as a resident of a suburban community. She said that she did not experience herself as "different" from her white peers because of her ability to purchase the same things.

Angela, the biological daughter of a European American mother and an African American father who self-identified as white, described feeling uncomfortable self-identifying as "black" on her college applications. She defined being black as an economic category, a category to which she did not belong by virtue of her *economic status* and cultural training. Moreover, she resisted self-identifying as black, although her school counselor identified her as black on the basis of her father's African ancestry. Like Mimi, Angela equated being middle class with having a white identity: "I associate myself with being white." Since she identified herself as a member of a privileged economic class, self-identifying as white meant not being "underprivileged" and not being poor. In Angela's interpretive framework, claiming a white identity meant claiming her class identity as a middle-class person. Neither Mimi nor Angela had experienced material deprivation or social stigma as academic achievers in their peer groups. Neither reported any encounters with antiblack racism or any form of racialized discrimination. Their definition of whiteness excludes poor whites and links a culturally white identity to a middle-class position. Academic success and not being excluded from the middle class thus were the signifiers of white cultural identity.

The experience of becoming culturally white was class-linked and regionally specific to the suburbs for these women. The process of acquiring a white cultural identity may not occur in the same manner or at all among individuals who grow up in predominantly middle-class communities of color, multiracial suburban communities, working-class suburban communities, or lower-income white urban communities.

WHITE IDENTITY AS AN EXPRESSION AND EMBODIMENT OF INDIVIDUALISM

Interviews with the daughters of European American and Asian American (born and raised in Asia) women revealed a constellation of ideological conditions under which African-descent girls acquired a white identity. In addition to experiencing racial neutrality, they had been encouraged to define themselves primarily as individuals. In their attempts to establish a link with their daughters, the mothers minimized phenotypic differences and instead emphasized their daughters' class identity and their identity as individuals. Frankenberg describes this perspective as "power-evasive" or "color-blind." Being raised white and middle class emerged as being linked to learning to privilege specific ideological positions, namely the tendency to self-identify first as an individual with no links to a specific racialized or ethnic community.

Angela reported that she had not been conscious of being treated as a member of a racially visible or stigmatized group before attending the University of California. This brown-skinned woman of visible African ancestry, who *continued to self-identify as white* despite being counteridentified by other students (including her friends of European descent who self-identify as white), described being unconscious of any antiblack racial discrimination before attending Berkeley. She had not experienced herself as racially visible at all. She described the differences between her experiences and those of brown-skinned students who self-identified as black in her high school.

> *Angela:* I went to a black student union meeting once. The black students talked about all the times they felt biased against or discriminated against. I sat there and listened. I had never [experienced racial discrimination]. Like they talked about not getting into classes because they were black. Nobody would talk to them because they were black. I've never, ever felt that.[29]

Like the white feminist Minnie Bruce Pratt, who stated that until she lost her racialized gender privileges as a white, married, heterosexual woman she had never experienced herself as a member of a stigmatized or oppressed group, my informants argued that they were not conscious of belonging to a stigmatized group and that they had never experienced discrimination. All had been taught (like their white peers) to be *indifferent* to racial issues. Thus, in addition to being a racially neutral site, white identity involves indifference to race(ism) or racialized issues. Blackness is conflated with being oppressed, and whiteness is conflated with the privilege of "normalcy." The families of the women I interviewed, like their neighbors, took the position that racial identity was not important in their lives.

Ayesha, a woman who was raised by a white mother and a black American father, delineated individualism as both a white cultural practice and as an ideological position. While she described her father in terms of his relationship to a larger black political community, she described her mother as an individual unconnected to a larger community. Her mother's individualism was presented as a salient aspect of her white identity; her lack of commitment and responsibility to a specific community were presented by Ayesha as a signifier of her whiteness. Ayesha cited her obligations to a racialized community as defining her in opposition to her white mother, who interpreted her problems as individual issues, not as collective ones.

> *Ayesha:* My mother. Just certain things that she did were in a lot of ways distinctively white. . . . Also I think, her being a white woman, she doesn't really have any connection [to a racial community], whereas my father definitely has a community . . . with a historical situation. He has a definite connection [to a racial group]. Whereas my mother seems to be very individualistic. . . .

She can turn her back on everything and say I'm going to be my own person, the hell with this whole thing [social problems].[30]

Her mother's identity as a white woman enabled her to respond to her environment in a certain way—to isolate herself and make decisions as an individual. In other words, she did not have to claim a racial identity, the identity of a member of a racial group.

WHITE IDENTITY AS A COMFORT ZONE

Feeling comfortable—unself-conscious and not engaging in self-censorship—in the presence of people who self-identify as white emerged as yet another necessary social condition for the enactment and acquisition of a white cultural identity. Being culturally white requires being familiar with and comfortable functioning in milieus culturally controlled and dominated by whites. My informants defined the white experience as growing up and feeling comfortable with middle-class people who did not self-identify as members of a *racialized* group, being familiar with their cultural norms, and, most important, feeling comfortable interacting with middle-class whites. Individuals who self-identify as black generally learn within the family at a very early age to maintain a certain suspicion and social distance with nonblacks. In order to survive in a white-dominated society, blacks have learned to censor themselves, not to be completely open in their interactions with whites.[31] In contrast, not feeling the need to restrict the topics discussed to limit the interaction is a sign of white identity.

This "comfort zone" emerged as one of the primary distinctions between African-descent women who self-identified as black or biracial and those who self-identified as white. Whitney, an eighteen-year-old olive-skinned woman with naturally blonde and curly hair who had been adopted and raised by a white family, summed up her relationship to whites in this way.

> *Whitney:* To tell you the truth I feel comfortable around white people because I've lived with them my whole life. I'm not really [self-conscious], whereas my [black boyfriend] doesn't trust white people. . . . He's not, like, paranoid, but he's more cautious around white people than he is around black people. Whereas I'm not that way.[32]

African-descent women like Whitney who have previously self-identified as white are distinguished by their high level of comfort in social interactions with European Americans who do not claim a racially marked identity. They have learned to feel comfortable in racially exclusive milieus that exclude most people of African descent. It is the shift to seeing whites as *racially* other that signals the beginning of the loss of white identity.

Challenges to White Identity: Puberty, Dating, and the Loss of Racial Neutrality

Disjunctions between my informants' experiences as racially neutral and their counteridentification by their peers as nonwhite began around puberty. Several women described first becoming conscious of the limits that their physical appearance (brown skin, curly hair, and other biological markers of African ancestry) placed on their ability to experience the world as white at puberty. In retrospect, speaking as blacks, these women interpreted these experiences as disruptions, but they did not relinquish their white cultural identity in response to these incidents of rejection, which I shall refer to as "boundary events" (after Barth).[33] Not being desired by their male peers as dating partners and being excluded by their male and female friends from full participation in the dating game did, however, force them to acknowledge that they were perceived as "different" by their peers.

Formal dating rituals (for heterosexuals) in suburbia generally begin in junior high or high school. The public selection of an individual as a desirable partner is a critical way of both expressing allegiance to a social group and affirming one's membership in a social network. It was at this moment that many of my female informants first became conscious of being marked as racially nonwhite by their peers and began the process of "losing" their position of racial neutrality. Whitney described how her sister and white friends pressured her to date the one black male in her high school.

> *Whitney:* High school is such a time when you're just really exposed to the dating atmosphere, and it's exciting and everybody thinks it's cool if you're [dating]. . . . I didn't date the first two years . . . [in high school]. Not that I wasn't interested in guys. Not that I didn't [stutters], I think [long pause], I don't know. A lot of [my experiences] were racial [pauses]. I think I had some problems because I was black. And . . . practically all of my [adoptive

European American] sister's friends and all of my friends were trying to get me and this black man set up. They were pushing for us to go out together so it was like automatically assumed that because we were both black that we should [date]. . . . Why was it that I could only date a black man? [34]

Whitney never dated the black man, and two years later she began dating one of her peers who was not of any known or visible African descent. She did not date any self-identified black men until she began attending the University of California at Berkeley.

Jessica, a twenty-one-year-old woman who was raised in a suburban community by her Anglo-American mother, a single parent, described how she began to lose her position of racial neutrality when she entered junior high school. When asked to describe how this transformation in her consciousness and identity occurred, she immediately described her relationships with her white male peers.

> *Jessica:* Growing older and being in a community that was predominantly white and not having the same interactions with white boys that my friends were having . . . not being ostracized [by peers] because I was [socially] accepted to a large extent. But in terms of [dating] relationships with boys and men . . . I wasn't accepted as having those intimate relationships with [white] boys that my [female] friends were having at those ages.[35]

The experiences of Rebecca, an eighteen-year-old Jewish woman of African descent, echo those of Jessica with regard to being excluded from the potential pool of dating partners by white male peers:

> *Rebecca:* In junior high . . . other people [my female peers] were going out with [white] boyfriends and I always recognized the fact that I was not—I was not chosen by the [white] guys at school.

An analysis of their dating relationships reveals that patterns of exclusion and antiblack racism began to operate in my informants during puberty. For women of color, being selected by a male as a "public" romantic partner is an important aspect of the white socioeconomic-cultural experience. During puberty, they became aware that they were not desired by their male peers or pursued by them as potential romantic partners. In fact, dating emerged as the critical arena for initial confrontations with racism. A twenty-one-year-old woman who grew up in an all-white town in northern California described a change in her consciousness about her white identity when she entered junior high school.

> *Jessica:* It wasn't that people often referred to me in racial terms. It's just that I became more aware of myself as being different [from peers]. I came to the realization that I wasn't white, but I still lacked a racial consciousness. I wasn't aware of my racial identity. I was just aware that I wasn't white.

How did Jessica become aware of this difference? Dating and marriage are two critical arenas where the marking and enforcement of "difference" occurs. Ruth Frankenberg's research on interracial relationships revealed that white women are socialized across class and region in the United States to see blacks as, at best, inappropriate dating and marital partners, and, at worst, dangerous and deviant.[36]

During puberty, dating becomes an arena where the boundaries of whiteness are drawn by the exclusion of individuals of known African descent from the pool of dating partners. A woman must be desired and publicly recognized as the legitimate romantic partner of a white male in order to maintain a white cultural identity. Her peer groups must affirm and support the selection of the partner for her to be seen as white. Silence about their African ancestry also plays a role for such women. The peer group must either be unaware of the African ancestry or choose to ignore it and not emphasize it as significant marker of difference in order for a white cultural identity within one's peer group to be maintained.

However, being rejected by their male peers did *not immediately* result in either the relinquishment of a white identity or of the acquisition of a black or biracial identity. That occurred only *after* these young women arrived at Berkeley. These women were able to fully reinterpret their experiences in junior high school and high school only after they had relinquished their white cultural identity.

Becoming Black at Berkeley: Leaving a White Cultural Identity at Home

> Identity is not static. It's constantly changing. It's constantly evolving. So while perhaps during their first two years at Berkeley [multiracial] students decide to identify as black or Chicano, or

Asian, that identity could change in two years. . . . Racial identity is constantly going to change.[37]

Tamala, a woman of African and European descent who was adopted at birth, had had very limited contact with blacks. As she described it, before attending the University of California she had been a white person. When I interviewed her she was in the process of acquiring a black cultural identity. She was being culturally retrained by her African American boyfriend and peers in the black campus community at Berkeley.

> *Tamala:* Before I came to Cal I was white. I was all white culturally. . . . [Here] I am perceived as black. I'm treated as black so I don't have a problem with being black. . . . But it's a difficult situation. It's really hard.[38]

With one exception, all of the women described a shift in their identity and their consciousness during their first two years in college. Attendance at Berkeley was the common shared cultural experience and the most recent significant event in their lives. At the time of the interviews, they were between the ages of eighteen and twenty-five years and were adjusting to the climate of heightened racial consciousness and ethnic politics on the Berkeley campus.

The Berkeley experience challenged their ideology of individualism. They were no longer able to be "just individuals." Their prior identity as racially neutral (read "white") middle-class girls was abruptly challenged. The politicized communities of color would not allow them to avoid claiming a nonwhite racial identity. At the moment that they became conscious of their cultural whiteness (like their monoracial peers of no known African ancestry) they were encouraged to embrace and assert a post–civil rights "black" identity by their incorporation and recruitment into the black campus community. According to the *Diversity Project Report,* a report produced by the Institute for the Study of Social Change, "a process of racial and ethnic crystallization takes place at Berkeley. This process may be described in terms of the current literature on race as one of racialization, a development where social relations that were formerly defined in terms or factors other than race come to be defined in racial terms." [39]

The heightened sense of racial and ethnic consciousness that exists at Berkeley pressures students of any African ancestry to recog-

nize and claim a black racial identity as part of their campus socialization process. In addition, allegiance to one's racial group must be demonstrated in terms of dating preferences and participation in racially
based social clubs and professional, political, and academic organizations.[40] Social spaces are visibly racialized spaces on the Berkeley campus by the institution of "ethnic" parties that exclude whites. These
racialized events and spaces generate ethnic group solidarity while also
marking individuals who participate as racially marked members of
a group.

Angela, an eighteen-year-old raised by her exclusively European-
descent biological mother and an adoptive stepfather, felt uncomfortable in all-black environments but not in exclusively white environments. Her best friends were white. She dated white men exclusively
and self-identified as white despite her obvious African American features.

> *Angela:* At the beginning of the year I was invited to all of the Afri-
> can American activities that they have here [at Berkeley]. I went
> to some of these events and I [when] I was walking down Sproul
> Plaza, some black guy called out at me "Sistah, Sistah," . . . they
> would just call me. I kinda felt uncomfortable because I feel that
> I'm just [an individual] and I don't need to stick together with any
> [group]. I just need to be myself.
> *FWT:* In what way do you feel that you can't be yourself at those
> black campus events?
> *Angela:* Well . . . I'm there because I'm black so I'm black when
> I'm there. So I'm supposed to act black.[41]

Note that it was her presence at a specific social event that defined
Angela as black ("I'm black when I'm there"). Angela did not feel
comfortable in social spaces racially marked as nonwhite—spaces that
excluded white people. Exclusively black locations imposed a black
cultural identity on Angela that contradicted the white social identity
she acquired as a child and adolescent. She was not comfortable in
black spaces because, as a person who self-identified as black on her
college admissions application and was identified by others as black
based on her skin color and physical appearance, she was unable to
assert a white cultural identity in this setting. Being in a social space
that excluded white people, and racialized whites by this exclusion
process, forced Angela to align herself racially with blacks. Angela de-

scribed feeling uncomfortable being pressured to ally herself with a racial group (although she was allied with whites). She described wanting to just be "me"—an individual—and emphasized how her status as an individual was denied in this setting.

Angela did not wish to be racially "marked" or visible as black because it contradicted her core identity as a racially neutral *middle-class* person. She experienced herself as neutral, just like her middle-class white peers who were not under pressure to embrace a black identity. At one point during the interview Angela described black students as "extreme" and implied that blacks are deviant, in opposition to *her* identity as a "normal" person.

> *Angela:* They're more aggressive. They've always been more aggressive [in social interactions]. . . . They've always been like, well, fighting for their equality and stuff. They've been really violent [unlike whites].

For Angela, blackness emerged only in relation to a "normal" identity—normal being those individuals who are not visible because of their cultural conformity. A white identity emerges as an unmarked cultural identity that is predicated on not being excluded from white social circles and not being included in all-black cultural settings that intentionally exclude nonblacks. Social spaces that are racially marked as "not white" by the presence of blacks and the exclusion of whites prevent multiracial women from asserting their white cultural identity.

Acquiring a Paradigm: Learning to See through a Racial Lens

A change in perception emerged as one of the most important indicators of the shift from a white identity to a black or biracial one. My research revealed a link between interpretive framework and the experience of being white culturally. My informants described being white as a way of perceiving and responding in social interactions. Whiteness emerged as an interpretive frame—a way of explaining and understanding social relations. In other words, it is an analytical posture used to decode social interactions. Whitney, a woman who self-identified as white before arriving at Berkeley, described the shift in her interpretive frame generated by her romantic relationship with her boyfriend, who embraced an African American identity. Her immersion in African American studies courses and the African American community provided her with an alternative paradigm, a way of interpreting her social world that was not "color- or power-evasive."[42] Her ability to decode racist assumptions and ideas became nuanced.

> *Whitney:* Raishan was talking to this [black] woman at the bank. And she goes, "Yea, when you make your millions." And this white woman, who also worked at the bank, overheard them. And she goes, "How is he going to make millions, he's not a rapper or an athlete." See, that's a racial statement because she doesn't think that blacks could—are capable of doing anything except for being a rapper or an athlete. But I wouldn't have caught on to that if I hadn't been more aware like I am now . . . in high school I would have caught on to that. I'm more cued to that type of thing. I'm a different person now.[43]

Whitney had been culturally retrained through her relationship with her boyfriend and had begun to learn how to recognize everyday racism—something that children who grow up in households with parents who self-identify as black are often taught at an early age, although learning to recognize everyday racism can be taught by a parent who does not have a black identity and may not be taught to children by their African-descent parents.

A critical shift from a white identity to a biracial or black identity occurred for several women when they began exclusively dating men who embraced an African American identity. Establishing romantic relationships with black men also signaled to their parents and peers that they were embracing and privileging their African American ancestry over their cultural training as racially neutral. Dating relationships were no longer framed as just a matter of "individual choice" but instead became political decisions. Several women described feeling deprived of their ability to choose when they found themselves being encouraged to date men who were of African heritage and being rejected by some European American male peers. Rebecca described how her Russian Jewish American mother responded to her shift to dating men who identified as black.

> *Rebecca:* And my mom is wondering, "[When] are you going to date a white person?" . . . She feels hurt because she sees me identifying with my African American cultural [heritage], and my [black father] didn't raise me. He didn't do anything for me . . . especially when we have a conversation about who I'm dating and

almost everybody that I bring home is black. Almost everybody. And all the pictures on my wall. Almost everybody is black. . . . And I don't think she realizes that it's not a choice that I have. I mean it kinda was because I kind of made the switch [from a white to a black identity] on my own, but it wasn't really like if I wanted to make a conscious choice to be white, I have the option.[44]

Rebecca also described a pattern of subtle rejection and an increased awareness that she was not perceived as physically attractive by her male peers. She was not "chosen" and did not actively pursue white men in dating relationships, so she found herself being selected by men of African American descent. Aesthetics seemed to play a key role in the politics of exclusion as my informants got older. Judged (by European American men) on the basis of their physical attributes, they found themselves unable to compete with their female peers whose features more closely approximated the popular ideals of European American beauty.

Rebecca, like other women, also began to shift her identity away from a racially neutral one that emphasized individualism, and toward a racialized collective identity that emphasized her political and cultural connection to an African-descent community by dating men who embraced an African American identity.

SELF-CENSORSHIP: INCREASED SOCIAL DISTANCE
AND THE LOSS OF THE COMFORT ZONE

The comfort zone, characterized by an absence of self-censorship, did not survive in the politicized Berkeley campus, where an ethic of color-blindness was not embraced or defined as desirable by a vocal segment of the student body. As a result, my informants reported an increase in self-censorship and increased social distance between themselves and their parents. They began to censor themselves in front of people who did not self-identify as black or biracial. They learned that there are topics that are taboo in the presence of people who claim a racially neutral identity. This knowledge was accompanied by the loss of their parents' racial neutrality. Relatives who had been perceived as racially neutral became racialized. As Whitney learned to experience the world as a self-identified black, she began to experience increased cultural distance between herself and her adoptive mother. She gradually relinquished her previous ideological framework. This is illustrated by her recollection of a home visit with her mother.

> *Whitney:* We were talking to Vincent's roommate. Vincent's room-
> mate is black but he always [dates] white women. And I felt my-
> self—when we were telling my mom about this one white girl
> that he brought over and . . . we didn't tell her what race she was.
> But we were just talking about him bringing home the ugliest
> women. "They're so ugly." And I go, "Yeah, Mom, and they're—"
> I stopped myself. "Yeah, Mom, and they're all white women." I
> can't tell my mom that. You know I never would have said that in
> high school. . . . But I find myself [thinking] in this kind of men-
> tality. Like thinking, Whitney, think of your biological parents.
> That was them. Black and white . . . it's little things like that are so
> hard and I feel that I can't [talk about this]. I haven't shared this
> with my mom yet. . . . Maybe I'm afraid that she won't understand.
> That she can't understand because I'm [learning from the black
> community] that white people don't understand [racism] or can't
> identify with [racial] problems, so that's where I'm in a conflict.[45]

Several women brought up the issue of their mothers not being able to
understand them as black or biracial women. Once they had acquired
an interpretive framework that was different from their mothers', they
no longer saw themselves as occupying the same position as their
mothers and did not evaluate their relationships in the same way. Whitney's relinquishment of a white identity and her acquisition of a black
identity involved learning to make the distinction between whites and
blacks in terms of what topics should be censored in the presence of
nonblacks. She began to see her mother as not able to engage in a culturally competent fashion in discussions that addressed racial identity
and racism.

Conclusions

The experiences of African-descent girls who shifted from a white to
a black or biracial identity reveal that the one significant aspect of
the construction of "white" identity is an interpretive framework that
privileges individualism and racial neutrality. This essay both supports
and expands the research of previous feminist scholars of whiteness by
providing specific case studies of African-descent girls raised in suburban communities and their acquisition of a color- and power-evasive
paradigm that enabled them to construct a racially neutral (white)
identity. This essay also shows that a white identity is available (prior

to attending a university) to a segment of the economically privileged and residentially segregated African-descent female community.

The African-descent women I interviewed had a white identity available to them as children growing up in middle- and upper-middle-class suburban communities. This identity was contingent on their being raised in residentially, socially, and socioeconomically segregated milieus. Such segregation has specific ideological consequences for the construction of white identity among African-descent women of multiracial heritage. African-descent women who have biological markers of "difference" but are not culturally or economically distinct from their peers may acquire a white identity as children. However, my research also reveals the limits of white identity claims after puberty and after women of visible African ancestry relocate to a politicized campus community.

In this essay I provide compelling evidence that a white, and later a black, identity is socially constructed and can be enacted under specific economic, demographic, and social conditions. All the women I interviewed stated that they had learned a great deal about their heritage and their identity by enrolling in African American and ethnic studies courses. These courses compensated for the lack of information they had received at home from their parents and served to reposition them both culturally and racially. Courses in African American/black studies and ethnic studies provided an anchor for the identity transition of students who had previously self-identified as white. This has implications for the cultural training of European American students of no known African heritage. It suggests that students of exclusively European descent could not only unlearn to see themselves as racially neutral but could also be taught to privilege a cultural connection to their African American cultural heritage as Americans, even if their cultural training and experiences prior to college did not give them access to a black cultural identity.

The Black Power movement and the Civil Rights movement played critical roles in the institutionalization of a reconstructed black identity accessible to African-descent students from a range of sociocultural backgrounds. During the 1960s and 1970s U.S. blacks fought for the establishment of academic departments and programs centered on the experiences and contributions of black Americans. Through course curricula and campus events, black/African American studies and ethnic studies departments have provided African-descent and other students with access to alternative paradigms that challenge the discourses of individualism and power evasion. At the University of California women of African-descent are socialized into a post–civil rights black identity that privileges and centers their African American heritage as *more politically* and socially relevant than their non-African (Asian and European) heritage.

Further research, particularly longitudinal studies involving a larger and more diverse sample of women and men from a range of socioeconomic-economic and regional backgrounds, is needed to evaluate the impact of class on the construction of racialized gender identities. Studies that examine differences *within* families between siblings who may acquire different racial identities are also needed. Since I did not have access to the siblings of my participants, I am unable to theorize about the impact of these identity shifts on siblings and other members of the family system.

I cannot say anything about the experiences of African-descent women in *working-class* suburban communities. Ethnographic studies that do not neglect the experiences of working-class, middle-class, and upper-middle-class African-descent suburban residents are needed to expand our understanding of the *meaning* of a white (and hence black) identity in various socioeconomic-economic and regional communities. This study challenges the notion that racial identities are fixed, natural, and unmalleable even in the face of phenotypical constraints. It also suggests that despite the persistence of overt antiblack racism in the contemporary United States, Asian American and European American mothers may play a pivotal role in transferring a racially neutral identity to their daughters. Moreover, the cultural practices and ideologies of mothers generate a racially neutral milieu in which their mixed-race daughters experience themselves as unmarked. My research demonstrates that a *racially neutral* experience and cultural identity are available (at least prior to puberty and attendance at a university) to an economically privileged segment of the African-descent female community raised by Asian or European American mothers.

Notes

I thank Ara Wilson, Gloria Cuadraz, Jennifer Pierce, Naheed Islam, Sarah Murray, John Wolfe, and Jonathan W. Warren for their insightful comments and suggestions on the first draft of this essay. This essay also benefited from the critical reading and comments of my colleagues at the University of Washington, Caroline Chung Simpson and Judith Howard. Finally, I thank Kristin Luker at the University of California at Berkeley, who inspired me to write this paper, which is based on a study I began while enrolled in her graduate seminar on qualitative research methods.

1 Suzanne Caruthers, "Catching Sense: Learning from Our Mothers to Be Black and Female," in *Uncertain Terms: Negotiating Gender in American Culture* ed. Faye Ginsburg and Anna Lowenhauptísing (Boston: Beacon Press, 1990); Patricia Hill Collins, *Black Feminist Thought: Knowledge, Consciousness, and the Politics of Empowerment* (London: HarperCollins Academe, 1989).

2 Kathleen Blee, *Women of the Klan: Racism and Gender in the 1920s* (Berkeley: University of California Press, 1991); Ruth Frankenberg, *White Women, Race Matters: The Social Construction of Whiteness* (Minneapolis: University of Minnesota Press, 1993); Minnie Bruce Pratt, "Identity: Skin Blood Heart," in *Yours in Struggle: Three Feminist Perspectives on Anti-Semitism and Racism,* ed. Elly Bulkin, Minnie Bruce Pratt, and Barbara Smith (Brooklyn: Long Haul Press, 1984); Karen Sacks, "How Did Jews Become White Folks," in *Race,* ed. Steven Gregory and Roger Sanjek (New Brunswick: Rutgers University Press, 1994), 78–102.

3 Virginia Dominguez, *White by Definition: Social Classification in Creole Louisiana* (New Brunswick: Rutgers University Press, 1986); Ruth Frankenberg, "Whiteness and Americanness: Examining Constructions of Race, Culture, and Nation in White Women's Life Narratives," in *Race,* ed. Steven Gregory and Roger Sanjek (New Brunswick: Rutgers University Press, 1994), 62–77; Sacks, "How Did Jews Become White Folks?"

4 Signithia Fordham and John Ogbu, "Black Students' Success: Coping with the 'Burden of Acting White,'" *Urban Review* 18 (1986). This essay departs from Fordham and Ogbu's ideas of "acting white" by examining the experiences of African-descent women who had not acquired a black identity before attending college.

5 Constance Perrin, *Belonging in America: Reading between the Lines* (Madison: University of Wisconsin Press, 1988).

6 Ibid., 5–7.

7 Elizabeth Atkins, "For Many Mixed-Race Americans Life Isn't Simply Black or White," *New York Times,* June 5, 1991.

8 Reginald Horsman, *Race and Manifest Destiny: The Origins of American Racial Anglo-Saxonism* (Cambridge: Harvard University Press, 1981); Alexander Saxton, *The Rise and Fall of the White Republic: Class, Politics, and Mass Culture in Nineteenth Century America* (New York: Verso, 1990); David Roediger, *The Wages of Whiteness: Race and the Making of the American Working Class* (New York: Verso, 1991); bell hooks, "Representations of Whiteness in the Black Imagination," in *Black Looks: Race and Representation* (Boston: South End Press, 1991); Toni Morrison, *Playing in the Dark: Whiteness and the Literary Imagination* (Cambridge: Harvard University Press, 1992); Vron Ware, *Beyond the Pale: White Women, Racism, and History* (London: Verso, 1992); Ruth Frankenberg, *White Women, Race Matters;* Charles Gallagher, "White Reconstruction in the University," *Socialist Review* 94, nos. 1–2 (1995): 165–87; Tomas Almaguer, *Racial Fault Lines: The Historical Origins of White Supremacy in California* (Berkeley: University of California Press, 1994), 17–74.

9 For a discussion of the transformations and expansion of the "white" category see Sacks, "How Did Jews Become White Folks?"; Noel Ignatiev, *How the Irish Became White* (London: Routledge, 1996); Jonathan Warren and France Winddance

Twine, "White Americans, the New Minority? Non-blacks and the Ever-Expanding Boundaries of Whiteness," *Journal of Black Studies,* in press.

10   Warren and Twine, "White Americans, the New Minority."

11   During the first phase of this research project, I recruited volunteers who had been raised in multiracial families of *any* ethnic or racial background. After conducting interviews with two students of Asian and European American heritage, I decided to restrict my focus to students of known African descent. The history of slavery and the concentration of African Americans primarily in the rural South and the urban North has generated a unique experience that distinguishes African Americans, as a group, from American Indians, Asian Americans, and European Americans. I further decided to restrict this study to individuals who had one parent who self-identified as black or African American. This provided not only a "control" but also a common denominator that facilitated a more nuanced analysis of racial consciousness and racial labeling within multiracial families.

12   Francine Winddance Twine, Jonathan W. Warren, and Francisco Ferrandiz, *Just Black: Multiracial Identity* (New York: Filmmakers Library, 1991).

13   All names of participants used in this paper are pseudonyms. No names of specific suburban communities are used, although the names of larger geographical regions and the names of states have been retained.

14   Transcript of interview conducted on March 30, 1991.

15   Transcript of interview conducted on October 5, 1990.

16   William Sharpe and Leonard Wallock, "Bold New City or Built-up Burb? Redefining Contemporary Suburbia," *American Quarterly* 46, no. 1 (1994): 1–30.

17   Ibid., 7.

18   Arlie Hochschild, *The Second Shift: Working Parents and the Revolution at Home* (New York: Viking Press, 1989).

19   Nancy Chodorow, *The Reproduction of Mothering: Psychoanalysis and the Sociology of Gender* (Berkeley: University of California Press, 1978); Evelyn Nakano Glenn, Grace Chang, and Linda Rennie Forcey, *Mothering: Ideology, Experience and Agency* (New York: Routledge, 1994).

20   Suzanne Caruthers, "Catching Sense."

21   Transcript of interview conducted on November 25, 1991.

22   John Langston Gwaltney, *Drylongso: A Self Portrait of Black America* (New York: Random House, 1980).

23   Transcript of interview conducted on October 15, 1990.

24   Transcript of interview conducted on April 8, 1991.

25   Transcript of interview conducted on November 25, 1991.

26   For a discussion of how mixed-race African-descent people continue to be constructed as unqualified for the white category, see Virginia Dominguez, *White by Definition: Social Classification in Creole Louisiana;* and F. Floyd David, *Who Is Black? One Nation's Definition* (University Park: Pennsylvania State University Press, 1991). For a discussion of the classification of African-descent people from North Africa, see Soheir Morsy, "Beyond the Honorary White Classification of Egyptians: Societal Identity in Historical Context," in *Race,* ed. Steven Gregory and Roger Sanjek (New Brunswick: Rutgers University Press, 1994).

27   Sharpe and Wallock, "Bold New City," 11.

28   Transcript of interview conducted on May 10, 1991.

29 Transcript of interview conducted on November 25, 1991.

30 Transcript of interview conducted on October 24, 1990.

31 Philomena Essed, *Everyday Racism: Reports from Women of Two Cultures* (Claremont, Calif.: Hunter House, 1990). This book compares the experiences of African-descent women (Surinamese) living in the Netherlands with those of African American women living in the San Francisco Bay area. Essed found differences in the cultural training of U.S. black American women and African-descent women in Holland. African-descent U.S. women had been trained as children to see and respond to everyday occurrences of racism in a sophisticated manner while Surinamese women generally lacked this training. In addition, Essed found that the socialization process for African American children (in monoracial black families) included learning how to deal with racism. In other words, African-descent children raised by two self-identified black parents in U.S. homes are taught to distinguish between covert and overt racism and to censor in the presence of nonblacks and whites. Hence, their early cultural training cues them to detect subtle forms of racism, which distinguishes them, in most cases, from children raised by European Americans in the United States.

32 Transcript of interview conducted on March 30, 1991.

33 Fredric Barth, ed., *Ethnic Groups and Boundaries* (Boston: Little, Brown, 1969), 294.

34 Transcription of interview conducted on March 30, 1991.

35 Transcript of interview conducted on March 20, 1991.

36 Frankenberg, *White Women, Race Matters*, 71–101.

37 Transcript of interview conducted on October 15, 1990.

38 Transcript of interview conducted on February 15, 1991.

39 Institute for the Study of Social Change, *Diversity Project: The Final Report* (Berkeley: Institute for the Study of Social Change, 1991), 44. This report, which examines the impact of the dramatic demographic shifts in the student population at Berkeley on campus life, is based on interviews conducted between February 1989 and April 1991 with 291 students and sixty-nine focus groups divided along lines of race. In addition to surveying student attitudes on affirmative action and other issues, the report illuminates the socioeconomic-political terrain that students from diverse racial and socioeconomic-economic backgrounds must negotiate on entering Berkeley.

40 For a more detailed discussion of the role that dating partners play in the identity shifts of multiracial college students, see "Heterosexual Alliances: The Romantic Management of Racial Identity," in *The Multiracial Experience: Racial Borders as the New Frontier,* ed. Maria P. P. Root (New York: Sage, 1996).

41 Transcript of interview conducted on November 25, 1991.

42 Frankenberg, *White Women, Race Matters*.

43 Transcript of interview conducted on March 20, 1991.

44 Transcript of interview conducted on May 13, 1991.

45 Transcript of interview conducted on March 30, 1991.

Laboring under Whiteness

Phil Cohen

Exam question: Some people are born white; others achieve whiteness; and some have whiteness thrust upon them. Discuss.

A few years ago it would not have been possible to set this exam question, let alone discuss it in the classroom. But whiteness has, in the last few years, undergone a radical reinvention.[1] The new whiteness is in many respects the obverse of the old. It is self-conscious and critical, not taken for granted or disavowed; it is the visible focus of open conflict and debate, not the silent support of an invisible consensus of power; for those to whom it is primarily addressed it is a source of guilt and anxiety rather than of comfort or pride; above all, it issues from a perspective that privileges a certain black experience of racism and insists that racism is primarily a white, not a black, problem. In this story, whiteness is the new white man's (and woman's) burden; their task is first to recognize and then to help lift its oppressive yoke by acknowledging its function as a badge of racial exclusion and privilege.

This "alternative" whiteness has a precise genealogy. It was first put together in the United States in the aftermath of the Civil Rights movement in the 1960s; it proceeded from a critical reflection on the particular history of slavery, settler colonialism, white European immigration, and black segregation that constitutes the trajectory of white supremacism in North America.[2] The issue was taken up and developed further by those concerned at the way the white feminist and antiracist movements were unconsciously reproducing, and sometimes actively promoting, a new form of color-blindness in the name of political unity.[3]

Two assumptions lie at the heart of this ambitious enterprise. First, whatever local variations there might be in its form or content, the ideology of white supremacism is the paradigmatic form of racism, and it permeates the whole of society and its body politic; second, as a discourse of the West—in both its association with the American frontier and in its larger geopolitical sense—whiteness belongs to a transatlantic culture of racism premised on a common Eurocentric worldview dating back to at least the eighteenth-century Enlightenment.[4]

From this starting point, it seemed entirely plausible to follow in the footsteps of the abolitionists of the 1830s and build a new transatlantic wall against racism.[5] If black Britons entertained a special relationship with their American cousins, in terms of common African roots and the Middle Passage, then surely this must help promote the traffic in contemporary antiracist ideas between the two continents. Of course there are different models as to how this can best be achieved. American afrocentrics and black roots radicals in Britain make a more or less common cause of cultural authenticities forged against white domination. And what could be more rewarding or exciting than a journey across fractured histories and geographies of oppression to discover an integral black identity?[6] An alternative itinerary offers the prospect of a "black Atlantic" in which ethnic absolutisms of every kind are transcended through the diasporic medium and hybrid forms of its traveling cultures.[7]

Whatever the outcome of the debate within black cultural politics between ethnic fundamentalists and postmodernists, it is already clear that both positions have contributed more than their fair share to the confusion about the terms in which whiteness can be located on both sides of the Atlantic. In one case whiteness is reduced to an essentialized biological medium of racial supremacy and then conflated with an equally simple-minded model of European hegemony, which, for example, is supposed to have impressed itself in much the same way on the USA as on the "third world." The history of racism thus becomes the story of white Europeans oppressing black non-Europeans on the basis of skin color; whites are intrinsically racist, and a black European is a contradiction in terms.[8]

Alternatively, skin color is treated as a purely social or discursive construct, in such a way that it becomes virtually a free-floating signifier; what it can be made to mean is no longer circumscribed by any corporeal reality outside its representation in language or the social text. As for the European tag, this takes on a curious fixity as a historical sediment of colonialism within the archaeology of knowledge. The story of antiracism thus becomes the struggle of white Europeans to deconstruct their whiteness and decolonize their Eurocentrism in order to abolish or transcend their racial significance.

Both positions offer a certain rhetorical consolation, but there is growing recognition that neither offers much purchase on the complexities of the encounters that are currently taking place in and across racial and ethnic divides.[9] The meaning of whiteness is no more exhausted by its biologization within "color racism" than by ethnicizing its appeal as an item of "cultural racism" or Eurocentrism. Indeed, the issue is significant precisely because it puts in question the distinction between color and culture as mutually exclusive terms of discrimination. To think whiteness requires us to rethink both racism and the way racism speaks the body.

Labor's Two Bodies and the Habitus of Race

The standpoint adopted here draws heavily on recent psychoanalytic thinking about identity and difference and also on certain recent developments in social history that focus on race as labor's "other scene."[10] From the first perspective we get the idea of race as an empty category or degree zero of representation, an "X marks the spot" that is not Y, a difference placed outside language and inside the body by a discursive operation that is necessarily subject to unconscious disavowal and repetition. This "spot" marks what is otherwise somatized as unrepresentable about difference and its desire, and makes it available as a shared place of origins and destiny. This imaginary place functions as the indelible sign of blessing or curse visited not just on bodies but on the body politic. Whether race is cultivated as beauty spot or blemish, elective affinity or derogation, it thus becomes a central reference point for a "narcissism of minor differences" that is worked up by the operation of power into a major site of civic inclusion and exclusion.

The next step in the argument tries to suggest why these "natural" symbolisms of race are so often anchored to particular attributes or divisions of labor, here considered in its broadest sense as any practice that works on given matter to reconfigure its value and meaning. We start from the fact that each mode of production, even the most rationalized, has its own habitus;[11] in other words, a set of customary rules, rituals, and invented traditions into which subjects are inducted and which holds them unconsciously in certain frames of mind about who or what is fitting where within the general framework of social production. The habitus creates imagined communities of labor that both govern particular workplace cultures and shape the way different kinds of work are evaluated in society as a whole. The habitus of slavery, feudalism, artisanal, industrial, and post-Fordist production all differ vastly, but they all index certain attributes of gender, age, class, and ethnicity to positions within the overall social division of labor. But what gives the habitus its binding power? Certainly not just the slave master's whip or the tyranny of petty masters, the dull coercion of industrial work discipline, or the impersonal regulation of technobureaucracies! Even the prospect of starvation, poverty, beatings, unemployment, or social stigma associated with a refusal to play the game does not quite explain why people go on doing it. And why is the spell not necessarily broken by a revolution in material or social technologies? Is it because a rather more seductive and intimate form of subjection is also at work?

Insofar as the human body is alienated by and from the labor processes in which it is engaged—for example, when it is turned into a puppet, a robot, a beast of burden, or a more or less redundant appendage (and the form of alienation varies according to different regimes of social production)—then this sets in motion a compensatory desire for a unitary and ideally productive body-of-labor whose power no longer depends on any means outside itself. The habitus is magically transformed into a kind of second womb that will give birth to a new man or woman, the embodiment of living labor freed once and for all from the dead hand of alienation.

Such fantasies of self-sufficient combination may be worked up into full-blown revolutionary utopias; more often they are articulated through myths of origin and entitlement which support purified definitions of the work habitus in terms of "species-specific" qualities of labor. The secret society, the craft fraternity, the work gang, the closed shop, the workers committee, the cell of militant cadres, even the specialist niche on the Internet are examples.[12] Each in its way furnishes a special genealogy of labor powers, indexed to particular patrimonies and prides acquired through rituals of initiation which invariably place restrictions on entry.

The almost exclusive masculinism of this project is underpinned by the maternal body that provides its unconscious but disavowed model. To belong to this body is to acquire a special pedigree, a principle of consanguinity, which is often transmuted into an almost mystical sense of ownership and control over the means of self-production. Coal is in your blood. You are an East Ender born and bred. You have the soul of a seafarer. Not surprisingly, these tropes are strongest in contexts where real and imagined communities of labor most closely interlock, where children follow parents into the same occupational habitus, and growing up is essentially an apprenticeship into a fixed inheritance. There is the sense of an almost congenital link between origins and destinies, providing a template for what we might call the protoracialization of labor power.

It was almost inevitable that such communities should come to be widely regarded as forming a "race apart" from the rest of society. This term has been variously applied to miners, dockers, fishermen, sailors, farmworkers, foresters, sharecroppers, peasants, costermongers, and artisans of every kind.[13] But from just these ranks has arisen the counterclaim that labor constitutes the backbone of the nation, even a chosen people. This should not surprise us, for the same trope is at work, except that it has been masculinized; labor is now the hidden armature of the phallocentric body politic, stiffening its resolve against outside interference, erecting defenses against the forces of decadence within.

It is at this point that the machinery of representation goes into reverse. For no sooner has this ideal body-of-labor been created than its integrity is threatened from both within and without by an "antibody of labor" that represents, usually in an exaggerated or grotesque form, the very alienations that have been disavowed. The state of abjection felt to be consequent on separation from the means of self-production is thus projected onto particular groups whose faces do not fit within the immediate work habitus (i.e., "wrong" age, race, gender, or ethnicity). These become the hidden hands that are secretly at work undermining the patrimony of labor.[14]

This is a double act, in which each figure mirrors the other's moves; social antagonisms or conflicts of interest derived from divisions of labor are thus overlain with a second, even more lethal animus. For example, those who are selected as members of labor's Other Body are also identified as potential traitors to the Cause, prior to and quite independently of anything they may or may not have done to earn that title in the course of actual struggles. Their symbolic crime is that they either openly present the "unacceptable face" of labor or else represent capacities that are otherwise lacking in its body politic and hence give the lie to the ideal "plenitudes" being claimed.

This is a self-fulfilling prophecy, of course, since groups marginalized as a result of this kind of treatment are also much more likely to be mobilized to undermine customary solidarities.[15] But this should not fool us into thinking that the closing of ranks is merely a defensive gesture grounded in an accumulated experience of real betrayals. It is always accompanied by a sense of satisfaction that prejudices are being confirmed; that certain individuals or groups have been made to reveal their true but hidden essence, which has always and already been ascribed to them as the "enemy within." The figure of the blackleg or scab is first created as the negative of an *imagined* community of labor before it is concretely personified by the act of strike breaking; no one taking on that role in the narrative of class struggle is ever not already "in character."

The final stage of the argument suggests that the empty category of race functions as a key operator of split labor representation and, en route, becomes a fully fledged component of its history. There has been much research into how distinctions between manual and mental, waged and unwaged, free and unfree, skilled and unskilled, regular and irregular, productive and reproductive labor become racialized;[16] particular attention is paid to how this process serves to institute or legitimate a range of inequalities between locally "sedimented" and immigrant populations as sources of labor power.[17]

On the antiracist left this is often still described in terms of some crude ruling-class conspiracy in which racist ideologies are beamed down at exploited and oppressed populations with the design or effect of "dividing and ruling" them.[18] Alternatively popular racism is read as symptomatic of some "necessary" false consciousness, one that provides a commonsense explanation for social ills and disadvantage, in terms not of underlying structural causes but of immediately perceivable effects — viz. bad housing or unemployment is blamed on the immigrant or ethnic minority presence rather than on the workings of the free market economy.[19] Both explanations are underpinned by a purely economistic rationale in which the needs or logics of capitalist development require the importation of a reserve army of cheap migrant labor from the "periphery," on which the nation-state then impresses special, and often stigmatizing, forms of racial regulation. In this perspective whiteness is a pure epiphenomenon, a cosmetic that masks the real underlying causes and effects of racism.

More recently there has been a shift in emphasis to examine the forms of working-class self-activity that produce cultures of racism "from below." This is seen not just as a defense of relative economic privilege or as a complaint about real or imagined deprivation but as a means of constructing identities that offer to resolve, however magically, certain lived social contradictions.[20]

A psychological dimension is thus added to the argument. At the same time, the idioms of racialized identity are no longer treated as a simple "projection" of dominant or subordinated ideologies or class interests but as a site of cultural negotiation between them. This process also involves nonclass—i.e., gender or generational—positions. Finally, instead of operating with some undifferentiated model of white racial supremacy and its global permeation, a space is opened up for the comparative analysis of different forms of racism in particular contexts.

This approach is still in its infancy and inevitably runs into difficulties attendant on trying to combine psychoanalytic theory with the concerns of labor history. Recently, for example, David Roediger has done much to anchor the formation of white ethnicities and their patterns of racialization in the USA to a concrete historical analysis of class structure, and in particular to the emergent culture of the American labor movement.[21]

Although Roediger's work perceptively pinpoints some of the dynamics of racial envy and ambivalence in white ethnicity, it is somewhat vitiated by its classical Marxist model of unitary class subjects conjoined to a no less reductionist Freudian model of their psychic economy. Much of his argument relies on an essentialized notion of "working-class psychology" as some kind of defensive adaptation to common material circumstances of immigration. But if we want to understand the invention of a white race at the heart of the American Immigrant Dream, it would perhaps be better to consider the latent rather than the manifest content of the dream work itself. What is being displaced or condensed in and by this figure? In more general terms, what is not being recognized in the daily residuum of labor under particular regimes of alienation so that what is wished for in its place takes the form of a racialized white or black body?

In order to unravel this conundrum we need to take a somewhat different approach to understanding race as labor's "other scene." We might argue that considering race as "degree zero" provides labor with two equally phantasmagoric body images. The first is a sublime body that leaves nothing to be desired because it is endlessly productive or entirely self-regenerating in and through its racial genealogy; its immaculate condition speaks of an innate freedom that transfigures the toils of labor into a "species-specific" site of redemption. The second is an inferior but mortal body driven by desires that are disciplined, disfigured, and ultimately destroyed in the process of its own daily reproduction through labor. Its "race," its whiteness, adds only a further sense of insult to the injuries this body sustains in its intercourse with the real world.

Through the device of this dual body, a labor process hated for what it signifies about lack can be emotionally invested as an index of pride and even privilege in being a race apart. But at the same instant this position is reversed into its opposite. Labor becomes the white backbone of the nation standing firm against its antibodies—those who are forced to figure the unacknowledged underside of exploitation. This transubstantiation has nothing directly to do with the content or status of real jobs; for example, unskilled manual work can be simultaneously whitened by being made to signify a proletarian ethnicity or macho sexuality and blackened by association with "dirt." [22]

Within this framework black labor is made to represent the predicament of a mortal but degenerative body enslaved by desire; blacks at work both represent the graven image of generic pain and suffering and lend their bodies to a certain eroticization of its punishing effects. White bodies, by contrast, are made to function as vehicles of a "birthright in freedom" that resists or transcends any such bondage; they always and already have the keys to the New Jerusalem.

Blacks are thus allowed to function as universal symbols of human exploitation and oppression, but only under two limiting conditions: either it is their natural lot, in which case they bolster by contrast the claims to collective self-emancipation staked on behalf of white labor; or they may slough off the chains imposed by black bodies and claim their "rightful" spiritual inheritance as part of a universal "consanguinity of labor power." Alternatively, blacks may be allowed to keep and celebrate their bodies, but outside the discourse of labor and its project of emancipation. Black physicality is then split into an aestheticized sublime and a dangerous sexuality produced through radical desublimation. Black athleticism in all its forms can then be safely acknowledged and even fetishized as the art of noble savagery, while at the same time any actual intercourse with white bodies remains the object of secret fear, fascination, and more or less brutal repression.[23]

There are several things worth noting about this structure. To begin with, it rests on a masculine fantasy of labor-as-castration and its denial. It is *this* anxiety—of separation from the nurturant womb of labor power—and its sublation in a regime of physically punishing work that overdetermine the sexual politics of black-white labor relations. At the same time, the problematics of emasculation involves a notion of unfreedom that conflates the regimes of chattel slavery, indentured labor, and wage labor, while at the same time leaving the real and unequal differences between them intact. It is in terms of this set of equivalences and the counterinsistence on their specifics that ideological debates around black-white labor relations have taken place.[24]

One thing, however, is not permitted within this framework, and that is any kind of transracial working-class alliance based on recognizing the real historical individuality of black labor. Instead, a narcissistic connection between labor and the white body is facilitated as a means of denying the symbolic wounds and real injuries of growing up working class. This in turn enables a deal to be struck between the masculine autonomies bought by the family wage and submission to the petty despotisms of the capitalist work discipline.[25]

This trade-off lies at the heart of white laborism and what might be called its system of double indemnity. For it then becomes possible for white male workers to rationally attack blacks for taking their jobs or cheapening their labor, and hence threatening the family's livelihood; at the same time, at a more unconscious level, blacks are both envied insofar as they are not "emasculated" by the disciplines of work or domesticity and hated for showing the "real face" of physical toil that had been hidden under the sign of whiteness.

The final difference race makes to labor is the reversal of its dematerialization under postmodern capitalism. This is a complex process that requires some unraveling. The original aristocratic distinction between those with breeding and those who merely bred was premised on a model of a race and class in which freedom from selling one's labor power and control over carnal instinct were the joint conditions and marks of a superior moral and mental condition of humanity. Whiteness was both the visible sign and the invisible guarantee of this disconnection between desire, labor, and the body, which was the foundation of Enlightenment humanism.[26]

This ideal of refinement through cultivated pursuits was subsequently combined with more utilitarian and "bourgeois" notions of mental and physical fitness as an index of racial or national health; nevertheless, whiteness as a principle of class/race distinction was still anchored to distance or difference from crudities of mind and body associated with the act of laboring. The civilizing mission was precisely to impose a measure of refinement and/or health on those who had the misfortune to engage in it.[27] It was in and against this model that labor's two bodies were constructed, and labor aristocracies elaborated their own set of racialized distinctions to set themselves apart—as skilled men with regular family wages—from the world of the casual unskilled and indigent poor, most of whom were women, children, and immigrants.

It must be remembered that all this occurred at a time when working and living conditions were conspicuously dirty, dangerous, and degrading—and often resulted in injury, chronic illness, and premature death.[28] It was these material realities that gave so much force to the mechanisms of splitting and denial at work in labor's dual-body politics. But times have changed. In the Western capitalist countries the struggles of labor movements through the nineteenth and twentieth centuries have been largely successful in changing immediate conditions for the better. A price has also been paid: labor's gains forced industrial capital to shift to ever higher ground from which to maintain its rate of profit. In the West this was achieved by replacing the old labor-intensive forms of industry with automated technologies, rationalizing the work habitus through the application of informatics and the development of more flexible employment patterns, and through the growth of work based on bureaucracy, marketing, and personal servicing rather than the production of goods.[29] Additionally, of course, with the growth of multinational corporations operating on a global scale, production was shifted to low-wage economies in the third world.[30]

Although the new "post-Fordist" labor forms entail their own kinds of physical and psychological stress, they do not engage the body in an obvious process of degradation; the system is rather more subtle and contradictory than that. In a world where the employee is supposed to model the corporate image (including nowadays its equal opportunity policies) and where impression management is the name of the game (and even often of the job), the "right" physical appearance and social skills are required alongside the necessary vocational credentials.[31] Certainly in the dream jobs to which so many young people in the West aspire—airline hostess, dancer, lifeguard, rock musician, athlete, etc.—what is being sold is socialized body power rather than labor power in the traditional sense. But at the same time, the process of social production has become increasingly dematerialized; in the information flows that regulate the movements of global capital, the essential inputs are entirely disembodied and abstracted from living labor.[32]

Race and gender have thus become much more material in determining access and status within the immediate work habitus but are now largely immaterial to its wider conditions of reproduction. At the level of recruitment and promotion within internal labor markets, faces now fit as coded signs of "lifestyle," but all of this is entirely irrelevant to the productivity of the computerized systems of faceless interfaces that these "faces" operate. At the point at which globalization makes racism and sexism finally redundant in principle, in practice it strengthens their hold over local labor histories.

At a local level, then, the contradictions proliferate. Those who have the credentials to win the "clean" white-collar jobs consign the dirty jobs and those who do them to the dustbins of history; yet the new "white" jobs also become destabilized by global pressures of corporate downsizing. Meanwhile, among the rank and file who cannot gain entry to the new work habitus, certain types of traditionally white manual work take on a hyperinflationary value, not so much because of skill or wage level, but because they require or permit the public display of masculinities that have otherwise become redundant and dysfunctional. Certain types—the construction worker, the trucker, the rigger, the cowboy, the steel worker, the miner—stake out the new frontiers of white laborism and sometimes push beyond them. Their praises are sung, in country and western music, in buddy movies, in soft-porn magazines and comics, in corporate advertising, and in television serials, often with strongly homoerotic overtones. This new ideal body-of-labor is at once firmly rooted in the work habitus and highly mobile. These men are at home wherever they go. They are celebrated for being ruggedly individualistic *and* for restoring a lost sense of physical male fraternity and pride—and not just to the working classes but to the nation as a whole. They have indeed been invented as the standard-bearers of a new white race.[33]

Yet many young white people have abandoned these "ideal types" of manual labor as sites of identification because they no longer correspond to any realizable aspiration. The growth of youth unemployment as a structural feature of Western economies throughout the 1980s cut a whole generation off from any kind of work apart from that offered by the hidden economy.[34] The whole habitus of manual labor was simultaneously reorganized in order to dismantle the customary practices of working-class apprenticeship.[35]

The emergence of a "skinhead youth international" closely allied to movements of the far right and with transatlantic links is one symptom of these changes. Yet it still seems remarkable that what started as a local and somewhat sardonic metastatement about a white English ethnicity associated with the dying culture of costers, dockers, and cockneys in the East End of London should develop into an international badge of popular white supremacism.[36]

At least one of the things that made this possible was the ease with which the skinhead "uniform"—shaved head, Doc Martens boots, T-shirt, jeans, and suspenders—could be abstracted from any specific reference or content in local social history and projected as a generic transnational image of white labor. It was easy precisely because this labor had been emptied of any content apart from its "color." What it worked on and reconfigured with new value and meaning was precisely whiteness. And by the same token, this whiteness now signified its own transcendence of any determinate work habitus. Which is perhaps one reason why this version of proletarian hardness was so popular among unemployed youth.

Yet once whiteness floats free of any social anchorage and becomes a pure narcissism of physical difference, its inner emptiness stands revealed. One defense against this consists in reinscribing whiteness within an alternative but no less imaginary community—that of the nation, modeled no longer on the state but around local analogues of labor's body. Nationalisms of the neighborhood, the football team, even the family can serve as supports for unofficial forms of immigration control directed against those whose faces do not fit the habitus of white male territorialism. This device is one way the most powerless and disadvantaged groups can imagine themselves to be some kind of local ruling class. For at least "we rule round here" (not them).[37] And yet precisely because the nation has become such a fluid and unstable construct, this is a tactical essentialism that often raises more contradictions than it resolves.[38]

An allied strategy consists in elaborating a cultural politics around skin and the body, playing with elements of the color code while conserving the significance of whiteness as a natural symbolism of race. The early skins, in fact, used facial cosmetics to give themselves a "black look"; today, dark suntans are de rigueur among white unemployed youth, if only because they are supposed to speak volumes about a hedonistic lifestyle far removed from the workaday world and the degradations of slum city. If you have nothing to do all summer but hang out in the street or park, then "sunbathing" on the invisible tropical beach beneath the broken paving stones and withered grass means that at least you have something to show for it. Yet exhibitionistic darkening, whether achieved by artificial or "natural" means, is almost always ambiguous. At one level it may describe a more or less envious identification with the pleasure principles of black culture, as Roediger suggests; but at another, far from repudiating the privileges of whiteness, it is a means of reasserting their validity on the part of those who in real terms are largely denied their enjoyment.

The payoffs for this move come both from its positive equation between rich and poor as members of the same racially exclusive leisure class and from the negative reworking of this position in popular racial conspiracy theories that posit a secret alliance between the political elite and blacks to promote their joint interests as parasites living off the white working class. Here is a paradoxically postmodern form of white supremacism that cultivates hybridity through mimicry and masquerade in order to strengthen its claims to speak for the race. It is a skin politics that enables young people who are born of the wrong side of the tracks to imagine they have the best of the white and black worlds, while in reality they have the worst of both.[39]

The whiteness of the old imperial racism was modeled on an aristocratic aversion to labor. As Lord Milner put it when he was watching some of his troops washing in a stream during the Battle of the Somme in the First World War, "I never knew the working classes had such white skins." It is a matter of considerable debate among labor historians as to how much of this whiteness washed off on a working class systematically treated as a race apart.[40] The whiteness of the new "postmodern" racism starts much closer to home, for, as I have tried to argue, it is based on the fetishism of certain "ideal types" of manual labor and their abstraction into displaced images of the body politic. It is no coincidence that this is occurring at a time when laborism and working-class politics generally are in retreat throughout the Western world.[41] Through the medium of its racialized and sexualized bodies, labor comes to reoccupy a central place in public imaginations of the nation, a place from which it has long been evicted in the field of political ideology. Yet, as we shall see, this provides a very unstable field of identifications for young white people who have to grow up working class.

A Working-Class Racist Is Something to Be

The transcript below is an edited extract from a discussion with a group of ten- and eleven-year-old white boys attending a primary school in London's docklands. The discussion was recorded as part of a research project investigating cultures of racism among young people in working-class neighborhoods of the inner city and evaluating different approaches to antiracist work with them.[42]

At the time the tape was made (1988), a large area of derelict docklands on both sides of the Thames was being rebuilt into what was supposed to be a new international financial and commercial services complex. The area was lavishly landscaped and equipped with yachting marinas, supermarkets, restaurants, and a whole range of other leisure facilities, all designed to attract a large yuppie population to move into the new private estates that were being constructed in and around the old waterfront. The project was the flagship of Mrs. Thatcher's enterprise culture and set out to prove her claim that private capital could regenerate public amenity. Under the slogan "Go with the Flow" the declared ambition was to install a major relay point in the global circuit of capital with certain secondary "trickledown" benefits to a local working-class population whose way of life had been all but demolished by the closure of the docks.[43]

At the heart of New Docklands was the Canary Wharf development, and the terms and extent of its failure epitomize the fate of the whole ill-judged scheme. As the economic bubble burst, firms could not be lured in by "imagineering" alone. Canary Wharf had no takers and went into liquidation. The New Docklands became a surreal Chirico ghost town. The promised jobs and other benefits did not materialize. Youth unemployment rose.

From the beginning the plan was opposed by a vigorous campaign bringing together trade unions, the local Labour party, and community groups on both sides of the river; but they were no match for a Tory government still riding high on a wave of national popularity following the Falklands War and determined to grind the last vestiges of socialism into the dust left by the bulldozers. With their backs increasingly to the wall, the campaigners began to take a leaf out of Thatcher's patriotic cookbook. Under the slogan "Give Us Back Our Land" they painted a picture of a beleaguered community of freeborn Englishmen and women invaded by foreign despotism and fighting a desperate rearguard action to preserve an ancient heritage from destruction.[44]

It did not, unfortunately, take much to give this plot a racist twist, and before long the local Bangladeshi community found itself in the front line of attack from local groups campaigning on a platform of "rights for whites" and claiming that the indigenous cockneys and East Enders were being driven out by foreign immigrants with the connivance of the state.

In part this movement evoked a tradition of white laborism that had developed amongst the dockworkers and their families since the turn of the century. At that time Ben Tillet, the dockers' leader, had been at the forefront of a campaign to introduce legislation to curb immigration from abroad. The Aliens Bill of 1905 was aimed primarily at Jews but provided the model for later legislation against black immigrants.[45] The dockers also had close links with the seamen's union, which, following the race riots of 1919, was successful in campaigning for the preferential hiring of white labor on British ships.[46] And more recently it was London dockers who marched in support of Enoch Powell's negrophobic "Rivers of Blood" speech in 1968.[47]

Much of the impetus for white laborism came from the local Irish population, who originally built the docks and subsequently settled in the area, providing much of the leadership and rank and file of the dockworkers' organization. They also played a prominent role in local Labour politics, a contribution which by the early 1980s had become increasingly controversial, with accusations of corruption on the part of an "Irish Mafia" becoming increasingly frequent. The Labour parties in the dockland boroughs were anyway changing in both composition and ideology, with an influx of young middle-class "radicals" setting a new agenda around equal opportunities, antiracism, and gay rights. In one famous incident, a gay rights activist nominated to an apparently safe Labour seat lost by a large majority to a Liberal Democrat whose platform emphasized the importance of giving priority to established "community interests." This result was no flash-in-the-pan protest vote. White working-class voters felt that their Labour party, the party of white laborism, had been taken over by an unholy middle-class alliance of gays, blacks, and feminists armed with alien ideologies. They deserted in droves to the Lib Dems, who pandered to their fears and spoke of the need to ensure that traditional patterns of family and community life were preserved. Racial violence against ethnic minorities continued to increase throughout the decade, and the British National party, a far right racialist organization, succeeded in establishing a presence in many dockland areas, culminating in the election of its first local councillor in 1994.[48]

This, then, is the background against which our research took place. Northside Primary School, where the tape was made, had an almost exclusively white student body drawn from ex-docker families. This was partly because the school deliberately tried to keep alive an imagined sense of working-class community even as its real infrastructures were collapsing. The school was part of a broader movement to reinvent local traditions of white laborism as a defense against the drastic changes taking place in the docklands. The school's curriculum and ethos were as deliberately old-fashioned as the building itself. Parents and grandparents who had gone to the same school could be sure that their children would be singing many of the same hymns, taking part in the same historical pageants, and learning the same English lessons as they had done. The rationale behind the curriculum was the need to provide a sense of stability for children who were growing up in the largest building site in Europe, and who needed the sense of security that traditional forms of learning and discipline provided at a time when so many of the familiar landmarks of their childhood were being bulldozed around them.

Some of the children who attended the school had been actively involved in a series of racist attacks against the few black families who had been moved into one of the most rundown estates in the area. The head was concerned that something should be done. The school had a policy of disciplining any child found guilty of making racist remarks, and claimed to have silenced even the most vociferous offenders. At the same time, the head permitted the expression of racialist views in a mock election, since that was an education in the workings of democracy. Standing against its red (Labour), blue (Tory), and purple (Lib Dem) rivals, the white (racialist) party won easily on a program of voluntary repatriation for black immigrants. So at one level the local culture of racism was explicitly outlawed while at another level it was being given a legitimate space of representation.

Nevertheless, the head thought that an outsider, a supposed expert in this kind of thing, might play a useful role. As he put it, it was a question of letting these kids get it off their chests. "Lance the boil, Mr. Cohen, lance the boil." The medical metaphor should perhaps have warned me of what was to come when I took a group containing some of the hard-core racists out of school for a preliminary discussion, which, with their permission, I taped. It was clear that they had been waiting a long time for an opportunity to "say what we really feel about blacks," as one of them put it. This is what they had to say:

NATAL ATTRACTIONS

PC: Let's look at this thing about being British. Some of you, from what you've said, feel very proud to be British. It brings everyone together. Now what about black people who feel they're British? They're born here, after all. They're also going to feel proud of being British, aren't they?

Darren (in a small voice): Yes, that's right.

Mark (loudly): Oh come off it. Jesus Christ!

John: I've got a Scandinavian name. God knows when, it must be one of my really early ancestors—so I feel I'm British because I go back all down the line.

PC: That's an important point. People who feel they're British come from all different parts of the world, from Europe, from Africa, from India.

John: I didn't originate from Scandinavia.

Darren: One of my ancestors came from Denmark, but they went to South Africa so I'm South African.

John: It's probably my great-great-grandfather who got married to an English woman. Heysens is a strictly British name, yeah, cos I looked it up.

PC: Well, what do you mean by British? British Welsh, British Asian, British English, or what?

John: It's English. I've got Saxon blood in me. I can't actually find out the meaning of the word [Heysens] but it's something to do with ley lines, power lines. I feel good to have a British name.

Mark: But if their parents are born in Africa (no, Darren, I'm not saying against you) . . .

Paul: Or any country . . .

John: And they're born in this country, then to me they're not British. Different colors . . .

PC: So it's not where you're born . . .

John: Yes, it's where you're born.

PC: Oh, well, if it's where you're born . . .

John: And the color.

PC: Ah, that's different. They're two different things.

Mark: No, no, no. They're mixed together.

PC: Well, there may be a lot of people who are born here, whose mothers are British, who may also be black.

John: Oh, that's an insult to me!

PC: Why?

John: You put me in the category of being black. If I were born in this country, black, and my parents weren't British, I know for a fact I'd have my brains (I was going to say something else) kicked out of me.

PC: Why?

John: Cos I'm black, which I'm not.

PC: You're just imagining if you were, because you know black people have a hard time of it.

John: Cos I know the resentment against blacks. It will always be there.

MORE THAN SKIN DEEP

Alan (speaking for the first time): Say you had a suntan, a white person might think you was black, and go up to you and stab you in the back.

Mark: You can't say that, cos John's got blond hair and black people have black hair.

John: Hold on a moment [turning to PC, rather threateningly]. Are you against whites?

PC: Why do white people want to get a suntan? They spend a lot of time and a lot of money going on expensive holidays abroad so as not to look white. What's all that about?

Alan: Cos they think it looks nice.

Paul: Like Peter Hills (a boy in the school). He acts all flash cos he's been to America and he's got all brown.

John: That don't make him look black. Does it make him look like a toilet cleaner?

Alan: If they had black hair and brown eyes and they was sunburnt, and say you thought it was a black person and you went up behind them and stabbed them . . .

John: What, with blond hair?

Alan: Black hair.

Mark: When we played the black kids at Drakes [a local youth club], the folks were all cheering us on because they didn't like black people.

John: Me and Paul play for Drakes. It's all white. Well there's one half-caste—that Michael—he's a nigger—he's small for his age and fat.

Darren (in a small voice): Well I don't think there's much difference between a white and a half-caste actually, because one of my best friends is a half-caste.

John and Mark (mimicking Darren's stutter): Half a caste, half a caste. You mean half-caste, stupid.

Mark: Miss X is German and she's got blond hair and blue eyes.

Paul: So has John.

Darren: We've got a Chinese teacher.

John: Yeah, and I hate her. She goes "Ah so."

Mark: We've got two black teachers.

John: I know and I hate them. They act all flash and walk around as if they own the place. But they are real divs. One of them can hardly speak English . . . just got off the banana boat, my dad says.

Mark: I've met plenty of blacks and I've had some stabs in the back from them personally.

Paul: Knives?

ANTIBODY POLITICS

John: Hold on, Darren wants to say something. We're treating Darren as one of us, even though he isn't British.

Darren: Do you go down Deptford High Street often?

John: I've heard that if any white person goes down there they gets mugged. The niggers just hang about all day sunning themselves, which is a waste of time for them, but then some poor kid comes along on his way home from work and they nick all his money.

Paul: My mum went over there [Deptford] once and she was nearly mugged. There's a video shop where they all hang out.

Mark: Me and John are going to school in Deptford, and that is a black area, you know. A blacks' paradise over there!

John: Niggers galore!

Mark: They all clan together, don't they. They help each other out, but they wouldn't lift a finger to help one of us.

John: It was the same with the Jews. If they had a cousin they'd buy off their cousin, and that cousin would buy off another cousin, who would buy off their dad, and the dad would buy off the granddad.

PC: Well, it looks as if you're going to have to come to terms with black people if you're going to school in Deptford. You're going to have to learn to live with them and get on with them, whether you like it or not.

John: No. If they call me anything. I'm going to show them what I'm made of—all the business. I'm going to kick their heads in.

Darren: Well, I went down there with my friend and we didn't see anything like that. We just went shopping in the market.

Mark: The other day we was down the market this side of the water and we saw this geezer come up out of a manhole and he was speaking some foreign language. I dunno what it was—Russian, I think.

Paul: Yeah, probably was Russian cos they had one of their warships out there in the river. I saw one too, come out of the ground. He didn't know where he was. He started talking to these black muggers and they showed him where to go. They're probably working together in the sewers, you know. My dad says if Labour win [the election] the Russians are gonna take over the Surrey Docks and maybe the whole of London.

PC: I think the Russians probably have enough problems of their own at the moment. But how many of you think that if Labour gets in it will be bad for the area?

Chorus: They're rubbish . . . They're all pooftas . . . wankers . . . Lib Dems forever, etc.

PC: Well, what do you think would be good for the area? What would you like to see happen here positively? And what are the bad things that you would like to see something done about?

At this point a flip chart was introduced and we wrote down the group's suggestions. The main items are summarized below:

What We Want Round Here	*What We Don't Want Round Here*
A swimming pool	Bulldozers
A cinema	Houses for rich people
More white people	More black people
More jobs	Gays, snobs, medallion men
More space to play	Car parks

My Dad Says . . .

How are we to read this text? One of its riches is precisely that it is open to so many different interpretations and hence is useful in promoting debate. My understanding of it has shifted focus considerably over the years and will no doubt continue to do so as times and theories change. But for present purposes I am concerned with the light it may shed on some of the themes I introduced at the beginning of this essay.

It may be well to begin by clarifying the text's status as an example of racist discourse. These are the views of children on the cusp of adolescence, for whom issues of identity and difference, power and relationship to the wider society are of increasing concern. But these are also children who are having to grow up working class at a time and in a place where the customary links between these terms have snapped. And this is especially the case for boys. The kind of male occupational succession that once underpinned the habitus of dockwork is a thing of the past. The question, then, is how do these boys use their whiteness to grapple with or evade this problem? How are categories of race, nation, or ethnicity mobilized to reinvent or replace the culture of white laborism? Is this culture something to which these boys are still somehow being apprenticed, or can it only be imagined as an inheritance, as part of a collective memory of a world they have lost?

I do not think it helps to hear this text simply as a reiteration of received adult opinion. The notion of adult ventriloquism—of the adult speaking through the child—is a popular view among teachers, who often blame working-class children's bad attitudes and behavior, including racism, on parental influence or failure. Not only does this let the school itself off the hook, but it goes along with a deficit model of working-class cultures which is itself based on a highly dubious and indeed racist notion of intelligence. For the underlying assumption is that reason and tolerance are the prerogatives of an enlightened and educated middle class, while unreason, prejudice, and ignorance (and hence racism) are the congenital lot of the masses as long as they resist the civilizing mission of the school. An alternative view is clearly called for!

Although at several points in the discussion the boys used "my dad says" to preface a racist remark, I think this phrase must be understood as a ritual invocation used to authorize the statement rather than as an index of literal quotation. In a matrilocal culture where it is mum's word rather than dad's that is law, and where the paternal metaphor no longer maps out a territory to be conquered in the world of work, its discursive citation here has a double compensatory function: it enables the boy to speak from the place of the father, and hence to assume in language a manhood that cannot be guaranteed through labor; and at the same time it lends an aura of legitimacy to racist statements of which the child is well aware most adults (including the interviewer, teachers, and possibly parents) disapprove and sometimes actively censor. But if my dad says, then it's OK.

It is significant that the first "my dad says" is used to reverse the traditional imputations of ignorance and to authorize the application of the deficit model to black teachers rather than white pupils. The scandal seems to be that the state has put a black in place of a white as a source of quasi-parental authority over the child—a metaphorical form of "transracial adoption" that reverses the normal procedure and symbolically threatens the sanctity of "traditional family values."[49] But there is a class as well as race dimension to this generational saga.

In this discourse, the presence of a black, a Chinese, or indeed any ethnic minority in a position of direct personal authority over whites is taken as a sign of their having "taken over" not only the local power structure but the government of the country as well. "They" have become part of the ruling class. "They" have taken not only our jobs and houses, but our exams as well. And now "they" are running "our" schools. Remember that in this case the school itself encouraged a proprietorial attitude on the part of white parents. However, this takeover is described here not in structural terms but through the idioms of male adolescent territorialism—the teacher is acting "flash" as if he owned the place. On the street and in the playground this might be countered by the usual formula of ritual insult leading to physical injury as the gangs fight it out to see "who rules round here." But in the educational setting the issues cannot be settled in such a straightforward fashion.

The cited insult—"div"—means "dimwit" and is a popular term of abuse among children; it associates stupidity with being a "mummy's boy" or crybaby (i.e., someone who has not yet been properly weaned). It also, of course, echoes pedagogical sarcasm directed against less academic children, who often get their own back by using the term not directly against teachers, but against those who will one day take their place—the brighter, more middle-class pupils who supposedly are not streetwise. In this case, however, the child's word is put into the father's mouth, whence it is directed as a racist insult against the teacher. In this game of trading places the black teacher has been put into the shoes of the working-class child, whose father has replaced him as the sole arbiter of knowledge. It's a double whammy.

En passant a racist theory of intelligence is mobilized against the very form of class hegemony by which it is normally subsumed and legitimated in the hidden curriculum and pedagogy of the school. The very idea that blacks could teach whites something is held up to ridicule as a contradiction in terms. In this discourse a black teacher is an oxymoron. Sanctioned by "my dad says," the school counterculture can then safely deploy racist idioms not just against black pupils, but in a more general attack on the official middle-class values of the school. And if these values include multiculturalism or antiracism, so much more grist for the mill.

Finally, note how easily the deficit model used by some teachers to construct the white working class as "racists apart" is used by them in return to transfigure themselves into the backbone of the nation, defending a hereditary Englishness which blacks qua immigrants can never possess. Whiteness has here become a corpus of knowledge that is not so much learnt as passed from hand to mouth, taken in with mother's milk, a language to which only the native-born English mysteriously have access.

What's My Line?

In making it possible for the son to speak through the father via the hidden medium of his mother tongue, racist discourses provide a kind of inverted system of apprenticeship to a cultural inheritance that can never be lost because it is innate, and not dependent on learning through labor. But if it is not a case of adult ventriloquism but the other way round, does this mean that most of the discussion transcribed above is mere adolescent fantasizing—a projection of identity conflicts that will soon be resolved? Is racism merely a phase these boys are going through, something they will grow out of with a little help from some friendly antiracists? Or, alternatively, is racism an ideology that appeals only to those who have never grown up—eternal adolescents locked in a narcissistic daydream of absolute identity (whiteness) and pure difference (blackness)? Is right-wing fascism, like left-wing communism, an infantile disorder?

Without entering into the details of this debate, it is perhaps enough to caution against any model that reduces racism to individual or group psychopathology, authoritarian personalities, or the like.[50] It is too complex and normative a phenomenon for that. But I think it is clear from the transcript that what these boys are working at, albeit with the raw materials of white supremacism, is the task of growing up. And what they have to grapple with is a set of contradictions which, far from being simply the product of their florid fantasy lives, are structurally part of the British social formation.

We can see this in the opening discussion about national, ethnic, and racial identifications. These elements are strenuously juggled in order to avoid the possibility that black British, like black teacher, could be anything other than an absurd oxymoron. But in attempting to define who they are in terms that make black and British mutually exclusive categories, these boys get themselves into a real twist. Or, to put it another way, they get trapped in the chronic double bind that is endemic to this particular language game.[51]

John starts with a classic, we might say premodern, statement of racial lineage. In terms of nationality his ancient pedigree is evidently Scandinavian, yet he feels he is British because he goes back "all down the line." At the moment he said it, I had an image of him as a young Viking. Perhaps his family romance was a kind of Norse saga centered on an exotic parent who had crossed the North Sea on a marauding expedition![52] His actual account of his family history was rather vague. But if his great-great-grandfather had actually married a local English girl, then it all made more sense.

The docks in this area once specialized in trade with the Baltic states. Many of the old houses were built of Scandinavian timber scavenged by dockworkers. There were Finnish and Norwegian seamen's missions in the area right up until the docks closed. Some of the sailors must have jumped ship and settled down with local girls. This intermarriage with foreigners was not always popular with the local lads, but on the whole it was tolerated, even at times encouraged. Because, of course, it whitened the area, set it off as a cut above the rest of the waterfront with its "tiger bays," its "dangerous and disreputable" multiracial mix of Lascars, Malays, Chinese, and Africans. In terms of local labor history, then, "Scandinavian" became interchangeable with "British" as a synonym for "white."[53]

John does not know this history, and indeed almost all its material traces have been effaced from the local landscape by the closure of the docks. But this leaves him with a puzzle about his patronym—Heysens. He cannot square the circle at this level; naming, unlike whiteness, requires a story to locate it within a myth of origins and destiny.[54] His assertion of the "strictly British" nature of his obviously Scandinavian patronym indirectly points to what it has come to stand for and yet conceals within the suppressed history of white laborism—

a whiteness that in this context "dare not speak its name" because it would give away the game.

Cut off from pursuing that line of inquiry, his search for a stable identity leads him in another direction, to the English and to "Saxon blood." In other words, to a racial myth of national origins that makes the Saxons, and in particular King Alfred, the founding fathers of ancient English liberties associated with the rights of the common people in their struggle against the Norman and other foreign yokes;[55] the source, then, of a popular patriotism that did much to transform the laboring classes from "a race apart" into "the backbone of the nation."[56] John may well have learnt the details of this story at school, but he has put it here to quite particular use. It provides the missing link to a genealogy that has apparently been buried in the meaning of his name. The evocation of a Saxon bloodline leads him straight into the druidic underworld—to ley lines, invisible conduits of magnetic energy running under the earth, linking up centers of sacred power into a unified body/soul politic of Arthurian legend. And all this is suddenly in John's grasp by virtue of the magic contained in his name!

We seem to be dealing here with a mystical but still material version of labor's ideal body and its power of social combination. By his own account, the construct makes John feel part of something vastly bigger than himself and also immensely strong. Perhaps the device offers an oceanic feeling of self-sufficiency in which all the tensions generated by these disjunctive identities might dissolve.[57] This young Viking with Saxon blood, bearing proudly a strictly British but all too foreign sounding name, whose Englishness depends on Celtic traditions, is certainly looking for some such escape route. But the more he tries to discover a purified sense of origins, the more hybrid he becomes. The more he seeks a stable and singular identity, the more destabilized it becomes. That is the nature of the double bind.

John and his friends retrace the steps of a vain and self-defeating quest for an internally consistent definition of racial and national identity that has accumulated more and more contradictions over the past hundred years.[58] Thus encumbered, they must wrestle with the niceties of *jus sanguinis* and *jus sol,* the crux of British immigration policy since the war. It is here that the impossibility of producing a watertight system of classification to ensure that if you are black you cannot be British, and vice versa, strikes home.

"Bred in Britain" echoes a sense of the indigenous that works at a purely local level as a device of racial exclusion—for example, in the rhetorics of rights for whites campaigns—but it clearly is not a wide enough category to deprive settled ethnic minority populations of their right to British citizenship; nor is it much use for denying their entitlements to public amenities and resources. John's move is to anchor Britishness to "Anglo-Saxon blood," and hence to whiteness per se. But this is either too restrictive—Vikings and Scandinavians, not to mention the Celtic fringe, no longer count as part of the union—or too inclusive—if all British are white, it follows that all whites must be British!

Many of the anomalies created by official classification systems in the attempt to juggle competing claims of biological, legal, cultural, historical, and geographical entitlements in fact derive from the conflation of racial and national categories operating at different levels of determination.[59] When I tried to distinguish between *jus sol* and *jus sanguinis,* Mark was in a sense right to correct me and say no, they're mixed. In fact, these boys combine them to produce an axiomatic definition that is certainly internally consistent and corresponds to the commonsense racist view: the British are those born in Britain of white parents. Yet, as the following section shows, even this watertight definition cannot quite abolish the anxiety of influence created by growing up in a multiracial society.

White under the Skin

No sooner does whiteness emerge as the kernel of these boys' identity than it becomes problematic as a source of lethal misrecognition. Reduced to a matter of skin pigmentation, color is obviously a matter of relative rather than absolute difference. Alan worries that a white boy with a dark suntan might be mistaken for black and become the victim of racist attack. But help is at hand. The repertoire of racial binarism is not restricted to skin color alone. The presence or absence of all manner of somatic and behavioral features may be used for this purpose.[60] In this case hair color is tried as a new dividing line. Blacks can never be blonds and blonds can never be black! This may reinstate the blond, blue-eyed Scandinavian look as the ideal body type, but it does not solve Alan's problem of what to do about all those sunburnt whites with black hair and brown eyes whom racists will mistake for black.

Of course this is an entirely fictional problem set up to make the boys worry at what meaning to assign to physical features as markers of racial discrimination. The exchange between Paul and John swiftly and brutally resumes the actual social semiology of color's mise-en-scène. Bronzed bodies are a sign of affluence, expensive transatlantic holidays, and residence in exotic climes; by extension, brown is something even poor white boys can become just by sitting in the sun. But for John and his ilk, the important point is that in doing so they are still white under the skin. This metaphysical whiteness is difficult to articulate in the language of skin politics. John defines it by what it is not, reaching for an image of blackness that belongs to its symbolic function as an antibody of labor. The reference to blacks as toilet cleaners is not just about a menial job no whites in their right mind would do. It is not even saying that blacks are shit. They are associated with dirt because dirt is matter out of place. And blacks in this scenario have no place in the sun. They do not belong in the promised land of labor's freedom from labor.

The attempt to naturalize whiteness as self-enclosed surface fails to resolve the worrying ambiguity introduced by changing pigmentation. John's attempt to give color a fixed characterology still did not produce any positive depth. Whiteness is given content only when it is sociologically anchored by a narrative of real and imagined community. Mark and John here introduce the story of a football match at the local youth center in which their all-white team was cheered on from the terraces because they were playing a black team and "the folks don't like blacks." This youth center was, in fact, built as a last grand gesture by the old "Irish Mafia" and is widely regarded as a living monument to white laborism. But even this homely picture of volkish racism lending its voice to a nationalism of the neighborhood is marred by the presence of a "half-caste" who disturbs the symmetry of the scene.

The mapping of skin politics onto male territorial rivalries invariably racializes space. Skin as surface covers the whole body; it gives to it a single, all-enveloping color. The color coding of the body politic follows the same totalizing logic: an area is constructed as all-over black, or white, or Bangladeshi, or Jewish, irrespective of the relative density and composition of the different groups living within it. This is a form of "ethnic cleansing" that airbrushes quite large minorities out of the picture. One of the key issues in the local numbers game, in fact, is just how many immigrants it takes to effect a color change. In this part of the docklands at this time, even one black family seems to be one too many and to threaten whiteness.

Equally, even one mixed-race member of a football team is enough to disturb the polarities around which the racial narrative is organized.

John insists the "half-caste" is black, Darren that he is white. There seems to be no middle ground on which the meaning of these terms could be renegotiated. Or is there?

Tall Stories

Many of the discussions I recorded with this group contain a continual refrain of grievance and complaint about the personal injustices the boys had suffered as whites. This often took the form of feeling that something was going on behind their backs that was doing them down. In my view this is not just a paranoid fantasy aggravated by a general sense of political impotence; it has a more specific structure. The boys feel "stabbed in the back" by what they cannot see or articulate about the relationship between labor's two bodies. That is what is not being confronted in their version of whiteness.

I think we can get a glimpse of this in the section where the boys attempt to put into words some of their anxieties. Much of the discussion focuses on the theme of black street culture and crime and undoubtedly draws on moral panics about mugging orchestrated by the mass media.[61] But threaded through this is another vision—of a black El Dorado whose inhabitants sit around sunning themselves and living a life of ease on their ill-gotten gains. John's little vignette certainly seems to support Roediger's thesis about white working-class racism being driven by envy and resentment of blacks' free-and-easy lifestyle. Blacks are portrayed as criminally lazy and parasitic, enjoying themselves at the white workers-taxpayers' expense, and as rejoicing at being together, in their own self-sufficient community, having found a paradise they can call home. But I think Roediger underestimates the intensity of the ambivalence such narratives generate, and the consequences of disavowal.

What does it mean for these white boys that they cross the water to the other side and enter an alien world, which is also a paradise where they do not belong, and are robbed of what they have earnt by their own labor, either by blacks possessed of legendary powers of procreation or by Jews with their mysterious gift for self-enrichment? A psychoanalytic reading would note the fantasied contents of the mother's body, the black as phallus, the castration anxiety associated with labor, and the model of exclusionary intercourse as being key elements in the racialization of the male Oedipus. This would help to explain the manic glee of John's "Niggers galore" and its links with anti-Semitic constructions of Jewish community, and also the fantasy that underlies his plan to launch a campaign of racial harrassment when he moves to his new school. As he puts it, in a term that has a Jewish origin but has become associated with the East End criminal firm and its respectable "fronts," he is going to "do the business."[62] And that throwaway line is perhaps a clue to his real purposes. Under the auspices of his moral crusade for white rights, John is planning to embark on a criminal career—not only in the literal sense that if the police practice what they preach about their commitment to prosecute racial violence, John's activities will sooner or later land him in trouble with the law; but also in the symbolic sense that in making racism his business, so that in future his "productivity" will be measured by the number of heads he kicks in, he has transformed his laboring body into an engine of destruction. That is, into an antibody, which will do the work of racism.

Mark and Paul take another tack, one more likely to remain at the level of symbolization rather than being acted out. In a little folie à deux they construct a story about a criminal conspiracy between Russian Communists and black muggers to take control of the docklands and the whole of London. It is entirely appropriate that the main arteries of this antibody politic should be sewers not ley lines. Black and white underworlds meet in a single project of domination—a reworking, in the geography of the "other score," of the popular belief that an unholy alliance of middle-class lefties and black community activists had taken over the local state and was secretly using its power to disadvantage the white working class.

The credibility of the tale is guaranteed by "my dad says," and my dad says that Labour is to blame—the ultimate hidden hand out to stab the country and its erstwhile supporters in the back. Again, I think this citation is primarily a strategy of authorization for a very tall story. But it does contain, in addition, an appeal to political realism. For when it comes to formulating their own demands, the young people provide, in their own terms, a perfect résumé of the double-faced agenda of white laborism.

Behind Our Backs

At one point in the discussion John turned to me and asked rather aggressively whether I am against whites. Only in this moment of confrontation was the word *white* used. The rest of the time the references were coded and oblique.

It did not seem at the time that the boys were much concerned about my own position. But I should have known better. If ideology, as Althusser reminds us, works behind the backs of its subjects, then it always strikes when and where you least expect it.[63] On our return to school after this session, John suddenly got very anxious about what would happen to the tape. He was worried that I might show it to the head or to someone else in authority and get them all into trouble. I explained that it would be transcribed and the names and other details changed so that no one could identify either the school or them. This seemed to reassure him, and I thought no more about it. The next week, when I went into the school the head called me into his office. He looked angry and upset. There had been a complaint from one of the children in the group that I had used bad language. This could not, of course, be tolerated. Teachers must set a good example in terms of self-restraint. The boy's mother had been in to complain. If it happened again the project would be stopped. He did not seem particularly impressed by my denial of the charge. And, indeed, I did begin to feel as if I must have been guilty of some indiscretion—some of the things the boys said had made me very angry. The only way to find out was to listen to the tape. At this suggestion the head became even more agitated. Where was the tape? It should not have been made. What was going to be done with it? It should be erased. Even though we had explained at the outset that we would be making tape recordings as part of the research and had given the usual guarantees of confidentiality, this did not satisfy him now. No more taping!

What had happened here? Clearly my reassurances of the previous week had not been believed. John still thought that I would use the tape behind his back to expose his racist beliefs and activities, and, as he admitted later, "have him taken away and put in prison." So rather than have his bad language—his racist discourse—used as evidence against him, he had then gone behind my back to the head and accused me of using bad language. Perhaps he also secretly hoped that I would be taken away and put somewhere where I would be incommunicado. He had thus neatly turned the tables on me, put me in his boots, in the attempt to get me to feel as paranoid as he was. I was being put in the position of a naughty boy, while he, using the head as a kind of ventriloquist's dummy, tried to shut me up.

It was not, in fact, difficult to feel that people in this school were doing what they could to undermine the project. Support from the other staff had been minimal. I got a sense of a closing of the ranks against an unwelcome intruder. I was in effect a potential "blackleg" who didn't belong in this imagined community of labor; my work threatened to undermine theirs. In other words, I was given the same treatment as was daily meted out to the Vietnamese and Bangladeshi communities, just as earlier it had been experienced by the Jews. As for the tape, this had ceased to be a medium of mechanical reproduction—it now stood directly for the racist discourse it recorded. The racism was no longer in the school or in the community, or in even the children's acts or words; it was in the tape. And so it could be simply erased, the record wiped clean, by the press of a button.

On a Screen Near You

Racism proceeds by erasure. There is the genocidal impulse of ethnic cleansing. There are the campaigns to "clean up our estate" by getting rid of "undesirables." And there is the wiping out of whole histories from the maps of civilization drawn for the benefit of those who are supposed to lack it.

Ironically, in view of its project, what this erasure produces is memory. Not a false memory, or a full memory, but a memory that bears the traces of a repression. A screen memory. In other words, a graphic image bound up with a strong impression of some formative moment, which nevertheless covers over an even more traumatic event. Covers over, but does not wipe out, for what remains encoded in a subliminal organization of the body image is still there waiting to speak, to be decoded and embodied in a narrative.

I have tried to show that the habitus of white laborism provides a screen memory of this sort; that it provides a space of representation for vivid images of labor's alienation and the struggle to overcome. As such, it generates a language in which contradictions can be handled through mechanisms of splitting and denial to flesh out the surface narratives of race with human incident.

As the case study shows, those who are learning to labor under whiteness also actively produce it as they negotiate the crisscrossing positions of gender, generation, race, and class within specific local contexts. In some cases this identity work has become racialized explicitly as memory work, as an attempt to retrieve a labor history seen as an exclusively white inheritance. For these boys, though, it is more a question of finding in the idioms of race a form of apprenticeship to masculinity that will convert the ideal body-of-labor into an adolescent body ideal. I have suggested that in order to do this they must locate whiteness in specific social relations that simultaneously destabilize its meanings and make it untenable as a site for remaking working-class identities.

Although this double bind increases the likelihood of random outbursts of racial violence and rage, it also has a more hopeful side. For it is precisely at this point where the cover story no longer works that a dialogue between labor's two bodies, the sublime and the abject, becomes possible outside its fixture in the racial binary. Once or twice in the discussion with the boys we glimpsed this potential space. It is there in the split second John puts himself in a black boy's shoes as the target of his own attacks, only the next instant to slip back into his accustomed place. Why else does he need to deny so quickly that any shift in position is possible—to avow that racial hatred will "always be there"? And it is there in Darren's resolute resistance to the massive pressures to conform to the peer group ideology.

Darren comes from South Africa and knows all about racial apartheid "from the inside." He is John's main, indeed only, adversary in the debate, and he suffers the consequences. For he interrupts the flow of racist discourse in more than one way. He has a stutter, which, of course, gets worse when he becomes agitated. John and Mark cruelly seize on his speech impediment to ridicule his defense of hybridity. Yet what their mimicry amplifies is not his despair but theirs. For they are not able to entirely wipe out what Darren is struggling so bravely to put into words: that it is not necessary to go on laboring under whiteness. His stutter, like that of the trickster, becomes a sign of the fact that labor's two bodies are inseparable, and that somehow they have to learn to talk to each other in a language that is not organized around infernal oppositions.

Italo Calvino puts it like this: "The inferno of the living is not something that will be; if there is one, it is already here, the inferno we live every day, that we form by being together. There are two ways to escape suffering it. The first is easy for many: accept the inferno and become such a part of it that you can no longer see it. The second is risky and demands constant vigilance and apprehension: seek and learn to recognise who and what in the midst of inferno, are not inferno, then make them endure, give them space."[64]

Notes

1   For an account of this development, see David R. Roediger, *Towards the Abolition of Whiteness: Essays on Race, Politics, and Working Class History* (London: Verso, 1994), and the editor's introduction to this volume. In seeking to make a contribution to this debate, the present text offers a very preliminary draft of a larger and more historically grounded argument about the racial formation of the English working class, which I am developing in current research. I am very grateful to Catherine Hall, Avtar Brah, and Nora Rathzel for their comments and criticisms of this early effort, and also to Ruth Frankenberg for all her editorial efforts.

2   The pioneering work in mapping out the terms of a comprehensive historical account has been done by George Rawick, *From Sundown to Sunup* (New York: Harcourt, 1972); Alexander Saxton, *The Rise and Fall of the White Republic: Class Politics and Mass Culture in Nineteenth Century America* (New York: Verso, 1991); David R. Roediger, *The Wages of Whiteness: Race and the Making of the American Working Class* (New York: Verso, 1991); and Theodore Allen, *The Invention of the White Race*, vol. 1: *Racial Oppression and Social Control* (London: Verso, 1994).

3   Notably in bell hooks, "Representations of Whiteness," in *Black Looks: Race and Representation* (Boston: South End Press, 1992), 165–79; Toni Morrison, *Playing in the Dark: Whiteness and the Literary Imagination* (Cambridge: Harvard University Press, 1994); Vron Ware, *Beyond the Pale: White Women, Racism, and History* (London: Verso, 1992); and Ruth Frankenberg, *White Women, Race Matters: The Social Construction of Whiteness* (Minneapolis: University of Minnesota Press, and London: Routledge, 1993).

4   The term was first given theoretical status by Samir Amin in *Eurocentrism* (London: Zed Press, 1989) and has since taken off as a popular buzzword. Amin's classical Marxist model of Eurocentrism as capitalism's myth of origins has been challenged in some poststructuralist accounts; see, e.g., Robert Young, *White Mythologies: Writing History and the West* (London: Routledge, 1990).

5   See R. J. M. Blackett, *Building an Antislavery Wall* (Baton Rouge: Louisiana State University Press, 1983); on the transatlantic alliance against slavery and on the more general context, see the contributions to P. Lovejoy and N. Rogers, eds., *Unfree Labour in the Development of the Atlantic World* (London: Cass, 1994).

6   For a general overview of the cultural politics of roots in Britain see Kwesi Owusu, *Storms of the Heart: An Anthology of Black Arts and Culture* (London: Camden, 1988).

7   This position is argued cogently by Paul Gilroy in *The Black Atlantic: Modernity and Double Consciousness* (London: Verso, and Cambridge: Harvard University Press, 1993). Homi Bhabha, *The Location of Culture* (London: Routledge, 1994), develops the most convincing poststructuralist account of the making of diasporic identities in both the colonial and postcolonial worlds. See also the contributions to Ali Rattansi and Sallie Westwood, *Racism, Modernity, and Identity: On the Western Front* (Cambridge: Polity, 1996).

8   See Herbert Aptheker, *Anti-racism in U.S. History: The First Two Hundred Years* (New York: Greenwood Press, 1992), on the history of the antiracist movement in the United States. There is no study of similar depth for Britain, but see Caroline

Knowles, *Race, Discourse, and Labourism* (London: Routledge, 1992), for a comparison between pre- and postwar discourses of left antiracism.

9   There is now a considerable revisionist or antiessentialist literature. Recent sub-
stantive contributions that include useful overviews of the debates include Floya
Anthias and Nira Yuval Davis, *Racialised Boundaries* (London: Routledge, 1993);
David Theo Goldberg, *Racist Culture: Philosophy and the Politics of Meaning* (Cam-
bridge: Blackwell, 1993); and the contributions to *Race, Culture, and Difference,* ed.
James Donald and Ali Rattansi (London: Sage, 1992).

10   There are some interesting points of convergence between Lacanian and post-
Kleinian perspectives, particularly in recent discussions of racism as a "narcissism
of minor differences." Michael Rustin, ed., *The Good Society and the Inner World*
(London: Verso 1991) has drawn of elements of both problematics in elaborating
the notion of race as an "empty category"; Kristeva's model of abjection and the un-
canny as generative structures of feeling about the Other (Julia Kristeva, *Foreigners
to Ourselves* [London: Allen and Unwin, 1993]) also shows traces of Kleinian as
well as Lacanian influence. There do, however, remain important differences in
emphasis between the two perspectives. Lacanians such as Sibony (Sibony, *Le
Nom et le corps* [Paris: Seuil, 1994]), and Slavoj Žižek (*The Sublime Object of Ideology* [London: Verso, 1989]) link the dynamics of racist desire and its compulsive
repetitions to the disavowal of difference. Kleinians continue to stress the role of
racist constructs as a form of defense against anxieties associated with loss of identity. Both perspectives have considerably influenced the argument developed here;
they offer a more sophisticated reading of structures of unconscious representation active in racist discourse than the mechanical repression models found in the
classical Freudianism of Joel Kovel, *White Racism: A Psychohistory* (New York: Pantheon, 1970); or K. Theweleit, *Male Phantasies* (Cambridge: Polity Press, 1993).

11   The concept is developed by Pierre Bourdieu in *The Field of Cultural Reproduction*
(Cambridge: Cambridge University Press, 1993).

12   For the persistence of preindustrial forms of labor organization and culture in
forms of resistance to capitalist work discipline, modernity, and the law, see
Christopher Hill, *Change and Continuity in Seventeenth Century England* (London:
Penguin, 1974); E. P. Thompson and D. Hays, *Black Acts, Whigs and Hunters* (Lon-
don: Allen Lane, 1985); M. Rediker, *Between the Devil and the Deep Blue Sea:
Merchant Seamen, Pirates, and the Anglo-American Marine World, 1700–1750* (Cambridge: Cambridge University Press, 1987); Peter Linebaugh, *The London Hanged:
Crime and Civil Society in the Eighteenth Century* (London: Penguin, 1993); and
above all John Rule, *The Labouring Classes in Early Industrial England* (London:
Longman, 1986), and Rule, *Albion's People: English Society, 1714–1815* (London:
Longman, 1992). The significance of this cultural conservatism for the ideology
of laborism is discussed in John Marriott, *The Culture of Labourism: The East End
between the Wars* (Edinburgh: Edinburgh University Press, 1991); and Zigmunt
Bauman, *Memories of Class* (London: Routledge, 1982).

13   The image of particular sections of the working class as constituting a race apart,
as inhabiting an unknown or "dark" continent, is a recurrent theme in much public commentary published during the Victorian period, and one which for obvious
reasons was much used by the urban social explorers. The frequency of this term

is noted by Linebaugh, *London Hanged;* Louis Chevalier, *Laboring Classes and Dangerous Classes in Paris during the First Half of the Nineteenth Century,* trans. Frank Jellinek (New York: H. Fertig, 1973), notes the function of the term in characterizing the "dangerous classes." Anne McClintock, *Imperial Leather: Race, Gender, and Sexuality in the Colonial Context* (London: Routledge, 1994), discusses the use of the term in the context of sexual politics and the late Victorian culture of imperialism. The term continued to be applied to dockers and miners up until the 1960s, and still characterizes many local narratives. For a further discussion see Phil Cohen, *Island Stories* (London: University of East London Press, 1997).

14   The role conspiracy theories of labor play in cultures of working class racism is a greatly underresearched area, but see the discussion in Robert Miles and Annie Phizaclea, *Labour and Racism* (London: Routledge, 1980).

15   The use of Irish migrant laborers to undermine wage bargaining or as strike breakers was prevalent in Victorian Britain; in the Edwardian period, Lascars and African seamen were similarly substituted for English labor on British ships. Both practices were instrumental in the early development of white laborism and have been extensively documented in collections of research studies edited by Kenneth Lunn (*Hosts, Immigrants, and Minorities: Historical Response to Newcomers in British Society, 1870–1914* [Folkestone: Dawson, 1980] and *Race and Labour in Twentieth Century Britain* [London: Cass, 1985]) and D. Frost, ed., *Ethnic Labour and British Imperial Trade* (London: Cass, 1995).

16   Two famous examples of this kind of racialized class struggle narrative are Engel's characterization of the Irish (Friedrich Engels, *The Condition of the Working Class in England* [Oxford: Blackwell, 1971]) and Robert Blatchford's view of Jews in Merrie England. Many similar characterizations can be found in working-class autobiographies from the Victorian and Edwardian periods. For a discussion of this whole phenomenon see K. Malik, *The Meaning of Race* (London: Routledge, 1996).

17   Robert Miles has done much to map the racialization of divisions of labor in the British context. See Miles, *Racism and Migrant Labour* (London: Routledge, 1982).

18   In its cruder versions the divide-and-rule thesis is nowadays confined to far left antifascist groups in Britain.

19   Miles, *Racism and Migrant Labour,* for example, stresses the formal adequacy of commonsense racism as an explanation of economic disadvantage or decline, but still regards these explanations as false in the sense of misrecognizing or reversing the true relation of cause and effect.

20   For examples of this process see Phil Cohen and David Robins, *Knuckle Sandwich: Growing Up in the Working Class City* (Harmondsworth: Penguin, 1978); and Les Back, *New Ethnicities and Urban Youth Cultures* (London: University College London Press, 1995).

21   See Roediger, *Wages of Whiteness.*

22   The two bodies of theory outlined here draw on the psychoanalytic theory of body images developed in Françoise Dolto, *Image inconscient du corps* (Paris: Seuil, 1982); and Sami Ali, *Corps real, Corps imaginaire* (Paris: Seuil, 1981). The historical origins of this dual image in the divine/mortal body of the feudal monarchy are analyzed in Ernst Hartwig Kantorowicz, *The King's Two Bodies: A Study in Mediaeval Political Theology* (Cambridge: Harvard University Press, 1986); its transposition into aristocratic genealogies of race is discussed in A. Devyver, *Le Sang Epure*

(Brussels: Louvain, 1984); and its subsequent sublimation in bourgeois/democratic versions of the body politic in E. Mirzoeff, *Bodyscapes* (London: Routledge, 1995). Žižek, *The Sublime Object of Ideology,* shows that this principle of "dual organization" of power is nevertheless still active in positions of subjection within the modern nation-state. The cultural linkage of two bodies to notions of purity/impurity and natural symbolisms of difference is suggested in Mary Douglas, *Natural Symbols* (London: Penguin, 1973); and Douglas, *Purity and Danger* (New York: Praeger, 1966).

23 See Kovel, *White Racism;* and Kobena Mercer, *Welcome to the Jungle: New Positions in Black Cultural Studies* (New York: Routledge, 1994), for two contrasting accounts of this particular dialectic of racial and sexual repression.

24 For a general discussion of the freedom/unfreedom debate as it relates to the status of wage labor see Hill, *Change and Continuity in Seventeenth Century England.* On the relation between slavery and ideologies of freedom under capitalism see Thomas C. Holt, *The Problem of Freedom: Race, Labor, and Politics in Jamaica and Britain, 1832–1938* (Baltimore: Johns Hopkins University Press, 1992); Orlando Patterson, *Freedom in the Making of Western Culture* (London: I. B. Tauris, and New York: Basic Books, 1991); and David Brion Davis, *The Problem of Slavery and Western Culture* (Ithaca: Cornell University Press, 1966, and Oxford: Oxford University Press, 1988). On the specific terms of transatlantic comparison between chattel slavery and wage labor see Blackett, *Building an Antislavery Wall;* Betty Fladeland, *Abolitionists and Working Class Problems in the Age of Industrialization* (Baton Rouge: Louisiana State University Press, and London: Macmillan, 1984); Marcus Cunliffe, *Chattel Slavery and Wage Slavery: The Anglo-American Context, 1830–1860* (Athens: University of Georgia Press, 1979); and the contributions to Lovejoy and Rogers, *Unfree Labour in the Development of the Atlantic World.*

25 For a discussion of the trade-offs involved in family wage bargaining in working-class cultures see Joanna Bourke, *Working Class Cultures, 1880–1960: Gender, Class, and Ethnicity* (New York: Routledge, 1993).

26 Tzvetan Todorov, *On Human Diversity* (Cambridge: Harvard University Press, 1993); and Kristeva, *Foreigners to Ourselves,* stress the tensions between racism and the humanistic project of the Enlightenment. Etienne Balibar, *Race, Nation, Class—Ambiguous Identities* (Cambridge: Polity, 1991), suggests the continuities. The question of whether antiracism should be considered an antihumanism in Althusser's sense is discussed in Phil Cohen, "Sur l'antiracism et l'antihumanisme," *Lignes* 25 (1995).

27 See Norbert Elias, *The Civilising Process* (Manchester: Manchester University Press, 1991); and also Phil Cohen and H. Bains, eds., *Multi-Racist Britain* (London: Macmillan, 1988). Robert Miles, *Racism after Race Relations* (London: Routledge, 1994), gives a good summary.

28 For a discussion of the relation between material conditions of working-class life and labor and their forms of representation see Chevalier, *Labouring Classes and Dangerous Classes.*

29 For the debate on Fordism and post-Fordism see Bob Jessop, *Fordism and Post-Fordism* (Lancaster: Lancaster University Press, 1991).

30 On the economic impact of globalization and its cultural implications see Arjun Appadurai, "Disjuncture and Difference in the Global Cultural Economy," *Public Culture* 2, no. 2 (1990): 1–24.

31   See Arlie Hochschild, *The Managed Heart* (Berkeley: University of California Press, 1983).

32   On the abstraction of living labor and its relation to contemporary cultural forms see Fredric Jameson, *Postmodernism, or, The Cultural Logic of Late Capitalism* (London: Verso, 1992); and John Stallabrass, "Gargantua," *New Left Review* 234 (1995).

33   The reconstruction of working-class masculinities around idealized figures of manual labor and their homoerotic dynamics has not, as far as I know, been the subject of recent study, but for a discussion of postmodern imagery of manual labor see J. Bettie, "Class Dismissed? *Roseanne* and the Changing Face of Working-Class Iconography," *Social Text* 13, no. 4 (1995): 125–49.

34   On the impact of youth unemployment and the hidden economy see R. Holland, *The Long Transition* (London: Macmillan, 1990); and the contributions to *Schooling for the Dole? The New Vocationalism,* ed. Inge Bates (London: Macmillan, 1984).

35   See Bates, *Schooling for the Dole?*

36   Two recent American studies of skinhead culture, Mark S. Hamm, *American Skinheads: The Criminology and Control of Hate Crime* (Westport, Conn.: Praeger, 1994), and Jack B. Moore, *Skinheads Shaved for Battle: A Cultural History of American Skinheads* (Bowling Green: Ohio State University Press, 1994), explore many of their forms and functions in relation to a reinforcement of popular sexism and racism but miss the element of mimicry and masquerade highlighted in Hebdige's pioneering study: Dick Hebdige, *Hiding in the Light* (London: Methuen, 1987).

37   For a discussion of white male territorialism and its relation to racism see Phil Cohen, *Home Rules* (London: University of East London Press, 1994) and Barnor Hesse et al., *Beneath the Surface: Racial Harassment* (Aldershot: Avebury, 1992).

38   For an approach to the contemporary deconstruction of the nation see Homi Bhaba, ed., *Nation and Narration* (London: Routledge, 1990).

39   See Simon Jones, *Black Culture, White Youth: The Reggae Tradition from JA to UK* (London: Macmillan, 1988).

40   John Mackenzie and P. Duane, eds., *Imperialism and Popular Culture* (Manchester: Manchester University Press, 1986), document the extent to which imperialist and racist stereotypes informed popular culture during the Victorian and Edwardian periods. Gareth Stedman Jones, *Languages of Class* (Cambridge: Cambridge University Press, 1983), argues that this was a major element in the remaking of labor politics along more conservative lines. R. Price, *An Imperial War and the Working Class* (Routledge, 1976), however, on the basis of a study of popular responses to the Boer War, argues that jingoism was largely a lower-middle-class phenomenon and did not greatly enthuse working-class people. For a general overview of the dominant class and race discourses of this period, see D. Lorimer, *Colour, Class and the Victorians* (Leicester: Leicester University Press, 1978); and Catherine Hall, *White, Male and Middle Class* (Cambridge: Polity Press, 1992).

41   For an empirical study, see Barry Hindess, *The Decline of Working Class Politics* (London: McGibbon and Kee, 1971). For a structural analysis, see A. Gorz, *Farewell to the Working Class: An Essay on Post-Industrial Socialism,* trans. Michael Sonenscher (London: Pluto Press, 1984). The political debate on the decline of working-class politics can be found in Martin Jacques, ed., *The Onward March of Labour Halted* (London: Lawrence and Wishart, 1984); and Jeremy Seabrook, *What Went Wrong* (London: Gollancz, 1978).

42   This work was carried out at the Institute of Education between 1986 and 1988.

43 See the discussion in Doreen Massey, *Docklands: A Microcosm of Thatcherism* (London: Forum, 1994).

44 This is discussed in "All White on the Night: Narratives of Nativism on the Isle of Dogs," in *Rising in the East*, ed. Michael Rustin (London: Lawrence and Wishart, 1996).

45 On the Aliens Bill and working-class anti-Semitism see Steven Cohen, *That's Funny, You Don't Look Anti-Semitic* (Manchester Books, 1986) and the discussion by Feldman, in *Metropolis, London: Histories and Representations since 1800*, ed. David Feldman and Gareth Stedman Jones (London: Routledge, 1989). On popular responses to the Jewish presence see A. Lee, "Working Class Response to the Jews in Britain," in *Hosts, Immigrants, and Minorities*, ed. Kenneth Lunn (Folkestone: Dawson, 1980).

46 See J. Jenkinson, "The Glasgow Race Disturbances of 1919," and N. Evans, "Regulating the Reserve Army," both in *Race and Labour in 20th Century Britain*, ed. Kenneth Lunn (London: Cass, 1985).

47 See Bill Schwarz, "The Only White Man in There," *Race and Class* 38, no. 1 (1986).

48 See Runnymede Trust, *Neither Unique nor Typical* (London: Runnymede Trust, 1993).

49 For the debate on transracial adoption and family values see Ivor Gaber and Jane Aldridge, *In the Best Interests of the Child: Culture, Identity and Transracial Adoption* (London: Free Association Books, 1995).

50 For a discussion of psychological reductionism see *Changing the Subject*, ed. Valerie Walkerdine (London: Routledge, 1987).

51 For a discussion of racist discourse as a language game built around a double-bind system see Phil Cohen, "It's Racism What Dunnit," in *Race, Culture, and Difference* ed. James Donald and Ali Rattansi (London: Sage, 1992).

52 On Freud's theory of the family romance and its relation to processes of identity formation see Martha Robert, *The Origins of the Novel* (Brighton: Harvester, 1980).

53 See Stan Hugill, *Sailortown* (London: Cassel Books, 1984); and Eve Hofstettler, *A Short History of the Isle of Dogs* (London: Island History Trust, 1991).

54 On the symbolic function of naming see Ernst Cassirer, *Symbol, Myth, and Culture* (New Haven: Yale University Press, 1979).

55 On the theory of the Norman yoke and its influence as a myth of racial and national origins centered on the theme of the "freeborn Englishman" see Leon Poliakov, *The Aryan Myth: A History of Racist and Nationalist Ideas in Europe* (London: Weidenfeld and Nicholson, 1974).

56 On traditions of popular patriotism and their relation to working-class struggle see H. Cunningham, "The Language of Patriotism," and Linda Colley, both in *Patriotism: The Making and Unmaking of British National Identity*, ed. Raphael Samuel (London: Routledge, 1989). For a more detailed study see Margot C. Finn, *After Chartism: Class and Nation in English Radical Politics, 1848–1874* (Cambridge: Cambridge University Press, 1993); and Linda Colley, *Britons — Forging the Nation, 1707–1837* (New Haven: Yale University Press, 1992).

57 On the "oceanic feeling" of racial identification see Daniel Sibony, *Le Nom et le corps*.

58 P. Rich, *The Politics of Race and Empire* (Oxford: Oxford University Press, 1992), develops a useful historical analysis of the role discourses of race and empire have played in the development of a sense of political community in Britain.

59 See Anthias and Davis, *Racialised Boundaries,* for a good discussion of anomalies in

racial classification as an outcome of power struggles within and between ethnic minorities in Britain.

60 See Sander Gilman, *Difference and Pathology* (Ithaca: Cornell University Press, 1985).

61 For a discussion of "moral panics" around mugging and black crime see Centre for Contemporary Cultural Studies, *The Empire Strikes Back: Race and Racism in Seventies Britain* (London: Hutchinson, 1984).

62 For a study of mythologies associated with East End crime see Dick Hobbs, *Doing the Business: Entrepreneurship, the Working Class, and Detectives in the East End of London* (Oxford: Clarendon Books, and New York: Oxford University Press, 1989).

63 For a discussion of Althusser's theory of ideology and its limitations as model for understanding racism see Phil Cohen, "Sur l'antiracisme et l'antihumanisme."

64 Italo Calvino, *Invisible Cities* (London: Secker and Warburg, 1986).

Island Racism: Gender, Place,

and White Power

Vron Ware

HE United Kingdom lurches from one manifestation of its prolonged identity crisis to another. The end of empire, the prospect of European federalism, demands for Scottish devolution,
the crumbling of the monarchy, the political impasse over Northern
Ireland, all combine to produce regular paroxysms of conflict and uncertainty over the meanings of Englishness and Britishness at the end
of the twentieth century. Within the context of national decline, the
memory of Britain's victory over Nazism is routinely employed by different groups of people to demonstrate an instinctive hatred of fascism
and intolerance in the British national character. Almost continuously
since the 1940s, however, there have been many other voices, both
within and outside the established political parties, insisting on the
harm being caused to "British culture" by the presence of former colonial subjects. The desire of the most extreme group in this contingent
to "Keep Britain White" erupts periodically to shake the complacent
afterglow of the nation's apparently invincible antifascism. The two
episodes I describe below are recent examples of a political crisis that
both reveals and produces deep anxieties about the state of Britain
today, and which is often expressed through an overt language of "race"
and white supremacy.

In September 1993 a member of a neofascist group called the
British National party (BNP) was elected as a local borough councillor in the East End of London. Although Derek Beackon was in office
for only nine months, his initial success and the accompanying rise
in racist attacks in that area were deeply shocking to many people

throughout the country.[1] The media responded to the election with outrage: overnight, pictures of jackbooted, Nazi-saluting thugs covered the front pages of newspapers under headlines such as "Votes, Fists and Boots for the BNP," "Sieg Heil . . . and Now He's a British Councillor," and "Day Cockney Pride Turned to Shame: Growing Threat from Europe's Evil Boots Boys." Crowing over their moment of glory and refusing to accept any responsibility for the vicious racist attacks that accompanied their presence in the area, BNP leaders brandished placards bearing the simple message "Rights for Whites" at hostile television reporters. By intervening in the local politics of housing allocation and manipulating existing racial tensions, these men had applied their nationalist and xenophobic rhetoric to a very small place; but, as I shall discuss later, in doing so they raised the specter of a wider, national community of long-suffering, angry whites, seething with resentment at what they saw as the iniquities of multiculturalism.

The second episode also involved members and supporters of the far right waving the flag for England, but this time as spectators of the national sport. On the night of February 16, 1995, a so-called friendly football match between Ireland and England was called off when riots broke out in the crowd. English fans tore out seats and threw them onto the pitch, injuring many spectators who happened to be in the way. The next day, the press and television news showed pictures of men shouting, fighting, bleeding, and, in the case of some of the England fans, giving Nazi salutes. Chants such as "When we get deported, this is what we say . . . we are England, we are England, God save our Queen"; "Fuck the Pope"; "No Surrender to the IRA"; and "Sieg Heil" were cited as evidence that representatives of England's "yob culture" had traveled to Dublin with the intention of warring with the Irish. Neo-fascist groups left their calling cards on the seats, confirming the presence of the political factions thought to be responsible for coordinating the violence. Headlines spoke of the shame felt by many peace-loving soccer fans who had gone to enjoy the game; shame, too, was the reaction of the government and soccer spokesmen in the face of scrutiny by the international media. England's football hooligans, who had caused so much grief and bloodshed in mainland Europe in the last decade, had once again revealed the unacceptable and uncontrollable face of English national pride.

Neither episode can be understood adequately taken out of the context in which it happened. The various meanings attributed to events such as these are clearly affected by concurrent discourses on race, criminality, masculinity, and national identity. The BNP election, for example, took place shortly after Winston Churchill, a Tory MP, had called attention to the problems caused by having large numbers of immigrants in British cities. The soccer riot took place during the Anglo-Irish peace talks—many of the "yobs" interviewed were open about their desire to sabotage the process. Only a few days earlier a government minister had resigned because he was worried that the European union would require Britain to relax immigration controls. This had prompted more public debate about the number of black settlers and non-European migrants within Britain and the consequences of "opening the floodgates" to allow more in. The scenes in Dublin must be viewed in the context of the behavior of English football fans in Britain and in Europe over the previous decade. Viewed as an ongoing symptom of "the thuggery attached like a cancer to the English game," as one newspaper put it, the occasion prompted further calls for strengthening the law to prevent suspected rioters from leaving the country or from attending matches, even if they had no previous convictions.

Yet if we consider the images of fanatical patriotism produced by these events, I believe it is possible to draw instructive comparisons between them and to use them as a basis for a discussion of gender, racism, and nationalism. First, in each case there was a tension between, on the one hand, the idea that the English hooligans, thugs, and yobs had acted outside the bounds of acceptable English behavior; and, on the other, the shameful knowledge that they represented a symptom of social and cultural decline rooted in the country's very real problems. Second, in each instance the concept of shame was used to describe the overwhelming collective reaction of the nation. Third, although the election of Derek Beackon happened in a very specific locality, which enabled it to be passed off as an aberration, it also involved discourses of racism that carried meaning for the nation as a whole, as I shall argue shortly. Conversely, the eruption of national chauvinism in football can be seen to represent a temporary truce between rival gangs forged out of fierce and often territorial loyalty to local teams. Finally, and most relevant to my own argument, both critical moments evoke images of exclusively male behavior; it is as though violent racism, nationalism, and xenophobia were being expressed by young unemployed men whose naturally aggressive energies would once have been channeled into manual labor or some legitimate form of warfare. One commentator, recognizing the symptoms of "collective male psychology," lamented that "there is no wilderness left for brutal young men to spend their energies in taming" now that "the Armed Forces are being run down to a skeleton crew and the Empire is gone."[2] In an article that began, "As every man knows who knows himself," the same writer explained why men require particular kinds of outlets for their instinctively violent behavior: "The male of the species feels a deep need to belong. It may even be the deepest of his psychological needs, comparable with the maternal instinct in women (who feel their most intense attachments to individual children, and men, but who famously don't take so easily to corporate life with other women). Men naturally organise themselves into groups, with rules and traditions, albeit often enough 'invented traditions.' In this country especially, they also like badges of identity." Although we learn from this extract why it is that women are rarely found on the football terraces exhibiting collective loyalty and group aggression, there is no mention of the politics that might inspire some young men to organize and identify themselves as neo-Nazis. Instead, the writer expresses the familiar idea that it is "natural" for men to bond together on the basis of group identities in a way that would be "unnatural" for women. Violence and aggression are then prerogatives of masculinity; femininity implies an instinctive loyalty to husband and family and, by implication, a lack of concern with collective identities, nationalist or otherwise.

By talking about these depictions of masculinity I want to raise questions about the role of women in the articulation of racism and white supremacy. What is the significance of women's absence from these often terrifying images of violent racism—of white men doing things to other men—and what does this tell us about male domination and the profiles of different kinds of racism? There are several other questions that flow from this apparent invisibility of women, which, in my view, indicate the crucial importance of analyzing gender issues in relation to racism. First, if the fighting and brutality are figured as aspects of masculinity, are there corresponding types of femininity associated with racist activity? In other words, are there particular forms of racism that can be identified with women's behavior? If so, what are they—and are they seen as potentially dangerous, for example, as comparable with physical intimidation? And where should one look for signs of women's racism if the dominant images and voices are mainly of male hooligans, male fascists, and male politicians?

In this essay I will examine different aspects of the BNP victory in an attempt to understand how intricately gender and class are interwoven in discourses of racism in contemporary British politics. First, it seemed important to investigate what lay behind the shocking images of white working-class (or rather, nonworking-class) masculinity that dominated media representation of the event. The absence of women from the photos and headlines seemed questionable, particularly since their anger and frustration about their own living conditions percolated through the lengthier written reports on the inside pages. Second, looking beyond superficial media coverage of the election, gender was clearly a significant factor in the construction of a local, exclusively white, organic community fostered by political parties responsible for administering social housing and other public resources. Third, the specific characteristics and dynamics of the area in which the election took place also demanded attention, not just because it happened in the heart of one of the most contested territories in London, but also because it was a reminder that the spatial aspects of social conflict are inseparable from the social, political, and economic.

Female Racism

Before discussing the election of the fascist Beackon in more detail, however, I want to link the concerns discussed above to an ongoing, if somewhat intermittent, feminist debate on gender, racism, and ideologies of whiteness. I can still recall my excitement on first reading Adrienne Rich's essay "Disloyal to Civilization" while riding the New York subway, hardly able to read the words on the page they felt so right and so timely. It was Rich's idea of a history of "female racism" that so intrigued me, for that was precisely the problem we were grappling with in Britain in 1980. How was the far right attempting to mobilize women in support of racist and fascist policies, and on what grounds could feminists appeal directly to women to take an antiracist stand? At that time there was little theoretical discussion of the links between race and gender, although few could deny the very real and divisive effects of racism in feminist politics. I discuss this period in more detail in *Beyond the Pale: White Women, Racism, and History;* here I want to emphasize both the novelty and the radical nature of Rich's intervention at that time. Her essay contains many other right and timely observations, particularly those about the paralyzing effect of white women's guilt: "An analysis that places the guilt for active domination, physical and institutional violence, and the justifications embedded in myth and language, on white women not only compounds false consciousness; it allows us all to deny or neglect the charged connections among black and white women from the historical conditions of slavery on; and it impedes any real discussion of women's instrumentality in a system which oppresses all women, and in which hatred of women is also embedded in myth, folklore, and language."[3]

Now, rereading the same essay with my own project on "female racism" in mind, I am intrigued by the way Rich repeatedly stresses the role of patriarchy in pressing women into active and passive racist service. Having identified the futility of white guilt and the problems arising from ignorance, she reminds her readers that white women, too, are locked into a system of oppression that ought to give them special insight into the structures of racism: "The passive or active instrumentality of white women in the practice of inhumanity against black people is a fact of history. . . . But beneath that indisputable fact—or overarching it—there are other facts. White women, like black men and women, have lived from the founding of this country under a constitution drawn up and still interpreted by white men, and, under which, even if the Equal Rights Amendment should finally pass, there would still, given the composition of the courts, be no guarantee to *any* woman even of equal rights under the law."[4]

To claim that the systems of white supremacy and patriarchy are connected is one thing, and no one could really argue with the "facts" in this example. Almost twenty years after the publication of Rich's essay, however, I do not think it is possible to talk so confidently about the unitary category of "women" and to generalize about the effects of white male domination on the huge and diverse group of people contained under this heading. However, Rich is quite clear about her motives in calling attention to "female racism" without wanting to overemphasize its significance. Further on, she writes: "We have a strong antiracist female tradition, despite all efforts by the white patriarchy to polarize its creature-objects, creating dichotomies of privilege and caste, skin-color and age and condition of servitude. It is that tradition—rather than guilt feelings or 'liberal' politics—that I wish to invoke in this paper." In Rich's view, it is important for feminists to acknowledge the history of "female racism" in order to begin to express genuine solidarity with black women. Like her, I believe that a sense of accountability rather than guilt or denial is essential to an active political stance against racism. By calling attention to the ways white women have historically collaborated in the oppression and exploitation of black men and women, Rich "outed" a problem that was almost taboo in the more enthusiastic quarters of women's liberation politics, in Britain certainly. But today it is clear that we need to know more about how (and why) women engage in racist activity if we are to understand how white supremacy addresses different groups of people and how it works in conjunction with other systems of domination. It is no longer sufficient to argue that all white women are born into a racially divided and patriarchal world that they have not helped to create. Throughout the 1980s and 1990s feminist theorists have argued persuasively that issues such as social and economic status, ethnicity, and sexuality intervene to complicate the construction of the female subject. In the intervening years since the publication of "Disloyal to Civilization," the voices of black women and women of color have long since removed any grounds for shock at the idea that white feminists might not be immune to practicing "female racism." One result is that the project of exploring the active and passive instrumentality of women in racism is already under way in some very interesting and important work, particularly in historical studies. The activities of the Women's Ku Klux Klan, for example, have been examined in fascinating detail by Kathleen Blee; British women's place in colonial societies is also being scrutinized, and new information is coming to light concerning the role of women in collaborating with the Nazis.[5] Although there has been less focus on women's involvement in contemporary forms of racism, Ruth Frankenberg's exploration of gender and the social construction of whiteness highlights the importance of looking at the details of everyday life.[6] It is appropriate here to acknowledge the significance of Lillian Smith's earlier work on the foundations of white racial prejudice in the family and home. Although she focused on the American South, her attempt to discuss the psychology of racism through acknowledging black women's roles in rearing white children must surely resonate with the histories of segregated colonial societies, particularly the Raj, where the ayah was a central figure in many British children's early lives. Smith's extraordinary book *Killers of the Dream* describes how women and men are born into a world that teaches children the ideology of white supremacy with their mothers'—and nurses'—milk:

> From the day I was born, I began to learn my lessons. I was put in a rigid frame too intricate, too complex, too twisting to describe here so briefly, but I learned to conform to its slide-rule measurements. I learned that it is possible to be a Christian and a white southerner simultaneously; to be a gentlewoman and an arrogant callous creature in the same moment; to pray at night

and ride a Jim Crow car the next morning and feel comfortable in doing both. I learned to believe in freedom, to glow when the word *democracy* is used, and to practise slavery from morning to night. I learned it the way all of my southern people learn it: by closing door after door until one's mind and heart and conscience are blocked off from each other and from reality.[7]

The value of Smith's work lies partly in its description of how the ideology of white supremacy constructs and positions everyone as having a racial identity. In doing so it refuses to confine questions of race and racism to a world of people judged to be black; and by focusing on lessons learned in childhood Smith's analysis implicates mothers as well as fathers. In other words, she allows her readers to glimpse how concepts of whiteness are socially constructed in everyday life and can be experienced as aspects of gender relations from the earliest moment. In her reconstruction of the domestic worlds of the South, Smith also constantly reminds her readers that the whiteness of which she speaks is a product of that geographical area; it is a differentiated whiteness crossed by regional, local, and "ethnic" factors.

The Isle of Dogs

In this essay I want to examine the representation of men and women expressing racist sentiments in a particular location to see whether racism is being constructed as a gendered form of aggression—or protest—and what relation it bears to social class. This will require an examination of several layers of racism, looking not just at outbursts of abuse and physical violence but also at more silent forms of white hostility and discrimination: those structured into local institutions of power and those articulated by the powerless. While there is no space here to include empirical research, I would also like to consider the implications of the way racism is projected onto a wider audience. For example, if racism is shown to be associated with particular types of masculinity, this is likely to have a misleading effect on strategies to counter it.[8] One of the dangers with this approach is that, if racism (and fascism) is seen to be something that white working-class men do to black working-class men, many people may feel either unconcerned or intimidated in the face of it. Instead, the fact that the imagery of racism is largely male dominated, and a working-class phenomenon, as I shall shortly demonstrate, ought to ring alarm bells about the importance of gender and class in analyzing the continuing appeal of white supremacy.

On September 16, 1993, Derek Beackon, a long-standing member of the British National party, won the election in the Millwall ward of London's Isle of Dogs by a mere seven votes. The slogan that propelled Beackon to victory was "Rights for Whites," and his election propaganda dealt mainly with housing issues in the Isle of Dogs. It appeared from interviews carried out in the streets that few people who voted for the BNP cared about its underlying policies and the ideologies that had formed it as a political faction. "Rights for Whites" had struck a chord among those who felt their housing needs had been passed over in favor of the local Bangladeshi population, and their votes were a form of protest by those estranged from political power.

Like most of the fascist groups that have formed and reformed since the 1950s, the BNP surrounds itself with an aura of violence and thuggery. Just a few days before this election, the police failed to prevent or arrest a group of white men who rampaged down the main street that ran through the heart of the Bengali community in nearby Spitalfields, smashing windows and attacking passers-by. On the night of the election a gang of Hitler-saluting BNP supporters were caught on national television news rushing down a back street, pulverizing a hapless white man who happened to be in their way, and throwing bricks and bottles at a contingent of antiracist demonstrators outside the polling station. Meanwhile, a young man named Quddus Ali lay in a coma after having been attacked by a racist gang only a few days before, and nine young Bengalis were arrested during a peaceful vigil outside the hospital where he lay. Following the election the level of racist violence directed against the local Bengali community rose dramatically. The police disclosed that the number of reported racial incidents had risen nearly 300 percent in the four months since the election, and that the perpetrators appeared to be mainly white men in their twenties and thirties. In one such attack, Muktar Ahmed, aged nineteen, almost died after he was cornered by a mob while walking home with friends one evening in an area previously considered "safe" from racist gangs.

Racist violence is certainly not a new phenomenon in urban Britain, but the combination of organized physical intimidation and brutality being carried out in an area where a fascist candidate had been democratically elected had not been seen since the late 1970s. Then, a similar group called the National Front enjoyed a brief period of popularity in local elections, winning one seat in the north of England

and coming dangerously close in several other areas—including East London. Although it is often impossible to prove hard-and-fast connections between BNP members and specific assaults, it is clear that the physical presence of groups like the BNP invariably gives rise to a local increase in violence and intimidation toward those they perceive as their enemies. At the same time, the BNP is also drawn to areas in which racial tension is apparent because it gives them a foothold from which to begin mobilizing. In southeast London, where the BNP headquarters is located, four young black men have been murdered in the last few years, each the result of an unprovoked attack by a gang of white males. In the most recent case, in April 1993, eighteen-year-old Stephen Lawrence was fatally stabbed as he waited at a bus stop with friends. The police failed to make any arrests despite being given incriminating evidence by local people familiar with the activities of racist gangs. Because of this failure to convict anyone for Lawrence's murder, the Conservative Council, in whose borough the BNP was based, refused to evict the fascist group. Without more binding evidence of the BNP's involvement in the violence, they maintained, they had no legal right to do so. Their readiness to tolerate the BNP led to some of the worst confrontations between police and antifascist protesters since the late 1970s; and was only in 1995 that the council backed down and ordered the BNP to close its headquarters.

One result of the violence at the football match in Dublin in February 1995 was the greater media exposure of the paramilitary neofascist group known as Combat 18. Formed as a splinter group from the BNP three years earlier, it is reported to be a tightly organized and disciplined collection of small cells of members. Internal documents indicate the group's commitment to violence, robbery, and arson as a strategy to provoke "race war" on the streets, which they believe will lead to segregation and, eventually, repatriation.[9] Combat 18 has been implicated in attacks on antifascist activists who have been targeted by the far right in different parts of the country: in January 1995, for example, an attempt was made to kill a prominent member of the Kent Anti-Nazi League by setting fire to her house while she and her family slept.

The fact that the neofascists came near to murdering a woman in this last incident is a reminder of the way that they attempt to intimidate their opponents into silent retreat through violence, regardless of their age, gender, or racial identity. Yet all the earlier assaults were on young male victims, and their assailants were nearly always identified as men in their twenties and thirties.

This discussion seems to have taken us a long way from an analysis of "female racism". Yet perhaps at the same time it has helped to illustrate the problem of trying to analyze the dynamics of gender when racism is represented solely in terms of almost pathological male-on-male violence. By bringing in other factors—of class, locality, and history, for example—it is immediately possible to overlay this rather one-dimensional account with a more complicated web of social relations.

It should be evident from its name that the Isle of Dogs is no ordinary place. The "island" is actually a peninsula in the Thames that lies just east of the City of London and north of the Greenwich meridian. In the eighteenth and nineteenth centuries the area was excavated to become the center of the London docks serving the empire, and it came to be populated by dockers and their families as well as by seamen living a more precarious existence. Heavy bombing during the 1940s saw much of the island flattened, and industrial decline and new developments in shipping led to almost complete abandonment of the docks by the 1970s. The remnants of the island's established working-class community, which had traditionally included migrants from the former colonies, were either rehoused in substandard public housing or relocated to suburbs such as Dagenham, the site of a huge Ford plant, or to new towns in Essex such as Harlow. Meanwhile, the post-1940s period also saw large-scale settlement of migrants from the Sylheti district of Bangladesh, drawn to the borough initially by the relatively high proportion of privately rented property in adjoining areas such as Spitalfields. As the pattern of migration changed and the demand for family accommodation increased, Bangladeshi settlers were moved into council blocks that were considered undesirable by the majority of white residents.[10] The 1991 census showed that Bengalis constituted almost 23 percent of the borough's residents, and a more recent local educational survey shows that more than half the borough's pupils are from families whose parents came originally from Bangladesh.[11]

Various plans for redevelopment of the derelict docks were stalled by successive governments until 1981, when the Tories assigned the area, along with neighboring sections of riverside, to the nonelected London Docklands Development Corporation (LDDC) for complete refurbishment. The result was the largest redevelopment site in Europe —directly affecting more than fifty thousand people living in mainly working-class communities—and a financial disaster for many leading developers and their clients. Now, more than a decade later, it is the visual impact of the contrast between great extremes of wealth and deprivation concentrated in a small space that is most likely to strike the visitor. One architectural guide to the area begins:

> London's Docklands contains one of the worst collections of late 20th century building to be seen anywhere in the world. It is a marvel, if it were not so embarrassing, that so many very bad buildings from the same period can be found in such a comparatively small area of the city, massed so closely, and so incongruously together. Like chalk screeching down a blackboard, the conjunctions of one plastic looking facade against another, of vast glass office walls against the charm of what was once the noble entrance to the London Docks, of a clutch of mock-Tudor bijou homes in a wasteland of roadworks, or the grotesque marriage of a ziggurat of flats with the former Free Trade Wharf of the East India Company on the Highway in Wapping make you want to cringe and cry with the hopeless crassness and vulgarity of it all.[12]

As this extract implies, the eight-square-mile area, running along a nine-mile stretch of the River Thames east of the city, represents an extraordinary and unsuccessful experiment in the creation of new forms of urban space. At an early meeting of the LDDC, the first chief executive, Reg Ward, called it a "virgin site: a blank canvas upon which we can paint the future." Of course, this ill-chosen remark reveals the extent to which earlier forms of settlement and investment had already been removed from sight in the minds of the developers. Peter Dunn and Loraine Leeson, founders of the Art of Change and the Docklands Community Poster Project, describe the disjuncture between the desirability of the place and its proximity to undesirable neighbors:

> Later as luxury housing became a prominent feature of the development, the politics of the view entered the frame—those who had spent vast amounts of money for their "View of the River" did not want it marred by the sight of crumbling tenement blocks and unsightly council estates. This was dealt with at first by retaining the dock walls to screen off the new developments and, where possible, using gates and video surveillance to enhance their exclusivity. Strategic tree planting was also used to mask the

unsightly. Finally, if all else failed, the Development Corporation provided money for the refurbishment of council properties *but only those that affected the view.*[13]

As a symbol of late capitalist aspirations, the construction of Canary Wharf by multinational property developers Olympia and Yorke is an eternal monument to the greed and stupidity of a government determined to enforce the redevelopment over the protests of communities that had little to gain from proximity to the precarious world of finance and investment.[14] Situated in the Isle of Dogs at the center of the LDDC zone, the silver 245-meter tower of Canary Wharf (the building, 1 Canada Square, is referred to by the name of the development as a whole), designed by Cesar Pelli, is visible for miles around, hubristically changing the skyline of the city itself. The developers considered its physical location crucial because it is situated midway in the time zone between New York and Tokyo, within easy reach of London's financial center. Its position on the digital highway must indeed have seemed more attractive than the fact that it might potentially bring regeneration to an area in industrial decline. Its method of construction and the origins of the materials used to build and decorate the development are staggering in terms of both technology and cost. According to an informative press guide, the imposing red marble used to line the interior of the huge atrium at the base of the tower was imported from Uruguay; the contrasting green marble was excavated from a quarry in Italy, closed forty years previously but reopened specifically for this purpose. The four hundred-odd trees that line the walkways and miniboulevards linking different parts of the complex were purchased from a nursery near Hamburg, Germany, where they were first planted in the 1940s. In order to achieve uniform shape the trees had been moved every four to five years to prevent them from establishing deep roots. They had been transported, at a cost of well over £1,000 each, on individual trucks to their new home on the Isle of Dogs: instant symmetrical trees standing (with the help of cables because they have such shallow roots) as a sign of a new City Beautiful, built from scratch out of the ruins of an older industrial order. Interesting, then, that in the artists' impressions of the development before it was completed not one member of the crowd relaxing in the café society of Canary Wharf's various plazas appeared to be anything other than white. Despite its investment in the solid and permanent qualities of marble, the construction of Canary Wharf coincided with the recession, and Olympia and Yorke was forced to sell the buildings because there was no one willing or able to pay the rent.

The contempt in which the local inhabitants of the island were held is clearly demonstrated by the scale of the building, inside and out. The Docklands Light Railway, built to connect the new commercial district with the City of London, began with one carriage and is now unable to expand beyond two; until late 1995 trains were scheduled to run only during business hours; they ended at nine in the evening and did not run at all on weekends. A ride along the elevated track through the Isle of Dogs provides a remarkable view from the frontier between steel, glass, and waterfront developments on one side, and dilapidated 1960s housing projects on the other. At the time of the 1993 election there was still one supermarket, serving yuppies and locals alike, their different connections to the place reflected in their method of payment at the checkouts. According to the same press guide, himself a native of the island, the use of plastic credit cards instead of cash provokes great derision, not only because it leads to longer queues but because it also marks the owners as class enemies: newcomers and outsiders.

These details of urban deprivation and overdevelopment do not on their own account for the bitterness and resentment expressed in the vote for the BNP at the local election in September 1993. Shortly afterward Stuart Hall expressed the rage many people felt at the predictability of the white, racist response:

> That terrible moment recently when we woke up to find the official form of the liberal democratic process had seen a fascist elected in the Isle of Dogs brought home the brutal reality of a community that was expunged and an area flattened to give rise to that monument to Thatcherism, Canary Wharf—this fetishistic totem that can't even rent itself. In one small area an abandoned white population is left. Then, it is into this cauldron that you drop some Bangladeshis.
>
> How difficult it is to tell the story of why Canary Wharf is there, and what happened to those old communities. It is so much easier to blame the blacks.[15]

Imagined Communities

Beneath the images of brute masculinity and shattered complacency that emerged in the days of attempted analysis and postmortem it was possible to see the outlines of a complex social ecology encompassing decades of history, tradition, myth, and very real political neglect. As I shall demonstrate, the media drew pictures of the Isle of Dogs as a very particular zone of London, partly, it seemed, to explain and reassure the nation that a democratic vote for fascism could not, or was less likely to, happen anywhere else in the country. In this way it was possible to read the result as an aberration from the British sense of fair play and a typical response from a media usually concerned to play down racism and deny its effects. On the other hand, the fact that the area can be described as an island allowed it to be seen both as an isolated spot and as an allegory for the predicament of Britain itself. The danger of this ambiguity, which allowed the small island to stand for the larger island nation, arose from the way the very real racism articulated in the Isle of Dogs could be amplified and made to speak for wider white communities.

In a sample of media representations of place and community that appeared the day after Beackon's shallow victory it is possible to catch a distorted glimpse of this social ecology. One tabloid wrote: "The Isle of Dogs hangs like a tear-drop into the Thames. Yesterday it had good cause to cry. For years its face was a source of Cockney pride. A place of kith and kinship to warm the cockles of every East Ender." The same paper went on to describe the impact of the Dockland development as a gold rush that had brought financial rewards for yuppies far beyond the reach of East Enders: "A cockney community began to die as daughters were forced to move far away from their Island mothers. Sons went their separate ways. And strangers, they claimed, walked in their steps." [16]

The area has also been repeatedly described as "the loop of land known to millions only from the title sequence of *EastEnders*." [17] The *Guardian* referred to it as "this introverted community stranded in a loop of the Thames" and as an area famous for three things: "it's that nipple hanging from the belly of the Thames you see in the map on TV's *EastEnders*; it was the birthplace of Millwall football club; and it houses one of the world's greatest follies." In another reference to Canary Wharf, the same paper referred to the building looming over the area "like a school bully." [18] The *Independent* described the Isle of

Dogs as "an outcrop of land almost entirely surrounded by the Thames" where recent developments had created a "siege mentality among the indigenous population."[19] The *Observer* stated that "in many ways the people of the Isle of Dogs live in a time warp. The 'island' is cut off from the rest of East London in a meandering noose of the Thames."[20]

The relationship between the local and national islands is further complicated by the marking of the fiftieth anniversaries of the Second World War. The commemoration of events such as the Battle of Britain, D-Day, or the Blitz, in which large areas of London, including the Isle of Dogs, were destroyed, involves a celebration of British nationalism that was once defined against the threat of Nazism. How could anyone explain the appeal of this new breed of Nazis in an area that had almost died to keep Hitler's army out? The emphasis on the sense of shame and shock provoked by this traditional East End community's vote for the BNP marginalized the nonwhite residents further, particularly the Bangladeshis, who were perceived to be jumping the housing queue by having large families and making themselves homeless in order to be rehoused more quickly. However, since the racist language of postwar immigration debates in Britain routinely employs metaphors of invasion and warfare, it would not be far-fetched to argue that the Bengalis had been cast in the role of invaders who were being permitted to succeed by stealth where Hitler had failed with bombs. Their status as non-British interlopers emerged in interviews with residents who were asked why they had taken the step of voting for the BNP. Less visually striking than the pictures of fists and boots illustrating the events surrounding the election were the quotes from women who gave vent to their different varieties of hatred. One pensioner who said she usually voted Labour added that the Bengalis were "dirty pigs who bring disease into the group and spit everywhere. I'm not prejudiced, but they've got two wives and get about £300 per week. We have to pay. We work all these years and it is for them. This country is finished."[21] Another woman, aged twenty, was quoted as saying: "I would love them if they weren't in my block. We are running alive in cockroaches. They are taking over aren't they? I'm for the BNP." A young mother made no apology for voting for Beackon: "I'm stuck up in a tower block with no chance of anything. I'm not saying I've got more right to live here, but I find their smell awful. . . . Here, we just don't mix with different religions. We just don't mix."[22]

It is worth examining this vocabulary of intolerance to consider the significance of three things: (1) who is articulating it, (2) what it

represents about the idea of cultural mixing, and (3) the way it con-
jures up images of the migrant as a source of pollution. Taking the
last point first, the journalists interviewing the white residents selected
quotes that expressed a classic racist view of outsiders as vermin whose
standards of personal hygiene and propensity for breeding made them
a danger to the indigenous community. The pig is a familiar icon of
dirt, greed, slovenliness, and poverty, often found in descriptions of
working-class urban life in the industrial city. In his famous account
of Manchester, the "shock city of the 1840s," Engels interprets the
presence of pigs in Little Ireland as a further sign of the depths into
which the immigrants had been forced to sink: "Heaps of refuse, offal
and sickening filth are everywhere interspersed with pools of stagnant
liquid. The atmosphere is polluted by the stench and is darkened by the
thick smoke of a dozen factory chimneys. A horde of ragged women
and children swarm about the streets and they are just as dirty as the
pigs which wallow happily on the heaps of garbage and in the pools of
filth."[23] It is hardly necessary to point out that the East End itself was
represented, not so long ago, through precisely the same tropes of danger and disease. By calling her Bengali neighbors "dirty pigs who bring
disease into the group" the Englishwoman from the East End resorted
to a familiar metaphor of life-threatening dirt, pollution, and disease
once found in "horrid little" slums like the one described so vividly by
Engels. The mention of cockroaches supplies a more modern menace
to this scene. As Stallybrass and White argue in their essay "The Sewer,
the Gaze and the Contaminating Touch," it was the metaphor of the
rat that so powerfully conveyed the creeping horror of physical and
moral "dirt" that threatened the nineteenth-century European city.[24]
Although cockroaches have figured less dramatically in the topogra-
phy of the city than rats, their untouchable insect bodies are still able
to evoke a demonized Other,[25] particularly in the way they conjure up
infestation and failure to control "dark" natural forces.

The powerful imagery of filth and vermin conveyed by these racist
comments also demands attention because of what it infers about the
process of cultural mixture. Within the few sentences quoted there are
many elements of "difference" that suggest complete incompatibility
between the Islanders and the Bengalis: the threat of disease precludes
any easy proximity; personal habits such as spitting and intolerance of
different smells make separate living spaces desirable; the mention of
"two wives" suggests a degree of female subordination that is not only
unthinkable but also illegal in British society; last, the question of dif-

ferent religions sits rather lamely at the end of the list. For religion here must surely mean way of life rather than actual faith, a way of life that encompasses all of the above transgressions. The mosque is made to symbolize not just another set of beliefs about God, but also another set of values, allegiances, and loyalties that places the believers apart from the majority. Religion is called on to justify the apparent impossibility of living harmoniously with people who seem to have different personal and moral habits and who are seen to be taking all the rewards of society for themselves without contributing anything in return.

The third point of significance in the comments of the women interviewed is that they supposedly represent a specifically female point of view. As I have already suggested, most of the intolerable habits involve domestic space; smells, spitting, cockroaches, and the bringing in of disease all represent threats to the home. Nor is it surprising that women should call attention to the alleged custom of Bengali men having two wives, as it suggests a totally different basis for gender relations within the family. Although the quote suggests that the crime consists of claiming social security payments illegally to support this arrangement, it must also be inferred that the practice of polygamy is unfair to women, and therefore can be seen as a mark of an inferior civilization.[26]

Finally, the woman who claimed to be "stuck up in a tower block with no chance of anything" expressed the anguish of the unemployed, impoverished young woman who is a victim of a totally inadequate social policy. It is perhaps ironic that this construct of the dutiful young mother who stays at home with her children, acting entirely in accord with the most conservative ideology, becomes a cipher for racial intolerance through the vulnerability and powerlessness that it comes to articulate. As I shall argue below, the enduring image of a seemingly passive, but wronged, white femininity can be seen to occupy a central place in the contemporary histories of racist domination and female subordination.

In this context of social deprivation and despair, the media represented the BNP vote more as a protest than as a genuine demand for fascist government, a cry to be heard above the confusing rhetoric of political multiculturalism and the babble of very un-British voices. The fact that this cry came largely from women helped to present it as a far more authentic and heartfelt appeal for justice than the macho violence of the racist thugs. In the days that followed, however, more considered articles that discussed the local politics of housing, education, health, and other issues helped to explain, or at least make sense of, the underlying tensions that had led to Beackon's success. Among these discussions it emerged that both the residents of the Isle of Dogs and their political representatives had exhibited an unusual degree of attachment to the place over many decades. In 1970, for example, a group of men and women barricaded the road into the Isle of Dogs and declared the island an independent state to protest consistent neglect by local and national governments. They elected as president dockworker, communist councillor, and poet Ted Johns. As in many other parts of the East End, the political traditions of the community included the radical left as well as the potential for supporting fascism. It is important to point out that the totally undemocratic activities of the LDDC during the 1980s and 1990s had met with some highly creative forms of resistance and objection expressed by the indigenous communities. Michael Keith and Steve Pile point out in an essay entitled "The Politics of Place" that "there were (and are) specific geographies to these protests: people organized in different ways and at different times in different places. The notion of Docklands became a symbol around which people mobilized; a way in which residents identified their neighbourhood; and an administrative and economic zone; an imagined geography and a spatialized political economy—a way of seeing and a way of life." [27] Although many of the organized protests were successful in that they brought different groups together and forced the issue of "the local people" onto the political agenda, the locals were largely frustrated in their attempts to oppose the LDDC. In the aftermath of the BNP election, however, it was not the development corporation that was seen to be responsible for bringing the cauldron to the fire. The success of Derek Beackon revealed that many people were utterly disillusioned by the efforts of both of the established political parties—Labour and the Liberal Democrats—to improve the area. Above all, the election was linked to a local power struggle between the two parties that centered on housing allocation policy.

Island Sons and Daughters

For several years the Liberal administration of Tower Hamlets, an area extending from the edge of the city to Canning Town in East London, had devised a housing policy for residents of the borough that assured them that their children would be housed within the same area, in spite of the relatively high number of homeless families in need of accommodation. This policy was then applied to the Isle of Dogs, where housing resources were even scarcer and where there was a substantial homeless population consisting, partly, of Bengalis. Promising housing priority to "island sons and daughters," their propaganda repeatedly stressed that the families of existing island residents would be rehoused in the same area, implying that newcomers would have to wait their turn or live elsewhere. The rival Labour group argued that the propaganda distributed by the Liberal Democrats had deliberately tried to scare the local white population into thinking that the Labour Party would not only abolish the sons and daughters scheme when it gained control but would also discriminate in favor of Bengalis and other ethnic minorities. It was claimed that the Liberals had published fake leaflets purporting to come from the Labour Party in order to stir up resentment against ethnic minorities.

Faced with these allegations, the national Liberal Democratic Party immediately launched an investigation of the charge that its local representatives had produced racist election material during the preceding two years. The resulting report concluded that the material was indeed guilty of "pandering" to racism by encouraging white voters to believe that their resentment and anxiety about the Bangladeshi section of the community were soundly based. The investigating panel had examined the wording and presentation of several incriminating leaflets produced by the local administration in the period preceding the election. One such leaflet, an issue of the local Liberal newsletter *Focus*, demonstrates how the sense of an exclusively white community was created through an appeal to family, hostility to nonwhites, and a spurious sense of local, class-based tradition. The front of the newsletter describes how the Labour Party opposes the Liberals' sons and daughters scheme for the island because the Commission for Racial Equality would "take a dim view of it." On the reverse side, a questionnaire headed "HAD ENOUGH?" asks three questions:

1. Do *you* believe that new homes should go to Islanders not homeless families?
2. Do *you* believe that the Island should have an Island Sons and Daughters scheme like Liberal Neighbourhoods?
3. Do *you* believe that your island Councillors should listen to Islanders and not the Commission for Racial Equality?
   THEN PLEASE LET US KNOW TODAY . . .
   FOCUS SAYS: "ISLAND HOMES FOR ISLAND PEOPLE"[28]

It is worth repeating here that the constant use of "island" is a metonymic substitution for the nation as a whole. I would also suggest that the whole concept of "Sons and Daughters" is tacitly addressed to women as mothers. The appeal to keep families together in one place can be read as an attempt to exclude all those who cannot claim natural kinship with the group. By calling on residents to ignore the advice of the Commission for Racial Equality, the leaflet constructs that kinship as white and gendered, and in doing so naturalizes the community as both homogeneous and rooted organically in the soil.

Another leaflet, produced after the election but in time to be considered by the inquiry, is also worth examining for the way it addresses different kinds of white fears. Titled *Focus Fights for Mrs X,* the leaflet bears a single image of a menacing, unmistakably black, male figure in the pose of a boxer. The text describes the plight of Mrs. X, a "74 year old decorated during the war" who lives alone on a "dangerous" housing estate in an area controlled by Labour. Describing her predicament and that of other pensioners living next door, the leaflet ends, "Is this any way to treat those who endured the Blitz, and risked their lives for our country? Is this the welcome fit for heroes?"

The report produced by the inquiry found this second leaflet offensive in that it suggests that blacks are partly responsible for the state of fear endured by Mrs. X. The report also drew attention to the repeated references to the war, which construct the leaflet's audience as white, excluding the immigrants who had settled there since 1945 and recasting them as invaders. What the report did not do was analyze the way the two images—aggressive black masculinity and vulnerable white femininity—work together to suggest something even more insidious than simple cause and effect in the context of Mrs. X's situation. These constructions derive their apparently hidden (but no less effective) meanings from the historical memory produced by centuries of slavery and colonization. The image of the defenseless white woman whose safety is threatened by the predatory and violent black male can be traced back to discourses of white supremacy, as I argue in *Beyond the Pale*. In the context of later twentieth-century British racism, this couplet was revitalized by Enoch Powell in 1968 when he drew a portrait of the white female old-age pensioner marooned in a street taken over by "negroes." The specter of this helpless female figure, surrounded by people of alien cultures who had respect for neither her person nor her way of life, was a potent symbol of racism over the following two decades. By resorting to that well-worn and instantly recognizable image, the Liberal Democrat leaflet is therefore able to express the idea that these very local issues are connected to a wider national problem caused by the presence of black people in British cities. Once again the specter of impoverished and neglected white womanhood is seen to articulate the tired old refrain that "we just don't mix."

Everyday Social Networks

In this brief and preliminary account of an alarming episode in the dismal history of British racism, I have done little more than call attention to the crucial importance of gender in understanding how communities are divided hierarchically along racial lines. The figures of the embittered cockney "mum" fighting to have her grown-up children rehoused in her own neighborhood; the pale, tense young woman held prisoner in a tower block overrun with cockroaches and foreign smells; and the frail pensioner, afraid to leave her flat for fear of being mugged by blacks, are powerful icons in the construction of a white working-class femininity that stands as a symbol for the wider racially defined community suffering from years of political and economic neglect. Although these images are less visible in the media than the tattooed bodies of the young white males who periodically kick their way into the headlines, the deceptive passivity they seem to represent demands investigation all the more urgently. We have seen how racist propaganda can construct a mystical white kinship through appeal to family, tradition, and association with place that can then erupt with physical and verbal violence to assert itself. The media represent racism as a gendered set of activities in which men and women play different but interconnected roles: in this context the overwhelmingly male violence directed at young Bangladeshi men on the streets cannot be easily separated from the sneers of women who stay at home complaining of vermin, foreign religions, and overbreeding.

One important reason why we should reject this traditional military model is that it avoids the whole question of what happens when women are violent and active in neofascist organizations like the BNP. So far I have focused on women as potential supporters of racist policies rather than as active members of avowedly racist and fascist organizations. This is another aspect of gender and white supremacy that requires attention, again partly because there seems to be so little evidence at present that women are significantly involved in such groups, but has been neglected within feminist studies. As Kathleen Blee says in the introduction to her book on the Klan:

> Extremist right-wing and reactionary women are nearly absent from studies on women in political movements, which have focused on progressive and women's rights movements or, to a lesser degree, on antifeminist movements. We have no clear evidence whether this paucity of research comes from the unimportance or numerical insignificance of women in extreme right wing organizations or whether women are assumed to be pacifist, social welfare oriented and apolitical. It is likely however that the omission of women from studies of extremist rightwing movements limits, and perhaps minimizes, scholars' assessment of the consequences of reactionary politics. Traditional (and male-centered) definitions of politics that focus on workplaces, electoral contests, courts, and organized voluntary associations ignore the political effects of actions and organizing in neighborhoods or through kin and informal networks.

Blee's interviews with Indiana women who were active members of female Klan groups in the 1920s reveals important clues about the way racism is sustained and spread through everyday social networks. It would appear that the neighborhood is a crucial site for producing and sustaining the white supremacist attitudes that are fostered and expressed along existing fault lines of gender and class relationships:

> Informal conversations among women—dismissed as insignificant gossip by contemporary men and Klan historians—fuelled one of the Klan's most powerful weapons. Rumor did not spread randomly; the WKKK used tightly organized bands of Klanswomen to ensure its dispersal across the state. The impact of the "poison squad of whispering women" was profound. Women's poison squads could spread stories to every corner of the state within 24 hours. Even when the story in its entirety was known to be false, doubts lingered, as a woman in central Indiana attested: "Many of the rumors possibly had a degree of truth in them so you could not deny it all but it was not the truth as it was told." [29]

This extract makes a neat connection between the organized, gender-segregated activities of Klan members and the way racist ideology was reproduced within gendered social worlds, using existing networks of communication as well as specially devised ones—the "poison squads." This throws new light on the involvement of white women in the fearful dynamics of lynching in the United States. Although it is well known that whites of all ages and classes flocked to witness lynchings, it is not hard to imagine the role of white women as conveyors of gossip and innuendo about the alleged deeds that led to the attacks on the mainly black victims. This is not to say that men are not involved in the process of spreading rumors or malicious gossip, but rather to recognize that those with restricted access to political power are capable of finding alternative means to express their political viewpoints.

It is instructive to look at the dynamics of class and gender in sustaining racist and fascist policies in other historical periods and in other parts of the world. In particular, the growing literature on the collaboration of German women with Nazi policy deserves attention. In an article on women and the Nazi state, Matthew Stibbe argues that

> at first sight the Third Reich would appear to be an area in which the importance of women as actors in history could not be easily demonstrated. . . . Nevertheless, as historians are increasingly coming to recognise, the success of nazism depended not on one single all-embracing factor but on its ability to enforce a dynamic integration of a variety of conflicting interests, not least those of women, who at the time constituted half of the German population. For example, although the male vote for the Nazis during the Weimar republic was always higher than the female, the difference did narrow in the early 1930s and in some protestant areas was even reversed. In particular, it seems that many younger women who had not voted before cast their first ballot for nazi candidates, which suggests that there was something in the party programme which positively attracted them.[30]

The project of researching the role of women in supporting a totalitarian regime such as Nazi Germany raises important theoretical questions about using gender as a tool of analysis. The difficulty in interpreting the different roles taken by women in the Third Reich is discussed by Adelheid von Salden in an article on feminist historiography of Nazism.[31] Arguing against the representation of women as either victims or perpetrators, she suggests that it would be more fruitful to look for differences among women that reveal a wide range of relationships to and experiences of the regime. She also makes the point that using a simplistic binary of the private versus the public sphere obscures the many ways in which women were involved in supporting, voluntarily or not, the structures of the Third Reich.

This growing recognition of the complexities involved in thinking about gender in relation to various forms of white supremacy connects directly with my discussion of Adrienne Rich's concept of "female racism." Earlier I suggested that it was important to go beyond the idea of women being drawn into actively or passively supporting racism as an aspect of their subordination to men, arguing that it might be more productive to analyze gender and racism in relation to a particular place and time in order to demonstrate the intricacies of social relations that give rise to white supremacist activity. Below I summarize five main areas that require further investigation if we are to understand more about the gendered dynamics of local forms of whiteness.

First, it is important to study the ways that ideas about race and racial difference move between the private and public realms of everyday life: the home itself, the street, the school playground, the clinic, the hospital, the church, the supermarket, and other places of congregation. It is important here to look critically at the concept of gendered space, as increasingly high rates of unemployment in traditionally male sectors and the availability of part-time work for women have meant that many more men are now involved in what were once exclusively female domains. In an area like the Isle of Dogs, for example, it is not uncommon for men to take children to and from schools and nurseries and to spend time with them in parks, playgrounds, and health centers. On the other hand, a women's group based in an area of the East End adjacent to the Isle of Dogs reported many incidents of aggressive and abusive behavior from white women of all ages on buses, in the streets, and within housing estates.[32] More research is needed on the spatial aspects of community life, including procedures and sites of exclusion as well as cohesion and solidarity. Clearly this does not mean looking solely at white women's lives but at the cultural geography of specific locations as well.

Second, we need to know more about codes and styles of masculinity and femininity that express ideas about cultural superiority and difference: does gossip, for example, operate differently among certain types of women than among men? Again, members of the women's group referred to above had "overheard" older white women traveling on buses and talking loudly about the fact that they had seen Asian women with cockroaches in their hair. How do different styles of dress articulate such powerful ideas about patriarchy, independence, or incommensurable foreignness? How does the body become an emblem of difference that gives rise to vicious racial hatred or repressed desire? Myriad questions like these need to be addressed if we are to break through the surface tension of everyday life in order to analyze how gender figures in the psychological construction of whiteness.

Third, and related to this last point, it is important to acknowledge that while gender can articulate different forms of racism, the reverse can also be true. Ideas about what it means to be white, for example, defined against the racialized "other," are also implicated in the social construction of gender. For those who absorbed the fleeting accounts of the dominant media but had little interest or time to reflect on the complexities of the episode, the violence perpetrated by those attracted to the xenophobic rhetoric of the BNP is likely to represent an aspect of masculinity that is both patriarchal and active in defending the "racial" community. The tired voices of beleaguered mothers summon up a version of white femininity that is passively concerned with the task of trying to reproduce the racial purity longed for by their menfolk. This traditional military model sustains the mistaken belief that women cannot be actively involved in violent racist and fascist practices, and asserts a rigid norm of heterosexuality in which men and women must conform to strict codes of behavior in order to qualify as "white."

Fourth, as the episode in the Isle of Dogs demonstrates, it is clear that the history of a particular place, whether it comprises a few miles square or a whole country, can be reconstructed by political factions in order to divide inhabitants along lines of racial and cultural difference. These versions of history invariably appeal to a sense of family in relation to place, and as the infamous sons and daughters policy demonstrates, it is possible to construct an exclusive white kinship in the name of local democracy, a kinship that implicitly appeals to a form of matriarchy in its desire to protect the rights of its offspring. Gender, as well as class and race, becomes an essential factor in analyzing this powerful concept of racialized community.

Finally, it is necessary to return to the images of white masculinity with which I began. If it is possible to demonstrate that "female racism" (to borrow Adrienne Rich's phrase again) has a status in the media that is different from the more violent, and more visible, forms of racism so often identified with men, then it is also essential to make connections between them. In other words, what do the wives, daughters, girlfriends, and mothers do while the men are warring on the streets? To what extent is the racist violence committed mainly, though not exclusively, by men, carried out with the knowledge and support of the women with whom and among whom they live? And what difference does it make if an individual man or woman decides to speak out against racism in a community—how does gender affect the articulation of antiracism and the manner in which it is represented? In the spirit of Rich, who counterposed the history of "female racism" with a "strong female antiracist tradition," I would like to suggest that through closer analysis of these sorts of questions it might become possible to undo the illusory cohesion of whiteness as an ethnic or racialized form of kinship, whether attached to a local or a national community.

Notes

A version of this essay appears in *Feminist Review,* no. 54 (Autumn 1996): 65–86.

1   Derek Beackon was elected to represent the Millwall ward of Tower Hamlets on September 16, 1993, in a council bye election. He was subsequently ousted by a Labour candidate in the local elections in May 1994. Since then he has stood in other local elections in East London, as the BNP continues to contest seats in targeted areas.

2   Geoffrey Wheatcroft, "What They Really Are," *London Daily Telegraph,* February 17, 1995.

3   Adrienne Rich, "Disloyal to Civilization: Feminism, Racism, Gynephobia," in *Lies, Secrets and Silence* (New York: Norton, 1979), 301.

4   Ibid., 284.

5   Kathleen Blee, *Women of the Klan: Racism and Gender in the 1920s* (Berkeley: University of California Press, 1991). With regard to colonialism, I am thinking of Ann Laura Stoler's essay "Carnal Knowledge and Imperial Power" in *Gender at the Crossroads of Knowledge,* ed. Micaela di Leonardo (Berkeley: University of California Press, 1991); also Alison Blunt, *Travel, Gender and Imperialism* (New York: Guilford Press, 1994); and Nupur Chaudhuri and Margaret Strobel, *Western Women and Imperialism: Complicity and Resistance* (Bloomington: Indiana University Press, 1992). For new work on women in Nazi Germany see Adelheid von Salden, "Victims or Perpetrators? Controversies about the Role of Women in the Nazi State," in *Nazism and German Society 1933-1945,* ed. David F. Crew (London: Routledge, 1994), and Alison Owings, *Frauen: German Women Recall the Third Reich* (New York: Penguin Books, 1995). This list is merely indicative of this rapidly expanding area of study.

6   Ruth Frankenberg, *White Women, Race Matters: The Social Construction of Whiteness* (London: Routledge, 1993).

7   Lillian Smith, *Killers of the Dream* (London: Cresset Press, 1950), 15.

8   For example, one of the most vocal groups currently opposing the BNP is Anti-Fascist Action, whose slogans and symbols match the violent and masculinist tone of their opponents. Most, if not all, of their stickers feature a fist or a boot smashing a swastika; the special edition of their publication targeting soccer supporters is entitled "Fighting Talk."

9   *Observer* (U.K.), March 5, 1995.

10   J. Eades, *The Politics of Community: The Bangladeshi Community in East London* (Aldershot: Avebury, 1989), 26–29.

11   Centre for Bangladeshi Studies, *Routes and Beyond: Voices of Educationally Successful Bengalis in Tower Hamlets* (London: Centre for Bangladeshi Studies, 1995).

12   Stephanie Williams, *Docklands* (London: Phaidon Architecture Guide, 1993), 8.

13   Peter Dunn and Loraine Leeson, "The Art of Change in Docklands," in *Mapping the Futures: Local Cultures, Global Change,* ed. Jon Bird, Barry Curtis, Tim Putnam, George Robertson, and Lisa Tickner (London: Routledge, 1993), 138.

14   Ibid., 137.

15   Stuart Hall, *New Statesman and Society* (December 1993).

16   *Daily Mirror* (U.K.), September 18, 1993.

17   *Sun* (U.K.), September 18, 1993. *EastEnders* is a popular television soap opera based in a fictional square in East London.

18   *Guardian* (U.K.), September 18, 1993.

19   *Independent* (U.K.), September 18, 1993.

20   *Observer* (U.K.), September 19, 1993.

21   *Observer* (U.K.), September 18, 1993.

22   *Independent* (U.K.), September 18, 1993.

23   Friedrich Engels, *The Condition of the Working Class in England* (Oxford: Blackwell, 1971), 71.

24   Peter Stallybrass and Allon White, *The Politics and Poetics of Transgression* (London: Methuen, 1986), 143.

25   Ibid.

26   In *Beyond the Pale: White Women, Racism and History* (London: Verso, 1992), I have written at length about how the status of women was (and still is) often cited as an index of how civilized a particular society was (or is). Many early women's rights campaigners, for example, argued that the roots of women's oppression lay in primitive societies, and that evolutionary forces would compel them toward greater equality with men (106); I have also argued that many British feminists in the late nineteenth century were convinced of their duty to spread Christian civilization throughout the empire in order to help save women from the patriarchal customs of heathen, and therefore "backward," cultures (160).

27   Michael Keith and Steve Pile, "Introduction: The Politics of Place" in *Place and the Politics of Identity,* ed. Keith and Pile (London: Routledge, 1993), 14. See also Dunn and Leeson, "The Art of Change in Docklands"; and Jon Bird, "Dystopia on the Thames," in Bird et al., *Mapping the Futures.*

28   *Political Speech and Race Relations in a Liberal Democracy. Report of an Inquiry into the Conduct of the Tower Hamlets Liberal Democrats in Publishing Allegedly Racist Election Literature between 1990 and 1993* (London: Liberal Democratic Party, 1993).

29   Blee, *Women of the Klan,* 148.

30   Matthew Stibbe, "Women and the Nazi State," *History Today* (November 1993): 35–40.

31   Von Salden, "Victims or Perpetrators?"

32   Following Derek Beackon's election in 1993 a broad-based women's group was set up in an attempt to mobilize Bangladeshi women to register to vote against him in the election the following year.

Minstrel Shows, Affirmative Action
Talk, and Angry White Men: Marking
Racial Otherness in the 1990s
David Wellman

Affirmative action, in education and the workplace alike, is leaking poison into the American soul. . . . It is time for America once again to try living with inequality, as life is lived. —Richard J. Herrnstein and Charles Murray, *The Bell Curve: Intelligence and Class Structure in American Life*

The Bell Curve authors say aloud what others of their race tend to whisper: Descendants of slaves would be well advised to repress any feelings they have of entitlement or envy. If that attitude can be brought about, we would be a happy and stable society, much like a modern version of an antebellum plantation. —Andrew Hacker, *Nation,* July 10, 1995

It's open season on black people. —Howard Stern, media shock-jock

FACTUAL representation and logical argument were the initial victims in this political hunting season. That was the usually conservative *Los Angeles Times*'s conclusion three days after Governor Pete Wilson persuaded a majority of the University of California Regents to end policies that take race and gender into account in admissions, hiring, and contracting decisions. Wilson's first kill in the hunt for anti–affirmative action votes had been bagged, the paper editorialized, through "distortions and misrepresentations so complete that facts seemed segregated from the decision."[1] Shocked by the Regents' contempt for evidence to justify their decision, the *Times* observed that "the sweeping reversal makes no sense in terms of logic or education." The editors concluded, "In this debate, who wanted to be bothered with pesky things like facts?"

Anyone who has taken the time to make a case for affirmative action knows the feeling and shares the frustration. No matter how compelling the argument, how statistically significant the facts, or how detailed and scientific the data, the opponents of affirmative action are never persuaded. Regardless of the evidence presented or the logic used, the answer is always the same: Don't bother me with facts.

What's going on in this high-stakes dispute over the future of equality in America? Why are facts treated as bothersome details to be ignored in the debate which some fear signals a return to antebellum racial policies? Why are facts virtually irrelevant in this ugly argument?

I think it's because the dispute is not about affirmative action. Something else is going on. But that something else is not visible when one accepts anti–affirmative action talk at face value. To see what's really at stake one needs to revisit a distinctively American art form that was concocted in the 1830s, when songs, dances, and skits based on southern plantation stereotypes and purporting to represent black life during slavery became wildly popular. The performers were mostly white men in black greasepaint. The audience was also mainly white: foreign immigrants from Europe, native migrants from rural America. Neither audience nor performers knew much about southern plantations or black life.

The art form was called the minstrel show.

Until recently, minstrelsy was assumed to be mostly about race and racial imagination. But that was before contemporary historians took another look. It now turns out, writes Thomas Holt (president of the American Historical Association), drawing from and synthesizing recent historical research, that minstrel shows were never just about race.[2] Other issues were being worked in these skits. Complicated political, economic, and social dislocations were being negotiated. Minstrelsy had little to do with the objects of ridicule onstage. It wasn't about the actual lived experiences of black Americans. The unannounced object of attention was *white* America. Minstrel shows, historians are now convinced, provided an opportunity for white, heterosexual, male American identities to be fashioned and expressed. In minstrel theaters, white (male) Americans could appropriate and use elements of black life to negotiate problems posed by the larger society. Minstrelsy linked global political-economic forces to the everyday experiences of white (male) Americans. The minstrel shows soothed white anxieties, they reassured white men who they were not: not black, not slave, not gay.

One hundred years later another kind of minstrel show is being staged. Instead of Aunt Jemimas, Uncle Toms, and city slicker dandies, a new cast of equally outrageous characters has been constructed: quota queens, unqualified beneficiaries of preferential treatment, reverse discrimination victims, and angry white men. Instead of applying greasepaint, the performers in this minstrel show hide behind clever linguistic constructions. Rather than speaking in dialect, they talk the language of "fairness," "color-blindness," and "meritocracy." While the content has changed, this modern minstrel show provides another stage for constructing and expressing white (especially heterosexual male) identity. And like its earlier incarnation, the new minstrelsy assures white men who they are not: not unqualified recipients of unfair advantage, not responsible for past racial injustices, not beneficiaries of government assistance.

Like the minstrel shows of an earlier era, anti–affirmative action talk is not just about race, even though the apparent objects of ridicule and derision are mostly African Americans. And also like minstrelsy, the talk is not based on facts or the actual lived experience of black Americans. Like their counterparts in the previous century, the "scholarship" of affirmative action's major intellectual critics (Nathan Glazer, Christopher Jencks, Glenn Loury, Thomas Sowell, Shelby Steele, and William Julius Wilson) is not "scholarly" in any serious sense of the term. The data they use are outdated and flimsy. Assertion substitutes for argumentation; anecdotes pretend to be systematic evidence; mystification masquerades as social science; and fantasy is treated as truth. It is a remarkable performance.[3]

Listening to the affirmative action minstrels, one would think that daughters of black brain surgeons are numerous, and that they are routinely elbowing out the better-qualified sons of poor white coal miners; that America has been ravaged by "quotas"; that an epidemic of "reverse discrimination" has raged across North America; that the economic playing field has been tilted against white males; that misguided "liberal" intentions have produced a sorry state of "unqualified" university students in black and brown bodies, tortured by "victim-focused identities"; that policies recognizing race are unnecessary because racial discrimination is rare in America.

Like old-time minstrelsy, the symbols, narratives, and imagery performed by the modern minstrels are rooted in caricatures. "Quotas," writes one bit player in the show—John Ellis, former graduate dean at the University of California at Santa Cruz—"are for affirmative action what the gulag was for the Soviet system."[4] Without explaining how or why, and resting his case solely on hyperbole, Ellis apparently is saying that Soviet prison camps and quotas are equally repressive assaults on human liberty. The "analysis" is driven by stereotypes. Thus the central images and themes in these new routines bear little resemblance to the actual lived experience of Americans—black or white. Anti–affirmative action minstrelsy has very little relationship to documented sociological "truths."

Consider the following:

One of the tall tales affirmative action minstrels love to tell is that the policy rewards the wrong people. It "creams off" the talented tenth in communities of color and leaves out the "truly disadvantaged" majority.

Actually, the matter is more complicated than that. While affirmative action does help affluent members of targeted communities, its benefits extend considerably beyond the fortunate few. Serious research suggests that affirmative action increases the demand for "lowly" educated as well as "highly" educated black Americans, the reason being that enforcement of affirmative action policies moves blacks up into semiskilled, service, blue-collar jobs as well as management and white-collar positions.[5] Writing in the *Yale Law Journal*, William L. Taylor reports that affirmative action provides "upward mobility for less advantaged minority workers."[6] A significant number of minority medical students, concludes Michael Drake, Dean of the Medical School at the University of California, San Francisco, are the children of low-income and low-job-status parents.[7]

What about the quota skit? The one in which a chorus of white men chants (but without rhythm), "Oh Lord! All my troubles due to quotas." Has "preferential treatment" transformed the racial and gendered appearance of America's occupational and economic face?

Hardly. The new minstrelsy notwithstanding, the Supreme Court actually outlawed quotas in 1978. Race and gender, it ruled, could not be the sole criteria in affirmative action decisions. Race and gender had to be included along with a range of factors. Thus, race-based remedies for past discrimination could require only good-faith efforts aimed at achieving certain goals or objectives. And as a cursory review of workforce data indicates, even these goals are seldom met. Although African Americans represent 12.4 percent of the U.S. population, they account for only 4.2 percent of doctors, 5 percent of college professors, 3.7 percent of engineers, 3.3 percent of lawyers, 1.4 percent of architects, and 6.5 percent of the construction trades. Employment data for Latinos are not much different. And though women are an absolute majority of the nation's population (51.2 percent), they constitute only 22.3 percent of all doctors, 8.3 percent of engineers, 24.6 percent of lawyers, 16.8 percent of architects, and 2.2 percent of the construction trades.[8]

According to reports issued in the 1990s by the Census Bureau, little progress has been made in narrowing the income gap between blacks and whites, despite public policies created to increase economic equality between the races.[9] In 1993, the median income for black men employed full time was $23,020, about three quarters of the $31,090 earned by white men, a proportionate disparity reduced only slightly since 1979. For women, a narrower income gap between blacks and whites widened slightly in the fourteen years between 1979 and 1993. Black women, whose median income was about 92 percent of white women's in 1979, saw that slight disparity widen by 1993, when black women earned $19,820 compared with $22,020 for white women.

The discrepancy between wealth in black and white communities is even more dramatic than the income gap. In a study comparing middle-class whites and blacks earning between $25,000 and $50,000, two sociologists recently unearthed a remarkable finding. While the net worth (the value of all assets less debts) of white Americans in this income category was $44,069, the net worth of African Americans in the same category was only $15,250! And when they compared net financial assets (family assets excluding equity accrued in a home or vehicle), they discovered that while wealth declined radically in both communities, the gap between them was enormous: $6,988 versus $290.[10]

What about "reverse discrimination"? Listening to the affirmative action minstrels, one would think a huge wave of discrimination against white men had swept over America.

But that's not what a law professor at Rutgers writing for the Department of Labor discovered in his review of three thousand discrimination opinions by federal district and appeals courts from 1990 to 1994. He could find only one hundred reverse discrimination cases. And a "high proportion" of these claims lacked merit. Reverse discrimination was established only six times, or 0.2 percent of all cases![11]

What about the angle of the economic playing field? One routine in the new minstrel show features a dialogue between two white-faced characters complaining about losing their advantage. "The playing field is tilted against us," proclaims a Joe Sixpack stereotype.

White men actually *have* lost ground in the last twenty years. Their median income has fallen steadily from $34,231 in 1973, when it peaked, down to $31,012 in 1992. But lost ground does not mean lost advantage. Black and Latino men, who earned less to begin with, have also lost ground, earning, respectively, $22,369 and $20,049 in 1992. Women's income, while rising in the last two decades, remains substantially below that of men. In 1992, the median income for white women was $21,659; for black women it was $19,819; and Latina women earned $17,138.[12]

The persistence of the white male advantage shows up in other ways as well. In 1980, for example, blacks with college educations had a higher unemployment rate than white high-school dropouts.[13] And the 1989 National Academy of Sciences report on the status of black Americans demonstrates that although the earning power of both white and black males with a high school degree deteriorated between 1969 and 1989, the *white male's lowest earnings were higher than the black male's top earnings*.[14] Finally, analyzing the economic penalties for blackness, a Princeton political scientist concludes: "Even after controlling for a wide range of non-race-related differences, black men's wages remain about 10 to 20 percent below white men's wages. The monetary return for an additional year of education or labor market experience remains noticeably lower for blacks than whites."[15]

One of the show-stopping skits performed by affirmative action minstrels is constructed around a tragic figure: the "unqualified recipient of preferential treatment." White audiences in California especially love this character. People slap each other on the back when it is performed. They vigorously shake their heads in agreement as the character confirms their worst suspicions about why their son didn't get admitted to Berkeley. They clearly resonate. Certain Asian audiences also enjoy this routine. It makes them feel very "American."

These audiences have no time for university administrators and faculty who patiently explain that under the thirty-five-year-old California Master Plan for Higher Education, the University of California must provide a place at one of its campuses for all students from the top 12.5 percent of the state's high school graduates. Race, ethnicity, and gender play no role in determining who is *eligible* to attend the University of California. These audiences don't hear the words that say

60 percent of the University of California entering class is admitted on academic criteria alone. Another 36 percent is admitted on the basis of academic achievement and supplemental criteria that include ethnic identity, physical and learning disabilities, educational disadvantage, low income, special talents and experiences. This audience does not hear that 96 *percent* of the students are academically eligible. "Qualified." They don't hear the words that say it is no longer possible to exclusively use quantitative criteria for determining academic eligibility to Berkeley because more applicants to that campus have straight-A (4.0 grade point) averages than there are openings in the freshman class.[16] This audience doesn't hear the words telling them that a mere 4 percent of the freshman class is admitted by exception. They don't hear that only 1,300 students in the entire UC system in 1994 technically did not fall within the top 12.5 percent of high school graduates. And more important, they don't hear that students admitted by exception have *demonstrated the capacity to do college-level work* and are therefore "qualified" students. Further, these students possess special talents and life experiences that enrich the educational environment. Many are student-athletes and gifted artists.[17]

Certain middle-class black audiences are moved by a version of this skit. Accepting the minstrels' construction of "qualified," and figuring it applies to them, they worry that the tragic "unqualified" figure will be defeated by "victim-focused identity" problems. The fear is real. Life is not easy for students of color attending historically white universities. But, like other characters in the show, this one is conjured. The minstrels provide no credible evidence to document negative consequences of victim-focused identities. Statistical inaccuracies are ignored or pursued in the face of counterevidence. Thomas Sowell, for example, insists that victim-focused identities explain why the graduation rate is only 27 percent for African American students at Berkeley. He persists in using this figure even after a Berkeley vice chancellor wrote to him explaining why it is incorrect.[18]

Interestingly, neither audience nor performers show much concern for the "unqualified" but wealthy white recipients of the preferential admissions policies practiced by expensive and exclusive Ivy League colleges. No one appears to worry about "victim-focused identity" among Harvard's "legacies." In 1988, more than one in six of Harvard freshmen (280 of 1,602) had fathers who had attended Harvard. If these alumni children were admitted at the same rate as other applicants, their numbers would drop by nearly two hundred. That figure is more than the total number of students of color enrolled in the entire 1988 entering class.[19] The "legacy," however, is not a character in the affirmative action minstrel show.

The final skit brings down the house. A figure dressed to look like a professor appears onstage. He (for some reason the character is typically performed by a male) speaks in very earnest, measured, and authoritative tones. Pretending to be objective, and acting like he is troubled by the words he is forced to say, he delivers a long, scientific-sounding discourse on the state of race relations in the United States. Using the language of science, spicing his assertions with numbers, invoking the historical "record," and speaking philosophical talk, he weaves together the necessary symbolic and discursive elements to make his performance credible. The performance is so well executed that very few people detect the distortions, manipulations, and omissions necessary to make it believable. At the end, doing a marvelous imitation of Irwin Corey's Professor Longhair, without a shred of documentation, he announces that discrimination is no longer practiced in America. The problem is quotas, reverse discrimination, and victim-focused identities leading to a breakdown of traditional values. And that is why affirmative action is not only unnecessary but counterproductive and un-American, he proclaims.

The audience goes wild.

The performance works because a large proportion of the audience need not go back very far in their own family histories to encounter vivid tales of discrimination, ostracism, or humiliation. Whether worn as ethnic badges or experienced as hidden injuries of class, the audience members have constructed identities for themselves based on narratives of perseverance, toughness, independence, and self-help. There is no room in this construction to acknowledge at least two massive stagings that made possible this narrative of heroic uplift. So the minstrel academic never mentions the extraordinary assistance the government provided to white men through the New Deal in the 1930s and the GI Bill after World War II.[20] The performance is believable because he fails to remind his audience that no matter how precarious their comforts may be now, fifty years ago they were very dependent on "government handouts." It is credible because the history against which he judges blacks is neither relevant nor accurate.

He also fails to mention the carefully documented, persuasive scholarly evidence that demonstrates how racial discrimination is currently practiced in U.S. life. Research based on matched pairs of job seekers has been available since at least 1986, when pairs of white and black 1983 high school graduates in Newark, New Jersey, were matched for academic achievement and sent out to find employment. These young people were actually seeking work—this was not an experiment. Although both groups were equally successful in obtaining employment in the manufacturing sector of the economy, the differences were dramatic in the service sector, where whites were four times more likely than blacks to be fully employed.[21] Updating and elaborating on this study, R. J. Struyk, A. Turner, and M. Fix conducted 576 hiring audits in Chicago and Washington, D.C., during the summer of 1990.[22] The researchers carefully matched young black and white men for their education, job qualifications, and experience. The young men were also coached to display a similar demeanor. All were college students who were dressed conventionally and described as "articulate and poised." Despite these crucial commonalities, the young men were treated quite differently by potential employers. The white applicants were three times more likely to be hired in the service sector than their black counterparts.

The gap between myth and reality is not surprising when one realizes that anti–affirmative action talk is minstrelsy, not serious intellectual-political discourse. The traditional minstrel show was not about facts or scholarly evidence. And neither is its contemporary counterpart. The old-time minstrel show was effective, popular, and believable to white audiences *despite* its poor fit with "truth." And so is the modern version. Like the earlier art form, the current minstrel show is not just about "the facts" as performed in these skits. Other, unacknowledged issues are at stake.

Like the era when traditional minstrelsy was most popular, today's America is experiencing economic and cultural dislocations of earthquake proportions. Then, it was abolitionism, western expansion, and the making of an urban working class. Now, it is fiscal mismanagement, job flight, increased economic inequality, and political gridlock. One consequence of this shifting sociological terrain is that white, heterosexual working-class males, together with a majority of other Americans, are losing ground. But *not* because of affirmative action. This is particularly obvious in California.

Following a decade of extraordinary economic growth, California in 1990 had surpassed most nations in output and income.[23] The state's gross domestic product reached $700,000 billion. The state added 2.6

million jobs between 1979 and 1988. Average income per capita increased in real terms during the 1980s. California became the principal engine of U.S. economic development.

That engine was derailed, however, by the Reagan-Bush era of increased corporate consolidation and supply side economics, which triggered a recession in 1991–94. Colliding with fiscal mismanagement and political gridlock, the state economy was dramatically forced off its tracks.[24] Between 1991 and 1994, virtually every key function of state government was cut by one-fourth to one-third. The state dropped precipitously from one of the top-ranked states in per pupil spending on public schools to thirty-eighth. California currently has the largest average class size of any state. The school maintenance backlog is forty-five times the national average. The state lost close to 1.5 million jobs between 1990 and 1992: 900,000 in wholesale and retail trade, 200,000 in manufacturing, 150,000 in construction, and 70,000 in agriculture. Unemployment, the worst since the 1930s, peaked at 9 percent in 1993. The official poverty rate jumped radically in two years: from 12 percent in 1990 to 18.2 percent by 1993. Almost overnight, California dropped unceremoniously to one of the ten poorest states in the union (just above Arkansas).

The California experience is not unique. During the last quarter century, the United States has exhibited the most rapid growth of wage inequality in the Western world. Wage data since 1973 show that while the wages of people at the top have climbed in recent years, the wages of those at the bottom have fallen steadily.[25] Despite a sustained increase in the real gross domestic product, the majority of American workers have experienced a decline in real wages.[26] Not surprisingly, many working-class Americans believe their children's lives will be worse than theirs. A Harris poll conducted for *Business Week* in 1995 indicates that only half of the parents interviewed expected their children to have a better life than theirs. And three quarters of these parents believed that the American dream will be even harder to achieve in the next decade.[27]

California's decline and the increasing income inequality in the United States are *not,* however, attributable to affirmative action. And none of the symbols, narratives, or imagery constructed by affirmative action discourse explains these troubles.

But that's not what the talk is supposed to do. Like the earlier period when minstrelsy first emerged, economic and political dislocations are only one part of the story. The other part is that national and personal identity issues were/are surfacing at the same time. At the very moment when the political-economic landscape is being radically reconfigured in disturbing directions, whiteness and maleness are becoming increasingly visible and marked. Thus, political-economic troubles are *experienced* as racial and gendered, rather than class, grievances.

Until recently, the categories "white" and "male" were taken for granted. Being white and male was being "normal." The taken-for-granted world of white, male Americans, then, was their normalcy, not their whiteness or their gender. As a result, the privileges that came with whiteness and masculinity were experienced as "normal," not advantages. But that is no longer possible. The normal has been made problematic by people of color and women, who have, through their visibility, challenged assumptions once taken for granted. As a consequence, white males are suddenly made to feel "white" and "male," something new to most of them. In experiencing these new categories, white men have discovered what nonwhites and women living in a predominantly white male (and heterosexual) world have always known: Life in a racial and gendered category is not always comfortable. Thus, white men are beginning to experience what they previously took for granted: for middle-class men, this is a sense of privilege; for working-class men, it is feeling beleaguered and besieged.

Like masculinity, racial advantage is routinely taken for granted by white men. Unless disturbed, it is interpreted as "normal." Usually it is not even noticed. But when this advantage is challenged, it is defended. That is why unions have fought to maintain exclusionary practices when ordered by courts to admit black workers.[28] That is why white Americans began leaving the Democratic party as early as 1936, when blacks first became members, and have been transforming the Republican party into the Party of Whiteness ever since.[29] That is why so many white (male) Americans cry "foul" when forced to relinquish unrestricted access to occupational and educational opportunities. They do so, however, *not* because they are antiblack racists, but rather because they are defending normal, routine institutional practices which, *in their experience,* are racially neutral.

No mystery, then, why the affirmative action show is so popular. No surprise that "equal opportunity" for African Americans is translated by Americans in white bodies to mean "reverse discrimination." Given the European American experience—historically and sociologically—equal opportunity for people of color *feels like* reverse discrimination for whites. Not because whites literally experience discrimination. They don't. But because, until recently, "equal opportunity" meant that white male Americans faced virtually no competition from blacks and women. That was "normal." Normal used to mean exclusivity; it meant white and heterosexual male. Affirmative action has disturbed that notion of normalcy. Whiteness and maleness can no longer be taken for granted. Affirmative action has made Americans in these categories newly conscious of their whiteness and maleness. And once they recognize these attributes and the benefits they bestow, white men understandably resist giving them up. That is why when white men lose the preferential treatment they traditionally enjoyed at the expense of blacks and women, they call it "reverse discrimination."

Until affirmative action was enforced, "all things being equal" routinely and practically *meant* that white men would get the job or slot in graduate school, or admission to law school. That was a "fact." It was normal, taken for granted. In 1964, 96 percent of all law students in the United States were male.[30] And it was "true" even when white men were *less* qualified than their racialized and gendered competitors. Affirmative action changed all that. Today, women constitute 43 percent of all law students.[31] Now white men actually have to *compete* against women and people of color. And sometimes that means they really do come in second, or even third. But given their historic-sociological experience, it is impossible for them to register that as "fair." It is beyond their comprehension. It *must,* therefore, have been produced by unfair practices or reverse discrimination. How else can it be explained? That is why talk about quotas and reverse discrimination is such a crucial component in anti–affirmative action discourse. These narratives articulate the experience and sentiment of white men in both senses of the word: they link *and* express their aggrieved sentiments. That is why so many men tell the same story about the job they lost to an "unqualified" woman or person of color. That is how "all things being equal" came to mean "reverse discrimination."

In addition to becoming problematic, whiteness has also lost market value in certain sectors during the past couple of decades. While by no means abolished, the wages of whiteness have been decreasing in some locations. Whiteness no longer receives the price it once commanded, especially in higher education, where a premium has been placed on people of color and women who "qualify" for scarce slots in freshman classes. Responding to demographic changes, shifting market shares, desegregation orders, and other reasons to diversify, some employers and many educators actively recruit people from these categories.[32] In these instances, the minimalist affirmative action injunction ("all things being equal," preference will be given to women and people of color) reverses past racial practices. Instead of benefiting white males almost exclusively, as it used to, "all things being equal" can now benefit previously excluded groups. This means, in effect, that the people in these categories are sometimes more highly valued than white males. Affirmative action, then, has inadvertently increased the market value of people of color and women (most noticeably in university admissions), driving down the historic premium paid to whiteness and maleness.[33]

Depending where one is located on the racial or gender divide, this state of affairs is either fair or unfair. But because the market has never been governed by the principle of fairness, talk about the decreasing market value of whiteness and masculinity being unfair sounds silly. No surprise, then, that the believability of affirmative action performances does not depend on how closely they correspond to "truth."

White Americans who embraced minstrelsy before the Civil War, to paraphrase Thomas Holt, did not do so simply to revile black people. And neither do white Americans who embrace the affirmative action minstrels. The serious business of minstrelsy goes unnoticed if one only interrogates the caricatures, stereotypes, and half-truths performed in these shows. What makes minstrelsy so deadly is not the inaccuracies, exaggerations, and vilifications it contains. Minstrelsy's most dangerous feature is that it stages the construction of racial selves. It marks racial otherness.

Minstrel shows, conclude historians Eric Lott, David Roediger, and Alexander Saxton, provided white Americans with an opportunity for posing traumatic questions about serious issues that connected their everyday lives to global-political phenomena. The issue for uprooted European peasants in pre–Civil War America was the foreign society and strange political economy they confronted there. For rural natives who had immigrated to cities, the issue was factory life and an alien wage labor system. The questions they posed were: What is America? Who is an American? Who is white?

The dynamics have changed in post–civil rights America. Issues once settled by earlier minstrel shows have been reopened. Whiteness and masculinity are no longer unmarked categories, experienced as normal and taken for granted. Racial advantage is no longer invisible. And while things were never equal, and certainly not all things, "all things being equal" doesn't guarantee white men first place anymore. The market value of whiteness has declined in higher education.

No surprise, then, that white Americans use affirmative action minstrelsy to raise some of the same questions posed 150 years ago: What is America? Who is American? What is whiteness worth? And what does "independence" mean? Some new questions are also posed: What is fair? Who is deserving? By what criteria are qualification and merit measured? What is my relationship to the structure of racial advantage and the African Holocaust practiced on American soil?

These issues are either settled symbolically or deflected on the minstrel stage. Affirmative action discourse enables Americans to fashion a new set of social selves; to construct whiteness and masculinity as *not*-affirmative action, or as the *opposite* of affirmative action. The modern minstrels represent these new identities as being self-made, self-sufficient, self-reliant, independent, hard working, disciplined, and tough. They mark white men as guys who play by the rules, live by agreements (even when they are unfair), and don't whine or complain. They are stoic and autonomous. "You got to roll with the punches, li'l black boy," Randy Newman sings.

> That's what you got to do
> You talk about the red
> we have talked about the blue
> Now we gonna talk about the white
> that's what we gonna have to do
> We had to roll with the punches
> yes we did
> we had to roll with 'em
> yes we did.[34]

For white men, affirmative action discourse symbolically settles traumatic private troubles caused by public global-political dislocations. It encourages them to feel superior. Perhaps, at least in this discourse, they can assure themselves that despite the ravages of increased income inequality, loss of jobs, and the devaluation of whiteness and masculinity, they are still—unlike weaker affirmative action recipients—independent, in control, and in charge. Real Men, the discourse tells them, don't need affirmative action.

In addition to inventing an identity, anti–affirmative action discourse also constructs whiteness as a space in which an identifiable set of embodied and learned social practices are performed.[35] So constructed, the practices associated with whiteness need not be restricted to white bodies. Thus, the space of whiteness is sometimes inhabited by nonwhite bodies performing practices that have come to represent whiteness. (Clarence Thomas's Supreme Court deliberations are an obvious example of this.)

But minstrelsy does more than construct a space for the white, masculine self. It also marks racial otherness. Whiteness comes to be marked as not-affirmative action. And in the process, racial boundaries are reinforced. Racial border crossing thus becomes more difficult. The ground people share goes unnoticed. Difference and otherness are (re)produced as the salient and relevant categories. Another mark for blackness also emerges. The earlier minstrels constructed a racial mark that identified the black other as "natural" entertainer, childlike, docile, and supersexual. The new mark modern minstrels are working on constructs the black other as affirmative action recipient: a dependent, undeserving, unqualified, ungrateful, and immoral trespasser.

This mark can be seen on university campuses where white students perform status degradation ceremonies that minimize or discount the accomplishments of black and Latino undergraduates. Color marks the students who are not "qualified" to be at the university; people who don't "belong," or belong but only in certain locations. "Are *you* still *here?*" black and Latino students at the University of California report being asked by their white counterparts, who express surprise when a semester or two has passed and the student of color is still on campus. "What are *you* doing here?" students of color are asked outside certain classroom buildings on campus. "This is a *science* building." "What is your major?" academically successful black students are likely to be asked, in an attempt to discount the achievement. "What is your SAT score?" white freshmen ask their black classmates, assuming the score is a low one. "I feel like I have 'Affirmative Action' stamped on my forehead," one African American undergraduate told researchers.[36]

Like earlier minstrel shows, the imagery and symbolism in affirmative action narratives are a constructed discourse, not a natural or inevitable feature of the American cultural-political landscape. The affirmative action minstrels know that framing helps determine the terms of discourse. They realize that certain questions produce desired answers. Thus, they know that two-thirds to three quarters of white men polled over the last two decades favor public policies that compensate for past discrimination. They also know that when asked if they favor policies that promote quotas and preferential treatment, the same men will say no in much the same proportions.[37] No accident, then, that affirmative action has been constructed to mean race, quotas, and preferences. The affirmative action minstrels have framed the discourse strategically. Initially presented as "remedial action" by the Johnson and Carter presidencies, affirmative action minstrels hired by the American Enterprise Institute and the Hoover Institution writing in journals like *Public Interest* and *Commentary* transformed talk about the policy into "reverse discrimination."[38] No accident, then, that white women are rarely the objects of anti–affirmative action talk, even though they are major beneficiaries of the policy. Perhaps that's because the affirmative action minstrels are marking racial otherness, not protesting unfair advantage.

At first glance counterintuitive, then striking and clever, the parallels between minstrel shows and affirmative action talk don't seem to generate much political traction. Indeed, one could conclude that the analogy leads to a strategic cul-de-sac. After all, how does one counter a performance that is effective *despite* its poor fit with the truth? How does one persuade in an argument that is not driven by facts?

One doesn't. And that's the point.

The distinctive feature of minstrelsy, whether performed in blackface or in academic robes, is not the accuracy of its claims, but rather that it uses African American lives to negotiate larger public troubles. These performances are powerful not because they are factual, but because they link together global political-economic forces and the lived experiences of white Americans. The minstrel analogy generates political torque, then, not because it replaces fiction with facts, but because it demystifies affirmative action talk; it gets backstage and unmasks the issues actually being contested. It therefore forces Americans to wrestle with the roots of our distress.

The analogy preempts easy formulations for long-simmering, deeply rooted social and political difficulties. It reminds us of what is at stake. And what is not. When the affirmative action debate is revealed to be minstrelsy, one sees through the linguistic disguises that have replaced greasepaint. Looking through these metaphorical lenses, one realizes that arguments over fairness, merit, and color-blind criteria are stand-ins for disputes over advantage, power, and control.

The analogy helps explain why so many Californians support

Governor Wilson's executive order abolishing affirmative action programs even though they know the action will be ineffective because the vast majority of state jobs are protected by federal civil rights regulations. And it also explains why they favor his attacks on university policies even though they know that only one-tenth of one percent of publicly funded scholarships are earmarked by race, and none of the money comes from taxpayers.[39] They don't support these policies because they suffer from "false consciousness"; rather, they support them because they know that anti–affirmative action minstrels needn't be politically effective to be successful. Performing symbolic acts that mark racial otherness is success.

The analogy also signals a warning to Americans defending the political ground won in earlier battles for civil rights. This terrain cannot be defended successfully by adding new faces, characters, and scripts to the modern minstrel show. That show has to be disrupted, not elaborated. The terms of discourse need to be shifted. New solutions must be theorized that negotiate the real problems posed by demographic shifts, corporate unaccountability, and the loss of jobs as capital pursues profit in the third world without blaming these troubles on people of color and women.

People who would protect affirmative action beachheads need to establish linkages between the everyday lives of white Americans and global-political issues in ways that avoid symbolic resolutions and focus instead on relations of power and advantage. To do that it is necessary to openly acknowledge the benefits of anti–affirmative action narratives: they *do* make white men feel better. They *do* provide culturally acceptable rationales for anger produced by events over which very few Americans have control. They *do* provide the ultimate American wedge issue for politicians. But these benefits, it must also be noted, do not come cost-free. They are expensive. Because anti–affirmative action talk is theater, it offers only symbolic resolutions. The price for immediate psychological and political advantage is long-range instability and possibly civil disorder as well. Affirmative action talk may make white people feel better momentarily, but the persistent problems that made the policy necessary will not have been resolved. Republicans may win on anti–affirmative action platforms, but America might not survive the divisions produced by the wedge that got them elected.

The minstrel analogy serves another political purpose. It reminds defenders of civil rights that whiteness and masculinity are in crisis, but *not* for the reasons cited by affirmative action minstrels. It suggests that the crisis can be negotiated only by disconnecting the difficulties experienced by white men from affirmative action and reconnecting them to the global political dislocations that produced the crisis in the first place.

Once released, the genies of whiteness and masculinity can never be put back into their bottles. And confronting them is not easy. But maybe those genies are an opportunity rather than an obstacle. Perhaps they can be used to pose the hard questions affirmative action minstrels don't dare raise, questions that point toward hope instead of despair. "This is my gift to white men," Alice Walker offered in a recent interview.

> Do try to decide who you are, *other* than "white man." You have to be something other than that. You have to understand that for people of color, and for colonized and brutalized and dominated people, that really is your name. Because that is the name that all of this evil stuff has been done under. "I'm a white man." "This is a white man's neighborhood." "This is a white man's drinking fountain. You stay away!" So we are just calling you what you have called yourself. But now, by your behavior, you can be something else entirely. Then you have a new name. What is it? What will it be? [40]

Notes

A number of people read drafts of this essay and provided especially helpful suggestions as well as moral support. Serious thanks to Ron Aronson, Dianne Beeson, Michael K. Brown, Terry Cannon, Greta Fields Clarke, Jan Dizard, Troy Duster, Ruth Frankenberg, Herman Gray, Ron Lembo, George Lipsitz, Jeff Lustig, Becky Thompson, and Al Young.

1   "Swatting Away Those Pesky Facts on Affirmative Action," *Los Angeles Times,* July 23, 1995, M4.

2   Thomas C. Holt, "Marking: Race, Race-Making, and the Writing of History," *American Historical Review* (February 1995): 1–20. Holt is summarizing Melvin Patrick Ely, *The Adventures of Amos 'n' Andy: A Social History of an American Phenomenon* (New York: Free Press, 1991); Eric Lott, *Love and Theft: Black Face Minstrelsy and the American Working Class* (New York: Oxford University Press, 1993); David Roediger, *The Wages of Whiteness: Race and the Making of the American Working Class* (New York: Verso, 1990); Alexander Saxton, *The Rise and Fall of the White Republic: Class Politics and Mass Culture in Nineteenth Century America* (New York: Verso, 1990); Robert C. Toll, *Blacking Up: The Minstrel Show in Nineteenth Century America* (New York: Oxford University Press, 1974).

3   For analyses of these performances, see Wendell Thomas and David Wellman,

"Testing Affirmative Action Hypotheses," manuscript, Institute for the Study of Social Change, 1993; David Wellman, "The New Political Linguistics of Race," *Socialist Review* 16 (May–August 1986): 43–62.

4   John Ellis, "Class-Based Affirmative Action: The Liberals' Desperate Fallback Position," *Heterodoxy* 3 (May 1995): 3.

5   Jonathan S. Leonard, "Splitting Blacks? Affirmative Action and Earnings Inequality within and across Races," *Proceedings of the Thirty-ninth Annual Meeting,* ed. Barbara D. Dennis, Industrial Relations Research Association Series (Industrial Relations Research Association, 1986), 57.

6   William L. Taylor, "Brown, Equal Protection, and the Isolation of the Poor," *Yale Law Journal* 95 (1986): 1713–14.

7   Michael Drake, "Statement on Medical School Admissions," *Higher Bounds* 2, no. 2 (1995): 21–23.

8   Willie L. Brown, "The Future without Affirmative Action," *San Francisco Chronicle,* April 4, 1995, A19.

9   Steven A. Holmes, "Census Finds Little Change in Income Gap between Races," *New York Times,* February 23, 1995.

10 Melvin L. Oliver and Thomas M. Shapiro, *Black Wealth/White Wealth: A New Perspective on Racial Inequality* (New York: Routledge, 1995), 94.

11 "Reverse Discrimination Complaints Rare, a Labor Study Reports," *New York Times,* March 31, 1995, A10.

12 Ramon G. McLeod, "White Men's Eroding Economic Clout Contributes to Backlash," *San Francisco Chronicle,* March 20, 1995.

13 Gertrude Ezorsky, *Racism and Justice: The Case for Affirmative Action* (Ithaca: Cornell University Press, 1991), 69.

14 Roger Wilkins, "White Racism Is Still the Problem," *Washington Post,* December 5, 1990.

15 Jennifer L. Hochschild, "Race, Class, Power, and the American Welfare State," in *Democracy and the Welfare State,* ed. Amy Guttman (Princeton: Princeton University Press, 1988), 161.

16 In the fall of 1989, approximately 21,300 California high school graduates eligible for the university applied for the 3,500 freshman slots open at Berkeley. More than 5,800 of those 21,300 students had straight-A (4.0) averages. Data derived from Institute for the Study of Social Change, *The Diversity Project* (Berkeley: University of California, 1991), 4.

17 William K. Coblentz, "UC Affirmative Action Benefits All," *San Francisco Chronicle,* May 12, 1995, A25.

18 Personal communication between author and W. Russell Ellis, vice chancellor for undergraduate affairs.

19 Jerome Karabel and David Karen, "Go to Harvard, Give Your Kid a Break," *New York Times,* December 8, 1990.

20 For detailed evidence documenting the ways government assistance privileged white men see Michael K. Brown, *Divergent Fates: Race and Class in the Making of the American Welfare State, 1935–1985* (forthcoming); George Lipsitz, "The Possessive Investment in Whiteness: Racialized Social Democracy and the 'White' Problem in American Studies," *American Quarterly* 47 (September 1995): 369–87; and Karen Brodkin Sacks, "How Did Jews Become White Folks?" in *Race,* ed. Steven

Gregory and Roger Sanjek (New Brunswick: Rutgers University Press, 1994), 78–102.

21 Jerome Culp and Bruce H. Dunson, "Brothers of a Different Color: A Preliminary Look at Employer Treatment of White and Black Youth," in *The Black Youth Unemployment Crisis,* ed. R. B. Freeman and Harry J. Holzer (Chicago: University of Chicago Press, 1986), 233–60.

22 R. J. Struyk, A. Turner, and M. Fix, *Opportunities Denied, Opportunities Diminished: Discrimination in Housing* (Washington, D.C.: The Urban Institute, 1992). Write to Research Paper Sales Office, P.O. Box 7273, Dept. C, Washington, D.C. 20044).

23 The following discussion is based on *California at a Crossroads* (pamphlet produced by Campus Coalitions for Human Rights and Social Justice [hereafter CCHRSJ], Oakland, Calif., May 1995).

24 For extended analyses of this development, see Richard Walker, "California Rages against the Dying of the Light," *New Left Review* (1995); Jeff Lustig and Richard Walker, "No Way Out: Immigrants and the New California" (occasional paper published by CCHRSJ, 1995).

25 Keith Bradsher, "Gap in Wealth in U.S. Called Widest in West," *New York Times,* April 17, 1995; William J. Wilson, "The New Social Inequality and Race-Based Public Policy" (lecture delivered to Aaron Wildavsky Forum, University of California, Berkeley, April 11, 1996).

26 Urie Bronfenbrenner, Stephen Ceci, Phyllis Moen, Peter McClelland, and Elaine Wethington, *The State of Americans: This Generation and the Next* (New York: Free Press, 1996).

27 *Business Week,* March 13, 1995, 80.

28 Herbert Hill, "Black Labor and Affirmative Action," in *The Question of Discrimination: Racial Inequality in the U.S. Labor Market,* ed. Steven Shulman and William Darity Jr. (Middletown, Conn.: Wesleyan University Press, 1989).

29 Robert Huckfeldt and Carole Weitzel Kohfeld, *Race and the Decline of Class in America Politics* (Urbana: University of Illinois Press, 1989).

30 Lee Teitelbaum, "First-Generation Issues: Access to Law School," in *Perspectives on Diversity,* ed. Rachel F. Moran (Washington, D.C.: Association of American Law Schools, forthcoming).

31 Ibid.

32 Decreases in the wages of whiteness should not be exaggerated. Despite a vigorous campaign to the contrary waged by affirmative action minstrels, a federal commission recently reported that while white men constitute only 43 percent of the workforce, they hold about ninety-five of every one hundred senior management positions in the country. (See Peter T. Kilborn, "Women and Minorities Still Face 'Glass Ceiling,'" *New York Times,* March 16, 1995.) And a California Senate Office of Research report claims that even though white men account for only one-third of the state's workforce, they hold 54 percent of the managerial positions in more than 15,750 of California's big companies. (See Robert B. Gunnison, "State Study Finds More Female, Minority Bosses," *San Francisco Chronicle,* March 28, 1995.)

33 In 1980, white males made up 40 percent of the University of California student population. They are now down to 24 percent. Women are up to 48 percent. (See Robert Scheer, "Angry Whites Should Check Wilson's Math," *Los Angeles Times,* July 25, 1995.)

34   Randy Newman, "Land of Dreams," Reprise Records, 1988.

35   For a discussion of whiteness as learned social practices, see Matt Wray, "Affirmative Action, Race Traitors, and the End of Whiteness" (paper presented to the California American Studies Association Conference, Occidental College, Los Angeles, April 26, 1996).

36   David Wellman, *Portraits of White Racism,* 2d ed. (New York: Cambridge University Press, 1993), 234.

37   John H. Bunzel, "Affirmative Re-Actions," *Public Opinion* 9 (February–March 1986): 45–49; Louis Harris, "Affirmative Action and the Voter," *New York Times,* July 31, 1995.

38   Empirical evidence for this reframing process can be found in William A. Gamson and Andre Modigliani, "The Changing Culture of Affirmative Action," *Research in Political Sociology* 3 (1987): 137–77.

39   "Scholarship Race: Affirmative Action Plays Almost No Part in Outcome," *San Jose Mercury News,* May 25, 1995.

40   Larry Bensky, "Telling Secrets: An Interview with Alice Walker," *San Francisco Focus,* September 1992, 75.

Bibliography

Aguirre Bernal, Celoso. 1985. *Joaquín Murrieta: Raíz y Razón del movimento chicano.* Mexico: Lito Publicidad Internacional.

Ali, Sami. 1976. *Corps Real, Corps Imaginaire.* Paris: Seuil.

Alibi F. E., and Jesús Nieto. 1975. *Sighs and Songs of Aztlan.* Bakersfield, Calif.: Universal Press.

Allen, Richard. n.d. "Empire, Imperialism and Literature." Manuscript.

Allen, Theodore W. 1994. *The Invention of the White Race.* Vol. 1: *Racial Oppression and Social Control.* London: Verso.

Almaguer, Tomas. 1994. *Racial Faultlines: The Historical Origins of White Supremacy in California.* Berkeley: University of California Press.

Amin, Samir. 1989. *Eurocentrism.* London: Zed Press.

Anthias, Floya, and Nira Yuval Davis. 1993. *Racialised Boundaries.* London: Routledge.

Antonowicz, Anton. 1993. "Fear and Bigotry Grip the East End." *London Daily Mirror,* September 18, 7.

Anzaldúa, Gloria. 1987. *Borderlands, la Frontera.* San Francisco: Aunt Lute.

———. 1990. "Haciendo Caras, Una Entrada, an Introduction," in *Making Face, Making Soul/Haciendo Caras: Creative and Critical Perspectives by Women of Color,* ed. Gloria Anzaldúa. xv–xxvii. San Francisco: Aunt Lute.

Appadurai, Arjun. 1990. "Disjuncture and Difference in the Global Cultural Economy." *Public Culture* 2.2 (Spring): 1–24.

Aptheker, Herbert. 1992. *Anti-racism in U.S. History: The First Two Hundred Years.* New York: Greenwood.

Arac, Jonathan, ed. 1986. *Postmodernism and Politics.* Minneapolis: University of Minnesota Press.

Atkins, Elizabeth. 1991. "For Many Mixed-Race Americans Life Isn't Simply Black or White." *New York Times,* June 5, 8.

Back, Les. 1995. *New Ethnicities and Urban Youth Cultures.* London: University College London Press.

Baldwin, James. 1955. *Notes of a Native Son.* Boston: Beacon. Reprint, 1984.

————. 1984. "On Being White and Other Lies." *Essence* (April): 80–82.

Balibar, Etienne. 1991. *Race, Nation, Class—Ambiguous Identities*. Cambridge: Polity Press.

Barth, Fredric, ed. 1969. *Ethnic Groups and Boundaries*. Boston: Little, Brown.

Barthes, Roland. 1967. *Elements of Semiology*, trans. Annette Lavers and Colin Smith. New York: Hill and Wang.

————. 1976. *Mythologies*, trans. Annette Lavers. New York: Hill and Wang.

————. 1977. *Image Music Text*, trans. Stephen Heath. New York: Hill and Wang.

Bates, Inge, ed. 1984. *Schooling for the Dole? The New Vocationalism*. London: Macmillan.

Bauman, Zigmunt. 1982. *Memories of Class*. London: Routledge.

Bensky, Larry. 1992. "Telling Secrets: An Interview with Alice Walker." *San Francisco Focus* (September), 75.

Bettie, Julie. 1995. "Class Dismissed? *Roseanne* and the Changing Face of Working-Class Iconography." *Social Text*, no. 45 (1995): 125–49.

Bhabha, Homi, ed. 1990. *Nation and Narration*. London: Routledge.

————. 1994. *The Location of Culture*. London: Routledge.

Bingham, Sallie. 1989. *Passion and Prejudice*. New York: Knopf.

Bird, Jon. 1993. "Dystopia on the Thames." In *Mapping the Futures: Local Cultures, Global Change*, ed. Jon Bird, Barry Curtis, Tim Putnam, George Robertson, and Lisa Tickner, 120–35. London: Routledge.

Birnbaum, Michele A. "'Alien Hands': Kate Chopin and the Colonization of Race." *American Literature* 66.2 (1994): 301–23.

Blackett, R. J. M. 1983. *Building an Antislavery Wall*. Baton Rouge: Louisiana State University Press.

Blauner, Bob. 1995. "White Radicals, White Liberals, and White People: Rebuilding the Anti-racist Coalition." In *Racism and Anti-racism in World Perspective*, ed. Benjamin P. Bowser. London: Sage.

Blee, Kathleen. 1991. *Women of the Klan: Racism and Gender in the 1920s*. Berkeley: University of California Press.

Blunt, Alison. 1994. *Travel, Gender, and Imperialism: Mary Kingsley and West Africa*. New York: Guilford.

Boggan, Steve, and Nick Walker. 1993. "East End Rivals Deny Dirty Tricks." *London Independent*, September 18, 2.

Boren, Lynda S., and Sara deSassaure Davis, eds. 1992. *Kate Chopin Reconsidered: Beyond the Bayou*. Baton Rouge: Louisiana State University Press.

Borman, Katherine, and Phillip Obermiller. 1994. *From Mountain to Metropolis: Appalachian Migrants in American Cities*. Westport: Bergin and Garvey.

Bourdieu, Pierre. 1993. *The Field of Cultural Reproduction*. Cambridge: Cambridge University Press.

Bourke, Joanna. 1993. *Working Class Cultures, 1880–1960: Gender, Class, and Ethnicity*. New York: Routledge.

Bradsher, Keith. 1995. "Gap in Wealth in U.S. Called Widest in West." *New York Times*, April 17.

Brasil, Joanne. 1985. *Escape from Billy's Bar-B-Que*. Navarro, Calif.: Wild Trees.

Bronfenbrenner, Urie, Stephen Ceci, Phyllis Moen, Peter McClelland, and Elaine Wethington. 1996. *The State of Americans: This Generation and the Next*. New York: Free Press.

Brooks, Peter. 1993. *Body Work: Objects of Desire in Modern Narrative*. Cambridge: Harvard University Press.

Brown, Michael K. Forthcoming. *Divergent Fates: Race and Class in the Making of the American Welfare State, 1935–1985*.

Brown, Willie L. 1995. "The Future without Affirmative Action." *San Francisco Chronicle*, April 4, A19.

Broyles-Gonzalez, Yolanda. 1990. "What Price Mainstream?" *Cultural Studies* 4.3 (October): 281–94.

———. 1994. *El Teatro Campesino: Theater in the Chicano Movement*. Austin: University of Texas Press.

Bunzel, John. 1986. "Affirmative Re-Actions." *Public Opinion* 9 (February–March): 45–49.

Butler, Tim, and Michael Rustin, eds. 1996. *Rising in the East: The Regeneration of East London*. London: Lawrence and Wishart.

Calvino, Italo. 1986. *Invisible Cities*. London: Secker and Warburg.

Campa, Arthur. 1946. *Spanish Folk-Poetry in New Mexico*. Albuquerque: University of New Mexico Press.

Campus Coalitions for Human Rights and Social Justice. 1995. *California at a Crossroads*. Oakland: Campus Coalitions for Human Rights and Social Justice.

Capeci, Dominic, Jr. 1984. *Race Relations in Wartime Detroit: The Sojourner Truth Controversy*. Philadelphia: Temple University Press.

Carby, Hazel. 1987. *Reconstructing Womanhood: The Emergence of the Afro-American Novelist*. New York: Oxford University Press.

Caruthers, Suzanne. 1990. "Catching Sense: Learning from Our Mothers to Be Black and Female." In *Uncertain Terms: Negotiating Gender in American Culture*, ed. Faye Ginsburg and Anna Lowenhaupt Tsing. Boston: Beacon.

Cassirer, Ernst. 1979. *Symbol, Myth, and Culture*. New Haven: Yale University Press.

Castañeda, Antonia, et al. 1972. *Literatura Chicana: Texto y Contexto*. Englewood Cliffs, N.J.: Prentice-Hall.

Castillo, Pedro, and Alberto Camarillo, eds. 1973. *Furia y Muerte: Los Bandidos Chicanos*. Aztlan Publication no. 4. Los Angeles: Aztlan Publications.

Center for Democratic Renewal. 1987. *They Don't All Wear Sheets: A Chronology of Racist and Far Right Violence, 1980–1986*. Atlanta: Center for Democratic Renewal.

———. 1991. *The Christian Identity Movement*. Atlanta: Center for Democratic Renewal.

———. 1992. *Quarantines and Death: The Far Right's Homophobic Agenda*. Atlanta: Center for Democratic Renewal.

———. 1994. *A Year of Intolerance: A Review of Hate Group Activities and Ideologies in 1994*. Atlanta: Center for Democratic Renewal.

———. 1995. *Paramilitary Right Moves Center Stage: Overview of Militias, Hate Groups, and Intolerance in 1995*. Atlanta: Center for Democratic Renewal.

Centre for Bangladeshi Studies. 1995. *Routes and Beyond: Voices of Educationally Successful Bengalis in Tower Hamlets*. London: Centre for Bangladeshi Studies.

Centre for Contemporary Cultural Studies. 1982. *The Empire Strikes Back: Race and Racism in 70s Britain*. London: Hutchinson.

Chabram, Angie. 1992. "I Throw Punches for My Race but I Don't Want to Be a Man Writing Us—Chica-nos (Girl, Us)/Chicanas—into the Movement Script." In *Cul-*

tural Studies, ed. Lawrence Grossberg, Cary Nelson, and Paula Treichler, 81–95. New York: Routledge.

Chabram-Dernersesian, Angie. 1994. "Chicana? Rican? No, Chicana-Riqueña! Refashioning the Transnational Connection." In *Multiculturalism: A Critical Reader,* ed. David T. Goldberg. Oxford: Blackwell.

Chafev, Ze'ev. 1990. *Devil's Night and Other True Tales of Detroit.* New York: Vintage.

Chaudhuri, Nupur, and Margaret Strobel. 1992. *Western Women and Imperialism: Complicity and Resistance.* Bloomington: Indiana University Press.

Chevalier, Louis. 1973. *Laboring Classes and Dangerous Classes in Paris during the First Half of the Nineteenth Century,* trans. Frank Jellinek. New York: H. Fertig.

Chock, Phyllis. 1987. "The Irony of Stereotypes: Toward an Anthropology of Ethnicity." *Cultural Anthropology* 2.3: 347–68.

Chodorow, Nancy. 1978. *The Reproduction of Mothering: Psychoanalysis and the Sociology of Gender.* Berkeley: University of California Press.

Chopin, Kate. 1969. *The Complete Works of Kate Chopin.* 2 vols. Ed. Per Seyersted. Baton Rouge: Louisiana State University Press.

Clifford, James. 1986. "Notes on Travel and Theory." In *Traveling Theory, Traveling Theorists, Inscriptions,* no. 5, ed. James Clifford and Vivek Dhareshwar. Santa Cruz: University of California Press.

Coblentz, William K. 1995. "UC Affirmative Action Benefits All." *San Francisco Chronicle,* May 12, A25.

Cohen, Phil. 1992. "It's Racism What Dunnit." In *Race, Culture and Difference,* ed. James Donald and Ali Rattansi. London: Sage.

———. 1994. *Home Rules.* University of East London Monograph. London: University of East London Press.

———. 1995. "Sur l'antiracisme et l'antihumanisme." *Lignes* 25.

———. 1996. "All White on the Night." In *Rising in the East,* ed. Michael Rustin. London: Lawrence & Wishart.

———. 1996. "Backbone of the Nation, Race Apart." In *Twenty Years,* Dockland Forum. London: Dockland Forum.

———. 1997. *Rethinking the Youth Question.* London: Macmillan.

Cohen, Phil, and H. Bains, eds. 1988. *Multi-Racist Britain.* London: Macmillan.

Cohen, Phil, and David Robins. 1978. *Knuckle Sandwich: Growing up in the Working Class City.* Harmondsworth: Penguin.

Cohen, Phil. 1997. *Island Stories.* London: Runnymede Trust, University of East London Press.

Cohen, Steven. 1986. *That's Funny, You Don't Look Antisemitic.* Manchester: Manchester Books.

Colley, Linda. 1992. *Britons—Forging the Nation, 1707–1837.* New Haven: Yale University Press.

Collins, Patricia Hill. 1990. *Black Feminist Thought: Knowledge, Consciousness, and the Politics of Empowerment.* Perspectives on Gender, no. 2. New York: Routledge. Reprint of London: HarperCollins Academic, 1989.

Culp, Jerome, and Bruce H. Dunson. 1986. "Brothers of a Different Color: A Preliminary Look at Employer Treatment of White and Black Youth." In *The Black Youth Unemployment Crisis,* ed. R. B. Freeman and Harry J. Holzer, 233–60. Chicago: University of Chicago Press.

Cunliffe, Marcus. 1979. *Chattel Slavery and Wage Slavery: The Anglo-American Context, 1830–1860.* Athens: University of Georgia Press.

Cunningham, H. 1989. "The Language of Patriotism." In *Patriotism: The Making and Un-making of British National Identity,* vol. 3, ed. Raphael Samuel. London: Routledge.

Darden, Joe, et al. 1987. *Detroit: Race and Uneven Development.* Philadelphia: Temple University Press.

Davis, Angela Y. 1981. *Women, Race, and Class.* New York: Random House.

Davis, David Brion. 1966. *The Problem of Slavery and Western Culture.* Ithaca: Cornell University Press. Reprint. Oxford: Oxford University Press, 1988.

Davis, Mike. 1992. *City of Quartz: Excavating the Future in Los Angeles.* New York: Vintage.

De Lauretis, Teresa. 1991. "Film and the Visible." In *How Do I Look? Queer Film and Video,* ed. Bad Object-Choices, 225–84. Seattle: Bay Press.

De Saussure, Ferdinand. 1986. *Course in General Linguistics.* Ed. Charles Bally and Albert Sechehaye, trans. Roy Harris. La Salle, Ill.: Open Court.

Devyver, A. 1984. *Le Sang Epure.* Brussels: Louvain.

Dockland Forum. 1996. *Twenty Years.* London: Dockland Forum.

Dolto, Françoise. 1982. *Image inconscient du corps.* Paris: Seuil.

Dominguez, Virginia. 1986. *White by Definition: Social Classification in Creole Louisiana.* New Brunswick: Rutgers University Press.

Donald, James, and Ali Rattansi, eds. 1992. *Race, Culture and Difference.* London: Sage.

Douglas, Mary. 1973. *Natural Symbols.* London: Penguin.

———. 1966. *Purity and Danger: An Analysis of Concepts of Pollution and Taboo.* New York: Praeger. Reprint. London: Ark, 1984.

Dunn, Peter, and Loraine Leeson. 1993. "The Art of Change in Docklands." In *Mapping the Futures, Local Cultures, Global Change,* ed. Jon Bird, Barry Curtis, Tim Putnam, George Robertson, and Lisa Tickner, 136–49. London: Routledge.

Dyer, Richard. 1988. "White." *Screen* 29.4 (Autumn): 44–64.

Dyos, H. J., and Michael Wolff, eds. 1977. *The Victorian City: Images and Realities.* Vol. 1. London: Routledge.

Eades, J. 1989. *The Politics of Community: The Bangladeshi Community in East London.* Aldershot: Avebury.

Elfenbein, Anna Shannon. 1989. *Women on the Color Line: Evolving Stereotypes and the Writings of George Washington Cable, Grace King, and Kate Chopin.* Charlottesville: University Press of Virginia.

Elias, Norbert. 1991. *The Civilising Process.* Manchester: Manchester University Press.

Ellis, John. 1995. "Class-Based Affirmative Action: The Liberals' Desperate Fallback Position." *Heterodoxy* 3 (May).

Ely, Melvin Patrick. 1991. *The Adventures of Amos 'n' Andy: A Social History of an American Phenomenon.* New York: Free Press.

Engels, Friedrich. 1971. *The Condition of the Working Class in England.* Oxford: Blackwell.

Essed, Philomena. 1990. *Everyday Racism: Reports from Women of Two Cultures.* Claremont, Calif.: Hunter House.

Evans, N. 1985. "Regulating the Reserve Army." In *Race and Labour in Twentieth Century Britain,* ed. Kenneth Lunn. London: Cass.

Ezorsky, Gertrude. 1991. *Racism and Justice: The Case for Affirmative Action.* Ithaca: Cornell University Press.

Falk, Pasi. 1994. *The Consuming Body*. Thousand Oaks, Calif.: Sage.

Fanon, Franz. 1982. *Black Skin, White Masks*. New York: Grove.

Fardon, Richard. 1990. *Localizing Strategies: The Regional Traditions of Ethnographic Writing*. Edinburgh: Scottish Academic Press.

Feldman, David, and Gareth Stedman-Jones, eds. 1989. *Metropolis, London: Histories and Representations since 1800*. London: Routledge.

Ferguson, Russell. 1990. *Out There: Marginality and Contemporary Art*. Boston: MIT Press.

Fine, Michelle, Lois Weis, Linda C. Powell, and L. Mun Wang, eds. 1997. *Off White: Readings on Race, Power and Society*. New York: Routledge.

Finn, Margot C. 1993. *After Chartism: Class and Nation in English Radical Politics, 1848–1874*. Cambridge: Cambridge University Press.

Fladeland, Betty. 1984. *Abolitionists and Working Class Problems in the Age of Industrialization*. Baton Rouge: Louisiana State University Press, and London: Macmillan.

Fordham, Signithia, and John Ogbu. 1986. "Black Students' Success: Coping with the 'Burden of Acting White.' " *Urban Review* 18.3.

Foucault, Michel. 1978. *The History of Sexuality*. Vol. 1: *An Introduction*. New York: Random House.

Frankenberg, Ruth. 1993. *White Women, Race Matters: The Social Construction of Whiteness*. Minneapolis: University of Minnesota Press, and London: Routledge.

Fregoso, Rosa Linda, and Angie Chabram. 1990. "Introduction." *Cultural Studies* 4.3 (October): 203–12.

Gaber, Ivor, and Jane Aldridge. 1995. *In the Best Interests of the Child: Culture, Identity, and Transracial Adoption*. London: Free Association Books.

Gallagher, Charles. 1995. "White Reconstruction in the University." *Socialist Review* 24.1–2: 165–87.

Galvan, Robert, and Richard Teschner. 1985. *El diccionario del español chicano*. Lincoln: Voluntad.

Gamio, Manuel. 1971. *Mexican Immigration to the United States*. New York: Dover. Reprint. Chicago: University of Chicago Press, 1930.

Gamson, William, and Andre Modigliani. 1987. "The Changing Culture of Affirmative Action." *Research in Political Sociology* 3: 137–77.

Garn, Stanley. 1961. *Human Race*. Springfield, Ill.: Charles Thomas Publishers.

Gates, Henry Louis. 1985. "Editor's Introduction: Writing 'Race' and the Difference It Makes." *Critical Inquiry* 12 (Autumn): 1–20.

————. 1991. "Critical Fanonism." *Critical Inquiry* 17.3 (Spring): 457–70.

————. "Art and Ardor." *Nation*, 493.

Gilman, Sander. 1985. *Difference and Pathology*. Ithaca: Cornell University Press.

Gilroy, Paul. 1993. *The Black Atlantic: Modernity and Double Consciousness*. London: Verso, and Cambridge: Harvard University Press.

Glazer, Nathan, and Daniel Moynihan. 1963. *Beyond the Melting Pot*. Cambridge: MIT Press.

Glenn, Evelyn Nakano, Grace Chang, and Linda Rennie Forcey, eds. 1994. *Mothering: Ideology, Experience, and Agency*. New York: Routledge.

Goldberg, David. 1993. *Racist Culture: Philosophy and the Politics of Meaning*. Cambridge: Blackwell.

Gonzales, Rodolfo. 1967. *I Am Joaquín*. Denver: El Gallo.

Gonzales-Berry, Erlinda. 1991. *Paletitas de Guayaba*. Albuquerque: El Norte.

Gordon, Avery, and Christopher Newfield. 1994. "White Philosophy." *Critical Inquiry* 20 (Summer): 737–57.

Gorz, A. 1984. *Farewell to the Working Class: An Essay on Post-industrial Socialism*. Trans. Michael Sonenscher. London: Pluto.

Grewal, Inderpal. 1994. "Autobiographic Subjects and Diasporic Location." In *Scattered Hegemonies: Postmodernity and Transnational Feminist Practice*, ed. Inderpal Grewal and Caren Kaplan, 231–54. Minneapolis: University of Minnesota Press.

Guerrero, Edward. 1990. "AIDS as Monster in Science Fiction and Horror Cinema." *Journal of Popular Film and Television* 18.3 (Fall): 86–93.

Gunnison, Robert B. 1995. "State Study Finds More Female, Minority Bosses." *San Francisco Chronicle*, March 28.

Gurganus, Allan. 1990. *White People*. New York: Ivy Books.

Gwaltney, John Langston. 1980. *Drylongso: A Self Portrait of Black America*. New York: Random House.

Hall, Catherine. 1992. *White, Male and Middle Class*. Cambridge: Polity.

Hall, Stuart. 1993. *New Statesman and Society* (December).

———. 1990. "Cultural Identity and Diaspora." In *Identity, Community, Culture and Difference*, ed. Jonathan Rutherford. London: Lawrence and Wishart.

———. 1980. "Encoding/Decoding." In *Culture, Media Language*, ed. Stuart Hall, Dorothy Hobson, Andrew Love, and Paul Willis. Birmingham: Center for Contemporary Cultural Studies.

———. 1980. "Race, Articulation and Societies Structured in Dominance." In UNESCO, *Sociological Theories, Race, and Colonialism*, 305–45. Paris: UNESCO Press.

———. 1985. "Faith, Hope or Clarity." *Marxism Today* 20.1 (January): 15–19.

———. 1986. "No Light at the End of the Tunnel." *Marxism Today* 21.12 (December): 12–16.

Halsell, Grace. 1969. *Soul Sister*. New York: World.

Hamm, Mark S. 1993. *American Skinheads: The Criminology and Control of Hate Crime*. Westport, Conn.: Praeger.

Hansberry, Lorraine. 1969. *To Be Young, Gifted, and Black*. Englewood Cliffs, N.J.: Prentice-Hall.

Haraway, Donna J. 1991. "A Cyborg Manifesto: Science, Technology, and Socialist-Feminism in the Late Twentieth Century." In *Simians, Cyborgs, and Women: The Reinvention of Nature*, Donna J. Haraway. New York: Routledge.

Harlow, Barbara. 1987. "Narratives of Resistance," *New Formations* 1 (Spring): 131–35.

Harris, Louis. 1995. "Affirmative Action and the Voter." *New York Times*, July 31.

Hartigan, John, Jr. Forthcoming. *Cultural Constructions of Whiteness: Racial and Class Formations in Detroit*. Princeton, N.J.: Princeton University Press.

———. 1996. "Disgrace to the Race: 'Hillbillies' and the Color Line in Detroit." In *Down Home, Downtown: Urban Appalachians Today*, ed. Phillip Obermiller, 55–72. Dubuque, Iowa: Kendall-Hunt.

———. 1997. "Establishing the Fact of Whiteness." *American Anthropologist* 99.2.

———. Forthcoming. "Green Ghettoes and the White Underclass." *Social Research*.

———. 1997. "When Whites Are a Minority." In *Cultural Diversity in the United States*, ed. Larry Naylor, 103–16. Westport, Conn.: Bergin and Harvey.

———. 1997. "Whites and White Trash in Detroit." In *White Trash: Race and Class in America*, ed. Matt Wray and Annalee Newitz, 41–56. New York: Routledge.

Heath, Steven. 1981. *Questions of Cinema*. London: Macmillan.

Hebdige, Dick. 1987. *Hiding in the Light*. London: Methuen.

Herron, Jerry. 1993. *After Culture: Detroit and the Humiliation of History*. Detroit: Wayne State University Press.

Hesse, Barnor, et al. 1992. *Beneath the Surface: Racial Harassment*. Aldershot: Avebury.

Hill, Christopher. 1974. *Change and Continuity in Seventeenth Century England*. London: Penguin.

Hill, Herbert. 1989. "Black Labor and Affirmative Action." In *The Question of Discrimination: Racial Inequality in the U.S. Labor Market*, ed. Steven Shulman and William Darity Jr. Middletown, Conn.: Wesleyan University Press.

Hill, Steven. 1976. *The Dockers: Class and Tradition in London*. London: Heineman.

Hindess, Barry. 1971. *The Decline of Working Class Politics*. London: McGibbon and Kee.

Hobbs, Dick. 1988. *Doing the Business: Entrepreneurship, the Working Class, and Detectives in the East End of London*. Oxford: Clarendon Books, and New York: Oxford University Press.

Hobsbawm, Eric. 1963. *Primitive Rebels: Studies in Archaic Forms of Social Movement in the Nineteenth and Twentieth Centuries*. Westport, Conn.: Praeger.

———. 1965. *Labouring Men: Studies in the History of Labour*. New York: Basic Books.

Hochschild, Arlie. 1983. *The Managed Heart*. Berkeley: University of California Press.

———. 1989. *The Second Shift: Working Parents and the Revolution at Home*. New York: Viking Press.

Hochschild, Jennifer L. 1988. "Race, Class, Power and the American Welfare State." In *Democracy and the Welfare State*, ed. Amy Guttman, 157–84. Princeton: Princeton University Press.

Hodor-Salmon, Marilyn. 1992. *Kate Chopin's "The Awakening."* Tallahassee: University Press of Florida.

Hofstettler, E. 1991. *A Short History of the Isle of Dogs*. London: Island History Trust.

Holland, R. 1990. *The Long Transition*. London: Macmillan.

Hollardnby, T. *Docklands*.

Holmes, Steven A. 1995. "Census Finds Little Change in Income Gap between Races." *New York Times*, February 23.

Holt, Thomas C. 1992. *The Problem of Freedom: Race, Labor, and Politics in Jamaica and Britain, 1832–1938*. Baltimore: Johns Hopkins University Press.

———. 1995. "Marking: Race, Race-Making, and the Writing of History." *American Historical Review* (February): 1–20.

hooks, bell. 1990. "Homeplace: A Site of Resistance." In *Yearning: Race, Gender, and Cultural Politics*. Boston: South End.

———. 1990. *Yearning: Race, Gender, and Cultural Politics*. Boston: South End.

———. 1992. "Representations of Whiteness in the Black Imagination." In *Black Looks: Race and Representation*, 165–79. Boston: South End.

———. 1992. "Representing Whiteness in the Black Imagination." In *Cultural Studies*, ed. Lawrence Grossberg, Cary Nelson, and Paula Treichler, 338–46. New York: Routledge.

Horsman, Reginald. 1975. "Scientific Racism and the American Indian in the Mid-Nineteenth Century." *American Quarterly* 27 (May): 52–168.

————. 1981. *Race and Manifest Destiny: The Origins of American Racial Anglo-Saxonism.* Cambridge: Harvard University Press.

Huckfeldt, Robert, and Carole Weitzel Kohfeld. 1989. *Race and the Decline of Class in American Politics.* Urbana: University of Illinois Press.

Huerta, Jorge. 1982. *Chicano Theater.* Ypsilanti: Bilingual.

Hugill, Stan. 1984. *Sailortown.* London: Cassel Books.

Husbands, C. 1982. "East End Racism, 1900–1980." *London Journal* 26.

Institute for the Study of Social Change. 1991. *The Diversity Project.* Berkeley: University of California Press.

Jacques, Martin, ed. 1984. *The Onward March of Labour Halted.* London: Lawrence and Wishart.

James, W. 1989. "The Making of Black Identities." In *Patriotism: The Making and Unmaking of British National Identity.* 3 vols., ed. Raphael Samuel. London: Routledge.

Jameson, Fredric. 1992. *Postmodernism: The Cultural Logic of Late Capitalism.* Durham: Duke University Press, and London: Verso.

Jefferies, Steve. 1989. "Matters of Mutual Interest: The Unionization Process at Dodge Main, 1933–1939." In *On the Line: Essays in the History of Autowork,* ed. Nelson Lichtenstein and Steven Meyer. Urbana: University of Illinois Press.

Jenkinson, J. 1980. "The Glasgow Race Disturbances of 1919." In *Hosts, Immigrants, and Minorities: The Historical Response to Newcomers in British Society, 1870–1914,* ed. K. Lunn. Folkestone: Dawson.

Jessop, Bob, Kevin Bonnett, and Simon Bromley. 1990. "Farewell to Thatcherism? Neoliberalism and 'New Times.'" *New Left Review* 179 (January–February): 81–102.

————. 1991. *Fordism and Post-Fordism.* Lancaster: Lancaster University Press.

Jones, Simon. 1988. *Black Culture, White Youth: The Reggae Tradition from JA to UK.* London: Macmillan.

Kantorovicz, Ernst Hartwig. 1953. *The King's Two Bodies: A Study in Mediaeval Political Theology.* Cambridge: Harvard University Press.

Karabel, Jerome, and David Karen. 1990. "Go to Harvard, Give Your Kid a Break." *New York Times,* December 8.

Kasaba, Kathie Friedman. 1996. *"To Become a Person": The Experience of Gender, Ethnicity and Work in the Lives of Immigrant Women, New York City, 1870–1940.* Binghamton, N.Y.: SUNY Press.

Katzman, David. 1973. *Before the Ghetto: Black Detroit in the Nineteenth Century.* Urbana: University of Illinois Press.

Keith, Michael, and Steve Pile. 1993. "Introduction: The Politics of Place." In *Place and the Politics of Identity,* ed. Michael Keith and Steve Pile, 1–21. London: Routledge.

Kilborn, Peter T. 1995. "Women and Minorities Still Face 'Glass Ceiling.'" *New York Times,* March 16.

Kim, Elaine. 1982. *Asian American Literature.* Philadelphia: Temple University Press.

King, Anthony D. 1991. *Culture, Globalisation, and the World System.* Binghamton, N.Y.: SUNY Press, and London: Routledge.

King, James C. 1981. *The Biology of Race.* Berkeley: University of California Press.

Kingston, Maxine Hong. 1976. *The Woman Warrior.* New York: Vintage.

————. 1981. *China Men.* New York: Ballantine Books.

Knowles, Caroline. 1992. *Race, Discourse, and Labourism.* London: Routledge.

Koloski, Bernard, ed. 1988. *Approaches to Teaching Chopin's "The Awakening."* Approaches to Teaching World Literature 16. New York: MLA.

Kovel, Joel. 1970. *White Racism: A Psychohistory.* New York: Pantheon.

Kristeva, Julia. 1993. *Foreigners to Ourselves.* London: Allen and Unwin.

Lambropoulos, Vassilis. 1993. *The Rise of Eurocentrism: Anatomy of Interpretation.* Princeton: Princeton University Press.

Land, H. *The Family Wage in Liverpool.*

Lawrence, Errol. 1982. "Just Plain Common Sense: The 'Roots' of Racism." In Centre for Contemporary Cultural Studies, *The Empire Strikes Back: Race and Racism in Seventies Britain,* 47–94. London: Hutchinson.

Leadbeater, Charlie. 1989. "Back to the Future." *Marxism Today* 24.5 (May): 12–17.

Lee, A. 1980. "Working Class Response to the Jews in Britain." In *Hosts, Immigrants, and Minorities: The Historical Response to Newcomers in British Society, 1870-1914,* ed. K. Lunn. Folkestone: Dawson.

Leonard, Jonathan S. 1986. "Splitting Blacks? Affirmative Action and Earnings Inequality within and across Races." *Proceedings of the Thirty-Ninth Annual Meeting,* ed. Barbara D. Dennis. Industrial Relations Research Association Series.

Levine, David Alan. 1976. *Internal Combustion: The Races in Detroit, 1915-1926.* Westport, Conn.: Greenwood.

Limón, José. 1977. "Agringado Joking in Texas Mexican Society." *New Scholar* 6: 33–50.

———. 1992. *Mexican Ballads, Chicano Poems.* Berkeley: University of California Press.

Linebaugh, Peter. 1993. *The London Hanged: Crime and Civil Society in the Eighteenth Century.* London: Penguin.

Lipsitz, George. 1995. "The Possessive Investment in Whiteness: Racialized Social Democracy and the 'White' Problem in American Studies." *American Quarterly* 47 (September): 369–87.

Lloyd, David. 1991. "Race under Representation." *Oxford Literary Review* 18.1–2 (1991): 62–94.

London Regional Liberal Democratic Party. 1993. *Political Speech and Race Relations in a Liberal Democracy: Report of an Inquiry into the Conduct of the Tower Hamlets Liberal Democrats in Publishing Allegedly Racist Election Literature between 1990 and 1993.* London: London Regional Liberal Democratic Party.

Lopez, Ian Hanley. 1996. *White by Law.* New York: New York University Press.

Lorimer, D. 1978. *Colour, Class and the Victorians.* Leicester: Leicester University Press.

Los Angeles Times. 1995. "Swatting away Those Pesky Facts on Affirmative Action." July 23, M4.

Lott, Eric. 1993. *Love and Theft: Black Face Minstrelsy and the American Working Class.* New York.

Lovejoy, P., and N. Roger. 1994. *Unfree Labour in the Development of the Atlantic World.* London: Cass.

Lunn, Kenneth, ed. 1980. *Hosts, Immigrants and Minorities: Historical Response to Newcomers in British Society, 1870-1914.* Folkestone: Dawson.

———, ed. 1985. *Race and Labour in Twentieth Century Britain.* London: Cass.

Lustig, Jeffrey, and Richard Walker. 1995. "No Way Out: Immigrants and the New California." Occasional paper, Campus Coalitions for Human Rights and Social Justice. Oakland: Campus Coalitions for Human Rights and Social Justice.

MacCabe, Colin. 1985. *Theoretical Essays: Film, Linguistics, Literature.* Manchester: Manchester University Press.

Maciel, Ysidro Ramón. 1971. "The Chicano Movement." In *A Documentary History of Mexican Americans,* ed. Wayne Moquin with Charles Van Doren. New York: Praeger.

Mackenzie, John, and P. Duane, eds. 1986. *Imperialism and Popular Culture.* Manchester: Manchester University Press.

MacLeod, Jay. 1987. *Ain't No Makin' It: Leveled Aspirations in a Low-Income Neighborhood.* Boulder, Colo.: Westview.

Madrid-Barela, Arturo. 1971. "Pochos: The Different Mexicans, an Interpretative Essay, Part I." *Aztlan* 7.1 (Spring): 51–64.

Malik, K. 1996. *The Meaning of Race.* London: Routledge.

Maloney, Michael. 1987. "A Decade in Review: The Development of the Ethnic Model in Urban Appalachian Studies." In *Too Few Tomorrows: Urban Appalachians in the 1980s,* ed. Phillip Obermiller and William Philliber. Boone, N.C.: Appalachian Consortium Press.

Mangan, J. A., ed. *Making Imperial Mentalities: Socialization and British Imperialism.* Manchester: Manchester University Press.

Marriott, John. 1991. *The Culture of Labourism: The East End between the Wars.* Edinburgh: Edinburgh University Press.

Marston, Sallie. 1989. "Public Rituals and Community Power: St. Patrick's Day Parade in Lowell, Massachusetts, 1841–1874." *Political Geography Quarterly* 8 (July): 255–69.

Martin, Wendy, ed. 1988. *New Essays on "The Awakening."* The American Novel 11. Cambridge: Cambridge University Press.

Massey, Doreen. 1994. *Docklands: A Microcosm of Thatcherism.* London: Forum.

Massey, Douglass, and Nancy Denton. 1993. *American Apartheid: Segregation and the Making of the Underclass.* Cambridge: Harvard University Press.

———. 1988. "Suburbanization and Segregation in U.S. Metropolitan Areas." *American Journal of Sociology* 94 (November): 593–625.

McClintock, Anne. 1994. *Imperial Leather: Race, Gender, and Sexuality in the Colonial Context.* London: Routledge.

McCoy, Clyde, and William Philliber, eds. 1981. *The Invisible Minority: Urban Appalachians.* Lexington: University Press of Kentucky.

McLeod, Ramon G. 1995. "White Men's Eroding Economic Clout Contributes to Backlash." *San Francisco Chronicle,* March 20.

Meagher, Timothy. 1985. "'Why Should We Care for a Little Trouble or a Walk through the Mud?' St. Patrick's and Columbus Day Parades in Worcester, Massachusetts, 1845–1915." *New England Quarterly* 58.1 (March): 5–25.

Meirer, August, and Elliot Ruwick. 1979. *Black Detroit and the Rise of the UAW.* New York: Oxford University Press.

Méndez, Miguel. 1986. *De la vida y el folclore de la frontera.* Tucson: Mexican American Studies Research Center.

Mercer, Kobena. 1991. "Skin Head Sex Thing and the Homoerotic Imaginary." In *How Do I Look? Queer Film and Video,* ed. Bad Object-Choices, 169–222. Seattle: Bay Press.

———. 1992. "'1968': Periodizing Politics and Identity." In *Cultural Studies,* ed. Lawrence Grossberg, Cary Nelson, and Paula Treichler, 424–49. New York: Routledge.

———. 1994. *Welcome to the Jungle: New Positions in Black Cultural Studies.* New York: Routledge.

Miles, Robert. 1982. *Racism and Migrant Labour.* London: Routledge.

———. 1994. *Racism after Race Relations.* London: Routledge.

Miles, Robert, and Annie Phizaclea. 1980. *Labour and Racism.* London: Routledge.

Mirzoeff, E. 1995. *Bodyscapes.* London: Routledge.

Moore, Jack B. 1993. *Skinheads Shaved for Battle: A Cultural History of American Skinheads.* Bowling Green: Ohio State University Press.

Mora, Pat. 1986. *Borders.* Houston: Arte Público.

Morrison, Toni. 1987. *Beloved.* New York: Knopf.

———. 1992. *Playing in the Dark: Whiteness and the Literary Imagination.* Cambridge: Harvard University Press.

Moss, Kenneth. 1995. "St. Patrick's Day Celebrations and the Formation of Irish American Identity, 1845–1875. *Journal of Social History* 29.1: 125–48.

Nelson, Dean. 1993. "Local Democracy Goes to the Dogs." *London Observer,* September 18.

Newman, Randy. 1988. "Land of Dreams." Reprise Records.

New York Times. 1995. "Reverse Discrimination Complaints Rare, a Labor Study Reports." March 31, A10.

Njeri, Itabari. 1990. *Every Good-bye Ain't Gone.* New York: Random House.

Oliver, Melvin L., and Thomas M. Shapiro. 1995. *Black Wealth/White Wealth: A New Perspective on Racial Inequality.* New York: Routledge.

Omi, Michael, and Howard Winant. 1986. *Racial Formation in the United States: From the 1960s to the 1980s.* New York: Routledge.

Osumi, Megumi Dick. 1982. "Asians and California's Anti-miscegenation Laws." In *Asian/Pacific American Experiences: Women's Perspectives,* ed. Tsuchida Nobuye. Asian/Pacific American Learning Resource Center and General College, University of Minnesota.

Owings, Alison. 1995. *Frauen: German Women Recall the Third Reich.* New York: Penguin.

Owusu, Kwesi. 1988. *Storms of the Heart: An Anthology of Black Arts and Culture.* London: Camden.

Paredes, Américo. 1966. "The Anglo-American in Mexican Folklore." In *New Voices in American Studies,* ed. Ray Browne, Donald Winkelman, and Allen Hayman. Lafayette: Purdue University Press.

———. 1976. "The Pocho Appears." In *A Texas-Mexican Cancionero.* Urbana: University of Illinois Press.

———. 1991. *Between Two Worlds.* Houston: Arte Público.

Paredes, Raymund. 1982. "The Evolution of Chicano Literature." In *Three American Literatures,* ed. Houston A. Baker Jr. New York: MLA.

Patterson, Orlando. 1991. *Freedom in the Making of Western Culture.* London: I. B. Tauris, and New York: Basic Books.

Peirce, Charles Sanders. 1931. *Collected Papers.* Cambridge: Harvard University Press.

Pérez-Torres, Rafael. 1995. *Movements in Chicano Poetry: Against Myths, against Margins.* Cambridge: Cambridge University Press.

Perkins, Linda M. 1983. "The Impact of the 'Cult of True Womanhood' on the Education of Black Women." *Journal of Social Issues* 39.3: 17–28.

Perrin, Constance. 1988. *Belonging in America: Reading between the Lines.* Madison: University of Wisconsin Press.

Pfeil, Fred. 1995. *White Guys: Studies in Postmodern Domination and Difference.* London: Verso.

Philliber, William. 1981. *Appalachian Migrants in Urban America: Cultural Group or Ethnic Group Formation?* New York: Praeger Scientific.

Poliakov, Leon. 1974. *The Aryan Myth: A History of Racist and Nationalist Ideas in Europe.* London: Weidenfeld and Nicholson.

Pratt, Minnie Bruce. 1984. "Identity: Skin, Blood, Heart." In *Yours in Struggle: Three Feminist Perspectives on Anti-Semitism and Racism,* ed. Elly Bulkin, Minnie Bruce Pratt, and Barbara Smith. Brooklyn: Long Haul Press.

Price, R. 1976. *An Imperial War and the Working Class.* London: Routledge.

Rainwater, Lee, and William Yancey. 1967. *The Moynihan Report and the Politics of Controversy.* Cambridge: MIT Press.

Rattansi, Ali. 1994. *Race, Modernity, and Identity.* Cambridge: Polity.

Rattansi, Ali, and Sallie Westwood. 1994. *Racism, Modernity, and Identity: On the Western Front.* Cambridge: Polity.

Rawick, George. 1972. *From Sundown to Sunup.* New York: Harcourt.

Reagon, Bernice Johnson. 1983. "Coalition Politics, Turning the Century." In *Home Girls: A Black Feminist Anthology,* ed. Barbara Smith, 356–69. New York: Kitchen Table Women of Color Press.

Rediker, M. 1987. *Between the Devil and the Deep Blue Sea: Merchant Seamen, Pirates, and the Anglo-American Marine World, 1700-1750.* Cambridge: Cambridge University Press.

Rendón, Armando. 1971. *Chicano Manifesto.* New York: Collier Books.

Rich, Adrienne. 1979. "Disloyal to Civilization: Feminism, Racism, Gynephobia." In *On Lies, Secrets and Silence: Selected Prose, 1966-78,* ed. Adrienne Rich, 275–310. New York: Norton.

Rich, P. 1992. *The Politics of Race and Empire.* Oxford: Oxford University Press.

Ridgeway, James. 1990. *Blood in the Face: The KKK, Aryan Nations, Nazi Skinheads and the Rise of a New White Culture.* New York: Thunder's Mouth.

Rieder, Jonathan. 1985. *Canarsie: The Jews and Italians of Brooklyn against Liberalism.* Cambridge: Harvard University Press.

Roberts, Martha. 1980. *The Origins of the Novel.* Brighton: Harvester.

Roediger, David. R. 1990. *The Wages of Whiteness: Race and the Making of the American Working Class.* New York: Verso.

———. 1994. *Towards the Abolition of Whiteness: Essays on Race, Politics, and Working Class History.* London: Verso.

Root, Maria. 1996. *Racially Mixed People in America.* Knobbier Park, Calif.: Sage.

Rosaldo, Renato. 1988. *Culture and Truth: The Remaking of Social Analysis.* Boston: Beacon.

Rule, John. 1986. *The Labouring Classes in Early Industrial England.* London: Longman.

———. 1992. *Albion's People: English Society, 1714-1815.* London: Longman.

Runnymede Trust. 1993. *Neither Unique nor Typical.* London: Runnymede Trust.

Rushdie, Salman. 1984. "Outside the Whale." *Granta* 2 (1984): 122–38.

Rustin, Michael, ed. 1991. *The Good Society and the Inner World: Psychoanalysis, Politics, and Culture.* London: Verso.

Ryan, Michael. 1988. "The Politics of Film: Discourse, Psychoanalysis, Ideology." In *Marxism and Interpretation of Culture,* ed. Nelson Cary and Larry Grossberg, 477–86. London: Macmillan.

Sacks, Karen Brodkin. 1994. "How Did Jews Become White Folks?" In *Race,* ed. Steven Gregory and Roger Sanjek, 78–102. New Brunswick: Rutgers University Press.

Said, Edward. 1983. "Traveling Theory." In *The World, the Text, and the Critic.* Cambridge: Harvard University Press.

Saldívar-Hull, Sonia. 1991. "Feminism on the Border: From Gender Politics to Geopolitics." In *Criticism in the Borderlands,* ed. Hector Calderón and José David Saldívar, 203–10. Durham: Duke University Press.

Sandoval, Chela. 1997. *Rhetorics of Rebellion: Flux at the Second Millenium.* Minneapolis: University of Minnesota Press.

San Jose Mercury News. 1995. "Scholarship Race: Affirmative Action Plays Almost No Part in Outcome." May 25.

Saxton, Alexander. 1990. *The Rise and Fall of the White Republic: Class Politics and Mass Culture in Nineteenth Century America.* New York: Verso.

Scheer, Robert. 1995. "Angry Whites Should Check Wilson's Math." *Los Angeles Times,* July 25.

Schneider, David, and Raymond Smith. 1973. *Class Differences and Family Structure.* Englewood Cliffs, N.J.: Prentice Hall.

Schwarz, B. 1996. "The Only White Man in There." *Race and Class* 38.1.

Seabrook, Jeremy. 1978. *What Went Wrong.* London: Gollancz.

Segrest, Mab. 1986. *My Mama's Dead Squirrel: Lesbian Essays on Southern Culture.* Ithaca, N.Y.: Firebrand Books.

———. 1994. *Memoir of a Race Traitor.* Boston: South End.

Sharpe, William, and Leonard Wallock. 1994. "Bold New City or Built-up 'Burb? Redefining Contemporary Suburbia." *American Quarterly* 46: 1–30.

Sherover-Marcuse, Ricky. n.d. "Unlearning Racism." Manuscript.

Sibony, Daniel. 1994. *Le Nom et le corps.* Paris: Seuil.

Smith, Lillian. 1978. *Killers of the Dream.* 1950. Reprint. New York: Norton, and London: Cresset.

Solomon, Barbara H. 1988. "Characters as Foils to Edna." In *Approaches to Teaching Kate Chopin's "The Awakening."* Approaches to Teaching World Literature 16. New York: MLA.

Southern Poverty Law Center. 1996. *False Patriots: The Threat of Anti-government Extremists.* Montgomery, Ala.: Southern Poverty Law Center.

Spelman, Elizabeth V. 1988. *Inessential Woman: Problems of Exclusion in Feminist Thought.* Boston: Beacon.

Spillers, Hortense J. 1987. "Mama's Baby, Papa's Maybe: An American Grammar Book." *Diacritics* 17.2: 65–81.

Spivak, Gayatri Chakravorty. 1990. *The Post-Colonial Critic: Interviews, Strategies, Dialogues.* Ed. Sarah Harasym. New York: Routledge.

Stallabras, John. 1995. "Gargantua." *New Left Review* 234.

Stallybrass, Peter, and Allon White. 1986. *The Politics and Poetics of Transgression.* London: Methuen.

Stange, Margit. 1989. "Personal Property: Exchange Value and the Female Self in *The Awakening.*" *Genders* 5 (Summer): 106–19.

Stedman Jones, Gareth. 1983. *Languages of Class.* Cambridge: Cambridge University Press.

———. 1984. *Outcast.* London: Penguin.

Stibbe, Matthew. 1993. "Women and the Nazi State." *History Today* (November): 35–40.

Stoler, Ann Laura. 1991. "Carnal Knowledge and Imperial Power." In *Gender at the Crossroads of Knowledge,* ed. Micaela di Leonardo, 51–101. Berkeley: University of California Press.

Stoler, Ann. 1989. "Making Empire Respectable: The Politics of Race and Sexual Morality in Twentieth Century Colonial Cultures." *American Ethnologist* 16.4: 54–74.

Strathern, Marilyn. 1991. *Partial Connections.* Savage, Md.: Rowman and Littlefield.

Streicker, Joel. 1995. "Policing Boundaries: Race, Class, and Gender in Cartagena, Colombia." *American Ethnologist* 22.1: 634–60.

Struyk, R. J., A. Turner, and M. Fix. 1992. *Opportunities Denied, Opportunities Diminished: Discrimination in Housing.* Washington, D.C.: The Urban Institute.

Swales, Martin. 1978. *The German Buildungsroman from Wieland to Hesse.* Princeton: Princeton University Press.

Taussig, Michael. 1987. *Shamanism, Colonialism, and the Wild Man: A Study in Terror and Healing.* Chicago: University of Chicago Press.

———. 1993. *Mimesis and Alterity.* London: Routledge.

Taylor, William L. 1986. "Brown, Equal Protection, and the Isolation of the Poor." *Yale Law Journal* 95: 1713–14.

Teitelbaum, Lee. "First-Generation Issues: Access to Law School." In *Perspectives on Diversity,* ed. Rachel F. Moran. Forthcoming from Association of American Law Schools, Washington, D.C.

Theweleit, K. 1993. *Male Phantasies.* Cambridge: Polity.

Thomas, Richard. 1992. *Life for Us Is What We Make It: Building Black Community in Detroit, 1915-1945.* Bloomington: University of Indiana Press.

Thomas, Wendell, and David Wellman. 1993. "Testing Affirmative Action Hypotheses." Manuscript. Institute for the Study of Social Change, University of California at Berkeley.

Thompson, Becky. 1996. "Time Traveling and Border Crossing: Reflections on White Identity." In *Names We Call Home: Autobiography on Racial Identity,* 93–110. New York: Routledge.

Thompson, E. P. 1980. *The Making of the English Working Class.* London: Gollancz.

Thompson, E. P., and D. Hays. 1985. *Black Acts, Whigs, and Hunters.* London: Allen Lane.

Thompson, Paul. 1993. "Strikers' Fury after Neo-Nazi Poll Win." *London Sun,* September 18, 7.

Todorov, Tzvetan. 1993. *On Human Diversity.* Cambridge: Harvard University Press.

Toll, Robert C. 1974. *Blacking Up: The Minstrel Show in Nineteenth Century America.* New York: Oxford University Press.

Turner, Roger, and Al Green. 1985. *Body Culture.* Toronto: Summerhill Press.

Twine, France Winddance. 1996. "Heterosexual Alliances: The Romantic Management of Racial Identity." In *The Multiracial Experience: Racial Borders as the New Frontier,* ed. Maria P. Root. London: Sage.

Twine, France Winddance, Jonathan W. Warren, and Francisco Ferrandiz. 1991. *Just Black? Multiracial Identity.* New York: Filmmakers Library.

Valdez, Luis. 1973. *Los Vendidos.* Film produced by George Paul.

————. *Early Works*. Houston: Arte Público.

Vergara, Camilo Jose. 1992. "Detroit Waits for the Millenium." *Nation,* May 18.

Vincendeau, Ginette. 1985. "Community, Nostalgia and the Spectacle of Masculinity." *Screen* 6.26 (November–December): 18–38.

von Salden, Adelheid. 1994. "Victims or Perpetrators? Controversies about the Role of Women in the Nazi State." In *Nazism and German Society 1933–1945,* ed. David F. Crew, 141–65. London: Routledge.

Walker, Richard. 1995. "California Rages against the Dying of the Light." *New Left Review.*

Walkerdine, Valerie, ed. 1987. *Changing the Subject.* London: Routledge.

Walkovitz, Judith. 1992. *City of Dreadful Delight: Narratives of Sexual Danger in Late Victorian London.* London: Virago.

Ware, Vron. 1992. *Beyond the Pale: White Women, Racism, and History.* London: Verso.

Warren, Jonathan, and France Winddance Twine. In press. "White Americans, the New Minority? Non-blacks and the Ever-Expanding Boundaries of Whiteness." *Journal of Black Studies.*

Wellman, David. 1986. "The New Political Linguistics of Race." *Socialist Review* 16 (May–August): 43–62.

————. 1993. *Portraits of White Racism.* 2d ed. New York: Cambridge University Press.

Welter, Barbara. 1966. "The Cult of True Womanhood: 1820–1860." *American Quarterly* 18.2, pt. 1 (Summer): 151–75.

Wheatcroft, Geoffrey. 1995. "What They Really Are." *Daily Telegraph,* February 17.

White, Deborah Gray. 1985. *Ar'n't I a Woman? Female Slaves in the Plantation South.* New York: Norton.

Williams, Brackette. 1991. *Stains on My Name, War in My Veins: Guyana and the Politics of Cultural Struggle.* Durham, N.C.: Duke University Press.

Williams, Stephanie. 1993. *Docklands.* London: Phaidon Architecture Guide.

Wilson, William Julius. 1978. *The Declining Significance of Race: Blacks and Changing American Institutions.* Chicago: University of Chicago Press.

————. 1987. *The Truly Disadvantaged: The Inner City, the Underclass, and Public Policy.* Chicago: University of Chicago Press.

Wray, Matt. 1996. "Affirmative Action, Race Traitors, and the End of Whiteness." Paper presented to the California American Studies Association Conference, Occidental College, Los Angeles, April 26.

Wray, Matt, and Annalee Newitz, eds. 1997. *White Trash: Race and Class in America.* New York: Routledge.

Wright, Winthrop. 1990. *Café Con Leche: Race, Class, and National Image in Venezuela.* Austin: University of Texas Press.

Yarbro-Bejarano, Yvonne. 1994. "Gloria Anzaldúa's *Borderlands/la frontera:* Cultural Studies, 'Difference,' and the Non-unitary Subject." *Cultural Critique* 28 (Fall): 5–28.

Young, Robert. 1990. *White Mythologies: Writing History and the West.* London: Routledge.

Žižek, Slavoj. 1989. *The Sublime Object of Ideology.* London: Verso.

Contributors

Rebecca Aanerud is completing doctoral research at the University of Washington, Seattle, in the Department of English. Her thesis, "Maintaining Comfort, Sustaining Power: Race, Social Change, and White Liberalism," examines conscious and unconscious racisms in U.S. films and literary texts from the late nineteenth century to the present.

Angie Chabram-Dernersesian is Associate Professor of Chicana/o Studies at the University of California, Davis. She is a member of MALCS (Active Women in Letters and Social Change). Author of numerous articles in feminism, ethnography, and criticism, she has coedited two special issues of *Cultural Studies* on Chicana/o cultural representations.

Phil Cohen is Reader in Cultural Studies at the University of East London, where he directs the Centre for New Ethnicities Research. His collected essays on education, labor, and cultural studies have just been published as *Rethinking the Youth Question*. His contribution to the present volume is part of a work in progress on historical and contemporary aspects of racism's other scenes, scheduled for publication as *Not Just the Same Old Story*.

Ruth Frankenberg is Associate Professor of American Studies at the University of California, Davis. She is author of *White Women, Race Matters: The Social Construction of Whiteness*. She has published several articles on racism, antiracism, and whiteness, including "'When We Are Capable of Stopping, We Begin to See': Being White, Seeing Whiteness," in *Names We Call Home: Autobiography on Racial Identity*. She is currently undertaking an interview-based study of spiritual practices in the contemporary United States.

John Hartigan Jr. is Assistant Professor of Sociology and Anthropology at Knox College, Galesburg, Illinois. His research on current popular and historical constructions of "white trash"—conducted, in part, as a fellow at the National Museum of American History, Smithsonian Institution—has appeared in *Visual Anthropology* and *Cultural Studies*. His ethnographic work in Detroit is detailed in *Cultural Constructions of Whiteness: Racial and Class Formations in Detroit*.

bell hooks is Distinguished Professor of English at City College in New York. She has published widely in feminist theory and history, race studies, cultural theory, and pedagogy. Her books include *Ain't I a Woman: Black Women and Feminism; Yearning: Race, Gender, and Cultural Politics; Black Looks;* and *Teaching to Transgress: Education as the Practice of Freedom.*

T. Muraleedharan teaches in the Department of English, St. Aloysius College, University of Calicut, Kerala, India. His work on film and postcolonial British nationalism is presented in his book *Gender, Race, and the Nation: Cultural Politics in Raj Cinema.* His article, "Women/Migrants/Victims and the Male Empire: The Redeployment of Racist and Patriarchal Notions in Raj Cinema," is forthcoming in *Critical Arts: A Journal for Cultural Studies.*

Chéla Sandoval is Assistant Professor of Cultural Theory in the Department of Chicana/o Studies, University of California, Santa Barbara. She has published articles in feminist theory in *Signs* and *Genders.* Her book, *Rhetorics of Rebellion: Flux at the Second Millennium,* is forthcoming in 1997.

France Winddance Twine is Assistant Professor of Women's Studies and Adjunct Assistant Professor of Anthropology at the University of Washington, Seattle. Her research and video productions engage intersections of race, class, and gender inequality within and across several national contexts. Her coproduced video, *Just Black? Multiracial Identity,* received the Special Jury Prize at the National Educational Film Festival of 1992. Twine is the author of *Racism in a Racial Democracy: The Maintenance of White Supremacy in Brazil,* and has published numerous articles on racial consciousness and antiracism. Twine is currently a Royalty Research Fund Scholar, writing a book on the meaning of whiteness and antiracism for white birth-mothers of African-descent children in Britain.

Vron Ware lives in London most of the time and the United States some of the time. She teaches cultural geography in the School of Humanities at the University of Greenwich, London, and is author of *Beyond the Pale: White Women, Racism, and History.*

David Wellman is Professor of Community Studies at the University of California, Santa Cruz, and Research Sociologist at the Institute for the Study of Social Change at the University of California, Berkeley. He is author of *Portraits of White Racism* and *The Union Makes Us Strong: Radical Unionism on the San Francisco Waterfront.*

Index

Strathern, Marilyn: and fractals theory of cross-cultural communication, 4, 27, 181, 182, 206 n.6, 213 n.53
Struyk, R. J., 319
Subordination, female, 127, 299–300
Suburbanites, 185, 186, 215–16
Superiority: whiteness as, 52, 70, 324
Supremacism. See White supremacism
Supreme Court, 314

Taussig, Michael, 165–66
Tautology: and white supremacism, 91–92
Taylor, William L., 314
Teatro Campesino, 132, 141
Terror: whiteness as, 26, 37, 169–72, 175–76
Thatcher, Margaret, 62
Thatcherism, 62–64, 79
"The Pocho Appears" (Paredes), 145–46
Third Reich, 306–7
Tillet, Ben, 258
Tío Tacos, 131
To Be Young, Gifted, and Black (Hansberry), 170
"To Live in the Borderlands Means You" (Anzaldúa), 127–28
Torres, Lourdes, 153
Tower Hamlets, 301–2
Tradition: in Britain, 63–64, 260–61
Training: diversity, 17–18
Transcoding, 69–70
Transnational identity, 150–54
Travel: theory of, 167, 172–75
"Traveling Theory" (Said), 172
Trope-ical family, 11–15
Tropes, 11–15, 202; in Gandhi, 81–82; Morrison on, 56; in representations of whiteness, 158 n.8; use of by Anzaldúa, 122; in white laborism, 247–48, 281 n.33. See also Stereotypes
Turner, A., 319
Twine, France Winddance, 5, 7, 27–28

Uncle Sam, 139
Unemployment, 254–55, 285. See also White laborism

United States, 5; current practices of discrimination in, 318–19; immigration control in, 6, 14, 128
Upper class, 13, 67, 83, 249

Valdez, Luis, 131, 133, 136, 141. See also Los Vendidos
Los Vendidos (Valdez), 130–44, 161 nn.51–56
Veterans Administration (VA), 8
Victim-focused identities, 317
De la vida y el folclore de la frontera (Méndez), 146
Vincendeau, Ginette, 77–78
Violence: and race, 68–69, 79, 81–82, 193–94, 210 n.40, 291–92

Wage slaves, 10
Wages of Whiteness (Roediger), 10–11
Walker, Alice, 328
Walker, Mr., 66, 73, 74
Wallock, Leonard, 220, 225
Ward, Reg, 294
Ware, Vron, 14, 23, 95; on Englishness, 29–30; on gender, 39; identification of female types by, 53; on reputation of white women, 43–44
"We Called Them Greasers" (Anzaldúa), 126–27
Wellman, David, 5, 14, 30
Wells, Ida B., 43
Wharton, William H., 127
White, Allon, 299
White, Michael, 208 n.20
"White" (Dyer), 169
White laborism, 244–82, 278 n.15, 285–86. See also Working class
White League, 59 n.33
White Man, 11, 12, 15, 158 n.8
White men, 13–14; advantages of, 330 nn.32, 33; and affirmative action, 315–18; authority over white women, 43–44; and "normal" state of being, 321–22; territorialism of, 255–56; tropes of, 11–13; unemployed, 254–55, 285 (see also White laborism)

Whiteness: acquisition of, 64, 76, 209
n.31; challenges to, 230–32; constructions of, 4, 10–11, 16–20, 22, 37, 52,
100–101, 112, 209 n.31; critical work
on, 2–3, 17–18; decoding of, 115, 117,
124, 155–56; demystification of, 119;
effects of, 17; effects of rhetoric on, 95,
98–99; expansion of, 225; hegemonic
quality of, 115–16; as interpretive
frame, 235–37; invisibility of, 5, 37, 61;
marking of, 45–50; multiple meanings
of, 10, 15, 25–26, 181–82; narrative
constructions of, 61; native constructions of, 115–16, 119–20, 122, 158 nn.8,
10; pluralization of, 25–26; as portrayed in the arts, 25; power versus,
25–26, 100–101; and racial dominance
(see Dominance: racial); as racial
neutrality, 222–24; reasons for examination of, 1–2, 107–10; reinscription
of, 8, 177–78, 255; social constructions
of, 28, 214–43; terms for (see Naming); on "the inside," 130–44; on "the
other side," 144–50; as universal, 3,
32 n.7, 60–61; as unmarked norm, 4,
5, 37, 61; unmarking of, 6, 37; whites'
reaction to blacks' conceptualization
of, 169. See also Literature: whiteness
portrayed in; Metaphors, for whiteness
White People (Gurganus), 22
White slavery, 10
White supremacism, 37, 256; Barthes on
rhetoric of, 86–96; discourses of, 303;
Fanon theories of, 88, 100–101; as form
of racism, 245; and identity, 3, 17; and
invisibility, 168; and naming of the

Other, 47; and nationalism, 255–56;
reinscription of by cultural practices,
177–78; and tautology, 91–92; and
white unmarkedness, 5
White trash, 13
White Woman, 11, 12, 303
White women: and affirmative action,
326; and racism, 286–90, 298–300,
305–6; reputation of, 43–44. *See also*
Women
Wilson, Pete, 311
Wilson, William Julius, 207 n.15, 313
Winant, Howard, 27, 182–84, 206 n.12
Woman of Color, 12, 15
Women: African American, 27–28, 214–
43; and colonialism, 289; and gender,
39; Mexican, 127, 138, 139–40; as
pochis, 149–50; poor white, 13; and
racism, 286–90, 298–300, 305–6;
as reflection of level of civilization
of society, 310 n.26; stereotypes of,
150–54; tropes of, 11–13, 82; undocumented, 125; and white cultural
identity, 232
Women's Ku Klux Klan, 289
Working class, 14, 23, 28–29, 210 n.39,
246–56; idealization of, 254; at local
level, 254–56, 259; and race, 246–56,
271–72, 320; as race apart, 248, 277–78
n.13; stereotypes of, 280 n.40. *See also*
White laborism

Yarbro-Bejarano, Yvonne, 159 n.23
"Yobs," 285
Young, Robert, 156, 164 n.88

Library of Congress Cataloging-in-Publication Data
Displacing whiteness : essays in social and cultural criticism /
Ruth Frankenberg, editor.
Includes bibliographical references and index.
ISBN 0-8223-2011-8 (alk. paper). — ISBN 0-8223-2021-5 (pbk. :
alk. paper)
1. Eurocentrism. 2. Whites—Attitudes. 3. Racism.
I. Frankenberg, Ruth.
HT1523.D57 1997
305.8—dc21 97-18562 CIP